MW01042608

GAY MALE

PORNOGRAPHY

LAW AND
SOCIETY

Law and Society Series
W. Wesley Pue, General Editor

gAy mAle

PORNOGRAPHY

An Issue of Sex Discrimination

CHRISTOPHER N. KENDALL

UBCPress · Vancouver · Toronto

15 14 13 12 11 10 09 08 07 06 05 04   5 4 3 2 1

Printed in Canada on acid-free paper

Library and Archives Canada Cataloguing in Publication

Kendall, Christopher N. (Christopher Nigel), 1966-
  Gay male pornography: an issue of sex discrimination /
Christopher N. Kendall.

  (Law and society series, ISSN 1496-4953)
  Includes bibliographical references and index.
  ISBN 0-7748-1076-9

  1. Pornography – Law and legislation – Canada. 2. Homophobia – Canada. 3. Pornography – Social aspects – Canada. 4. Butler, Donald Victor – Trials, litigation, etc. 5. Little Sister's Book & Art Emporium – Trials, litigation, etc. 6. Gay men. I. Title. II. Series.

HQ471.K46 2004   363.4'7'0866420971   C2004-903585-1

Canadä

UBC Press gratefully acknowledges the financial support for our publishing program of the Government of Canada through the Book Publishing Industry Development Program (BPIDP), and of the Canada Council for the Arts, and the British Columbia Arts Council.

This book has been published with the help of a grant from the Canadian Federation for the Humanities and Social Sciences, using funds provided by the Social Sciences and Humanities Research Council of Canada.

UBC Press
The University of British Columbia
2029 West Mall
Vancouver, BC V6T 1Z2
604-822-5959 / Fax: 604-822-6083
www.ubcpress.ca

For Jeremy

Contents

Acknowledgments

This book could not have been written without the energy and intellectual support of Professor Catharine A. MacKinnon at the University of Michigan Law School. Her commitment to change and passion for justice motivated me when I felt I had nothing left to offer. Her pioneering work on pornography and the links between homophobia and sex discrimination made this work possible.

Much of the preliminary research for this book was undertaken as part of the litigation surrounding the Supreme Court of Canada case of *Little Sisters Book and Art Emporium*. This case allowed me to meet and work with Professor Janine Benedet of Osgoode Hall Law School in Toronto. Janine and I prepared the legal factum used by the feminist group Equality Now in litigation before the Court. Janine successfully argued the case before the Court and our friendship has grown stronger ever since.

I also want to thank Andrea Dworkin and John Stoltenberg. Thank you for your strength and courage and for letting me be a part of your lives. I hope this work goes someway to ensuring that the battles you fight do not go unnoticed. You have given voice to a new generation of activists who remain committed to your goals and who will not stop until your vision of a just society is realized. I include among these Philip Galanes and thank him for his 1990 research into the anti-pornography ordinances and gay male identity. His groundbreaking and courageous paper motivated me to keep writing. Thank you also to the anonymous author of the 1985 UCLA study into the gay male pornography industry, referred to in this work. By saying what had to be said, you encouraged me to keep fighting for those who can't.

At the risk of leaving someone out, thank you also to Natalie Nenadic for reading and rereading so many of my papers and for helping me become my own person. Thank you also to Marc Spindelman for providing pages of comments on much of my work; Nairne Holtz, whose research skills made finding the impossible possible; and Wendy Adams, who spent many a late night with me at the University of Michigan making sure I kept writing, even though I often felt I had nothing left to say.

I would also like to thank my students and colleagues at Murdoch University for allowing me to experiment with new ideas. Thank you in particular to Dale Montgomery for formatting and typesetting what was clearly a word-processing disaster waiting to happen. Your fix-it skills are remarkable. Thank you also to the then Dean of Law, Professor Ralph Simmonds, for his generous financial support and to Linda McNamara for her brilliant editing skills.

I have been writing on the issue of pornographic harm and gay liberation for more than ten years. During that time, a number of law journals and books have helped me find my voice and have taken chances on my work when others would not. I would like to acknowledge the publishers of these publications in which some of the work in this book first appeared or which influenced its writing. A list appears on page 247.

I would also like to thank my family for instilling in me the value of being an individual, for encouraging me to respect myself and others, and for teaching me to stand up against prejudice and intolerance. My work may not make for easy reading but you have always supported me. What more could a son and brother ask for?

Finally, this book would never have been started or completed without the love and intellectual support of my partner, Jeremy Curthoys. Words alone cannot express my gratitude.

Introduction

FROM *BUTLER* TO *LITTLE SISTERS:*
WHAT WENT WRONG WITH GAY MALE LIBERATION?

On 20 December 2000, the Supreme Court of Canada ruled unanimously in the case of *Little Sisters Book and Art Emporium*,[1] a case concerning the right of Canada Customs to detain lesbian and gay male pornography, that gay male pornography violates the sex equality test for pornographic harm first set down by the Court in its 1992 decision in *R. v. Butler.*[2] In *Butler,* the Court ruled that legal efforts aimed at prohibiting the distribution of pornography were constitutionally sound because pornography undermined the rights of all Canadians to be treated equally on the basis of sex. In *Little Sisters*, the Court ruled that lesbian and gay male pornography should not be excluded from the same equality-based approach. The Court also held, however, that Canada Customs must not apply the test for harm first articulated in *Butler* in a discriminatory manner, such that non-harmful materials, be they heterosexual or homosexual in content, are wrongly detained.

Those who support the production and distribution of pornography have been quick to applaud the latter finding – a conclusion that feminists who oppose pornography have also long supported. But many of the people who support pornography have been notably silent on the central issue on which Little Sisters Book and Art Emporium, and those who intervened on its behalf, appealed and lost before the Supreme Court of Canada: the Court's finding that same-sex pornography can harm and, therefore, like heterosexual pornography, can be excluded from Canada. Despite the best efforts of Little Sisters and others to justify lesbian and gay pornography as life-affirming and liberating, Canada's highest court has now ruled unequivocally that gay and lesbian pornography, simply because it is gay or lesbian, is not harm-proof and is not, therefore, *Butler*-proof. This strengthens the sex equality analysis of pornographic harm articulated by the Court in its earlier free speech and equality jurisprudence and, in so doing, ensures that Canada remains at the forefront of judicial efforts aimed at ensuring that gender equity remains a central human and legal value. Despite this, little comment has been forthcoming from Little Sisters Bookstore and those who supported its litigation efforts about this aspect of the Court's findings. Instead, Little Sisters has focused solely on the Court's finding that there has been considerable discrimination and administrative error in the application of Canada's obscenity laws.

Gay activists might well celebrate the Court's ruling that inequality is harmful and that lesbians and gay men merit the same protections in this regard as non-gay Canadians. And yet, nothing of the sort was mentioned in the press releases following the Court's ruling in *Little Sisters*. Perhaps groups traditionally concerned with the eradication of inequality exemplified by pornography, as well as the other activist groups involved in this litigation, need to be reminded of what it was they were defending when they took this case to the Supreme Court of Canada. While the Supreme Court of Canada's recounting of the trial court's findings that Canada Customs discriminated against Little Sisters Bookstore deserves notice, those findings were not on appeal by anyone involved in the litigation before the Supreme Court of Canada. No one questioned that result before, during, or after the case was argued. What was contested in the *Little Sisters* litigation, and what Little Sisters Bookstore and those groups who intervened on its behalf lost decisively, were the questions of whether gay and lesbian pornography can do harm to equality rights, whether an equality harms-based test can validly apply to gay and lesbian materials, and whether Customs can legitimately stop pornography – any pornography – from entering Canada. Little Sisters argued that all three questions should be answered in the negative. The Court, supported only by the Attorney General of Canada and one intervener, Equality Now, rejected all these arguments.

This book analyzes the Supreme Court of Canada's refusal to throw out *Butler* and its refusal to permit harm to gay men and lesbian women to be an exception to its harm standards. Analyzing the Court's findings in this regard, I will argue that, in ruling that the harms-based test set out in *Butler* can apply to same-sex pornography, while also recognizing that Canada Customs cannot apply *Butler* in a discriminatory and homophobic manner, the *Little Sisters* case offers a rare opportunity for gay activists and anti-pornography feminists to unite in their struggle for systemic equality. Before this can occur, however, gay male activists must abandon what, I will argue, is a misguided defence of pornography, gay and non-gay alike.

Most of my comments will be directed specifically at gay men and their defence of gay male pornography for a number of reasons. To begin with, I am one and have a vested interest in the outcome of those litigation and social reform strategies allegedly undertaken on my behalf. Also, despite the claims of those who would argue that the feminist movement has abandoned its fight against pornography, much *has* been written in recent years by lesbian feminists in particular, outlining in considerable detail the harms that result from the production and distribution of lesbian pornography.[3] Much of their analysis is helpful to the arguments I make about gay male pornography, although it does not often address it squarely. I will focus on the central argument posed by gay activists and their supporters post-*Butler* and throughout the *Little Sisters* case: that gay male pornography is central to all that is gay male identity and thus can liberate us from the oppressions we face, and that any attempt to regulate it is homophobic and discriminatory. With the Supreme Court of Canada and those who have long argued that all pornography is an issue of sex discrimination, I will reject this assertion, arguing instead that gay male pornography will achieve only that which the homophobe has strived to do all along: the silencing of gay men by encouraging masculine mimicry and the public expression of the polar opposite of equality. The goal of systemic equality was at the heart of the Courts' findings in *Butler*. In *Little Sisters*, the Court ruled that gay men have a right to that equality and implied that we have a role to play in achieving it. This book asks gay men to acknowledge the validity of this finding and build on it, rather than ignore it as biased or dismiss it as unfounded.

There has been considerable academic and political effort by many gay men to defend gay male pornography as representative of a politic and identity to which all gay men must have access. This claim will be criticized and rejected. These arguments were central to the defence raised in the *Little Sisters* litigation. Adamant that it serves to affirm gay male sexuality, that it is different from heterosexual pornography, that it liberates and challenges heterosexuality as a compulsory social construct, and that it is necessary for the formation of a distinct gay male identity, many gay men have argued to justify the mass distribution of pornography as central to gay male "cultural history and political validation." Indeed, defenders of gay male pornography remain so adamant that the "right" to access pornography is integral to the struggle for gay liberation that present gay rights strategies continue to include an almost unquestioned assumption that any commitment to social equality for gay men must, of necessity, include a commitment to the unbridled production and distribution of gay male pornography.

With pro-pornography advocates asserting that attempts to regulate pornographic harm will achieve little more than the suppression of legitimate same-sex sexual expression, considerable public confusion also exists about the facts and reasoning in the *Butler* and *Little Sisters* cases, and about the role generally of pornography in the lives of gay men. Chapter 1 of this book unravels some of the misunderstandings surrounding *Butler* and what, I will argue, is the gay male community's misguided reaction to it. It clarifies what the case *does* say and what effect the analysis offered by the courts has on gay men in their struggle for equality. I argue that, far from being a threat to gay male identity, any judicial decision that recognizes the feminist call for sex equality does much to ensure the breaking down of those gender hierarchies that allow homophobia to exist in the first place. Important in this regard were the arguments made by the Women's Legal Education and Action Fund (LEAF) before the Court in *Butler*.[4] LEAF played a pivotal role in persuading the Court to restrict the distribution of materials that encourage actions that threaten equality and non-violence among citizens. Around nine years later, in its arguments before the same Court in *Little Sisters,* LEAF argued that same-sex pornography should be exempt from the sex equality analysis it advocated in *Butler.* This represents a remarkable about-face – one that, I will contend, was supported and possibly even provoked by the gay community's earlier attacks on LEAF's pro-*Butler* arguments and the gay community's own failure to understand what *Butler* stands for. Far from being a threat to the free expression of ideas, *Butler,* for the first time in legal history, moved in the direction of tackling the real specific acts caused by pornography – acts that result in individual and systemic inequality on the basis of sex. While much about the *Butler* analysis of pornographic harm can be improved on, LEAF's new line of reasoning, reinforced by the other pro-pornography interveners in the *Little Sisters* case, is, in my view, counter-productive, even oddly homophobic.

One might have hoped, given the amount of political effort expended by feminist women on behalf of gay men, before and after the onslaught of AIDS, that the gay male community might join in the feminist struggle for sex equality, so successfully articulated in *Butler.* Unfortunately, as Chapter 2 of this book explains, quite the opposite occurred. Many gay men severed their ties with early and present feminist commitments to social justice and instead embraced an ideology and a politics far removed from the fight for sex equality. This book as a whole aims to argue that, in doing so, gay men risk supporting a movement that – although they believe it promotes social justice – goes a long way toward ensuring that sexual and systemic equality will never be achieved.

Chapter 2, in an attempt to connect homophobia and sex discrimination, provides an analysis of the meaning of homophobia for gay men and society at large – what it does, who it benefits, and why, pursuing the connection that until gay men fully understand that sexism and homophobia are inextricably linked, they will not understand that their present drive toward manhood, best evidenced in their defence and promotion of pornography, is as anti-woman as that of heterosexual men, and as such, collaborates with all that is anti-gay male. Chapter 2 offers such an analysis within the context of the media coverage following *Butler* and during the *Little Sisters* hearings.

Chapters 3, 4, 5, and 6 detail the arguments on gay male pornography in *Little Sisters,* from its initial hearing before the British Columbia Supreme Court to its final hearing before the Supreme Court of Canada. Examining in considerable detail the arguments made by the plaintiff and pro-pornography interveners regarding the non-harmful effects of gay male pornography, and the writings of those who support these views, my conclusion is that the "sexual expression" defended as politically subversive and central to gay male liberation is far from liberating. Rather, it exemplifies and results in the inequality that the Canadian Supreme Court addressed in *Butler.* It typifies "expression" that produces actions that cause harm and, as such, harm gay men and, when defended, preclude gay liberation.

Chapter 3 describes the pornography defended in *Little Sisters*, pornography that would be freely distributed throughout Canada if pro-pornography arguments were not rejected and if effective measures aimed at stopping the distribution of pornography are not created. Although many gay activists have celebrated gay pornography generally, little coverage or analysis has focused on the actual materials that pro-pornography advocates would have us distribute throughout Canada without regulation. This chapter introduces the reader, via necessarily explicit description and quotations of some of the pornography at the centre of the *Little Sisters* litigation, to the types of materials that Little Sisters, LEAF, and others argued are mere sexual imagery, hence harm-free. Analysis of these materials reveals that gay male pornography epitomizes what it means to be male as socially defined. It offers gay men a choice: be violent and aggressive, hence masculine (read "male") or be non-masculine (read "the person over/upon whom that power should be exercised"), hence feminized, therefore "female" as socially defined. The resulting gender/power hierarchy, rather than challenging compulsory heterosexuality and male dominance, reinforces social norms that make heterosexuality compulsory and male dominance the interconnected and oppressive constructs that they are. The result of their embrace for gay men is self-hate and internalized homophobia. The result for society at large is but one more medium that, because it promotes rather than undermines a gender hierarchy in which "male" is top and "female" (read: all women and those gay men who fail to conform to the "male" construct and who are thus socially feminized) is bottom, is sexually discriminatory and helps maintain systemic inequality. It enacts and promotes, and relies for its sexual value upon, a hierarchy that keeps straight on top of gay by keeping all men on top of all women.

Chapters 4 and 5 query whether, given the nature and content of these materials, it is still possible to argue that they are harm-free and unlikely to have the negative individual and social impact that the Supreme Court attempted to address in *Butler*. Commencing with an overview in Chapter 4 of the men used to produce gay male pornography, and followed in Chapter 5 by an examination of the alarmingly high incidences of rape and domestic violence within the gay male community, these two chapters re-evaluate the arguments made throughout the *Little Sisters* litigation. Contrary to those who argue that gay male pornography is qualitatively different from heterosexual pornography, hence non-harmful, I will argue that the acts that result from its production and distribution are no less damaging than the acts resulting from other types of pornography. Far from being the fantasy or mere fictional representation that its promoters would have us believe it is, gay male pornography presents and therefore is a form of male sexuality and male power. It is this sexuality of dominance, of hierarchy, through which women are sexually violated. It is this sexuality that leads to the oppression of gay men as well. Gay male pornography, because it glorifies the masculine and denigrates the feminine, reinforces the male/female social dichotomy and hierarchy. And so, in addition to inflicting emotional and physical harms on those used to produce it, it strengthens those stereotypes that allow society to view certain behaviour as feminine, thus inferior, and reaffirms, because it sexualizes this dynamic, that it is unnatural to engage in a sexuality not premised on male/female polarity. It is, in essence, homophobic and results in those actions and practices that make homophobia and sexism a threat to physical safety and social equality.

This argument is further developed in Chapter 6, which posits that gay male pornography is an issue of sex discrimination and, as such, harmful to both gay men and the equality interest of society as a whole. I aim to demonstrate that, because gay male pornography teaches gay men sexually to reject an identity that challenges male supremacy, it *is* homophobic – telling gay men either to retain their degraded status as "female" or become the "real" men they should have been all along. Homophobia is aimed at silencing the expression of gay male identity – an identity that must be quashed because it has the potential to undermine gender male privilege and those gendered power hierarchies that result from the oppression of all those who are "female" as socially defined. Because it is homophobic, gay male pornography is a form of sex discrimination central to the maintenance of sexual and social inequality. Under the Supreme Court of Canada's decision in *Butler,* gay male pornography, like all pornography, thus *does* result in those harms springing from expression that undermines "egalitarianism, non-violence, consensualism and mutuality."[5] Given this, the arguments made in *Little Sisters* by advocates for pornography do not promote the interests of gay men as a group or gay male equality.

This conclusion is scrutinized in the context of the particular defences of pornography made in the *Little Sisters* case. In *Little Sisters*, much was made by a number of the interveners before the Supreme Court of Canada, but in particular by the Canadian AIDS Society, of the risk posed by *Butler* to the dissemination of those materials intended to promote safe sex. Other arguments were advanced that gay male pornography should not be restricted because it serves as a learning tool for young men and, in so doing, does much to reduce the alarming incidence of gay youth suicide. Chapter 7 queries these assumptions within the context of the materials defended in *Little Sisters*. My overall conclusion is that there is little reason to believe that the equality analysis advanced in *Butler* cannot be further developed legally and ultimately applied to those materials often wrongly defended as safe and life-affirming.

Focusing on the types of safe-sex materials now being distributed within the gay community, the emerging popularity of bareback or unsafe anal sex as promoted in gay male pornography, and ending with an examination of recent studies on the impact that the present gay male obsession with hyper-masculinity and body-image is having on young gay men who often feel unable to conform to this standard, this chapter argues that unless gay men recommit to a sexuality built on mutuality, respect and caring – that is, an identity politic built around sex equality – we may find that we are promoting a sexual identity that demands that self-respect and personal safety take a back seat, with potentially catastrophic results. Add to this a legal strategy that ignores those most in need of protection and one gets a legal and social interaction that sees life – gay life in this case – as expendable.

In *Little Sisters*, the plaintiff and those who supported it asked that gay male pornography be exempt from the equality-based test provided in *Butler*. They argued that failure to do so would undermine community efforts to protect gay men, young gay men in particular, from harm – self-inflicted or otherwise. This chapter argues that such an approach is backwards. It is exemption from a protection from harm that is harmful, not the protection itself. We cannot expect life-affirming change if legal exceptions are sought that advocate the antithesis of affirmation of life. To seek exceptions for promoting a sexual identity without equality jeopardizes gains already made and risks creating a model of protection that silences and penalizes those most in need of a voice.

In *Little Sisters*, the British Columbia Supreme Court found that, applying the *Butler* test, gay male pornography violated widely accepted equality prin-ciples. The British Columbia Court of Appeal agreed, as did the Supreme Court of Canada. Chapters 1 to 7 of this book lend support to this finding, responding to those who have argued otherwise. The question remains of how best to ensure that the equality test outlined in *Butler* and *Little Sisters* is im-plemented in a way that guarantees that those materials that do not violate this test are not denied entry into Canada, while those materials that do, are. In *Little Sisters*, it was revealed that Canada Customs' procedures for the sei-zure and detention of pornography at the Canada-US border had arbitrarily discriminated against lesbians and gay men. At the same time, much material that clearly does violate *Butler* was permitted entry. The lower courts outlined in detail the extent to which Canada Customs had failed to effectively imple-ment the *Butler* equality-based approach to pornographic harm. Chapter 8 examines these findings and considers how best to implement a system of legal regulation that avoids the discriminatory application of a test aimed at ending discrimination and that ensures that only those materials that result in those acts that are central to sexual and racial inequality are stopped, and materials that do not result in real, concrete harms are permitted. Thought control violates the Constitution. Stopping acts that keep others from living safely and equally, however, is a constitutional imperative. This is the position long held by anti-pornography feminists. While *Butler* takes a major step toward embracing this approach, it does not, in my opinion, go far enough toward addressing the acts caused by pornography.

The Supreme Court of Canada in *Little Sisters*, by reaffirming the equality rights test outlined in *Butler,* while at the same time recognizing the problems associated with state efforts to regulate Canada's obscenity laws, provided a victory for both lesbians and gay men concerned with the illegitimate exercise of state censorship and for those who have fought to address the harms of the production and distribution of pornography. In Chapter 8, I outline how those measures in place for regulating pornographic harm in Canada can be strengthened.

The *Little Sisters* litigation offers us the chance to implement these changes, and gay men have a role to play in ensuring that they are forthcoming. Indeed, the Supreme Court of Canada has provided a rare opportunity for both the gay male community and those who support the *Butler* equality-based approach to pornography to work together. The decision now requires that these groups align to ensure that the real harms of pornography are addressed in a manner that fairly and effectively implements the call for the elimination of those acts that violate the equality rights of all Canadians. While much can be done to rectify some of the more blatant abuses of administrative power outlined in *Little Sisters,* via education, for example, such that non-harmful materials are not targeted, it must be recognized that this will not be done without a reopening of the lines of communication between all those with an interest in how regulation of this sort occurs. Chapter 8 examines what this discussion requires and how best to achieve it.

My belief is that the best way to improve these efforts is to implement a system that empowers pornography's victims, female and male, gay and non-gay – an approach that allows those most harmed by pornographic acts to fight back against the agents of their harm. I argue that this can be achieved by implementing legislative changes that allow pornography's victims to take direct legal action on their own behalf against those responsible for their harms without relying solely on the state to act for them. The civil rights ordinances against pornography's harms, conceived by US legal feminist Catharine MacKinnon and US feminist writer Andrea Dworkin, offer and make possible such an initiative. While much has been written on the MacKinnon-Dworkin anti-pornography ordinances in the United States and in Canada, to date no one has examined these ordinances from a sympathetic and informed gay male perspective. *Butler* and *Little Sisters* offer an opportunity for such an analysis.

Overall, this book argues that the *Little Sisters* case provides an opportunity for gay men to rethink the role of pornography in our community, and the extent to which our defence of it continues to prevent us and others from achieving justice. It also offers strong support for an approach to equality that gay men and their supporters have rejected for too long and on which more gay men would do well to focus, given the clear links between sex discrimination and homophobia. Andrea Dworkin accurately notes that homosexuality is generally perceived as a failure to learn. If this book demonstrates anything, it will be that gay men today are "learning" but continue to read from the wrong book. They mimic but do not subvert. Gay rights have come to mean male dominant rights, the very essence of all that is anti-gay. Defined by the pornographic sexual exploitation of others, upon whose presentation and use we are told to construct our identity and community, we have now accepted and promote a model of identity that is more concerned with the use and abuse of others found in the form of sexual hierarchy than with liberation from that hierarchy.

What I long for is a gay male sexuality that includes and *is* compassion, sensuality, tenderness, intimacy, inclusive love-making, and the equality found only in a life-affirming reciprocity that does not depend on reciprocal harm. What has happened in the name of gay liberation is quite the opposite. Ultimately, gay men may find that they have at last achieved manhood and the power that comes with it. But at what price? Becoming a man, learning to be one, does nothing for gay male liberation. It ensures only that some of us become more heterosexually acceptable – a liberation tactic devoid of strategy, neither radical nor empowering. I hope that in reading this book, more gay men will be encouraged to question a discourse that for too long has denied us the right to speak.

Ultimately, this book will argue that what is needed is a definition of gay male sexuality and identity that is radically subversive – one in which erotic empowerment is linked to companionship, trust, and partnership. What is needed is an identity that rejects assimilation, masculine mimicry, and the notion that power over someone is sexy – one that instead finds strength in compassion, mutuality, and reciprocity. What is needed is the gay male rejection of a community and legal culture that has bought into the myth of male entitlement and that continues to valorize and eroticize sexist and homophobic power relations. What is needed is a community and identity that encourages justice-doing and that is based on mutual trust and the type of pleasure that can be found only in relationships built on equality – in other words, a community that embraces sex equality and turns its back on the homophobia and sexism presently permeating our sexual and social practices. Pornography, defended as equality, offers little hope for a rights agenda in which equality is in fact attainable.

gAy mAle

PORNOGRAPHY

1 Pornography as Inequality: A Perspective on Hate Speech and the Meaning of Sexism

> The effect of this [pornographic] material is to reinforce male-female stereotypes to the detriment of both sexes. It attempts to make degradation, humiliation, victimization, and violence in human relationships appear normal and acceptable. A society which holds that egalitarianism and non-violence are basic to any human interaction, is clearly justified in controlling any medium which violates these principles.[1]
>
> R. v. Butler *(Supreme Court of Canada)*

Combating the Real, Specific Acts of Pornographic Harm

In 1983, long before the Supreme Court of Canada was asked to tackle the constitutional validity of Canada's obscenity laws, American feminists Andrea Dworkin and Catharine MacKinnon drafted a civil rights ordinance for the City of Minneapolis aimed at addressing the real, specific acts directly caused by the production and distribution of pornography.[2] The ordinance, discussed further in Chapter 8, was designed to stop those materials that injure the public welfare by violating and discriminating against women. Its goal was to eliminate pornography as a systematic practice of exploitation and subordination that is central in creating and maintaining sexual inequality. Several attempts were made to pass legislation of this type throughout the United States; several overseas jurisdictions also recommended its implementation. In 1984, Indianapolis, Indiana, for example, passed such a law containing the following definition:

> *Pornography* shall mean the graphic sexually explicit subordination of women, whether in pictures or in words, that also includes one or more of the following:

1   Women are presented as sexual objects who enjoy pain or humilia-
    tion; or
2   Women are presented as sexual objects who experience sexual plea-
    sure in being raped; or
3   Women are presented as sexual objects tied up or cut up or muti-
    lated or bruised or physically hurt, or as dismembered or truncated
    or fragmented or severed into body parts; or
4   Women are presented being penetrated by objects or animals; or
5   Women are presented in scenarios of degradation, injury, abase-
    ment, torture, shown as filthy or inferior, bleeding, bruised, or hurt
    in a context that makes these conditions sexual; [or]
6   Women are presented as sexual objects for domination, conquest,
    violation, exploitation, possession, or use, or through postures or
    positions of servility or submission or display.

The use of men, children, or transsexuals in the place of women ...
shall also constitute pornography.

Materials that fit this definition were not banned by the ordinance but were
made civilly actionable as sex discrimination when the acts of coercing a person into performing for pornography, forcing pornography on a person, assaulting a person because of specific pornography, and trafficking in
pornography were engaged in. Materials in subsection 6 of the definition were
excluded from the reach of the trafficking provision, thus confining that provision to the most violent materials.[3]

This radical redefinition of pornography as a sexually discriminatory act,
rather than a point of view or mere idea likely to cause offence, sought for the
first time to allow those harmed by pornography's inequality and sexual exploitation to prove their harms and, in so doing, take action to stop those
responsible for their injuries from continuing to hurt them and others.

Canada has not adopted the MacKinnon-Dworkin civil rights approach to
pornographic harm. In Canada, the distribution of obscenity remains a criminal offence, not a civil or human rights claim. It also remains a community
standards law, not a sex discrimination law. In 1992, however, in the case of
Butler, litigation concerning the constitutionality of Canada's *Criminal Code*
obscenity provisions, the Supreme Court of Canada did accept, by interpretation, that because pornography is a threat to sexual equality, the *Criminal Code*
provision is constitutional.[4] Specifically, the Court ruled that obscenity laws
are unconstitutional if used to restrict pornographic materials on a moral basis, but are constitutional if used to address the harms that are discriminatory
on the basis of sex.

In *Butler,* the Supreme Court of Canada made no reference to the work of
either Catharine MacKinnon or Andrea Dworkin, nor did it refer to pornography

as a civil rights issue. More importantly, the Court did not specifically find that pornography caused specific, actual harms. Rather, the Court found only that Parliament was entitled to have a reasonable belief that harm was caused and could, as a result, pass legislation aimed at curtailing these harms. Subsequent cases have interpreted the Court's failure to state unequivocally that all materials, once found to be pornographic, are harmful, to mean that the Crown, in prosecuting those selling pornography, must prove beyond a reasonable doubt that each and every piece of pornography seized causes specific harm. This standard of proof has resulted in a situation where few *Criminal Code* prosecutions have been made post-*Butler*. Thus, while the Court recognized that pornography can reinforce "male-female stereotypes to the detriment of both sexes," with the result being a threat to society's equality interest, the Court – because it found only that Parliament could have *thought* that pornography violates community standards by harming women and equality – did not legally reframe pornography as a specific practice with real and actionable consequences, as MacKinnon and Dworkin did.

These distinctions are explored throughout this chapter. They have been raised at the outset, however, because, despite these significant differences, considerable effort has gone into attempts to convince other gay men and the community at large that *Butler* and the MacKinnon-Dworkin approach together threaten their fundamental freedoms by limiting their right to speak freely about sex and identity. Indeed, in the United States and Canada, many who are committed to the availability of gay male pornography leading up to the *Little Sisters* case condemned supporters of the civil rights approach to pornographic harm and blamed them for both *Butler* and the state seizure of gay male pornography that gave rise to the *Little Sisters* litigation.[5] Central to this counter-attack has been the claim that pornography, and gay male pornography in particular, is not harmful. Given this, *Butler*, which recognized pornography as a practice of sex discrimination (a practice that the MacKinnon-Dworkin ordinances seek to civilly address) is, for these people, wrong and a threat to gay male liberation. For others, although heterosexual pornography might arguably be an issue of sex discrimination, this is not an issue insofar as gay men and gay male pornography are concerned. For them, gay male pornography has little, if anything, to do with the harms of sex equality. *Butler*, for them, holds no value insofar as gay male liberation is concerned, and gay male pornography should be exempt from the sex equality analysis accepted in that case.

The present analysis criticizes these claims. This chapter begins with an examination of the Supreme Court of Canada's ruling in *Butler* that Canada's *Criminal Code* obscenity laws are constitutional and that any free speech justification for the distribution of pornography is outweighed by the equality guarantees codified in Canada's *Charter of Rights and Freedoms*. This is followed by an examination of the criticisms made by those who have queried the Court's finding in this regard, focusing on the argument that there is no proof pornography is harmful and that *Butler* is thus a threat to the right to free speech enshrined in the *Charter.* The chapter closes with an examination of the Court's failure to state that harm *has* been proven and the consequences (for both women and gay men) that have flown from this.

The gay community almost unanimously supported the Supreme Court's earlier decision in *R.* v. *Keegstra,* a case in which the Court upheld the constitutionality of Canada's *Criminal Code* hate propaganda provision as equality law.[6] I argue that the community's criticism of *Butler,* in which the Court recognized the harms of sex inequality, is inconsistent with this support. The Court in *Keegstra* did not require proof of a causal connection between hate propaganda and inequality. Rather, as in *Butler,* it found that Parliament was entitled to believe that harm could result and could, in consequence, pass laws aimed at stopping these harms. This was a finding that many gay men applauded. While this celebration is warranted to the extent that it put into perspective the links between hate speech and injury, given that the scientific literature on the harms of pornography demonstrates unequivocally that harm results, though there is little if any "scientific" evidence that hate propaganda results in harm, the subsequent criticism by gay men of similar reasoning in *Butler* is troubling. Gay men have readily accepted the Courts' harms-based arguments in the context of racist and religious hate speech as unproblematic. Yet, several decades of conclusive research on the harms of pornography is rejected, ignored, elided, and obscured by affirmative misrepresentations claiming that no harm has been, or can be, proven. This chapter highlights and rethinks this inconsistency.

The concerns of many gay men about *Butler*'s application is, in my analysis, misplaced and short-sighted. Rather than attacking the decision because it seeks to enshrine sex equality – a finding from which, as this book will show, all gay men stand to benefit – or reject it because of a misguided belief that pornography does not harm individuals or society's equality interest generally, gay men would do better to query the unwillingness of Canada's highest court to face the record of harm, which is ambiguous, head on. In *Butler,* despite the irrebuttable proof of harm laid out before the Court, the Court refused to conclude that pornography was harmful, that it caused injury. Rather, it found only that enough evidence existed for Parliament to believe that such harm "might" result, thereby allowing Parliament to pass laws aimed at controlling these harms. As will be explained, subsequent cases have interpreted this to mean that the Crown must now prove beyond a reasonable doubt (the criminal law standard) that pornography harms, and it must do so each time it wants to prosecute those who sell or possess pornography. Although the evidence of harm is strong, this standard is, in reality, a legal nightmare. This could have been avoided had the Court in *Butler,* accepting the absolute proof of harm presented to it, stated unequivocally that pornography causes harm, rather than finding that Parliament's suspicions in this regard are sufficient to pass anti-pornography laws.

Gay men have supported the conclusion that harm must now be proven each time the Crown tries to prosecute those who sell or possess pornography – a gay rights strategy that I will argue is naïve. This has ensured that Canada's anti-pornography laws are effectively dead. It has also ensured, however, that the same standard of proof is now applied to Canada's *Criminal Code* hate propaganda provisions – effectively ensuring that they too are dead. Gay men must take some responsibility for this unacceptable situation. Denying the harms of pornography, while demanding more action against the harms of hate speech, however, will not resolve it.

Butler should be applauded as a clear articulation of the need to fight sexism and discrimination in the pornography area. But *Butler* does not go far enough toward ensuring that those materials that do harm are stopped, while ensuring that those that do not are not. Cases post-*Butler,* examined in Chapter 8, expose some of the difficulties with the application of the *Butler* sex equality standard since the case was handed down. To my mind, the MacKinnon-Dworkin anti-pornography ordinances, now constitutionally sound in Canada as a result of the free speech versus equality analysis provided in *Butler* and *Keegstra*, offer such a guarantee. Without an ordinance-based approach and *with* the *Criminal Code* standard of proof now called for by the courts post-*Butler,* Canada's anti-pornography laws (and arguably its hate speech laws) are essentially left toothless. Gay men would do well to applaud the Court's recognition in *Butler* (as they did in *Keegstra*) that not all "speech" merits legal protection, and that equality matters, while working with others to ensure that effective legal measures are put in place that *do* address the harms of hate and sexual inequality generally. Rather than attacking *Butler* because there is "no proof" that sex discrimination is the end result of heterosexual pornography, demanding more and more proof every time anyone tries to do something about the harms that *do* occur and which have been proven, or rejecting it because gay male pornography is not an issue of sex discrimination, as in my analysis it *is*, gay men would be better off supporting those legal claims that do actually tackle the harms of all pornography head on – something that *Butler,* for reasons explained here, is not able to do.

R. v. Butler

On 21 August 1987, police seized most of the inventory, including all the videotapes and magazines, in the Avenue Video Boutique in Winnipeg, Manitoba.[7] The owner of the boutique, Donald Victor *Butler,* was subsequently charged pursuant to s. 159 (now s. 163) of the *Canadian Criminal Code*[8] for offences of possession and sale of obscene materials.[9] The Supreme Court of Canada in 1991 considered two constitutional questions concerning Butler's conviction. First, whether s. 163 of the *Criminal Code* violated his right to free expression as guaranteed under s. 2(b) of the *Canadian Charter of Rights and Freedoms* (the *Charter*)[10] and, if so, whether this section of the code could be demonstrably justified under s. 1 of the *Charter* as a reasonable limit prescribed by law.[11] The Court confined its examination to whether or not Parliament was constitutionally entitled to enact the obscenity provision in s. 163(8), which provides: "(8) For the purposes of this Act, any publication a dominant characteristic of which is the undue exploitation of sex, or of sex and one or more of the following subjects, namely crime, horror, cruelty and violence, shall be deemed to be obscene."[12]

This chapter considers the Court's analysis of the interaction between the right to speak and the right to participate in society equally and without discrimination.

Donald Butler argued that the test for obscenity in s. 163(8) prohibited him from asserting his constitutional right to free expression.[13] In the final analysis, the majority of the Court found that although s. 163(8) did violate Butler's constitutional right to free expression, Parliament's legislative mandate nonetheless constituted a reasonable limit on this right and was saved by virtue of the operation of s. 1 of the *Charter*.[14] The Court held that the overriding objective of the *Criminal Code* provision is to prevent harm to society – specifically, the harms that result from the production and distribution of pornographic representations and pictures that undermine the right of other people to live equally, without fear of harassment, violence, and other discrimination. State-imposed limits on the right to sell pornography were found justified when inequality resulted from the sale of these materials.

In its decision, the Court outlined the kinds of harms s. 163 of the *Code* aims to address and what kind of "expression" creates and promotes these harms. It is this analysis that is most groundbreaking in terms of Canada's approach to systemic equality. At a basic level, the Court reconceptualized the law of obscenity by abandoning the analysis of its justifiability traditionally offered by the courts. Specifically, quoting from the *MacGuigan Report*[15] on the effects of pornography, the Court noted that Parliament was entitled to limit the sale and possession of materials that result in sexism, misogyny, and gender inequality.[16]

The briefs in this case provided the Court with the overwhelming social and scientific evidence on the harmful effects of pornography on women, men, and thus on society as a whole – research from which the Court concluded that there is "sufficient reason for Parliament to believe" that pornography amounts to a practice of sex discrimination.[17] This evidence indicates that when rape is sexualized, women are more likely to be raped and subjected to sexual violence.[18] Findings on materials that are not violent but are nonetheless degrading or dehumanizing further indicate that pornographic materials "lower inhibitions on aggression by men against women, increase acceptance of women's sexual servitude, increase sexual callousness toward women, decrease the desire of both sexes to have female children and increase the belief in male dominance in intimate relationships."[19] The testimonies of women harmed during the production of pornography bolster these findings, as do the experiences of those whose partners have humiliated or terrorized them into imitating pornographic materials and who have been battered and psychologically abused by these same partners when they have refused to do so. Moreover, the testimonies of those women who report that pornography renders them open to harassment, or unable to function as equals in a society ripe with sexual inequality, strengthen the argument that pornography is a practice of sex discrimination and gender inequality.[20]

LEAF, in its factum in *Butler,* offered an accurate and revealing summary of the research conducted on the harms of pornography.[21] Commenting specifically on the materials seized in Donald Butler's store,[22] LEAF demonstrated that the vast majority of the subject materials at issue were visual ones in which women were presented as "used, hurt or abused for sex for men."[23] LEAF showed that these women are often presented as "being raped. Sometimes they act as if they are enjoying it; sometimes they scream, resist, and try to run."[24] The harms of pornography to women documented in the literature on harms were described to include "dehumanization, humiliation, sexual exploitation, forced sex, forced prostitution, physical injury, child sexual abuse and sexual harassment." Pornography was also argued to "diminish the reputation of women as a group, deprive women of their credibility and social and self worth, and undermine women's equal access to protected rights."[25] In sum, pornography was submitted to be "a practice of sex discrimination against individual women and women as a group."[26]

Relying on the literally thousands of empirical studies on this subject, LEAF showed that this work concluded that the circulation of such material leads to "an increase in the incidence of aggressive, harmful behaviour that make pornography a systematic practice of exploitation and subordination based on sex that differentially harms women."[27] Noting the harms inflicted on real women to produce pornography,[28] LEAF also persuasively argued that "if anything can violate a person's physical liberty and integrity more than a sexual assault, it is the mass marketing of that assault as sexual entertainment."[29]

Similarly, again within the context of sexual assault, LEAF, summarizing the groundbreaking work of experimental psychologists, noted that "when explicit sex and express violence against women are combined, particularly when rape is portrayed as pleasurable or positive for the victim, the risk of violence against women is known to increase as a result of exposure."[30] Referring to non-violent materials – that is, those that degrade and dehumanize women – the evidence demonstrates clearly that these materials also increase self-reported sexually aggressive behaviour.[31] This fact was noted to be well known to many women, who report that all these studies merely document what they know from their own lives – physical and psychological torture, sexual trauma, violence inflicted on them and their children, and a callous disregard for their right to live a life free of abuse.[32] And for those who are not subjected to physical violence per se, unequal treatment, sexualized through subordination, again remains the norm.[33]

LEAF's analysis is consistent with the evidence of other researchers and those women, men, and children who have been harmed by pornography. These findings were, for example, summarized by the US Attorney General's Commission on Pornography in 1986, which, reviewing all the studies conducted on the link between pornography and the unequal treatment of women to that date, accepted that an unequivocal causal connection existed between violent, degrading, and dehumanizing pornography and the systemic sexual subordination of women. With respect to non-violent materials, the commission concluded:

> [O]ur focus on these more violent or more coercive forms of actual subordination of women should not diminish what we take to be a necessarily incorporated conclusion. Substantial exposure to materials of this type bears some causal relationship to the incidence of various non-violent forms of discrimination against or subordination of women in our society. To the extent that these materials create or reinforce the view that women's function is disproportionately to satisfy the sexual needs of men, then the materials will have pervasive effects on the treatment of women in society far beyond the incidence of identifiable acts of rape or other sexual violence ... We feel confident in concluding that the view of women as available for sexual domination is one cause of ... discrimination [against women], and we feel confident as well in concluding that degrading material bears a causal relationship to the view that women ought to subordinate their own desires and beings to the sexual satisfaction of men ... The totality of the social science evidence ... is slightly against the hypothesis that non-violent and non-degrading [sexually explicit] materials bear a causal relationship to acts of sexual violence.[34]

In sum, the scientific and testimonial evidence accumulated for over thirty years proves overwhelmingly that pornography is a discriminatory practice based on sex that denies women the right to participate equally in society. It maintains sex as a basis for subordination, fostering bigotry and contempt sexually along gender lines and, in so doing, ensures that inequality remains society's central dynamic. The conclusions drawn from this evidence do not constitute an advocacy position. Rather, they are a description of the available facts.

In reviewing these facts, and in determining the constitutionality of legislation which, Parliament argued, would address these harms, the Court offered an understanding of pornography that represents considerable progress in balancing the right to free speech with the right to equality – a balancing process that the US courts continue to struggle with. In the final analysis, the Court in *Butler* offered a test for obscenity that recognized that the ultimate community harm to be addressed is the harm to equality by expression that makes "degradation, humiliation, victimization and violence in human relationships normal and acceptable."[35] Implicit in this reasoning is the conclusion that although free expression is a fundamental value, it is not the *only* value worth protecting and it does not always rank above other values. Indeed, the Court noted that any constitutional guarantee of free expression that develops without taking "the reality of substantive social inequality or the guarantee of legal equality into account," serves only to preserve, if not promote, present inequalities.[36] The Court further noted that "the harm caused by the proliferation of materials that seriously offend other values fundamental to our society is a substantial concern that justifies restricting the otherwise full exercise of the freedom of expression."[37]

Although the Court focused on the effect of pornography, once distributed, on equality, it should not be seen here as inferring that real women are not also physically harmed during the production of these materials. On the contrary, the Court did accept evidence of this fact,[38] relying on this evidence as further indication that pornography can be seen to be a tool of inequality through which those with power control those without it. Further evidence supports this point, showing that inequality and violence in the production of the material is real and often, but not always, self-evident from the material itself.[39] Once distributed, it serves to reinforce the very conditions of inequality that make its production possible in the first place.[40]

By focusing on these inequalities, the Court also specifically rejected the notion that pornographic "speech" should be limited to protect public morality. In so doing, it rejected an entire history of judicial reasoning concerned only with the preservation of majoritarian moral codes:[41]

> [T]his particular objective is no longer defensible in view of the *Charter*. To impose a certain standard of public and sexual morality, solely because it reflects the conventions of a given community, is inimical to the exercise and enjoyment of individual freedoms ... This is "legal moralism" – a majority deciding what values should inform individual lives and then coercively imposing those values on minorities. The prevention of "dirt for dirt's sake" is not a legitimate objective which would justify the violation of one of the most fundamental freedoms enshrined in the *Charter*.[42]

Rejecting immorality as the basis for prosecution, the Court instead defined the harms of pornography within a sex equality context, adding that "if true equality between male and female persons is to be achieved, we cannot ignore the threat to equality resulting from exposure to audiences of certain types of violent and degrading materials."[43] This conclusion can only be applauded in a society struggling with sexism and gender bias.

Accepting that the harm imposed by materials undermining equality is fundamentally a threat to society's interests in the equality of all persons, the Court explained that s. 163 of the *Criminal Code* could justifiably be applied with the following test in mind. Specifically, materials can be seized when they violate those equality values outlined by the Court as fundamental. These values are violated when the materials constitute "the undue exploitation of sex," as called for in s. 163 of the *Code*.[44] In determining whether the exploitation is undue, the Court explained that pornography can be usefully divided into three categories:

1   explicit sex with violence;
2   explicit sex without violence but which subjects people to treatment that is degrading or dehumanizing; and
3   explicit sex without violence that is neither degrading nor dehumanizing.

The Court then explained that in making the determination of what amounts to the undue exploitation of sex with respect to these three categories, the portrayal of sex coupled with violence will almost always constitute the undue exploitation of sex. Explicit sex that is degrading or dehumanizing will be undue if the risk of harm (to equality) is substantial. Finally, explicit sex that is not violent and neither degrading nor dehumanizing will not qualify as the undue exploitation of sex unless it employs children in its production. With respect to the second category, degrading or dehumanizing behaviour, the Court in *Butler* accepted the graphic, accurate description of the Manitoba Queen's Bench in *R. v. Ramsingh*,[45] in which the type of material that qualifies for this label was described as follows:

> [Individuals] are exploited, portrayed as desiring pleasure from pain, by being humiliated and treated only as an object of male domination sexually, or in cruel or violent bondage. Women are portrayed in these films as pining away their lives waiting for a huge male penis to come along, on the person of a so-called sex therapist, or window washer, supposedly to transport them into sexual ecstasy. Or even more false and degrading one is led to believe their raison d'être is to savour semen as a life elixir, or that they secretly desire to be forcefully taken by a male.[46]

Accepting this definition, the Court in *Butler* explained that degrading and dehumanizing sexual materials are harmful when they "place women (and sometimes men) in positions of subordination, servile submission or humiliation." These materials, the Court concluded, can be stopped because "they run against the principles of equality and dignity of all human beings."[47]

In *Butler,* the Canadian Supreme Court mandated that the overriding objective in limiting the production and distribution of pornography is the avoidance of harm to society[48] – the harm caused to real people from materials that exploit them and depict them as inferior and *unequal.*[49] In so ruling, the Court explicitly recognized that not all speech is equal and that some speech is in fact the source of inequality. The right to express oneself must thus be viewed within the context of real systemic inequalities and is not seen as absolute. In viewing the questions before it in this light, the Court took seriously the reality of sex discrimination in this setting, making sex equality a meaningful constitutional right.

Inequality Post-*Butler:* Gay Men Respond

Gay men's right to free speech has been too often silenced by a majority discourse that refuses to permit our ideas, politics, and pains expression. In the name of free expression, gay men have been subjected to oppression through hate speech that does little more than entrench our place in society as second-class citizens or, for those of us who have been completely denied any voice, as non-existent citizens. As US critical race theorist Mari Matsuda explains,

> [t]o be hated, despised and alone is the ultimate fear of all human beings. However irrational hate speech may be, it hits right at the emotional place where we feel the most pain. The aloneness comes not only from the hate message itself, but also from the government response of tolerance. When ... the courts refuse redress for hate messages and when attacks are officially dismissed as pranks, the victim becomes a stateless person.[50]

In *Butler,* by recognizing that some speech encourages and promotes societal acts that result in unequal treatment, and by recognizing the considerable personal toll inflicted on those subjected to hatred, the Canadian Supreme Court did much to advance the rights of all persons who do not benefit from a now recognized unequal distribution of power. Indeed, the fact that systemic equality is held out as a more fundamental right than the right to sell and possess materials that cause hatred and inequality represents an impressive leap forward for Canadian equality jurisprudence.

In reviewing the merits of the decision in *Butler,* it is worth highlighting again that for the Canadian judiciary, pornography had historically been viewed solely as a source of immorality and public indecency – an interpretation that, once applied, did little to address systemic gender inequality (or much else). Indeed, within the context of the lesbian and gay male community, this approach succeeded only in suppressing efforts to create, and ultimately express, a lesbian and gay male discourse aimed at undermining heterosexism and compulsory heterosexuality. In *Butler,* the Court rejected the judiciary's track record in this regard and sought instead to put in place a definition of harm that tackled inequality rather than indecency. It did so by stating that "true equality between male and female persons"[51] will not be achieved if "we ignore the threat to equality resulting from exposure to audiences of certain types of violent and degrading material."[52] The Court also held that employing morality as the measure of social harm could no longer be tolerated because "to impose a certain standard of public and sexual morality, solely because it reflects the conventions of a given community, is inimical to the exercise and enjoyment of individual freedoms."[53] Therefore, the approach offered by the Court – an approach that specifically rejected an assumed community-based need to protect social morality and which instead adopted an equality-based approach as the appropriate measure of systemic harm – provided a model for speech rights that finally aimed to protect those harmed by hate and inequality, while also permitting the legitimate expression of lesbian and gay male voices too long silenced by prejudice and intolerance.

Despite the considerable progress made as a result of its shift in thinking about the legal regulation of pornography and inequality, the reaction in the lesbian and gay male community post-*Butler* has been less than enthusiastic. In particular, many have been quick to attack *Butler* because, in their opinion, the Court based its analysis on evidence that did not "prove" that pornography was a cause of sexual inequality. Shortly after the decision in *Butler* was made public, Chris Bearchell, for example, a Toronto lesbian activist and writer, wrote in the main Toronto lesbian and gay newspaper that *Butler* was entirely the fault of feminist anti-pornographers who had simply "misunderstood" and manipulated the evidence of harm ultimately accepted by the Court. Commenting on LEAF's role in convincing the Court of the link between pornography and the harms of sex inequality, Bearchell stated:

> Canada's pre-eminent feminist law-reform organization, the Legal Education and Action Fund (LEAF) seems determined to curtail Canadians' newly enshrined right to freedom of speech before most of us ever get a chance to exercise it ...
>
> The Court did not make its decision because porn is proven to cause harm, but rather because it is believed by the Canadian public to cause harm and because this belief has been repeated often by expert witnesses in recent obscenity cases. And the fact that public and expert witnesses believe that porn causes harm is due to the success of the past decade's anti-porn propaganda campaign, carried out by a dubious alliance of right-wing Christians and such feminist anti-sex

crusaders as Andrea Dworkin and Catharine MacKinnon, who helped develop LEAF's strategy in the *Butler* case. Over the past few years, thousands of dollars have gone to support women's groups which actively spread this misinformation. The *Butler* decision evaded the question of proof by stating that such proof is unnecessary ...

It is a sad comment on our time that a moral panic about sexual imagery is led by feminists; that their energy is channelled into an anti-sex backlash ... In the face of a real problem that demands justice and power in their own lives for the abused, this brand of feminism perpetuates fear and intolerance instead, while it diverts attention from real causes of violence.[54]

Elsewhere, Bearchell wrote: "Discussions of whether or not pornography causes harm often degenerate into pointless haggles over whose experts have more credibility ... The debate about the relation of porn to violence is not really a scientific one, it's a political debate about the appropriateness of scapegoating pornography for deep-seated social problems. Porn is an easy target – it is visible, officially disapproved of and relatively controllable."[55]

In light of the evidence already outlined in this chapter, it is clear that Bearchell's reading of the work of Catharine MacKinnon and of the evidence that proves the reality of pornographic harm is on shaky ground at best. MacKinnon's work on pornography, best exemplified in her ordinances, targets pornography's role as a sexual practice. It is completely removed from the work of those who seek to control pornography as an idea or belief that undermines society's moral fibre. More importantly, however, MacKinnon's approach to pornography endeavours to allow those who have been harmed to seek redress by proving the causal connection Bearchell seems to want. This is a fact Bearchell and others simply overlook. Instead, these critics conflate her work with *Butler* in order to dismiss both because, as far as they are concerned, there is no proof that sexual inequality is the end result. In making this assertion, these writers ignore the harms inflicted on the real people who do claim to have been harmed by sexual violence and inequality and who for whom the evidence is clear that pornography played a role. In addition, however, they appear to be advocating a double standard that risks undermining the battle they themselves have fought, and in part won, in trying to get the courts and others to take seriously the concerns of lesbians and gay men who have been assaulted, victimized, and dehumanized as a result of materials that vilify them.

At its core, MacKinnon's work advocates a forum within which to allow those harmed by sex discrimination to speak and be taken seriously. She asks only that when women say, "this is what happened because of this material and this is why," that society listen and institutionally take seriously the assertions made. Her work is not confined to pornography, however. Indeed, she and many others have made similar arguments about hate speech, including anti-gay vitriol. And yet, if I am not mistaken, few (in Canada at least) have questioned those efforts. So why this apparent double standard when dealing with pornography? While it is true that the person reading a flyer that asks him to kill all fags might be provoked into rallying for gay rights, it is also true that another might actually take the message seriously and act on it. The fact that the former might be the case does not mean that the latter might not also prove true. Indeed, much time and effort by gay rights activists have gone into proving that the latter *is*, in fact, the end result in some cases. Similarly, while presentations of real women being hung and mutilated might teach some men that they are "turned off" by what they have seen, still others might discover that what they have seen excites them, whether or not they approve of that arousal or the treatment that causes it. And if women say that the source of this excitement results in direct physical harm being inflicted on them, do they not have the right to be heard and to a forum in which their claims are taken seriously? If a particularly brutal bashing occurs and we subsequently discover that the person responsible reads and takes seriously anti-gay hate literature, do we say "more proof please"? Or do we expect a forum within which to speak, within which to say, enough is enough, the connection is clear, stop it? The answer it seems, at least to those who know the reality of words that cause wounds, is an answer not foreign to most women. "Sexual imagery" does not cause harm and inequality. Pornography does. And *this* is what many have sought to stop. Nothing more. To the extent that some materials produce specific acts against women, then these women should be allowed to do something about it, and their concerns should not be dismissed as merely political or scapegoating. Similarly, not all speech that is negative toward certain groups produces violence and results in bigotry against minorities. No one has ever said otherwise. Nor would they be taken seriously if they did. But some does, and gay men have asked that *it* be taken seriously. Do not women with similar concerns merit the same consideration? To my mind, the distinction drawn by gay rights activists between the effects of anti-gay hate speech and pornography is inconsistent at best, particularly as the evidence favouring the control of pornography is much more documented and scientifically verified than the evidence used to control anti-gay speech. This is not to dismiss the effects of anti-gay hate propaganda material on gay men. Rather, it is to question the dismissal as inconclusive of the much stronger evidence used to stop pornography.

The Harms of Anti-Gay Vilification: No Proof Required?

The *Canadian Criminal Code* prohibits public expression that advocates or promotes genocide against people "distinguished by colour, race, religion or ethnic origin." Section 319(1) of the *Code* makes it an offence to communicate statements in a public place that incite hatred against these same people. "Sexuality" or "sexual orientation" is not a prohibited ground,[56] leading to repeated calls by lesbians and gay men for an immediate amendment to the *Code*. Accordingly, others, noted below, have argued that the *Code*'s under-inclusiveness should be challenged as a violation of the equality provisions guaranteed in s. 15 of the *Charter of Rights and Freedoms*. As of yet, federal government promises of change have not been forthcoming. This has led gay rights advocates to express concern that the government's failure to acknowledge the effects of hate speech on gay men and lesbians will do little more than encourage further discrimination, violence, and inequality. The evidence seems to support this claim, although, as tends to be the case with all forms of hate speech, no amount of proof that a link or causal connection exists will be sufficient to satisfy the cries of those who prefer a more absolutist approach to speech freedoms. These cries have not, however, tended to come from gay men. An examination of the extent of anti-gay vilification in Canada indicates why calls for more proof have not been forthcoming from those so quick to demand it in other circumstances. As the examples that follow demonstrate, gay men have been subjected to extreme forms of violence that are unquestionably and directly linked to anti-gay hate propaganda. It is not surprising, therefore, that gay men have led the charge for law reform aimed at curtailing the distribution of this material.

In February 1993, Jeffrey Kirk, a gay man living in Toronto, opened his mailbox to find a comic book published by Christ Is the Answer Inc., a Toronto-based organization linked with a Californian religious publishing network, Chick Publications. The comic book was also left lying in bus shelters and phone booths throughout the Toronto area and depicted the biblical account of the destruction of Sodom. Entitled "Doom Town," the comic shows the men of Sodom chasing a group of angels, saying, "We want to have sex with them." It then shows the same men succumbing to divine vengeance in the form of a rain of fire and brimstone.[57]

When asked to justify their actions, a spokesperson for Christ Is the Answer responded, "It's the word of God. It's what's in the Bible."[58] Kirk and many others disagree, arguing that the citation has less to do with divine Scripture than with the wishes of a homophobic born-again organization bent on encouraging violence against gays and lesbians.[59] As Kirk explains, "you can forgive the ancient Hebrews for saying these sorts of things, but not a contemporary group. There're basically saying, 'Let's kill fags' and that's unacceptable." Charles Campbell, who would later act as the lawyer employed to defend the right of Toronto gay bookshop Glad Day Books to import pornography, agreed, calling for the immediate amendment of Canada's hate speech laws to protect against the distribution of anti-gay speech: "I tend not to like the hate propaganda provision as it's open to abuse, but this comic book is definitely a direct advocacy of putting homosexuals to death. It's outrageous."[60]

Numerous other examples abound. In August 1998, for example, the *Regina Leader Post* announced that it would not reconsider its decision to run an advertisement that quoted passages from the Bible condemning "homosexual behaviour." The *Leader Post*'s general manager was quoted as saying that his newspaper champions freedom of the press and freedom of expression: "[W]e don't want to label ourselves as a newspaper where only certain select groups get freedom of expression." Gay groups were outraged, declaring the ads deeply hurtful, harmful, and disgusting.[61] Similar outrage was expressed when, in 1990, a full-page advertisement calling for days of fasting and prayer to dissuade God from destroying Vancouver during the Gay Games to be held in that city. Under the headline, "Time is running out," a group of unnamed evangelical leaders took out full-page ads that proclaimed that homosexuality is contrary to the Bible and that the Games "symbolize rebellion against God and will therefore bring disgrace to Vancouver. Those who in their public exercise of authority support and approve homosexuality place themselves and their followers under the judgement of God. History provides abundant evidence of cities and nations destroyed by internal moral decay."[62] Gay community leaders described the ads as an "intolerable diatribe," as "bigoted," and as an "outrageous use of selected biblical excerpts." A similar reaction was heard when, shortly after the ad appeared, a pamphlet produced by the Institute for the Scientific Investigation of Sexuality began to appear throughout Vancouver. Entitled *The Psychology of Homosexuality: Homosexuality Is a Crime against Humanity,* the flyer begins with this description of homosexual identity: "A person committed to homosexual habits is a loose cog. Aside from personal pleasure, his life is essentially pointless. The best he can do is stay out of the way and refrain from damaging the social machine; at worst he might foul its running and destroy it. He has no creative part in history – the end of his life will merely remove a bit of disorganisation from the social generator."[63]

At about the same time, REAL Women began distributing a pamphlet across Canada entitled *Laws Protecting Homosexuals or So-Called Sexual Orientation Legislation: How It Will Affect Canadians.* According to the pamphlet, the "homosexual movement" has a number of goals, one of which is to

SEDUCE THE YOUNG

The growing influence of pedophilia has been noted. One child sex ring in New York boasted over 20,000 customers. One report noted that:

"Pictures, magazines, films, videotapes depicting children in acts of actual sexual intercourse, sodomy, bondage, bestiality, sado-masochism acts (boy/boy, girl/girl) can be purchased for less than fifty dollars."

Many homosexuals, because they cannot procreate, must recruit – often the young. They also promote recruiting "straights." With new legislation such seduction becomes permissible and acceptable.[64]

As Kathleen Sam Banks explains, the above kinds of examples can and do occur on an almost daily basis in almost every Canadian city and town. Their theme is simple, their objective clear: the elimination of gay people on the basis of their sexual orientation.[65] This is a point best illustrated by a phone message on the answering machine of Canadian Liberty Net – a message that gay lobbyists successfully challenged in the courts as a violation of the anti-hate provisions in the *Canadian Human Rights Act,* which, unlike the *Criminal Code,* does prohibit anti-gay vilification.[66] The message said: "Hell, the ancient Celts used to take their queers and trample them into the peat bogs. That's not such a bad idea, maybe. Perhaps we have finally stumbled across the argument which will save the Burns bog in Delta from development because it is the only bog big enough to service the needs of the progressive city of Vancouver."[67]

Add to this the mass distribution of videotapes of a prominent TV evangelist encouraging the extermination of all gay people,[68] members of Parliament hiding behind parliamentary privilege to denounce gays as a threat to humanity,[69] portrayals of gay men as sordid and the embodiment of evil,[70] more anti-gay flyers that condemn gays for all eternity, and bumper stickers that read: "Kill a Queer for Christ,"[71] and what one gets is a pretty good indication that all is not well within the Canadian state, at least not for those for whom equality is not yet a reality.

The effect that speech such as the above has on lesbian women and gay men is clear. These words and the actions they provoke speak for themselves and in so doing, do much – including through material aggression – to silence those who cannot. As Banks again explains, those exposed to it suffer a loss of dignity and self-worth, with the end result that they begin to accept the prejudice, cease to speak out against those who attack them with words – if they survive – and ultimately cease to participate as full members of society;[72] silencing their own words, hiding their own identities, ultimately being ashamed of and making invisible that which the hatemonger aims to see disappear. As Banks rightly concludes:

> Implicit in these comments is the message that gay men and lesbians are genetically inferior, unhealthy, unworthy as human beings and certainly undeserving of any respect or dignity ... There can be little doubt that these statements are intended to elicit support from other like-minded thinkers, to encourage contempt for and discrimination against gay men and lesbians, and to remind gays and lesbians of their precarious safety in the community. These statements further serve to deny the gay and lesbian population as individuals and as a group the right to their dignity and equal status.[73]

Other arguments were advanced by LEAF in its submissions to the Supreme Court of Canada in *Keegstra*. LEAF argued that the wilful public promotion of hatred inhibits truth seeking because it intimidates disadvantaged persons from pursuing the truth: "Hatred promotes disadvantage and, as such, is a practice of discrimination ... enmity, ill-will, intolerance and prejudice produce exclusion, denigration and subordination. Stereotyping and stigmatization through hate propaganda shapes their social image and reputation, often controlling the opportunities of individuals more powerfully than their individual abilities."[74]

To some extent, LEAF's arguments for the need to restrict speech that silences and produces violence relied on the earlier work of Patrick Lawlor, Q.C., who, in 1984, had written a comprehensive report on hate speech and group defamation for the Attorney General of Ontario. In it, Lawlor argues that target groups are entitled to protection, not only against the actual physical violence that minority groups are all too well aware is caused by hate speech, but also against calumny, fear, and threat that infects and diminishes their lives.[75]

Lesbians and gay men are well aware that people do listen to hate speech and that it does result in harm, both physical and psychological. As M. Kirk and H. Madsen note with respect to anti-gay propaganda in the United States, "the excitable masses are listening," and there is no dearth of evidence to prove their point. The authors provide the following examples to make their point:

> While witnesses look on, a young man – a gardener for the city of San Francisco – is stabbed to death by four youths shouting "Faggot! Faggot!" In the same city, a lesbian is beaten in the face, knocked to the ground and kicked repeatedly while attackers scream "dyke" and "bitch."
>
> In New Jersey, three college-aged men are charged with entrapping a twenty-year-old gay at midnight in a shopping mall; after working him over and burning cigarettes in his face, they allegedly tied him by the ankles to their truck and dragged him down the road.
>
> In Winston-Salem, the killer of a gay man is released on probation, then murders another by cutting his throat and planting a butcher knife in his chest. (Prosecutors reportedly let the killer plea-bargain after concluding that jurors won't impose a stiff sentence for cutting a gay man's throat.)
>
> A statistical report of anti-gay violence in the Bay Area catalogues the following "favourite" implements of assault: knives, guns, baseball bats, bottles, crowbars, large boards without nails, large boards with nails, and chains.[76]

Although few statistics exist in Canada for anti-gay attacks, there is little reason to believe that similar stories are not as pervasive and real within the Canadian context, and much reason to believe that they are.[77]

Lawlor notes and accepts that hate speech results in violence[78] but also argues persuasively that almost as hurtful as the physical attacks on minorities is their perception, resulting from "what they hear, what they are told and what they witness, that their fellows do not care, that they are abandoned to their fate, that no protection is forthcoming."[79] Discussing racist speech, he notes:

> People ... seem to have only a blunted sense of what racial insults and discrimination do to the self-esteem, aspirations, and modes of life of the targeted individual or groups, and especially to the children. It can be and is too often devastating; they are treated as less than human, they are dehumanized. They react aggressively in anger, which usually only worsens the situation, frustrates the victim and drives the injury deeper; or supinely, they come to accept their stigmatization, as a fated fact of life, with all the misery and degradation that that entails.[80]

Perhaps the most publicized North American example of gays advocating the need to arrest the spread of what they perceived to be anti-gay messages is seen in those street actions that occurred throughout the continent, including Canada, before and after the release of William Friedkin's film *Cruising*. The film revolves around the sadistic killing of gay men by a man portrayed in the film as ridden by guilt and self-loathing. Set in a series of sado-masochistic bars and porn theatres in New York's gay district, the film documents the brutal murders of gay men "cruised" by the killer in these bars and clubs. Killing gays, we are led to believe, "exorcises the killer's own suspected homosexuality."[81] One scene, in which a fashion designer is knifed in a porn movie booth, juxtaposes the orgasm of a man getting whipped in the porn flick with the death agony of the designer. As Scott Tucker explains, the moral of this scene and many others in the film is that the wages of sin is death.[82]

Many gay men were quick to recognize the possibility that the film might encourage violence against gay men by persons wanting an excuse to assault them.[83] Referring to the film as "the most oppressive, ugly, bigoted look at homosexuality ever presented on the screen," the resolutely pro-pornography – an irony that will become clear later – *Village Voice* encouraged gays to block production of the film.[84] A flyer distributed throughout New York City read: "*Cruising* is a film which will encourage more violence against homosexuals. In the current climate of backlash against the gay rights movement, this movie is a genocidal act."[85] At a meeting attended by six hundred men to discuss the film, a journalist asked the men how many had been the targets of violence in the last year. More than half raised their hands.[86]

When asked at the meeting whether the hoped-for protests against the film violate free speech rights, the meeting's organizer proclaimed, "We're not attacking Billy Friedkin's right to make the film. We're just telling him we don't want it made off our backs. That's not censorship. That's self-defence!"[87] Another US writer agreed. Commenting on those who would defend the film on the basis of the First Amendment freedom of expression guarantees in the US Constitution, *Village Voice* journalist Richard Goldstein advocated for greater reliance on that country's equality provisions as found in the Fourteenth Amendment: "If you look behind the First Amendment to the people who are raising it as a defence to slur, you see that for the most part these people are white, male heterosexuals. The farther away you get from this nexus of authority, the less likely you are to find people who think freedom of speech means very much without the rest of the Constitution – especially the Fourteenth Amendment."[88]

In an interesting response to those who would require more proof that the type of violence glorified in *Cruising* might lead to an increase in anti-gay violence, Toronto-based writer Scott Tucker explained:

> During the protests, many gay men realized for the first time just what kind of struggle women are waging against media misogyny and abuse. Feminists at a recent conference on pornography watched a slide show of media assaults, epitomized by a *Hustler* cover showing a woman being fed into a meat grinder. That kind of imagery is big business, and with its images of gay men dying with their cocks hacked off and stuffed in their mouths, so is *Cruising*.
>
> Will the film directly provoke murders, as some claimed, or was this simply "rousing" rhetoric? Direct cause and effect is usually hard to prove, but films like *Cruising* can charge an already stormy atmosphere so that lightning finally strikes "at random." And the messages such a film carries help to keep us fearful and in our proper place in the hierarchy of power.[89]

Tucker's comments were made almost twenty years ago. Are gay men now any less aware of the effects of hate speech, any less wary of the effects of words that incite violence? I don't think so. When I ask gay men how it feels to be taunted, ridiculed, or terrorized with the label "faggot," and when I ask gay men how it feels to work in an environment in which colleagues are free to shout "queer" or "poofter" or "butt-fucker" without repercussion, these men reply that they feel silenced, threatened, emotionally insecure, incapable of working and hence vulnerable to dismissal at work, afraid of being assaulted at any time, reluctant to believe that they would have any recourse if they did report assaults against them, and wary of trusting those around them. When I ask gay men whether pamphlets encouraging the extermination of all homosexuals should be banned, I am told that these materials *must* be banned if gay men are ever to achieve equality.[90] And when I ask gay men whether they can "prove" that words alone undermine their ability to function, or whether words alone might actually encourage others to treat them in a violent manner or with disrespect and hostility, these men reply that "sometimes" people should just be believed and "sometimes" an exact causal connection is not required. And if they are lawyers, and if they are Canadian, they are quick to point out that Canada's highest court, in *Keegstra*, has now stated loud and clear that hate speech is an issue of inequality – *their* inequality – and that those who say they are hurt by hate speech should and must be believed. This, in turn, as indicated, has led many to call for an amendment to the *Criminal Code* so as to include sexuality as a ground that, like race and ethnicity, should not be the subject of vilification without legal recourse.

Women Speak: Does Anybody Listen?

Why not women? Why not pornography? Why not sex equality? What happened between Tucker in 1979 and Bearchell in 1990? The gay male commitment to limiting speech when it harms what they recognize as their interests is proven. Why are the decisions of courts and tribunals that acknowledge the effects of hate speech on gay men applauded but not those that acknowledge the effects of misogynistic speech on all women, lesbians included? Why now do many gay men advocate the rejection of a judicial decision that goes some way toward rethinking the effect of a kind of hate literature against half of humankind?

To heighten the contradiction, consider another example. In 1984, the *Body Politic*, a lesbian and gay newspaper in Toronto, ran an advertisement by Red Hot Video, one of Canada's leading distributors of heterosexual pornography. The paper justified its decision to run the ad on the basis that not to do so would constitute a violation of the company's right to free expression and risk undermining the rights of all people to speak freely about sexuality. In response, lesbian author Jane Rule, who (in another irony that will become clear later) testified on behalf of Little Sisters Bookstore (thus on behalf of the pornography it defended throughout its litigation), had this to say: "Sexual liberation is no more about raping women than it is about bashing queers. Would the *Body Politic* help publicize films that endorsed beating up homosexuals in the park, robbing and murdering them as an acceptable enhancement of manhood, sexually tantalizing? I think not. Yet it is argued that refusing ads for a firm which distributes films abusive to women is an act of negative censorship ... Gay men don't have to condone pornography degrading to women in the name of sexual freedom of expression."[91]

And yet they do. Why is that? Why do they condone *this* speech as "speech" but not the speech that encourages anti-gay violence? Those who attack the work of anti-pornography feminists from this perspective state or imply that pornography, as mere "sexual expression," does not harm, cannot harm – that is, that real people are not harmed as a result of its production and that its distribution does not and cannot, qua sexual, qua expression, result in those behaviours and attitudinal changes that lead to physical harm and undermine social equality.

The contradictions inherent in the arguments advanced by gay men in this regard are troubling. Aware of the effect of speech that promotes hatred, these men recognize that its protection does little more than deny those most harmed by it their right to speak, to obtain relief, and to experience change. Speech aimed at promoting violence against lesbians and gay men does just that – promotes violence against lesbians and gay men. This we know from experience, even if the scientific research to this effect has, of yet, not been forthcoming. So why then the opposition when women make a similar claim within the context of pornographic materials for which the scientific and experimental evidence of harm has been forthcoming?

Unfortunately, the decision of the Supreme Court in *Butler* has not helped resolve this schism over the need to prove harm. Indeed, a review of some of the judicial decisions post-*Butler* indicates that the gay community's call for more proof, in addition to harming women, may now in fact be being used to stop those actions gay men themselves have argued are harmful.

Contrary to the claims of pro-pornography advocates post-*Butler*,[92] there is *no* research that questions the findings and conclusions outlined by LEAF in *Butler*. The claim that such research exists is a misrepresentation.[93] Unfortunately, the Court in *Butler*, in repeating the outdated canard (advocated by gay and non-gay pornography advocates alike) that no such proof is possible, simply concluded that absolute proof and scientific accuracy is not required when attempting to balance speech freedoms within the context of undeniable systemic inequality.[94] Rather, harm "might" result and Parliament is thus justified in passing criminal laws aimed at preventing this possibility of harm. As Sopinka J. for the majority of the Court explained:

> While a direct causal link between obscenity and harm may be difficult, if not impossible, to establish, it is reasonable to presume that exposure to images bears a causal relationship to changes in attitudes and beliefs.
>
> Parliament was thus entitled to have a reasoned apprehension of harm resulting from the desensitisation of individuals exposed to materials which depict violence, cruelty, and dehumanization in sexual relations ... I am of the view that there is a sufficient rational link between the criminal sanction, which demonstrates our communities' disapproval of the dissemination of materials which potentially victimize women and which restricts the negative influence which such materials have on changes in attitudes and behaviours, and the objective.[95]

On one level, it is arguable that (given the Court's earlier judgments on speech, equality, and harm) this most recent finding that "a direct causal link between obscenity and harm may be difficult, if not impossible, to establish" but that it is not in any event required, was foreseeable. This does not, however, mean that such a link was necessary or accurate. In reaching its decision, for example, the Court relied specifically on its judgment in *Keegstra*, a case concerning Canada's *Criminal Code* hate speech provisions.[96] In *Keegstra*, the Court ruled that a "direct causal link" between hate speech and minority victimization did not exist but that this did not render the resulting harm any less real:

> Essentially, there are two sorts of injury caused by hate propaganda. First, there is harm done to members of the target group. It is indisputable that the emotional damage caused by words may be of grave psychological and social consequence ... Words and writings that wilfully promote hatred can constitute a serious attack on persons belonging to a racial or religious group, and in this regard ... these persons are humiliated and degraded ... A second harmful effect of hate propaganda which is of pressing and substantial concern is its influence upon society at large. The Cohen Committee noted that individuals can be persuaded to believe almost anything if information or ideas are communicated using the right technique and in the proper circumstances ... The threat to the self-respect of target group members is thus matched by the possibility that prejudice will gain some credence, with the attendant result of discrimination, and perhaps even violence, against minority groups in Canada.[97]

In *Keegstra*, the Supreme Court of Canada ruled that, insofar as hate speech is concerned, to require a strict causal connection between hate propaganda and harm before hate speech can justifiably be restricted is to deny our "historical collective knowledge of the potentially catastrophic effects of the promotion of hatred."[98] Gay men supported this finding but now query it within the context of pornography, demanding instead more proof that harm is caused by pornography. This is indefensible and, as the remainder of this chapter will show, politically naïve.

I am not convinced that the connection between the inequality of gay men and homophobic hate speech is impossible or in some cases even difficult to prove. Indeed, in reviewing the Court's reasoning in *Keegstra*, the reader is left somewhat puzzled by the Court's finding that a direct causal connection cannot be found between hate propaganda and harmful actions and attitudes. Note also, for example, the conclusions of McLachlan J. in the same case, who wrote that "[t]o view hate propaganda as 'victimless' in the absence of any proof that it moved listeners to hatred is to discount the wrenching impact it may have on members of the target group themselves ... Moreover, it is simply not possible to assess with any precision the effects that expression of a particular message will have on all those who are ultimately exposed to it."[99]

In recognizing that those who are the targets of hate are in fact hurt, one is left to ponder whether this is not "proof" that hate speech causes harm. If so, why then conclude that harm is difficult to pinpoint and thus not required? In a similar manner, Dickson C.J. noted that a lack of precision in proving harm does not make it acceptable to discount the concerns of those who claim to be harmed, particularly if those concerns are expressed within the context of undeniable systematic inequality and daily discrimination such as exists against minority persons: "The message of the expressive activity covered by s. 319(2) is that members of identifiable groups are not to be given equal standing in society, and are not human beings equally deserving of concern, respect and consideration. The harms caused by this message run directly counter to the values central to a free and democratic society, and in restricting the promotion of hatred Parliament is therefore seeking to bolster the notion of mutual respect necessary in a nation which venerates the equality of all persons."[100]

In advancing this argument, was the chief justice not admitting that he accepted the evidence before him that hate speech results in violence, unequal treatment, and a social hierarchy that differentiates along lines of race, sexual orientation, and so on? Could he not then have concluded that harm had been proven? Reviewing *Butler* in light of these considerations, it is arguable that the Court was attempting in *Butler* to reaffirm and strengthen its reasoning in *Keegstra*. In *Butler*, the Court again concluded that to require a direct, causal connection between the materials and harm was to ignore the real consequences of speech that promotes inequality and that, in the process, silences those most in need of a voice.[101] On one level, the Court's analysis is to be commended. In ruling, for example, that pornography can be seen to negatively affect individual attitudes and behaviours, and in the process create a substantial risk of harm to individual women and society at large, because society's equality interest will be threatened, the Court in *Butler* went a long way toward recognizing, and in so doing, making it possible to address, the many discriminatory effects of pornography. By taking seriously and listening to the voices of those harmed by pornography – by understanding, for example, that "images of a speculum inserted in a woman's anus, of a woman jerking off a pig, of a woman tied up, hooded and hanging from her breasts from the ceiling,"[102] actually say something, come from somewhere, and produce something about the accepted and expected and enforced roles of women and men in our society and that they promote discriminatory attitudes and behaviours – the Court put into perspective the meaning of and need for their opposite: namely, equality.

Hence, while there is much merit and good intention in this finding, unfortunately, in failing to acknowledge the proof that pornography *does* cause specific actions – or more precisely, in failing to acknowledge the evidence of the real, concrete, provable acts used to make it and that result from it – the Court risked embracing a theory of ideational harm, the mere belief, without proof, that harm "might" result. This approach, with its attendant risks, clearly built on *Keegstra*, in which the Court found that harm per se could not be strictly proven to arise from hate propaganda but that Parliament could nonetheless enact legislation aimed at combating racial vilification. And while both decisions go some way toward recognizing that inequality must be targeted, both are a long way from the harms-based theory of, for example, anti-pornography civil rights ordinances that *are* addressed to, and which recognize and accept as harmful, real, specific acts.

At a basic level, although recognizing that pornography is a practice of inequality, the Court in *Butler* nonetheless embraced an approach that risks attacking the idea that pornography harms, rather than the actual actions that do occur from its production and distribution. This is problematic and it was unnecessary. *Keegstra* did not have to form the basis of such an approach. There is sufficient evidence to support a finding of a link between hate speech and violence. Recent scholarship on the Holocaust shows that the genocidal killing of millions of European Jews was possible because ordinary Germans believed that Jews were subhuman and worthy only of extermination. Nazi hate propaganda both created and potentiated the idea that Jews should be extinguished – an idea that resulted in acts of systematic torture and extermination.[103] The connection between hate speech and action in this context is also one (as will be shown shortly) that many gay men have long held as fact, despite there being less scientific and experimental research conducted to prove it than exists on the connection between pornography and harms. We claim the connection, rightly, to be a given. Perhaps, in Canada at least, our arguments have been so widely accepted as valid that no one has felt the need to undertake research of the sort that has been conducted on the harms of pornography. In any event, there *is* evidence of a causal connection between pornography and specific acts of harm, and the Court in *Butler* could have relied on this evidence in upholding Parliament's enactment of the *Criminal Code* provisions in question. Unfortunately it did not. This in turn has left us with a less than satisfactory solution – an understanding of the causes of sexual inequality that, while accurate, is left, legally, without any teeth.

This last point becomes more evident once we examine the ways in which the *Butler* analysis of pornography's injuries has been applied by those charged with enforcing it. Shortly after *Butler* was handed down, for example, the Court of Appeal for Ontario was asked in the case of *R. v. Hawkins* to determine the legality of a number of prosecutions made pursuant to s. 163 of the *Criminal*

Code.[104] Much of the heterosexual pornography at issue in *Hawkins* consisted of videos that were described by the Crown as non-violent but nonetheless degrading and dehumanizing. The Crown, applying the definition of degrading and dehumanizing provided by the Supreme Court of Canada in *Butler*, argued that, in determining whether a work is degrading or dehumanizing, the focus must be on the manner in which sex is treated in the context of the material in question.[105] Degradation, it was argued, may be found in sexually explicit material where, for instance, people are, as clearly described by the Supreme Court in *Butler*, presented as sexual playthings, as sexual unequals, solely for the sexual satisfaction of others, or in subordinate roles in their sexual relationship with others, or engaging in sexual practices that sexualize and normalize humiliation.[106]

In *Hawkins*, the Crown submitted that once sexually explicit material is found to be degrading or dehumanizing, the substantial risk of harm to society's equality interest, as outlined by the Supreme Court in *Butler* and based on the considerable evidence before the Court in that case, is proven. In other words, once the Crown has proven that the materials in question have the qualities identified in *Butler*, namely sex plus violence or sex plus degradation plus inequality or discrimination, the inference of harm, based on the considerable evidence of harm placed before the Court in *Butler*, flows.

Unfortunately, the Ontario Court of Appeal in *Hawkins* rejected this argument, finding that in *Butler* the Supreme Court of Canada did find conclusively that harm always resulted from pornography. Rather, it found only that Parliament had a "reasoned apprehension of harm."[107] In other words, Parliament was entitled to think that harm might flow and could, accordingly, pass legislation aimed at stopping it. This legislation and the Supreme Court's decision in *Butler*, did not, however, according to the Court of Appeal, override the Crown's responsibility to prove harm beyond a reasonable doubt each and every time it wanted to prosecute under s. 163 of the *Criminal Code*.[108] As the Court in *Hawkins* explained:

> It is one thing, in my opinion, to find, in considering whether a limitation on this form of expression is justified under s. 1 of the *Charter*, that Parliament had a reasonable basis for concluding that harm will result from exposure to material which unduly exploits sex without demonstrating a causal link between the perceived harm and the material sought to be proscribed, and without actual proof of the harm. It is, however, quite another thing to find that the exercise of this constitutionally protected freedom creates the substantial risk of societal harm that is now an essential component of the offence when a person is on trial and subject to the full force of the law.
>
> Contrary to the Crown's submission, I cannot accept that *Butler* compels the conclusion that once the portrayal of sexually explicit

acts is found to be degrading or dehumanizing, it necessarily follows that the films are harmful and therefore obscene. In my opinion, it remains open to the court to find that the harm component of the offence has not been established. Just as there is a range of opinion as to what is degrading or dehumanizing, there is a range of opinion as to whether such matters causes social harm or the risk of such harm.[109]

A strong argument can be made that, based on the evidence before the Court in *Butler*, the Court in *Hawkins* misread the Supreme Court of Canada's decision in *Butler*. One could also argue persuasively that the Crown's analysis of *Butler* was both legally sound and socially more pressing and desirable. It is also true however that, given the Supreme Court's unwillingness in *Butler* to state unequivocally that harm results from pornography and that this conclusion was based on the considerable evidence before it, the decision in *Hawkins* and its effects were entirely foreseeable. To date *Hawkins* has not been overturned. Not surprisingly, the Crown seems to have decided that given the criminal burden of proof required and the costs and effort associated with proving what is now required in court, there will be few attempts to prosecute those who sell pornography. Indeed, to date there have been few successful post-*Butler Criminal Code* prosecutions.[110] In effect, Canada's anti-pornography laws are now frozen and of little use in the fight against the sexual inequalities caused by pornography.

While many will undoubtedly applaud this fact, I want to argue here that for gay men to do so is short-sighted. *Hawkins* has effectively seen to it that no pornography – straight or gay – will be stopped under s. 163 of the *Criminal Code*. But the decision represents much more than this, and its effects do not represent a victory for anyone seeking equality. Quick to call for more proof of harm, gay men have now received as a reward a judicial decision that risks stopping dead in its tracks their own struggle against those actions that cause harm. Indeed, there is hypocrisy in the claim that, within the context of criminal laws aimed at controlling systemic inequalities, an incredibly high standard of proof, and lots of it, must be presented every time the Crown tries to take concrete action to stop those materials that cause inequality. While gay men might applaud this finding within the context of gay pornography, in doing so, they should note that the same argument can be used to justify nonaction within the context of anti-gay hate speech. *Keegstra*, which gay men supported, like *Butler*, which gay did not support, stands for the proposition that harm is a "possibility," an "idea," rather than a fact. Proof beyond a reasonable doubt that harm results from hate speech must thus be advanced each time the Crown tries to stop it. It should not then come as a surprise that criminal prosecutions for hate speech, like those for pornography, have been few.[111] Knowing that it must now prove harm beyond a reasonable doubt each time it tries to prosecute those who distribute hate propaganda, in the same way that it must now do under the *Criminal Code*'s anti-pornography provisions, the Crown simply chooses not to. The standard required – a standard called for by those gay men who deny the harms of pornography – is simply too onerous. Hence, the gay community's call for more proof seems to have backfired, leaving us, like women, without the legal protections we deserve before we even get the chance to access them.

Conclusion: Making Harm Actionable

There are legitimate reasons to query the Supreme Court of Canada's ruling in *Butler* that absolute proof was unavailable and, in any event, unnecessary when tackling the harms of pornography – but not for the reasons thus far articulated by the many gay men who have attacked the decision. It may be that in *Keegstra* the Court had no choice but to draw this conclusion, given the lack of work undertaken at that point on hate speech and inequality. This was not, however, the case when *Butler* was heard. In failing to acknowledge this, the Court has left us with a judicial finding that is much weaker than it could have been. Indeed, we now find ourselves with a *Criminal Code* provision that is effectively unused and ineffective. This is a result that harms women, but it also harms gay men in their own struggle for equality. The challenge then is to find ways to ensure that the harms the Court acknowledged in *Butler* are addressed in reality.

The anti-pornography civil rights ordinances would ensure that the *Butler* sex equality analysis is given the teeth it needs to be proven effective, as subsequent chapters contend, by overcoming many of the enforcement problems evident post-*Butler*. Gay men have a role to play in ensuring that this approach is accepted and used. But such a role will not be forthcoming as long as gay men insist there is no evidence that pornography harms women. As this chapter has shown, this argument is both unsubstantiated and can just as readily be turned against those gay rights strategies that aim to fight the inequalities created by those materials that cause harm to gay men. More importantly, however, before gay men can assume a role in ensuring that effective measures are implemented to tackle the harms of inequality, they must also accept that pornography is not just an issue of harm for women.

Once it is accepted that an approach to pornography that targets sex discrimination is the correct approach, this does not mean that gay male pornography is exempt. On the contrary, once it is established that pornography is an issue of sex discrimination that results in harm – something, as we will see, that the ordinances allow us to establish while avoiding the numerous criminal law enforcement issues that have arisen post-*Butler* – gay men must accept that the pornography they defend as different from heterosexual pornography may in fact not be so different. Applying the definition of pornographic harm adopted in *Butler* and clarified in that provided in the anti-pornography ordinances, the remainder of this book argues that gay male pornography is not

Butler-proof and, as such, should not be exempt from any attempt to stop the harms it causes under an ordinance-based sex equality approach. On the contrary, I argue that by accomplishing little more than the reinforcement and promotion of those gender hierarchies central to sex discrimination and homophobia, gay male pornography is itself an issue of gender inequality. Specifically, it offers gay men little alternative but to conform to hyper-masculinity or to ape femininity. It thus results in a gay male liberation movement committed to gendered inequality, including gay male inequality, which results from heterosexual male dominance and the power sustaining it. Applying the harms-based test articulated in *Butler,* where materials pose a threat to systemic equality and violate society's sex equality interest, gay male pornography can be seen to result in harm. Therefore, those who *are* harmed must be given access to a justice system that remedies their injuries. The remainder of this book undertakes to demonstrate that gay male pornography does not merit an exclusion from the sex equality analysis at the centre of the Supreme Court of Canada's decision in *Butler* and that a legislative effort seeking to fairly and effectively implement this analysis is one all gay men should support. The *Little Sisters* case, a case that brings all these issues to the forefront, offers a rare opportunity for gay men to undertake a necessary re-examination of where it is we want to go in our struggle for equality. This book uses that litigation as a way of encouraging a much broader community debate about who we are, what we hope to achieve, and with whom.

2 Sex Equality and Homophobia

> However a man comes to perceive himself as "different" with respect to his relation to gender categories, in his sensual desires, in his passions, he comes to perceive himself in a cultural context which offers him the duality masculine/feminine to box himself into. On the one hand, he is "offered" the dominant sexist and heterosexist culture which will label him feminine and castigate him, and on the other hand, he is "offered" a very misogynist and hyper-masculine gay male subculture; he is invited to join a basically masculist gay rights movement. If he has the aesthetic and political good taste to find all of the above repugnant, he can only do what lesbians have been doing: invent. He has to move on in previously indescribable directions. He has to invent what maleness is when it is not shaped and hardened into straight masculinity, gay hyper-masculinity or effeminacy.[1]
>
> *Marylin Frye,* The Politics of Reality

Homophobia: An Issue of Sex Discrimination?

In *Butler,* the Supreme Court of Canada did much to ensure that sex equality was recognized as a legal and social mandate in Canada. The MacKinnon-Dworkin anti-pornography ordinances commit to the same end result but do so on a broader, international scale. The ordinances are also, as argued in Chapter 1, more effective at realizing their stated objective. Central to both approaches, however, is the claim that sexism must be challenged systemically and that true equality between the sexes cannot be achieved so long as women and some men are made inferior on the basis of gender.

A reading of the gay community's reaction to the *Butler* decision reveals considerable reluctance on the part of many gay men to see merit in this aspect of the decision. This, in turn, has led many gay men to dismiss the significance of the ordinances in their own lives. This is an unfortunate mis-reading of both *Butler* and the ordinances and one that stands in the way of a necessary alliance between gay men and those in the feminist community committed to eliminating sexual inequality. This chapter argues that gay men stand to benefit from any legal analysis that questions sex discrimination. More importantly, I argue that what is needed post-*Butler* is a re-examination of why and how sex discrimination and homophobia are linked and a careful articulation of why we would not have one without the other – a claim that, if accepted, allows us to then determine what both *Butler* and *Little Sisters* say about the value of gay male pornography and what gay men should do about it. But first, why sex equality?

To talk of sex discrimination is to talk of gender and the inequalities that arise within a society in which gender differences are polarized and hierarchi-cal – a society in which those who are "male" get privilege and those who are not, do not. I refer here not to gender as biologically determined but rather gender differences as socially constructed and as defined by specific behaviours that ultimately result in the gender categories "male" and "female." As MacKinnon explains, "[g]ender is an inequality, a social and political concept, a social status based on who is permitted to do what to whom. Male is a social and political concept, not a biological attribute, having nothing whatever to do with inherence, pre-existence, nature, essence, inevitability, or body as such."[2]

It is this social definition of male and female, with defining and rigidly enforced characteristics for each, that ultimately results in gender inequality. To reap the benefits awarded to those who are "male" in our society, one must worship and be all that is masculine – that is, a socially constructed set of behaviours and ideas that ultimately define who belongs to the male gender class and that determine who gets and maintains the power commensurate with male gender privilege. Under this system, "masculinity is seen as the authentic and natural exercise of male agency and femininity as the authentic and natural exercise of female agency."[3] To subscribe to masculinity, and to benefit from the privilege afforded "real" men, however, one must also sup-port compulsory heterosexuality – an ideology and political institution that embodies those socially defined sets of behaviours and characteristics that ensure heterosexual male dominance and that result in sexual inequality.[4] In this sense then, gender (a system of social hierarchy, an equality) and sexuality (through which the desire for gender is constantly reproduced) become in-separable. As MacKinnon again notes, within a system of gender polarity in which male equals dominance, female submission, "the ruling norms of sexual attraction and expression are fused with gender identity and formation and affirmation, such that sexuality equals heterosexuality equals the sexuality of (male) dominance and (female) submission ... Sexuality becomes, in this view, social and relational, constructing and constructed of power."[5] Heterosexual-ity must thus be enforced, made compulsory, because it is deemed necessary to ensure the survival of both masculinity and femininity, defined as male over female, through which male dominance over women is ensured. Lesbians and gay men challenge this requirement because they deny the inevitability of heterosexuality. Sexuality constructs men as superior to women, ensuring that gender remains hierarchical, ensuring that heterosexuality remains the norm through which gender inequality is maintained, requiring that those who challenge those norms through which gender remains polarized are penalized for non-conformity. As MacKinnon notes, "[s]exuality then is a form of power. Gender, as socially constructed, embodies it, not the reverse. Women and men are divided by gender, made into the sexes as we know them, by the social requirements of its dominant form, heterosexuality, which institutionalizes male sexual dominance and female sexual submission. If this is true, sexuality is the linchpin of sexual inequality."[6]

Once we see the extent to which heterosexuality made compulsory ensures the maintenance of gender as a system of dominance and submission, of sexual hierarchy, we can begin to see the extent to which anti-gay stereotypes play into and undergird sex inequality.[7] Together, sexuality and gender form the basis of institutionalized sexism. Sexuality, as constructed, represents the normative ideology of male superiority over women, and the hostility directed at lesbians and gay men finds its source in this power structure, aimed as it is at preserving compulsory heterosexuality. As Act-Up member Robert Goss notes, "[g]ay and lesbian sexual identities form a counter-practice that deconstructs the rigid definition of masculinity and femininity and social constructions based on these definitions. They transgress many dualistic strategies that support heterosexist sexual identities ... Gay and lesbian power arrangements [thus] challenge the unequal production and distribution of heterosocial power in our society."[8]

To this I would add, only as a clarification, that gay male power relations have *the potential* to challenge the patriarchal definitions of "male" and "female" through which those who subscribe to compulsory heterosexuality find privilege, *not* that present gay male power relations necessarily do so. To effectively challenge such definitions, the gay man must, as Frye explains, "be the traitor to masculinity that the straight man has always thought he was"[9] – a course of action upon which most, I will argue in the chapters that follow, have not embarked and which many apparently oppose. For those who do undertake such a challenge, however, the consequences are severe, for the notion that relationships (monogamous or otherwise) can function without gender inequality, without male power expressed over and in control of a feminized subordinate, sends a rather frightening message to those for whom gender inequality is so very important.

Lesbian activist Suzanne Pharr argues that homophobia works to maintain gender roles because it silences those men whose sexual identity and behaviour will, it is believed, "bring down the entire system of male dominance and compulsory heterosexuality."[10] This has led her to refer to homophobia as a "weapon of sexism," responsible for propping up those gendered stereotypes that are central to sexism and all patriarchal inequalities.[11] In a system built on sexual hierarchy, nothing is more threatening to those who benefit from it than the notion that there can be love and justice between equals, that inequality need not be. Gay men, to the extent that they choose to build same-sex relationships, monogamous or otherwise, based on mutuality, reciprocity, and respect – relationships which reject hierarchical gender roles and the sexually abusive relationships that result from gender polarization – are seen as a threat to male supremacy because they challenge the social constructions assigned to the definitions "male" and "female." Homophobia – which can be seen as a reaction to the actual or perceived violation of gender norms – is but one way to ensure that men do not violate those gender roles central to male power. For gay men, this results in silence, for fear of being identified, and ultimately results in invisibility. And this is exactly what homophobia is about: ensuring that gay men, to the extent that they do not conform, to the extent that they fail to partake in a system of sex inequality, are prevented from making public that which their enemies find so politically and socially subversive.

Anti-gay stereotypes can be seen to silence the public expression of non-heterosexual sexual identities and both foster and maintain "appropriate" gender-role behaviour,[12] ensuring that women and men do not violate those gendered norms central to male power and that all lesbians and gay men are suppressed and punished to the extent that they do. As Pharr explains,

> [t]o be a lesbian is to be perceived (labeled) as someone who has stepped out of line, who has moved out of sexual/economic dependence on a male, who is woman-identified. A lesbian is perceived as someone who can live without a man, and who is therefore (however illogically) against men. A lesbian is perceived as being outside the acceptable, routinized order of things. She is seen as someone who has no societal institutions to protect her and who is not privileged to the protection of individual males ... A lesbian is perceived as a threat to the nuclear family, to male dominance and control, to the very heart of sexism.[13]

Gay men, Pharr continues, are also perceived as a threat to male dominance, "and the homophobia expressed against them has the same roots in sexism as does homophobia against lesbians. Visible gay men are the objects of extreme hatred and fear by heterosexual men because their breaking ranks with male heterosexual solidarity is seen as a damaging rent in the very fabric of sexism. They are seen as betrayers, as traitors who must be punished and eliminated. In the beating and killing of gay men we see clear evidence of this hatred."[14]

There are numerous examples of the extent to which heterosexual male privilege relies on and ultimately insists on the preservation of gender inequality.

One obvious example, however, is the extent to which it is used to preserve "that bastion of patriarchal power, the nuclear family."[15] Patriarchy is the "manifestation and institutionalization of male dominance over women and children in the family and the extension of male dominance over women in society in general."[16] Lesbian and gay male relationships have the potential to reject hierarchical concepts of gender. They therefore challenge the notion that social traits, such as dominance and subordination, masculinity and femininity, equal and unequal, are needed. Because they do so, they are seen as challenging patriarchy and the male supremacy derived from it and are consequently punished for "not participating fully in [the] daily maintenance of women's oppression."[17] As Sylvia Law explains, "when homosexual people build relationships of caring and commitment, they deny the traditional belief and prescription that stable relations require the hierarchy and reciprocity of male/female polarity. In homosexual relationships authority cannot be premised on the traditional criteria of gender."[18]

Lesbian and gay male relationships and identities, because they can be interpreted to undermine that male/female split necessary for socially imposed gender inequality, are thus targeted for abuse. By subverting sex roles, and by choosing instead to build communities and relationships (monogamous or otherwise) premised on equality, reciprocity, and caring, lesbians and gay men have considerable potential to undermine the notion that relationships, and by extension society, must be divided hierarchically in order to function. As Marc Fajer explains, "one of the biggest contributions that gay people can make to society is to demonstrate the weakness of the bipolar model of gender and to attempt to rectify some of the harms it creates."[19]

As is clear from the examples offered in Chapter 1, much time and effort, often manifesting itself through violence and hostility, has been directed at silencing the public expression of any lesbian and gay male discourse and reality which challenges patriarchal privilege.[20] Indeed, so pervasive is anti-lesbian and gay male discrimination in our society that the consequences for any who dare to speak and challenge socially imposed definitions of "normal" are far from appealing or empowering: "[t]o be called a homosexual is to be degraded, denounced, devalued or treated as different. It may well mean shame, ostracism, discrimination, exclusion or physical attack. It may simply mean that one becomes an 'interesting curiosity of permissiveness.' But always, in this culture, the costs of being known as a homosexual must be high."[21]

For lesbians and gay men, the hostility directed at us ultimately ensures the suppression of lesbian and gay male public expression and visibility – a suppression deemed necessary for the maintenance of systemic inequality, linked to heterosexual privilege. As Jeffrey Byrne notes, "because of the vicious circle of labeling and silencing to which lesbians and gay men are subjected, the personal costs of coming out in a still largely heterosexist and often violently homophobic society serve to ensure the continued invisibility of lesbians and gay men."[22] And it is this invisibility that is at the heart of homophobia – a socially imposed muzzle aimed at silencing those whose very existence threatens to subvert gender male privilege.

To summarize then, homophobia can be seen as but one way of ensuring that gay men are bullied into rejecting any public expression of their sexual identity that undermines gender roles and the inequalities commensurate with them.[23] As Pharr explains, "misogyny gets transferred to gay men with a vengeance and is increased by the fear that their sexual identity will bring down the entire system of male dominance and compulsory heterosexuality."[24] Homophobia, which finds expression in gay bashing, employment discrimination, and familial and social ostracization, reminds all men that if they "break ranks with males through bonding and affection outside the arenas of war and sport," they will be "perceived as not being 'real men,' that is, as being identified with women, the weaker sex that must be dominated and that over the years has been the subject of male hatred and abuse."[25] The gay male, socially feminized, internalizes this misogyny and seeks to mimic, because he can, those behaviours and characteristics that will, he hopes, allow him to "pass" for the "male" he is supposed to be.

For gay men, mimicry and assimilation ensure that those gay men who are "visible" – those who refuse to be silenced, who refuse to conform – become the victims of greater physical and emotional abuse and discrimination. Because they continue to challenge the "normality" of gender polarity and in the process undermine male supremacy, these men will be brutally silenced. Those gay men who choose concealment, on the other hand, and who embrace and encourage that masculinity so central to male dominance do little more than sexualize their own oppression – making a fetish of that which ultimately silences them.

The desire to be identified as a man and reap the benefits of male privilege is, in a homophobic society, socially appealing. No one should underestimate the power of homophobia and the extent to which it literally terrorizes gay men into wanting to pass as "real" men. Nonetheless, gay men must reject the pressure to do so. A failure to do so only results in considerable individual and systemic harms. Indeed, at the risk of stating the obvious, it is clear that some men invest a lot of time trying to prove their manhood at the expense of someone else's freedom. They get a lot out of it and the harms that result are well documented. Gay men would do well to take these findings seriously, whether the harm that results from hyper-masculine role play be abuse directed at women or at other men. Recently, this point was brought into sharp focus by the experiences of a young American man, Joseph Oncale, who was the victim of sexual harassment at the hands of his male co-workers. What happened to Joseph Oncale can be read to send a clear message to gay men that gender is not something to be played with, mimicked, or adopted as a "life-affirming identity politic." Oncale's ordeal says a lot about what sex, gender, and sexuality mean socially. Indeed, what happened to Joseph Oncale is every bit as entrenched in homophobia as a baseball bat over the heads of two gay men daring to hold hands while walking down the street. Both create and depend on a gendered hierarchy and both are central to male dominance. Both reject equality, penalize mutuality, and applaud conformity, ridicule compassion, and celebrate contempt. Both are central to sexual inequality and very much an issue of sex discrimination. Therefore, gay men would do well to applaud any court decision that recognizes the need to eradicate the social stereotypes that harmed Oncale and that harm us. Put in context, this also means that gay men need to think carefully before condemning judicial pronouncements such as *Butler* and feminist legal efforts such as the MacKinnon-Dworkin anti-pornography ordinances that acknowledge the harms of sex inequality.

Joseph Oncale: Identifying That "Moment in Sexism Where Male Supremacy and Homophobia Converge"?

In August 1991, Joseph Oncale began work as a roustabout on an oil rig for Sundowner Offshore Services. Shortly after starting employment, Oncale's supervisor, John Lyons, approached him and stated, "You know you got a cute little ass boy" and threatened to "fuck him from behind." Remarks of this sort soon became a constant in the life of Joseph Oncale: "If I don't get you now, I'll get you later. I'm going to get you. You're going to give it to me."

John Lyons and two of Oncale's co-workers came close to "getting" Joseph Oncale, but they didn't have to "get" him physically (that is, rape him) in order to effectively destroy this young man's life. On one occasion, Oncale was grabbed from behind, pulled down onto his knees, and held immobile while Lyons unzipped his own pants, pulled out his penis, and placed it on the back of Oncale's head. A day later, Oncale was again forced to the ground while Lyons placed his penis on Oncale's arm. That same night, Lyons and another man attempted to rape Oncale while he was showering. He was, to quote Oncale, lifted off the ground by his knees while, "John Lyons grabs the bar of soap and rubbed it between the cheeks of my ass and tells me, you know, they're fixing to fuck me."

Joseph Oncale managed to escape from this assault and subsequently asked those charged with supervising his attackers to be removed from the oil rig. Before he could leave, however, he was again approached by Lyons, who stated, "You told your Daddy, huh? Well, it ain't going to do you no good because I'm going to fuck you anyway." Joseph Oncale left his job in November 1991 for fear of being raped, and to this day suffers "severe panic attacks and other episodes of long-term post-traumatic stress." Shortly after leaving the oil rig, "he became dizzy, numb in his hands, and had a rapid heartbeat, which symptoms he continues to attempt to control and treat with medication and counselling."[26]

Discussing the role of homophobia in propping up the inequalities central to the sex discrimination she challenges, Catharine MacKinnon writes, within the context of gay male sexual harassment: "It would be strange, if efficient, if a landmark sexual harassment case were decided in a homosexual context, simultaneously recognising that sexual harassment and employment deprivation in a same-sex context can be sex discrimination. But stranger things have happened than a simultaneous legal precedent for gays and for women sexually harassed by men – for reasons deriving from that moment in sexism where male supremacy and homophobia converge."[27]

Within her overall theory about the role of systemic gender polarity in maintaining the conditions that ensure workplace inequality, MacKinnon's foregrounding of the function of homophobia as a "weapon of sexism" has received little if any attention from the judiciary. Legal commentators too have all but ignored her analysis in this regard, while nonetheless writing extensively on what they claim to be her views on this subject. In sum, harassment within a same-sex context has rarely received the kind of equality analysis called for by MacKinnon and those who share her perspective[28] on the place of male dominance in the subordination of gay men and lesbian women and the social ramifications of workplace sexual harassment.[29] That is, until recently.

In December 1997, the US Supreme Court was asked to determine whether Joseph Oncale could sue for sexual harassment by his male superiors as sex discrimination under Title VII.[30] On 4 March 1998, the Court held that he could, explaining that Oncale's case should be remanded for further proceedings consistent with the Court's opinion that men who are taunted or abused by other men on the basis of gender are entitled to compensation for damages resulting from the sex discrimination to which they have been subjected.[31] Joseph Oncale ultimately settled his civil action out of court. Reading the Court's findings, however, it is clear that other men who, like him, are sexually victimized by their co-workers, will now be entitled to their day in court, should they want it. But what is also clear is that the Court now accepts the argument that sexual harassment must be looked at within the broader context of systemic sexual inequality and that homophobia and sex discrimination are not disparate forms of oppression.

Men on Men: Why Biological Sameness Failed to Protect Joseph Oncale

As far as I'm aware, Joseph Oncale is not gay. Nor are the men who sexually harassed him and threatened to rape him. Nor are the men who witnessed this abuse but failed to intervene. The question I want to ask, however, is, would it matter if they were? This might seem an odd question given the extreme violence to which Joseph Oncale was subjected. How, after all, could the sexual orientation of any of these men be relevant to the type of abuse that ultimately occurred? Unfortunately, the question is not as strange or uncommon as one might have hoped.

Lesbian legal academic Janet Halley, who, in a recent critique of Catharine
MacKinnon's efforts to assist Joseph Oncale, seems to imply that in a situation like that encountered by Oncale, any resulting trauma may have been
experienced only because the person complaining may actually have liked
what happened to him and simply could not deal with his own sexual desires
– in other words, that the facts of this case might be seen as representing little
more than a case of homosexual panic:

> [T]here is another way to imagine the case, and none of the facts
> published in the various court decisions can preclude it ... In this ver-
> sion it was Oncale ... who [was] homophobic. We can imagine that a
> plaintiff with these facts willingly engaged in erotic conduct of pre-
> cisely the kinds described in Oncale's complaint, or that he engaged in
> some of that conduct and fantasized about the rest, or indeed fanta-
> sized all of it – and then was struck with a profound desire to refuse
> the homosexual potential those experiences revealed in him.[32]

Halley continues: "[H]omosexual panic – the terror that some people feel
when they think that someone of their own sex finds them sexually attractive.
Homosexual panic can be extremely dysphoric. Some people might even say
that having a homosexual panic experience at work was unwelcome and sufficiently severe to alter the conditions of their employment and create an abusive work environment. Under *Oncale*, they can now sue for that."[33]

Halley's main objective in writing this article seems to be to warn those
feminists responsible for the Court's findings in *Oncale* of the need to acknowledge that the state is a site of sexual control and that by expanding federal
anti-discrimination laws to protect men who profess to have been harmed in
situations akin to those which harmed Joseph Oncale, feminist women such
as Catharine MacKinnon, who wrote the *Oncale* brief, risk stifling same-sex
sexuality: "federal antidiscrimination law may *implicitly* declare open season
on gay men and lesbians, leaving us unprotected from lawsuits that threaten
our very ability to work and learn. Moreover, insights provided by the same-
sex context precipitate concerns across the board. I ask here whether sex harassment enforcement has become sexuality harassment – a mechanism of social
control that pro-gay and feminist thought, alike, should find alarming."[34]

On one level, Halley seems to imply that the harms claimed by Oncale and
others do not result from being sexually harassed or abused, but rather from
the fact that men such as Oncale are uncomfortable with same-sex "sexual
desire," their own "homosexual potential" (read gay sex generally). The problem with such a claim is that in dismissing Oncale's ordeal as mere homosexual panic, she, like many before her, accuses the victim of sexual harassment
of overreacting, of not being comfortable with sex, of being too frigid and
unwilling to enjoy what many others *do* enjoy. Halley seems to imply that the

facts in *Oncale* can be seen as indicative of what gay sex is today and, as such, harmful to Oncale and others only because they are not yet prepared to deal with the apparently liberatory potential of homoerotic desire. In other words, if Oncale were more comfortable with gay sex, then what happened to him, because it *is* gay sex, would not have "upset" him.

Given what we know about what did happen to Joseph Oncale, it would appear that what we have here (perhaps for the first time) is a feminist writer asserting that within a same-sex context, rape *is* sex and, as such, non-harmful once accepted as something uniquely gay male. Indeed, Halley seems to imply that harm is undermined once we accept this fact and work toward a society in which those who fear and who are panicked by same-sex sexual attraction, apparently personified by the facts in *Oncale*, relax and learn to embrace it. Same-sex sexual harassment then, to the extent that there is a homoerotic element, is not harmful. Rather, once it is identified as or labelled gay male, it starts to represent little more than a type of sexual desire that should not be discouraged by those for whom sexual liberation is important. Instead, it should be encouraged because of the subversive potential of same-sex sexual relations generally.

There are a number of problems with Halley's arguments, many of which are further addressed in the chapters that follow.[35] For the time being, however, I want to respond to these claims by asserting that despite the best efforts of Halley and others to distinguish same-sex from opposite-sex harassment, what is clear from the *Oncale* case is that, insofar as same-sex sexual harassment is concerned, the sexual orientation of the parties harassing or being harassed is in many ways irrelevant.[36] The end result is the same: the continued sexualization of gender inequality and the power imbalances that are central to both homophobia and sexism. So long as Joseph Oncale as a straight man is subjected to ridicule and abuse along the lines of gender, gay men stand to lose their struggle for justice and women will never be treated equally. It is this connection between sexism and homophobia that is most central to the facts in *Oncale* and from which gay men have most to learn when examining the case.

To understand why the experience of Joseph Oncale is sex discrimination one needs to know a little bit about woman-hating and malestream culture. John Stoltenberg explains that "the system of male supremacy requires gender polarity – with real men as different from real women as they can be, and with real men's superiority to women expressed in public and in private in every way imaginable."[37] What happened to Joseph Oncale epitomizes why, as Stoltenberg so rightly argues, sexual "difference" is, for men, so vitally important. Indeed, what happened to Joseph Oncale epitomizes what transpires in a society in which gender differences manifest themselves sexually. By subordinating him through sexual violence and harassment, by creating a split between him and those who did all they could do to prove they were "real" men,

Joseph Oncale's attackers ensured that their victim was, at a basic level, stripped of male status and power, ridiculed as one to be used by those with it, and ultimately forced to assume the position of one without power.

Joseph Oncale was in effect rendered inferior for not being "man enough" to be the aggressor – that is, one for whom social empowerment is assured as a result of gender male privilege manifesting itself in sexual conquest. What happened to Joseph Oncale epitomizes what it means to be "male" as socially defined in our society. Indeed, the facts of *Oncale* are male supremacy in action. They tell us as men that we have two options: be domineering and in control, hence masculine, or be the person victimized sexually because of your inability or unwillingness to do so. The result for society is an imposed system of gender inequality in which "male" is top and "female" is bottom – a system in which men should and must, if they want to maintain the privilege that attaches to those who are male, reject any form of sexual expression that is non-hierarchical, non-abusive, and non-alienating (read equal).

Biologically, Joseph Oncale is a man. As such, he has the option socially of benefiting from male privilege. What we need to keep in mind, however, is that to those who abused him, Oncale was little more than an inferior – an unequal through which to valorize their own masculinity and strip him of his. To these men and others like them, biology is in many ways insignificant. What matters is the ability to reassert again and again who is in charge and to prove it by buying into a system in which those with power are those who practise and assert male dominance on those who cannot or who choose not to. What Joseph Oncale's ordeal tells us is that power does not depend on the biological capabilities of those who exert it – that is, it does not depend on an essentialized notion of gender. Harassment in an opposite-sex setting is harmful not simply because it involves a biological male violating a biological female, as the essentialist reading would have it, but because, as MacKinnon's feminist reading has it, it involves sexually abusive behaviour by those socially permitted to do it and socially defined by doing it. Similarly, within the context of same-sex harassment, the mere absence of biological "opposites" does little to undermine the very real harms resulting from an abusive power play in which "male" equals masculine, equals dominant. The forced coupling of two biological males does nothing to challenge (indeed, it only reinforces) those sexual and social power inequalities divided along gender lines if those behaviours central to the preservation of gender hierarchy (cruelty, violence, aggression, homophobia, sexism, racism, and ultimately compulsory heterosexuality through which heterosexual male dominance is preserved) are not themselves removed from the presentation of sexuality as power based.

What happened to Joseph Oncale took place because we live in a society that continues to insist on attaching benefit to male sexual aggression and the abuse that results from it. For women and men made socially inferior on the basis of gender, the acting out of sexual violence built on male/female polarity is but one more extremely forceful and effective tool with which to preserve that gender hierarchy necessary for social inequality. It is clear then that what happened to Joseph Oncale epitomizes all that *is* sex discrimination.

Why *Oncale* Should Matter to Gay Men: If It Can Happen to Him, It Can Happen to Us

But what of gay men? What does all of this have to say to them? Specifically, what does the case of Joseph Oncale say to us about sexism and its role in our lives? If we accept that what befell Joseph Oncale would not have happened if we lived in a society in which men were not obsessed with proving their gender adequacy and superiority, then it goes almost without saying that the violence to which some gay men are subject on an almost daily basis would not occur if the attitudes and stereotypes that resulted in Joseph Oncale being harassed did not exist. If we expand on the work of feminist authors well versed on the harms of gender inequality, it is clear that what we stand to learn from *Oncale* is that

1 the harassment of gay men (and of men perceived to be gay) is not a separate issue, which is of relatively minor importance in understanding the harassment of women but is, rather, an important aspect of policing culturally produced boundaries of both gender and sexuality; and,
2 sexist harassment can be seen as a pedagogy which schools women and men into normative heterosexuality.[38]

Gay men have done a lot to convince the courts that the types of discrimination they face should be taken seriously. I query though, given what we have learned from Joseph Oncale and others, how one *can* advocate for the eradication of homophobia without first understanding the role of sex discrimination in our society, without critically analyzing what gender stereotypes do, who they harm, and who they benefit. By failing to do so, do we not risk advocating a rights agenda that is responsible for encouraging those discriminatory harms that make homophobia and sex discrimination the oppressive and interconnected constructs that they are and always will be – unless they are challenged simultaneously? What happened to Joseph Oncale would not have occurred in a society in which men did not feel the need to sexually enforce their perceived right to dominate on the basis of gender superiority. Joseph Oncale was a victim of sexism because those who harassed him did so in the belief, socially sanctioned, that their masculinity entitled them to subordinate a gendered inferior.

For gay men, it should be clear that if we can do something to stop what happened to Joseph Oncale, that is, if we can move toward a society in which inequality achieved through sexual violence need not be, then a great deal can probably also be done to eliminate the abuses to which we, as gay men, are also subjected. For it is clear that without sex discrimination, there would not appear to be much need for homophobia. Without those gender hierarchies which are at the very core of sex discrimination, there would be no need to penalize those men and women who do not conform to the notion that sexuality must be hierarchical – men and women whose very existence threatens the power imbalances so crucial to maintaining sexual inequality.

Conclusion: Joseph Oncale as Pornographic Icon

So why then the inaction, even hostility, to *Butler*? Given the connections now evident between sex, gender, and sexuality, gay men might well applaud any judicial effort to eradicate but one of the many sources of sex discrimination, or so it would seem. In *Butler*, the Canadian Supreme Court offered society a judicial decision that recognized and attempted to address the harms of gender inequality. This is a decision that gay men should support, not condemn. And yet, the opposite has been the case. The remainder of this book attempts to determine why and does so specifically within the context of the present gay male defence of gay male pornography – a defence which, I will argue, prohibits gay men from understanding the links between homophobia and sexism and which also, because it is supported, ensures both remain in place.

Thus far I have argued that homophobia is a reaction to the perceived violation of gender constructs and is aimed at silencing gay men because the public expression of a non-hierarchical sexuality is viewed as jeopardizing male dominance, for which gender inequality is necessary. In concluding, it is helpful to again return to the ordeal of Joseph Oncale and ask, given what we now know about gender and sexuality, what occurs if gay men themselves partake in the very role play that allowed *Oncale* to exist in the first place? It is my firm belief that gay men today risk doing just this – a point no better illustrated than in the pornographic sexualization of inequality now evident in the production, distribution, and defence of gay male pornography.

What was done to Joseph Oncale could be and often is what appears on any page in any number of the gay male pornography magazines now available and recently defended in *Little Sisters*. I am not suggesting that the men who wanted to rape Oncale used or had even seen gay pornography. That isn't really the point. What I am saying, however, is that by making a game of that which did happen to Joseph Oncale, we do little more than prop up the types of gender inequalities that allowed it to take place and which daily result in the homophobic and sexist abuse of all those who are subordinated in the name of male supremacy. The question the remainder of this book poses is, can we as a community built on a historical struggle for sexual equality expect to achieve it if we do little more than sexualize and trivialize the very power structures and imbalances that are the source of our inequality? I think not, and I rather suspect that Joseph Oncale would agree.

The experience of Joseph Oncale typifies what gay male pornography justifies in the name of sexual freedom. But freedom to do what? If, as I argue in the next section of this book, gay male pornography valorizes and perpetuates the inequality to which Joseph Oncale was subjected and which further ensures that sexual harassment in the workplace and elsewhere is justified and normalized, then do we not as a community have an obligation to query its role in ensuring his oppression as well as our own?

I am not blaming gay men for the fate of Joseph Oncale. I blame a society in which harassment is justified in the name of sexual access and in which mutuality, reciprocity, and compassion for others is ridiculed and rejected. What I am saying is that what happened to Joseph Oncale can be challenged only by undertaking a radical transformation of these power dynamics, and this can occur only if we nurture and promote sexual relationships which *do* subvert gender conformity. Gay men have a role to play in this regard but only insofar as they do not buy into the power play now called for by so many in our community.

What was done to Joseph Oncale had nothing to do with his sexual orientation. It did, however, have a lot to do with enforcing those gender norms that ensure that the only sexual orientation to be afforded public expression is that which depends on the rejection of sexual equality. What happened to Joseph Oncale can and does happen to gay men, and the fact that we are gay when it happens to us does nothing to alter its individual and systemic injury. There is nothing liberating about abuse and nothing particularly empowering about any expressive medium that encourages it. Turning Joseph Oncale into pornography will not ensure that what happened to him will not happen to us and to all women, and although gay male pornography is not the source of all our woes, when examined in light of what *Oncale* says about gender, homophobia, and sex discrimination, it is, I think, quite clear that harassment, simply because it is sold and packaged as "just" sex, is anything but sexually emancipating or socially progressive. In *Butler*, the Supreme Court of Canada did much to address these issues – a reasoning strengthened in *Little Sisters*. The agenda offered is one that gay men would do well to embrace. The next chapter outlines why.

3 Sexualizing Masculinity, Normalizing Inequality: Gay Male Pornography Post-*Butler*

There is solid academic criticism of the equation of homosexual pornography with mainstream heterosexual pornography. Erotica produced for a homosexual audience does not and cannot cause the kind of anti-social behaviour generally or through stereotyping and objectification of women and children that Parliament apprehended might be caused in heterosexual obscenity. While heterosexual obscenity is often misogynist, that cannot be said of homosexual pornography.[1]

> *Submission of the appellant Little Sisters Book and Art Emporium, in the case of* Little Sisters Book and Art Emporium *v.* Canada *(2000)*

Little Sisters Book and Art Emporium v. Canada

In 1996, the British Columbia Supreme Court was asked by Little Sisters Book and Art Emporium, a Vancouver bookstore specializing in the sale of lesbian and gay books, magazines, and videos, to determine the constitutional validity of the legislative scheme that allows Canada Customs to restrict the importation of pornography into Canada.[2] The law governing the importation of goods into Canada is found in the *Canada Customs Act*[3] and the *Customs Tariff*.[4] Section 114 of the *Customs Tariff* prohibits the importation of "any goods enumerated or referred to in Schedule VII" of that statute. Schedule VII lists classes of prohibited goods and assigns each class a code number. Code 9956(a) deals with "obscene material" and prohibits the importation of those goods which can be described as "books, printed-paper, drawings, paintings, prints, photographs or representations of any kind that: (a) are deemed to be obscene under subsection 163(8) of the *Criminal Code*."

Section 163(8) of the *Criminal Code* was judicially interpreted and defined by the Canadian Supreme Court in *R. v. Butler.*[5] Essentially, code 9956(a) forbids the importation of materials caught by the *Butler* sex equality analysis for pornographic harm. Customs officials responsible for determining the legality of imported goods are expected to find guidance in *Customs Memorandum D9-1-1*, entitled "Interpretive Policy and Procedures for the Administration of Tariff Code 9956."[6] This memorandum incorporates a generally accurate summary of the present state of the law relating to obscenity, particularly in light of *Butler,* and is aimed at ensuring that Customs officials apply the reasoning in *Butler* when determining whether pornography can be imported into Canada.

In hearings before the Supreme Court of Canada, the appellant, Little Sisters, raised two main constitutional arguments, relevant to both s. 163 of the *Criminal Code* and the administrative procedures in place for applying s. 163 at the Canada-US border. Both related to the appellant's perception that its s. 2 and s. 15 *Charter* rights were unjustifiably infringed by Canada Customs legislation and the application of that legislation. The Court summarized these questions as follows:

> [T]he appellants argue that the "harm-based" interpretation given to s. 163 of the *Criminal Code* in *Butler,* does not apply to gay and lesbian erotica in the same way as it does to heterosexual erotica, or perhaps at all. Because the prohibition against importation of obscene goods contained in the Customs legislation is rooted explicitly in s. 163 of the *Criminal Code*, acceptance of this argument would mean that gay and lesbian publications would not be subject to the ordinary border regime applicable to other forms of expression.
>
> Secondly, the appellants say that the procedure laid down in the Customs legislation is so cumbersome and procedurally defective that it is incapable of being administered consistently with the protection of their *Charter* rights.[7]

Little Sisters was supported on both issues by six interveners. These included Equality for Gays and Lesbians Everywhere (EGALE), Canada's leading lesbian and gay legal lobbying and activist group, and LEAF (the same group that had successfully argued in 1991, in *Butler,* that pornography violated the *Charter*'s equality provisions). Apart from the Attorney General of Canada, the only intervener seeking to uphold the sex equality arguments raised in *Butler* was the international feminist rights group, Equality Now. In addressing both arguments, the Court supported the submission of Equality Now, ruling (per Binnie J.) that

[m]y conclusion on the first branch of the appellants' attack is that the *Butler* analysis does not discriminate against the gay and lesbian community. *Butler* is directed to the prevention of harm, and is indifferent to whether such harm arises in the context of heterosexuality or homosexuality. Nor in my view is the gay and lesbian community discriminated against in the Customs legislation, which is quite capable of being administered in a manner that respects *Charter* rights. The government *is* entitled to impose border inspections of expressive material. The obstacles experienced by the appellants and detailed at length by the trial judge were *not* inherent in the statutory scheme. The obstacles were, however, very real and in the end quite unjustified.[8]

In sum, the Court found that lesbian and gay male pornography could not be distinguished from heterosexual pornography, that the legislative scheme responsible for doing so was constitutionally valid, but the way in which the legislation had been applied was discriminatory as against lesbians and gay men. As for the constitutionality of the legislation itself, the majority held that it would be inappropriate to invalidate constitutionally sound legislation, but that steps must be taken to ensure that it was applied correctly and fairly – that is, in accordance with the equality rights to which the appellants were entitled. On this point, three members of the Court (Iacobucci, Arbour, and LeBel JJ.), while still agreeing that lesbian and gay male pornography should not be seen as any less harmful or any more important than heterosexual pornography, held that the Customs legislation was so vague as to be the source of misapplication and that, as such, the legislation should be struck out as unconstitutional. The minority in this instance would have preferred that regulation remain a criminal matter determined only once pornographic materials had already entered the country.

The *Little Sisters* case raises a number of constitutional issues. Of interest here is the Court's finding that same-sex pornography violates the *Butler* standard for pornographic harm and its finding that immediate action needs to be taken to stop what are clearly discriminatory and high-handed actions on the part of Canada Customs officials against lesbians and gay men. This latter finding makes it clear that the issue of how best to regulate the inequality arising from the production and distribution of pornography will not simply go away now that *Little Sisters* has been heard. Reform is required and it must, if it is to be effective, involve *all* persons with an interest in ensuring fairness and equality. What is also clear, however, is that, insofar as gay men and lesbians are concerned, the type of discussions needed to ensure effective change will not occur until the lesbian and gay community rethinks its present commitment to pornography as a central platform in the struggle for liberation.

The issue of how best to regulate pornography is analyzed in Chapter 8. First, however, it is necessary to undertake a critical examination of why it is that gay male pornography undermines the sex equality interests of gay men and society generally. Analyzing both the arguments made by Little Sisters and those who supported them and the types of materials that would be legally available in Canada had they won before the Supreme Court of Canada, I will argue that the Court's interpretation of the harms of gay male pornography was accurate. Specifically, analyzing some of the materials that were defended by trial and others that, while not themselves in issue, would now find protection had Little Sisters won, it is clear that gay male pornography does violate the *Butler* sex equality test for pornographic harm.

The Arguments: Gay Male Pornography – *Butler*-Proof?

In *Little Sisters*, the arguments made by those wanting to throw out Canada's anti-pornography laws all rely to some extent on one underlying theme: gay pornography *is* gay identity. This is evident in the arguments of the appellant Little Sisters Bookstore, for whom, its factum stated, "there is evidence, overwhelmingly and virtually uncontradicted, that gay and lesbian sexual imagery and text, including that which has been prohibited entry, is vital to gay and lesbian identity, dignity, self-worth, community formation, health and education."[9] In advancing this argument, Little Sisters relied on the testimonies of a number of pro-pornography academics and activists. Included in these was the testimony of Professor Tom Waugh, who had argued before the Supreme Court of British Columbia that "erotic materials in the gay community have not only functioned as erotica in the ordinary sense of the word, but as vehicles of education, of initiation, of community formation, of communication."[10]

The store also relied on the work of lesbian writer Pat Califia, who, when explaining why she emphasizes sexual explicitness in her work, testified at trial that "[w]ell, it's partly because I think that if you cannot find any fiction that describes people who are like you, people who have the kind of relationships you would like to have, people that have the kind of sexuality you would like to have, you begin to feel as if you're crazy. You don't exist. You're marginal, you're not important, and it creates a great deal of self-hatred and self-doubt. It also creates, I think, a lot of repression and just human misery."[11]

In this regard, it is worth noting the comments of Professor Gary Kinsman, who, also testifying on behalf of Little Sisters, opined: "[F]rom the sociological and historical research I have done there is this important relationship between the emergence of gay networks in the community, the availability of this type [of] erotic material."[12]

This is a view shared by the intervener LEAF, which, seemingly rejecting its own arguments in *Butler*,[13] argued in *Little Sisters* that pornography affirms same-sex sexuality by "presenting it as healthy, meaningful and empowering."[14] Relying on the work of Jerald Moldenhaur and Nino Ricci, the group continued its justification of lesbian and gay pornography by arguing that lesbian, gay, bisexual, and transgendered (LGBT) materials perform a critical role in developing and nurturing LGBT communities and cultures:

> [F]or gay people literature is a very important bond, a kind of glue within our community ... the way that we connect with our community is often through our literature, through our newspapers and through our books. [Jerald Moldenhaur, former owner of Glad Day Books]
>
> ... [V]alidation literature is literature which serves to say we are here, this is what we are ... ground breaking works in that sense in that they are establishing the right of a community to speak ... about a reality that is often not documented in mainstream sources, that is often reviled or stigmatized. And therefore ... these works perform the work that literature and art often perform. [Nino Ricci, author][15]

The same position is evident in the words of EGALE Canada in its factum before the Court, in which the group, professing to speak for all lesbians and gay men, explained that "sexually explicit lesbian, gay and bisexual materials challenge the dominant cultural discourse. They resist the enforced invisibility of our marginalized communities and thereby reassure us that we are not alone in the world, despite the apparent hegemony of heterosexuality. They reduce our sense of isolation. They provide affirmation and validation of our sexual identities by normalizing and celebrating homo- and bi-sexual practices, which mainstream culture either ignores or condemns. In short, they help us feel good about ourselves in an otherwise hostile society."[16]

In this regard, the group cited the work of author Tom Waugh, who has written that "[y]oung gay people who are growing up and who encounter gay erotica of some kind by accident or intentionally very often learn from this erotica for the first time that they are not alone, that the ... shame and stigma they have been feeling are unwarranted. They learn to discover that there are other people out there like them. They learn to acquire feelings of self-worth and dignity and belonging to a larger community."[17]

In a similar vein, EGALE continued: "[S]exually explicit lesbian, gay, and bisexual materials also empower us in other ways. For example, they make a valuable contribution to the historical and contemporary documentation of lesbian, gay, and bisexual existence and experience. In that respect, they are critical to the formation, evolution, and continued vitality of our communities."[18]

EGALE also cited the work of historian Karen Mitstysyn, who has argued that "[a]nyone who comes out [as lesbian, gay, or bisexual] knows the need usually to read literature and find out one's history or identity."[19]

To this, EGALE added: "All forms of sexual representation are part of an inherently political discourse about such fundamental issues as identity, humanity, passion, power, control, vulnerability, trust, respect, intimacy, and, of course, sexuality. Lesbian, gay and bisexual materials make an important contribution to that discourse. They thereby operate as a socializing force, provoking informed discussion among lesbians, gays, and bisexuals, through which we create networks, forge social and political ties, and develop vibrant communities."[20]

In this regard, EGALE again relied on the work of Waugh, who has argued that "[e]rotic materials in the gay community have not only functioned as erotica in the ordinary sense of the word, but as vehicles of education, of initiation, of community formation, of communication. In other words, they've played a lot of social roles in addition to their role as sexual arousal."[21]

Elsewhere, the same group argued that in addition to helping lesbians and gay men, same-sex pornography can be seen to be beneficial to society generally: "sexually explicit homo-erotic materials have liberating effects that benefit women as a whole, as well as lesbians and gay men. By subverting dominant constructs of masculinity and femininity, homo-erotic imagery and text challenge the sexism that is believed to be endorsed and reinforced by mainstream heterosexual pornography."[22] Attempting to distinguish gay pornography from heterosexual pornography, EGALE continued:

> The specific materials at issue in *Butler* consisted of mainstream pornographic videos produced for a heterosexual, predominantly male audience. In contrast, this case involves the systematic detention and seizure of sexually explicit homoerotic imagery and text, produced by and for lesbians, gays and bisexuals. The expressions conveyed by the *Butler* videos echoed the dominant refrain on sexuality, while the expressions conveyed in the materials at issue in this case are those of dissenting minority voices. The evidence establishes that the Customs Legislation silences a form of expression that challenges conventional notions of sexuality, undermines the cultural hegemony of heterosexuality, and thereby contributes significantly to the social and political vitality of our marginalized communities. In that respect, the expression at issue in this case enhances not only the values that underlie s. 2(b) of the *Charter*, but also those that underlie s. 15 (including respect for the equal worth and dignity of all human beings, and the elimination of prejudice and stereotyping based on sexual orientation).[23]

This too is a view shared by LEAF, which argued that "the equality rights of heterosexual women are also affected by the targeting of LGBT materials. These materials benefit heterosexual women because they may challenge sexism, compulsory heterosexuality and the dominant, heterosexist sexual representations which often portray 'normal' heterosexuality as men dominating women and women enjoying pain and degradation."[24]

While at first glance, many of these arguments seem legitimate, they soon lose their appeal once we reflect on the materials to which they apply. While it is undoubtedly the case that much legitimate lesbian and gay male literature has been unfairly suppressed, it is also true that many of the materials defended in *Little Sisters* or that would have been allowed into Canada had the bookstore and its supporters won were not mere "literature" as this word is commonly used. They were, in fact, pornographic, as defined by the Supreme Court of Canada in *Butler.* In making its arguments, for example, it is important to note that LEAF was doing so within the context of a case in which some of the materials denied entry into the country presented lesbian women being gagged and beaten. This is not something specifically mentioned by LEAF when it relies on the use of acclaimed lesbian author Audre Lorde, for example, while trying to defend the right of importers to import without restriction, but it is not something that can be easily swept aside as irrelevant. While it is one thing to argue that the types of materials defended by Lorde and others should not be restricted (a claim supported by parties on both sides of this case), it is quite another thing to use Lorde's work to support the production and distribution of materials that make possible the sexual liberation of women called for by Lorde and other feminist women.

LEAF's use of Audre Lorde to justify the production and sale of lesbian pornography is interesting, to say the least. The article that LEAF referred to is quite explicit in its rejection of the pornographic presentation of female sexuality. Specifically, Lorde calls for the realization of the erotic as the most self-responsible source of women's power, but states unequivocally that when she refers to the erotic, she is not referring to the pornographic. As gay male author Robert Jensen explains, moving the erotic away from the pornographic can make it easier to move away from "the limiting patriarchal definition of sex as fucking." Discussing Lorde's work, Jensen notes:

> She talks about the way in which women's erotic power is falsely cordoned off in the bedroom, made into "plasticized sensation," and confused with the pornographic. For Lorde, the erotic is a life force, a creative energy: "those physical, emotional, and psychic expressions of what is deepest and strongest and richest within each of us, being shared: the passions of love, in its deepest meanings."[25]

Given Lorde's description of the erotic – one that rejects the requirement that women be defined solely by the expectations of a male dominant sexuality through which women have no voice and no ability to self-empower – it is hard to imagine her justifying the use of some of the materials defended in *Little Sisters*, for as Equality Now explained to the Supreme Court of Canada, making specific reference to many of the materials defended by Little Sisters, LEAF, and EGALE, the use of materials that sexualize acts of coercion, violence, pain, and domination between women is not particularly liberating:

These materials sexually condition lesbian women to eroticize abusing, and being abused by, other women. The real violence that can
occur in lesbian relationships is also minimized to the degree that the
women abused in lesbian pornography are perceived as enjoying that
abuse. The idea that some women want to be the slaves of other women
is patterned on racist and sexist notions that it is right to dominate
certain individuals or groups because they want or deserve to be dominated. Black women and Jewish women, for example, have written of
the inequality they experience when acts of slavery and Nazism are
promoted as sexual. The abuse of women as and for sex remains abusive whether the perpetrator is a woman or a man.[26]

Responding specifically to the claim that these materials could be seen to
benefit women by challenging sexism, Equality Now continued:

Women cannot achieve equality if pornographers are given constitutional protection to define women's sexuality. It is pornography ...
that "silenc[es] already marginalized voices" and refuses to "free women
to shape their own lives independent of dominant norms." It is pornography that presents "heterosexist misrepresentations of lesbian
sexuality as perverse and deviant" and prevents lesbian "visibility in
the wider community" except among men masturbating to their abuse
and violation. The materials at issue in this appeal present lesbianism
as heterosexual dominance being acted out by women on women.
Equality Now submits that this misrepresents lesbianism.[27]

Hence, while it is true that non-harmful materials were denied entry into
Canada by Customs officials, it is also true that many of the materials that
were restricted were harmful. LEAF failed to acknowledge this distinction,
thereby encouraging the Court to allow materials very much opposed by Lorde
and some of the other writers the group relied on to make its point. Fortunately, the Court rejected LEAF's claims, finding that harmful materials,
whether lesbian or gay male, could not be saved simply because the people
used to produce, or the people ultimately using, these materials were lesbians
or gay men.

Although LEAF's arguments in *Little Sisters* refer specifically to lesbian
sexuality, nowhere in its factum did the group state that its assertions did not
apply to gay male pornography. This is a point noted by Equality Now, which,
again challenging the position taken by LEAF, reminded the Court that the
position taken by LEAF, Little Sisters, EGALE, and others, if accepted, would
allow the free distribution of materials that clearly violate the sex equality
interests of all Canadians, be they heterosexual women, lesbian women,

heterosexual men, or gay men. This is a valid argument. Indeed, the weaknesses in the claims made by those wanting to throw out legislation aimed at limiting the harms of pornography are made evident once we examine what types of materials their arguments, if accepted, would allow into Canada in the name of gay male identity.

Gay Male Pornography: An Overview of What Was Defended

The Supreme Court of Canada rejected the arguments put forth by Little Sisters and those interveners arguing on its behalf, ruling that there is nothing about the harms that result from lesbian and gay pornography that distinguishes it from the harms that result from the production and distribution of heterosexual pornography. Rejecting LEAF's position on sado-masochism, for example, the Court noted:

> The appellants, supported by the interveners LEAF and EGALE, contend that homosexual erotica plays an important role in providing a positive self-image to gays and lesbians, who may feel isolated and rejected in the heterosexual mainstream. Erotica provides a positive celebration of what it means to be gay or lesbian. As such, it is argued that sexual speech in the context of gay and lesbian culture is a core value and *Butler* cannot legitimately be applied to locate it at the fringes of s. 2(b) expression. Erotica, they contend, plays a different role in a gay and lesbian community than it does in a heterosexual community, and the *Butler* approach based, they say, on heterosexual norms, is oblivious to this fact. Gays and lesbians are defined by their sexuality and are therefore disproportionately vulnerable to sexual censorship.[28]
>
> The intervener LEAF took the position that sado-masochism performs an emancipatory role in gay and lesbian culture and should therefore be judged from a different standard from that applicable to heterosexual culture ... The portrayal of a dominatrix engaged in the non-violent degradation of an ostensibly willing sex slave is no less dehumanizing if the victim happens to be of the same sex, and no less (and no more) harmful in its reassurance to the viewer that the victim finds such conduct both normal and pleasurable.[29]

Elsewhere, the Court noted that within the context of the *Criminal Code* provision at issue in the case, "[t]he types of harm that *Butler* concluded might be exacerbated by obscenity are capable of being present in all human relationships, regardless of the sexual orientation of the individuals involved. There is no evidence that the homosexual community is immune from the kinds of problems that s. 163's obscenity provisions are designed to address. On the contrary, the evidence is, sadly, that gay and lesbian relationships suffer from physical, sexual and mental abuse in much the same way that heterosexual relationships do."[30]

Unfortunately, although ruling that gay male pornography violated *Butler,* the Court did not offer a detailed analysis as to why it is that gay male pornography specifically undermines society's equality interest, focusing instead on the right of Parliament to restrict the importation of pornography generally. While I support the Court's findings insofar as they refuse to distinguish gay pornography from heterosexual pornography, the Court's failure to offer a more thorough analysis of what gay pornography is and what it says risks leaving considerable room for pro-pornography advocates to argue that the Court simply failed to understand the meaning and significance of gay male pornography.

It is thus helpful to discuss and describe what gay male pornography is. While to some this might at first seem unnecessary, given the amount of pornography readily available to those who care to look at it, the need for discussion and description becomes evident once we realize the extent to which description and analysis of the source of the pornographic identity championed by those advocating its sale and production is lacking. In *Little Sisters,* the arguments in favour of the unbridled production and distribution of gay male pornography are clearly outlined. These arguments are examined and critiqued in Chapters 4, 5, and 6. However, it is important to note that a careful reading of the evidence and analysis presented in the case reveals a rather unsettling omission on the part of those defending the materials in issue before the Court. Indeed, for all the talk, for all the discussion of good versus evil, pro-sex versus anti-sex, progressive versus conservative, radicalism versus moralism in much of the written and oral evidence presented by pro-pornography advocates throughout this case, what is less well focused, indeed often entirely unmentioned, is the specific content of many of the materials the proponents of gay pornography are defending when they call for the courts to ignore *Butler* insofar as it applies to same-sex pornography.

Despite considerable effort to defend gay male pornography as a source of equality, justice, and freedom before, during, and after the *Little Sisters* hearings, there has been little description of what the materials in issue on this case look like and say, what their message is, and how these materials work. If gay male pornography is a source of affirmation, as it is said to be, the questions that need to be addressed are, what gay identity do they affirm, and what is it specifically about these materials that makes them affirm, indeed *be,* gay identity? If the materials are empowering, what is it about them that makes them be so? If this is equality, how do these materials promote and produce equality?

I have had an opportunity to review the materials in issue in this case, as well as other materials that, while not specifically defended before the Supreme

Court of Canada, would nonetheless be legal now had Little Sisters convinced the Court to allow the unrestricted distribution of gay male pornography in Canada. Many of these materials are summarized throughout this work.[31] They include some of the gay male pornography magazines, videos, and books that have been detained by Canada Customs since 1985. I summarized these materials in October 1999 over a two-day period at the Civil Exhibits Division of the British Columbia Court of Appeal. What is provided is a sampling of some of the materials at the centre of the *Little Sisters* litigation. As this book as a whole explores the role of gay male pornography in the lives of gay men and its broader social impact, an overview of those exhibits that are lesbian-specific or produced for a heterosexual audience will not be offered here, although much of the content and theme of those exhibits intended for gay male audiences are repeated in these materials, and even though a victory for Little Sisters would have ensured the free distribution of these materials in Canada.

Little Sisters ordered, and Canada Customs excluded as socially harmful, many of the materials described in this book. The other materials examined typify those ordered by other gay importers, such as Glad Day Bookstore in Toronto, and similarly prohibited as harmful. Still others are examples of materials that could be freely imported into Canada if the remedy requested by the appellant had been granted. Many were presented as exhibits at trial and were available to the Supreme Court of Canada when it decided whether or not gay pornography violates the *Butler* sex equality standard. This book offers an overview of some of the other pornography titles and products available to gay men today. Again, while these materials were not discussed in the *Little Sisters* litigation, they would nonetheless be protected by the arguments made by Little Sisters and others.

I created the summaries that follow by reading them into a tape recorder at the British Columbia Court of Appeal, Civil Exhibits Division, Vancouver, and later having them typed. As far as is possible, what follows is an accurate summary of what appears in the exhibits in issue in the *Little Sisters* trial. Other materials are as described in various gay male pornography video catalogues or magazines available throughout North America and Australia.

There were approximately two hundred exhibits in the *Little Sisters* litigation. Some of these materials do not violate the *Butler* equality mandate but were nonetheless detained by Canada Customs. This is a fact recognized by the Supreme Court and one that I discuss in Chapter 8 when analyzing how best to implement the *Butler* equality test in a way that is not discriminatory. For the time being, however, it is sufficient to note that of the two hundred exhibits before the Court, many do violate *Butler*. Of these, I offer a summary of approximately thirty.[32] Although some of the exhibits and materials described are more violent than others, it is again worth noting that Little Sisters and its advocates themselves drew no such distinction, requesting instead the dismantling of a system that would have allowed the sale and distribution in Canada of *all* the exhibits before the Court and *all* the materials described in this chapter. It is also unproven that gay sexual materials that do not show as much violence are necessarily less harmful than those that show aggression explicitly. Later in this book, I outline the disparate and connected ways in which violent and non-violent pornography work separately and together to undermine equality.

Before I do so, however, it is worth noting the views of those who took issue with others who did take the time to view and critique the exhibits in this case, particularly Equality Now. As one writer noted:

> Equality Now may be a newcomer to the sex wars in Canada. But its view is the one that many in the gay and lesbian community have been raging against for years. It's anti-porn, anti-sex, radical feminism run amuck. It has refused to learn even the most obvious lessons of the sex wars – that it's not nice to speak on behalf of people you haven't consulted with, and that censorship always comes back to haunt the least powerful, most marginalized voices within any community.[33]

This quotation was written by Canadian legal academic Brenda Cossman and is, to some extent, accurate. Censorship *does* hurt those least able to speak. But I refer here not to gay men denied their right to access pornography. Rather, I refer to those silenced and censored by those in their own community unwilling to hear their voices and their concerns. This is a fact of life that those who are gay or lesbian and who have questioned the role of pornography in our lives are familiar with. It applies with greater force to those who have been harmed by pornography but who, when trying to talk about it, are dismissed as ridiculous or reactionary.

Cossman's article, entitled "Return of the Loonies" – the loonies being those who don't support her pro-pornography crusade and who, because of this are the "enemy" in the sex war to which she refers – is remarkably polite when compared with the vitriol normally directed at anti-pornography gays and feminist women. "Moralistic," "conservative," "not really gay," "someone who just needs a good fuck," "a misguided fag to do MacKinnon's dirty work," "out of date," "intellectually passé," "simplistic," "emotive," "naïve." Reading this quote from Brenda Cossman, however, leaves me wondering what exactly she and other advocates for pornography are talking about or looking at when they talk about the pornography they defend in the name of gay liberation.

If the materials defended in *Little Sisters* indicate the gay identity defended by pro-pornography and pro-gay advocates, as they say they do, what has the Supreme Court of Canada just been told about homosexual identities? In answering this question, it is worth considering the lines below, found in an article in *Manscape Magazine*, not in issue in *Little Sisters*, but available none-theless from the plaintiff's bookstore: "Then I pushed him lower so my big dick was against his chest; I pushed his meaty pecs together. They wrapped around my dick perfectly as I started tit-fucking him like a chick. His hard, humpy pecs gripped my meat like a vice. Of all the things I did to him that night I think he hated that the most. It made him feel like a girl. I sighed, 'Oh, my bitch got such pretty titties! They was made for tittie fuckin, made to serve a man's dick.'"[34]

As in a great deal of written or pictorial gay male pornographic presenta-tions, what one gets from the above is a "source of affirmation" in which the physically more powerful, ostensibly straight male is glorified.[35] The linking of manliness with heterosexuality and overt masculinity is a common theme throughout many of these materials, with masculinity often gained at the ex-pense of a woman or ostensibly gay male's safety and self-worth.

Note, for example, the themes evident in *Movie Star Confidential*, a collec-tion of four comic strips defended at trial by Little Sisters as non-sexist.[36] Much of the content of this publication is either expressly violent or, at a minimum, degrading and dehumanizing. In the story, "Movie Star Confiden-tial," for example, the account follows an aging actress, Ms. Gingivitis, who longs for youth and beauty. The solution, the reader is told, is for her to bathe in substantial quantities of gay male sperm. She requests her robotic assistant to seek out fit, athletic, young men whom she can use for the purpose of filling a bathtub with sperm. He proceeds to frequent gay gyms and bathhouses until three hundred gay men are assembled to assist the woman, described as the "old bag," reclaim her youth. These men then proceed to ejaculate onto her while she sits in her bathtub. The experiment does not work and she turns into what appears to be an ape of some sort. She is portrayed as a sad, pathetic creature that remains vile and a laughingstock to be ridiculed by the gay men she has sought out – all of whom are presented as large, hyper-muscular young men with large penises. The result is a hierarchy drawn along the lines of gender, in which gay men, as men, are able to ridicule and subordinate an older woman who is disparaged for wanting to and failing to maintain her appearance. The misogynistic overtones are clear.

Often, women are not used or ridiculed in the pornography sold as gay male. This does not reduce the effects of sexism and misogyny evident in that which does. "Wolfbiorin the Viking," "Spartan's Quest," and "Harry Chess," for example – the three remaining stories in the *Movie Star Confidential* publi-cation – all promote violence or the sexual degradation of others along the lines of gender. Most of these comics sexualize large hyper-masculine men, many of whom are presented as enjoying sado-masochistic behaviour. Some are shown in torture chambers and others are described as "straight" men who are sexually aroused by inflicting pain on sexual subordinates (read: gay men) who, in turn, are described as enjoying the pain, humiliation, and degradation to which they are subjected.

This is a common theme throughout many of the materials seized by Canada Customs. *Playguy* magazine, for example, published by Modernismo Publications Ltd., and modelled along the lines of *Playboy* and *Penthouse*, offers photo spreads of young, muscular men and stories from readers, allegedly detailing real-life experiences.[37] One edition, sold by a number of gay bookstores in Canada, includes a story entitled "Provincetown Summer" that describes the experiences of a young gay male who, on completion of his sophomore year, finds a waitering job in Provincetown. He describes it as a boring place until he discovers that he can get sex at the local beach in the sand dunes. One quote from this story reads:

> I wanted to please my man. Though my nuts were about to pop, I clamped my ass cheeks around his meat and used a secret set of muscles to milk out his fuck stick. As I squeezed it and teased it, his cum filled nuts began to slap against the back of my thighs. "Give me your hole," he panted. "Roll over," he later gasped. Flipping me around, he hovered above me and mounted me from behind as he crammed his rock hard dick into my gaping crack. It occurred to me that there was something wonderfully degrading about taking it doggy style from a stud like Buddy. My tail end wagged like a dog at the thought that Buddy gave me a special treat. He grunted and growled. Another brutal thrust caused me to let go a yelp.[38]

Similarly, the December 1989 edition of *Advocate Men*, much like *Playguy*, features men who are youthful, muscular, or well toned and includes a number of photo spreads of the type of men often used in these magazines.[39] The story accompanying one of these collections of photographs reads:

> The first thing people notice about Glen Fargus, apart from his stern masculinity and animal sexuality is those muscles of his. It is easy to resent him when he remarks that he has never lifted weights but all is forgiven when Glen gives the reason for his physique. "I like to fuck a lot," he says. He is described as working as a foreman and although this requires a lot of heavy lifting, this is nothing compared to "the work I put into pumping some young stud's butt" ... "Sometimes my muscles get me in trouble. Some guys say I'm too rough during sex. I get into it and all the other guys end up all bruised. Like they say, no pain no gain."[40]

In the same magazine, in a story entitled "Night Watchman," we are provided with a scenario in which a gay man has a number of sexual experiences with married men. At one point, a non-gay male encourages another non-gay male to rape a gay man: "Now, fuck that hard ass man he told me yanking my cock hard and placing it against his hole. Shove that big cock up there until he screams. Fuck him man, you know how bad he wants it. Just do it until he screams and you load him full of cream."[41]

The story continues: "'The man's got a tight, tight pussy man,' Phil told me. He wrenched his hand free and slapped Saul in the back. 'Lean over and show this man your pussy ass.'"[42]

Another story, "The Plan," describes the sexual encounters of a young gay man in drag. It details how he is sexually used by an older man (who is described as not gay or a cross-dresser). The story, like those given above, draws a clear distinction between who is and is not the "man" in the sexual relationship and outlines what it takes to fit either the masculine or feminine role. In one quotation, the "straight" male says to the transsexual male, "what you want is me putting you on your knees. You want me stuffing money down your bra and fucking your face until cum runs down your chin while you are creaming your panties. You want fancy motel rooms and big double beds and my meat rammed up your ass. You want drive in movies with petting and kissing and my dick in your mouth. You want to be a lady and a tramp right?"[43]

At one stage, the younger man is forced to have sex in public. When he explains that he is worried about what people might see and say, the older man says, "Fuck em. You're my cunt. Not theirs."[44]

Frequently, sexual subordination is enforced through extreme forms of torture and violence, with masculinity again epitomized and celebrated in men who ridicule and emasculate others in the name of sexual pleasure. Those who are emasculated in these materials are often specifically described as gay male, while those who abuse them and who are iconized as sexual role models are described as straight, read "real" men. For example, the January 1990 edition of *MACII 19: A Drummer Super Publication* contains an article entitled "Prisoner" that details the torture and sexual mutilation of prisoners of war during a fictional military coup.[45] Many of the prison officers are described as "straight" and "real men" whose masculinity is shown through the sexual abuse of their prisoners, most of whom are belittled as gays, queers, and sissies. The rape and torture of one of these men is described as follows:

> The next day they started on him early. "Hi, I'm Sam," the man poked his head in the doorway. "Yer goin to be seein a lot of me. My friend Barney says ya got a tight ass," his sadistic sneer spelled trouble. Sam was tall and lanky with a country-hick shuck of brown hair, large nose and thick lips. He slipped off his belt. "I jes love to beat faggot ass," he smirked, swinging the leather across Steve's chest.

Steve grabbed the strap and pulled, trying to wrest the damn belt from the bastard. Sam tugged back, grinning, and Steve realized he'd made a mistake.

"I like faggots with spunk," Sam jerked the belt. "Makes me relish puttin em in thar place," he kneed Steve in the groin.

Steve's ears rang. He gasped for breath and tried to scrunch into a tight knot to ward off the incessant blows. The belt stripped across his arms and side. He yelped helplessly[.] "Please," he cried, and Sam kicked him in the ribs. Steve slumped over.

"Fuckin queer!" Sam yelled.

"Please," Steve whimpered.

Sam kicked him again. "Show me that faggot ass," Sam yelled.[46]

A similar theme is found in *Bear: Masculinity without the Trappings*, issue 9.[47] The emphasis in this magazine is on overt hyper-masculinity. Like *MACII 19*, many of the stories in this magazine mock gay men, describing them as "too feminine," and so on. One article, for example, quotes a trucker who, while bragging about the men who have "serviced" him at truck stops, says: "[T]ruckers sure know about the clean finger nail faggots taking up stalls all day playing footsies, tossing toilet paper and love notes at any pair of boots along side. Most truckers ignore them. Some want to kill them and others figure a blowjob for free is one hell of a lot better than tossing dollars at a whore."[48]

This publication, like many others, promotes violence and aggressive, non-egalitarian behaviour. The personals/classified ads at the back of the magazine typify this inequality in action. The theme throughout is hyper-masculinity found at the expense of someone else's liberty and self-worth. Merit is found in degradation. Rewards are attached to one's ability to use or be used. Equality is found, if at all, only in reciprocal abuse.

What all these examples provide is a sexualized identity politic that relies on the inequality found between those with power and those without it; between those who are dominant and those who are submissive; between those who are top and those who are bottom; between straight men and gay men; between men and women. From these and other materials, we are told to glorify masculinity and men who meet a hyper-masculine, muscular ideal. The result is such that men who are more feminine are degraded as "queer" and "faggots" and are subjected to degrading and dehumanizing epithets usually used against women, such as "bitch," "cunt," and "whore." These men are in turn presented as enjoying this degradation. In sum, they reinforce a system in which, as MacKinnon explains, "a victim, usually female, always feminized" is actualized.[49] Insofar as sex equality is concerned, the result is the promotion and maintenance of those gendered power inequalities that reject a non-assimilated gay male sexuality and ensure that homophobia and sexism remain intact.

In examining the exhibits before the Supreme Court in *Little Sisters*, many of them defended by Little Sisters and its supporters, all of them legal had Little Sisters won, we also get sexually explicit materials that sexualize racist stereotypes and degrade members of racial minorities for the purpose of sexual arousal. Gay Asian men, for instance, are presented as smaller and more feminine than their Caucasian counterparts and thus willing to be sexually subordinated by a more dominant, more stereotypical white male. An example of this type of publication is *Oriental Guys*. This magazine is, as its title indicates, a pictorial and written collection of articles and photographs of and about Asian men. A quick review of the magazine makes it clear, however, that, although about Asian men, the publication is directed at the Caucasian gay male market.

Oriental Guys presents photographs of young Asian men, usually posing by themselves. These photo spreads are often accompanied by articles with titles such as "Be My Sushi Tonight"[50] or "Behind Bars in Thailand,"[51] the latter of which discusses sex for sale in that country – a country where the sale and sexual use of young boys via sex tourism is rampant. The magazine does not present more than one young man at any one time. There is no apparent presentation of violence or physical pain. However, in accounts describing, among other things, older white men cruising Asian boys and male prostitutes, the magazine does focus on and sexualize the youth and race of those featured on its pages. In this context, young Asian men are described as "pearls of the orient," "easy to find," "accessible," and "available." Often, the photo spreads of young Asian men, shown face down with buttocks elevated, are accompanied by "news" articles that tell the reader how, for example, to recruit young Balinese men.[52] These, in turn, are accompanied by "letters to the editor" detailing the success of the magazine's readers' overseas conquests of young Asian men.[53]

The entire focus and content of this publication sexualizes racism and sexual exploitation. This is its intended result, and it is marketed as such. While degrading to Asian gay men, the theme promoted also justifies through sex the types of attitudes and inequalities that make racism and sexism powerful and interconnected realities. The white male is described as one who seeks out an inferior Asian other; the young Asian is described and presented as ready and willing to serve his sexual needs and fantasies. The white male is superior; the Asian male inferior. The resulting harm is an affront to all persons seeking equality.

In a similar vein, the reader is offered materials in which African-American men are presented as violent sexual predators with extremely large sexual organs who care only to emasculate white men through rape or, alternatively, are presented as sexually desiring to be the slaves of white men, who themselves need to reaffirm a masculinity threatened by the black male. With titles such as "Native American Drifter Hustles Man in Abandoned Mall" and

"Hawaiian Cocksucker Licks Cum from Peepshow Booth Floor," the collection of anecdotes in *Sex Stop: True Revelations and Strange Happenings from 18 Wheeler* is typical of this type of gay male pornography.[54] Many of the stories contained in it sexualize racial difference, sex with or between young boys, and incest.

In the story "Boy Buys Bicycle by Riding Man's Face," for example, the author describes how he and his friend were paid by an older African-American male, named Bill, for sex when they were boys. Meeting his school friend by the river, the writer explains his "surprise" when he realizes that the man who is going to pay him for sex is, in fact, African-American:

> I was shocked. A nigger! I had never even touched one. The thought made my flesh creep, but Bill just smiled and sat down on a fallen tree looking at us.
> "You tell anyone and I'd kill you!" Bobby John threatened. "You just let him suck on you and take the dollar. Bill likes white boys."
> Bill liked white chicken, for sure! As I discovered later on, Bill was sucking off Bobby John for a long time since he was much younger than I.

After Bill has finished with Bobby, he approaches the narrator, who writes:

> The black man stood up and looked at me. He wiped himself on his shirt and shook his head.
> "Would you like to have a slave like me, boy?"
> Bobby John assumed his cocky attitude, laughed and told him I was too green to own my own slave. But if I did, Bobby John was the way to get one. He would show me.

The story concludes with an editorial comment in which the editor of this collection of stories explains that "this gentleman is married and has grandchildren. He says he has never had any regrets and just loves to chase old black men when he can get away from his wife to do it."

In the name of identity, we are also offered materials in which gay men sexualize incest and sex with children, reinforcing the stereotype that gay men "recruit" by preying sexually on boys. With titles such as "Priest Has Bull Balls,"[55] a story in which a young man describes his first sexual encounter with his family priest, "South Dakota Sailor Fucks Boston Boy in Mouth,"[56] "Youth Lets Priest Play with His Cock,"[57] "Conservatives in South Dakota Call Youth Faggot While Raping Him,"[58] "Youth Sucks Off Brother,"[59] "Boy Sucks Off Married Soldier in Outhouse,"[60] and "I Was a Substitute Vagina,"[61] gay men are purported to reveal their "initiations" into sexuality as children through graphically presented sexual assaults by fathers, uncles, and older siblings.

These assaults are in turn presented as pleasurable for both the abuser and the child involved.

Throughout many of these materials, rape is normalized. Consent implied. In the story "Sucks Brother Off Before Wedding," from *Juice: True Homosexual Experiences*, for example, the writer describes being raped by his older brother and other men:

> When I was 8 ½ my brother Donald, who was about 13 then, decided he was going to have my cherry ...
>
> He crawled between my legs with that fuck pole of his. He located the hole and started to push. Naturally I felt like he was making a new hole ... I felt, like I truly had a telephone pole up there. The pain was excruciating but for some reason I enjoyed the thrill of debasement. I knew instinctively that I was a fucking slut. He fucked for what seemed like hours, and with the mixed feeling of pain and whoredom I survived.
>
> Whenever my parents would be absent from home, out would come his cock, hard as a fucking piece of steel, aimed at my asshole. He was just too butch for me to dare to raise my hand to him for fear of having the living shit beat out of me. I figured the best thing for me to do was to remain as passive as possible to keep from riling him.[62]

Explaining that this formed the basis of his preferred sexual experiences in adulthood, the writer then details another of his sexual encounters: "Once when I was about 25 I got raped by a powerful young guy that I had taken home to blow. I always say that was the best sex I ever had. Rape at that stage of the game was enjoyable. God he was good. He knew just what to do to a willing asshole that kept saying no. He took me with force and I fought him right to the bitter end and – thank God – he won out. When he got through with my asshole I knew I had had it. The bastard never came back though."[63]

The identity sold in these materials is one in which violence by one man against another man or men is presented as sexual for the persons involved and for the consumer of these materials. It is a common theme. Note, for example, the book *Entertainment for a Master,* specifically defended by Little Sisters, in which reciprocal battery, pain, and abuse are promoted as a form of equality: "Then I struck out at him. The leather was longer than a belt would have been. It allowed me to use it on the whole of both his cheeks. It left one broad stripe of red across the white expanse of muscle. He reared up. No amount of preparation would have steeled him so well that he wouldn't scream at the shock of the whipping. When, he moved, he jerked the rawhide holding his balls to Glen and the chains that joined the nipple, forcing his lover to experience a jolt of pain himself."[64]

Similarly, the magazine *Dungeon Master: The Male S/M Publication* presents men torturing other men in sexually explicit ways with hot wax, heat, and fire, while sexualizing this abuse as sexually arousing for the abusers, the persons injured, and again, the consumer.[65] The magazine *Mr. S/M 65* presents photographs of men being defecated on and who derive pleasure from eating and drinking excrement.[66] The film *Headlights and Hard Bodies* includes footage of men sexually using other men who are being pulled by neck chains, hit and whipped while tied to poles, penetrated by large objects and subjected to clamping, biting, and pulling of their nipples and genitals.[67] Men presented as "slaves" are shown in considerable pain but finding sexual enjoyment from the abuse inflicted on them. Those released from bondage kiss the man or men who beat them and thank them for putting them in their place with whips and verbal degradation. *MAC II* magazine, as mentioned above, glorifies sexually explicit torture in a military setting, while detailing the kidnapping, torture, and sexual mutilation of prisoners of war.[68] In a photograph in this magazine, two young men are shown confined in a cage. One, face down and bent over, is being slapped by an older man in a Nazi military uniform. Another is chained and hung in stirrups with a hand shoved down his throat.

What one sees in these and other examples of gay male pornography is an almost pervasive glorification of the idealized masculine/male icon. Cops, truckers, cowboys, bikers, and Nazis are eroticized, racial stereotypes are sexualized and perpetuated; muscle, "good-looks," and youth are glorified; and ostensibly straight (or at least straight-acting) men beat, rape, and humiliate descriptively (frequently stereotypical) gay men. Sadism, bondage, water sports, fisting, bootlicking, piercing, bestiality, slapping, whipping, incest, branding, burning with cigarettes, torture (of the genitals and nipples, with hot wax, clamps, and the like), child sexual abuse, rape, and prison rape are presented as erotic, stimulating, and pleasurable. In most, if not all these materials, it is the white, physically more powerful, more dominant male who is romanticized and afforded role model status. In those scenarios where male sexual partners take turns being the "top," the characteristics of dominance and non-mutuality remain central to the sexual act. In those photos where men are alone, positioned, and posed, their humanity is removed and they are transformed into an object. As Men against Rape and Pornography, a US activist group accurately explains, the man exposed becomes a non-human, an object waiting for you to do something to it or wanting to do something to you because he has what it takes to do so. The message sent is that some people want and deserve to have sex forced on them: they solicit this and they deserve this.[69] Either way, the result is a sexuality that is hierarchical and rarely compassionate, mutual, or equal. This was the conclusion first offered by LEAF in its submission to the Supreme Court in *Butler* in 1991. Specifically, in summarizing the materials before the Court in that case, LEAF argued:

Some of the subject materials present men engaging in sexual aggression against other men, analogous to the ways women are treated in
the materials described above. Men are slapped with belts. A man is
anally penetrated with a rifle. Men are presented as being raped. Men's
genitals are bound. They are in dog collars and in chains. Men lick
other men's anuses and are forced to lick urinals during anal intercourse. Men are presented as gagging on penises down their throats.
Men urinate on men and ejaculate into their mouths. Boys are presented with genitals exposed, surrounded by toys.[70]

These materials led LEAF to conclude that "[i]ndividual men are also harmed
by pornography ... LEAF submits that much of the subject of pornography of
men for men, in addition to abusing some men in the ways that it is more
common to abuse women through sex, arguably contributes to abuse and homophobia as it normalizes male sexual aggression generally."[71]

An overview of the materials available since *Butler* was first heard reveals
that, despite LEAF's change of heart, little has changed.

The materials summarized in this chapter provide but a small overview of
the content of the types of pornography available to and consumed by gay
men. They are, however, indicative of what is available and, if Little Sisters
and those who have intervened in the case on its behalf prove successful in
their bid to throw out the Supreme Court of Canada's *Butler*-based sex equality analysis of pornographic harm, would be readily available throughout
Canada. These materials and many more. Pornography is big business, and
gay male pornography sales are growing at a phenomenal rate. Mickey Skee,
the editor of *Adult Video News,* reports that the industry as a whole raked in
approximately US$2.5 billion. Of that, it is estimated that one-third to one-
half of all profits were from the sale and rental of gay male video porn through
mail order and video stores.[72]

This may be an understatement. As columnist Will Harris explains within
the context of the Australian market (a market not all that dissimilar from
that found in Canada), "today the Californian group sex scenes by the pool
are only a fraction of the diversity of the mostly US-produced gay porn videos
on the market. Now there are literally hundreds of titles on the shelves of the
gay pornography outlets, catering to just about every known sexual proclivity.
Canberra-based Champions Video has more than 800 titles on its shelves,
selling videos on group sex, nude wrestling, foot fetishes, bondage and S & M."
When you take into account that most people are probably unwilling to tell
market research companies how much they spent on foot fetishes in the last
financial year, the total sale estimates are probably conservative.[73] Indeed, the
average number of entries for the *Gay Video Guide*'s Erotic Video Awards ex-
ceeds five hundred videos each year, and *Adult Video News* reviews as many as
four hundred gay, bisexual, and transsexual videos each year. Add to this the

sale of magazine and paperback products such as those in issue in *Little Sisters* and the downloading and sale of gay pornography from the Internet, and what one gets is a remarkably lucrative business in which what you want is quite literally what you get. Log on to any number of the gay male pornography sites now available on the Internet, for example, and you, like the millions who do so on an almost daily basis,[74] will find and have the option of purchasing magazines, photo spreads, and videos of gay men having sex with animals, described on one Web site as:

ALL NEW: GAY FARM
HOT MEN AND ANIMAL FUN

We got donkeys
Horses
Pigs
Bunnies
Snakes
Monkeys
Chimps
Orang-utans
Hot Live Sex to Satisfy Every Taste

Exclusive Gay Farm Pixxx – Studs With Pigs, Donkeys, Chimps, Horses, Snakes and More
Free Guy-Monkey Pixxx!! Click Here[75]

Click on to any number of the sites that cater to men wanting photos of teenagers or young boys (marketed as "twinks") and you can access and buy photo sets, magazines, and videos of young, sometimes barely pubescent, boys, with titles such as "Boys Fucked for the First Time," "Virgin Serbian Boys 10-15 Fucked by NATO Soldiers," "Pass Me Another Young Boy, This One Is Split," "Brutal Young Fuck: Gang of Teenagers Ass Fucking One Boy in the Locker Room," and "The Sexual Exploitation of Jason: 4 Free Pages of Pics of Cute Twinkboy Jason Losing His Virginity to Older Boys and More."[76]

Should you not have access to the Internet, you have the option of ordering magazines, books, and videos of all of the above via mail order. Most mail order companies, for example, are more than happy to send you monthly updates of their catalogues of the latest releases and back-order selections. These catalogues offer the prospective buyer photos of the magazine and video covers he might want to purchase, with a brief description from those producing them of what he should expect from their purchase. They often show the type of men used to produce the video and the overall theme of the production. Should the buyer want more information on some of the men and themes marketed in these products, he can either buy magazines that show stills of new films[77] and which attempt to summarize the films and those used to produce them or he can buy an updated summary of some of the better-known porn "stars" and films as provided in publications such as the *1999 Adam Gay Video Directory*.[78] These publications summarize the films, rate them, and offer limited information about some of the better-known men who appear in gay male pornography videos and magazines. With titles such as "Don't Kiss Me I'm Straight," "Make it Hurt," "Torture Clinic," and " Fantasies of Black and White," these films provide the viewer with what gay men today are supposed to expect from their sexuality and the sexuality of those around them. Note, for example, the following descriptions of some of the videos available in 2000, as described in the *1999 Adam Gay Video Directory:*

DARK KNIGHTS 2

Synopsis: ... Bully Brooklyn shoves Danny around, threatening and taunting him. When they wrestle, Brooklyn is clearly in control, clobbering Danny with body blows. Brooklyn pulls Danny's shorts off, then his jock and fondles his dick ... Danny squeezes Brooklyn's nipples. Brooklyn enjoys this immensely and rewards Danny with more body blows. Brooklyn finally strips and sits on Danny's shoulders, pinning him and feeding him his cock. Breaking out the dildo, Brooklyn inserts it in Danny's ass and starts to beat off. Danny utters the five most beautiful words in the English language: "Come on me, please Sir" ...

Comments: This is fairly rough at first, but once we realized that it was a very physical dominant/submissive scene it became quite hot. Brooklyn alternates bullying aggressiveness with tenderness very effectively. Much of the action seems spontaneous and real, which is a definite plus.

Themes: Wrestling, Dildos, Humiliation[79]

BUSTIN' LOOSE

Synopsis: O'Donnell and Bradshaw bust drug dealers ... in a nightclub men's room after some intense fucking. Meek and nervous Ross is pulled over by big bad cop Stetson, who spirits the kid to a secluded torture-place and introduces him to the joys of whipping and rough anal sex. Sam Dixon is busted for tearoom sex with undercover Dick Forbes. In the lockup, Pierce and Davidson are put through Big House paces by sadistic turnkey Peter Dixon ...

Comments: ... there's a showstopper in the arrest and ravaging of John Ross. Everything about him is delectably vulnerable: his big eyes, his pale chest and belly, his shapely butt. And while he writhes and begs under daddy Bud's slaps and unsparing assault, Ross' dick just gets harder and ruddier and keeps spewing, resulting in a truly memorable scene.

Themes: Prisons, Cops, Orgies, Toilets[80]

These materials typify the identity that pro-pornography litigants, academics, and activists defend when they seek to strike down anti-pornography legislative regimes on the basis that gay male pornography equals gay male identity. Their effect? What is being advocated in the name of liberation and equality plainly creates, packages, and resells a sexuality that epitomizes inequality: exploitation and degradation of others; assertiveness linked with aggression; strength equated with violence, physical power, and the right to overpower; disrespect, intimidation, control of others, and lack of mutuality; humour found in the sexual debasement of another, and being hurt presented as pleasurable; violating and being violated presented as identity politics; and aggressive, non-consensual behaviour advanced as normal and sexually promoted as liberating. In sum, gay male pornography merges with an identity politics that personifies all that is masculine, hence gender "male," and which rejects all that is non-masculine, feminized, hence gender "female" – an identity through which, as Andrea Dworkin explains, gay men are not only penetrated like women but are expected to lust after pain and degradation like women are thought to under male dominance.[81]

By referring to the presentation of gay men as "feminized" and therefore "female," I am not suggesting that gay men and women are equally oppressed. Nor am I suggesting the harms of gay porn are exactly the same as those that result from the production and sale of heterosexual pornography. As Andrea Dworkin explains, "devalued males can always change status; women and girls cannot."[82] What I am saying, however, is that to the extent that some gay men reject socially defined "male" behaviour, and express a sexuality and politic that has the potential to subvert male gender supremacy, their behaviour is deemed unacceptable and is devalued as such. The gay male who does so is, as John Stoltenberg explains, "stigmatized because he is perceived to participate in the degraded status of the female."[83] Once "smeared with female status," the gay male assumes a position inferior to those who, not feminized, reap the benefits of male/female polarity.[84] Feminized men thus assume an inferior position in a gendered power hierarchy. And herein lies one of the very real harms of the gay porn defended in *Little Sisters*. It tells gay men that in order to become more valued, they must become more "male," less "female." It encourages them to do what they can do: "change status." In doing so, it, like all things homophobic, acts as a weapon of sexism.

Conclusion: Is It Harmful?
Not surprisingly, there are many who refuse to acknowledge the mere possibility of harm resulting from gay male pornography. Their arguments typically

paint a picture of a community in which inequality does not exist. Note, for example, the comments of journalist Paul Gallant:

> The Court's 1992 *Butler* decision has stuck us with the burden of common law that says images lead to action and that violent images lead to violent action – usually by straight men against straight women. Perhaps the best (but most unlikely) argument is that sex between men, and sex between women – and all the kinky representations of it we can muster – is indeed an exception. Nobody wants to be a separatist, but *Butler* leaves little room. For gay men and lesbians, sexual expression takes place in a self-contained, idyllic universe that has little effect on how women are treated in society. In homo couplings, societal inequalities between the genders don't come into play. There is more freedom in queer relationships, less worry about power going awry; the Supreme Court needs to acknowledge it.[85]

The summary of the content of gay male pornography provided in this chapter is indicative of what gay male pornography *is*. While content and presentation vary in degree and explicitness from one medium to another, what the above offers is an overview of what gay male pornography says and does. In arguing as they did before the Supreme Court of Canada that gay male pornography should be exempt from the sex equality standard set by the Court in *Butler*, Little Sisters Bookstore, EGALE, LEAF, and others defended or would have allowed the production and distribution of this, and they defended it as gay male identity – an identity which, like heterosexual pornography, glorifies those in our society who have always had the most power and who have always benefited from dominance and social inequality – white, able-bodied, middle-class, straight men. Like homophobia, gay male pornography silences those who refuse to do what they are told. The result for society, once accepted, is a sexual politic based on a male/female dichotomy – in essence, a remarkably accurate description of what it takes to get and maintain power and heterosexual male privilege.

Having looked at what gay male pornography is and what it says, given the similarities between it and heterosexual pornography, it requires considerable self-denial for gay men to argue that gay pornography is not harmful in much the same way that other forms of vilification are harmful. Indeed, in that its message is that "manliness is the only real virtue and other values are contemptible,"[86] one must ask whether this gay male identity will result in liberation, or whether in the name of liberation we are promoting a homophobic, hence sexist, politic that results in individual and systemic harms. In *Little Sisters,* the Supreme Court of Canada accepted that harm would result. The remainder of this book offers support for this finding.

4 Abusing Real People: The "Actors'" Perspective

No job
No money
No self-esteem
No confidence
All I have is my looks and body,
And that's not working anymore.
I feel washed up.
Drug problem.
Hate life.
HIV-positive[1]

> *1990s gay porn icon Joey Stefano (Nicholas Iacona),*
> *months before his death from a drug overdose*

A number of arguments were advanced in *Little Sisters* as to why lesbian and gay male pornography should be seen as harms-free, hence *Butler*-proof. In this chapter I want instead to provoke discussion on one aspect of the pornography industry and its possible effects that has received surprisingly little attention from gay and pro-porn activists alike. Specifically, I aim to query whether, in defending gay male pornography, gay men risk ignoring the dangers attached to an industry which is in a position to exploit and use men who are economically and socially disadvantaged for the financial gain and sexual gratification of other men (gay and non-gay alike). In *Little Sisters*, the Supreme Court of Canada specifically rejected the claim that same-sex pornography could be distinguished from heterosexual pornography, ruling that the harms analysis first articulated in *Butler* applied to gay and lesbian pornography and that gay pornography could, as a result, be regulated insofar as its distribution undermined the sex equality interests of all Canadians, including lesbian and gay male Canadians. The Court did not, however, make any reference to the harms that might arise during the production of this pornography. This chapter aims to fill this void and queries the claims of those who would argue that the production of same-sex pornography should be exempt from legal regulation because harms cannot result from it.

In *Butler,* the Supreme Court of Canada accepted the findings of feminist writers who, relying on the testimonies of women used to produce heterosexual pornography, established that direct physical and psychological harm is inflicted on real people in order to make some pornography, particularly visual pornography.[2] Some are coerced into pornography, and the pornography market provides a profit motive for harming people and treating them as second-class citizens.[3] A question not raised during the *Little Sisters* trial was whether similar harms might occur as a result of the production of gay male pornography. This chapter aims to explore this issue in more detail. My hope in doing so is that more gay men will commit to what I see as a necessary rethinking of those legal defences which, in arguing that gay male pornography should be defended at all costs, risk ignoring the very real costs paid by those who are exploited for another's sexual gratification, justified as gay male liberation.

Defending Linda Marchiano

In its submissions before the Supreme Court of Canada in *Butler,* LEAF outlined the harms suffered by the women used to produce heterosexual pornography. The most frequently cited example of this is found in the life story of Linda Marchiano (Lovelace). Marchiano's nightmare, described in her book *Ordeal,* exposes in her own words an industry quick to exploit for profit those women most psychologically and economically vulnerable and thus most easily abused and used during the production of pornography. Known by many for her role in the film *Deep Throat*, Marchiano's experiences at the hands of her ex-husband Chuck Traynor reveal an industry prepared to engage in sadistic, abusive, and non-consensual practices for the sake of financial gain. When testifying before hearings aimed at passing the MacKinnon-Dworkin anti-pornography civil rights ordinances in the United States, Marchiano described in detail the abuse inflicted on her from those responsible for the films in which she was used.[4] Her experiences serve as a necessary starting point for determining what, if anything, makes the gay male pornography industry substantially different enough from its heterosexual counterpart to excuse it from legal regulation.

In her book, Linda Marchiano details being used and abused by Chuck Traynor during a two and half year period, during which she was forced through physical, mental, and sexual abuse (often at gunpoint), and threats on her life and the lives of her family, to be involved in the production of pornography. When Marchiano told Traynor, whom she has described as "incapable of a sexual act without inflicting some type of pain or degradation upon a human being,"[5] that she wanted to leave him, Traynor made her his prisoner, refusing to let her out of his sight, holding a gun to her head while she was on the telephone, sleeping with a gun in the bed while next to her, and physically assaulting her if he thought she was trying to leave.[6]

Marchiano has documented that, during her time with Traynor, she was forced to prostitute herself to groups of men, and was introduced to various figures in the pornography industry and used by many of these men to produce pornography, ranging from films in which she was forced to have sex with a dog to the film *Deep Throat*. During the filming of the latter, which was again filmed at gunpoint, Marchiano described suffering a particularly brutal beating from Traynor, while the others on set refused to help her.[7] These beatings, ignored by those using her to produce the films from which they profited, became more regular and more brutal with each attempt to escape.

Linda Marchiano did finally escape from Traynor and the industry that supported him but continued to live with the trauma inflicted on her during her two and a half year "ordeal." When asked how she felt about the existence of the film *Deep Throat*, she responded:

> I feel very hurt and very disappointed in my society and my country for allowing the fact that I was raped, I was beaten, I was put through two and a half years of what I was put through. And it's taken me almost ten years to overcome the damage that he caused. And the fact that this film is still being shown and that my three children will one day walk down the street and see their mother being abused, it makes me angry, makes me sad. Virtually every time someone watches that film, they are watching me being raped.[8]

Marchiano's experiences are not unique. The abuse she has documented is one familiar to many of the women harmed during the production of pornography and from its distribution. From these testimonies, what we learn is that the documented harms of pornography include those of prostitution,[9] that many women entered the industry as children,[10] that many women felt trapped once they entered the industry and were unable to leave as a result of the abuse inflicted on them by pimps or as a result of drug addiction or because they felt they had nothing else to offer other than their bodies, and that many women have been physically coerced into making pornography.[11]

Despite the testimonies offered by these women, there are many who, while acknowledging that they have suffered horrific harms, nonetheless query whether the pornography industry is to blame. Often, in an attempt to strike down laws aimed at stopping the production of pornography, the experiences of these women are portrayed as resulting from some other external factor or simply as a "one-off," not indicative of the experiences of other women who have been reported as receiving considerable financial gain from the industry. American Civil Liberties president Nadine Strossen, for example, while condemning the abuse inflicted on Marchiano, writes that Marchiano should not be seen as representative of the pornography industry because what happened to her resulted from an abusive husband, not pornography:

> [I]n Marchiano's own case, it was not the participants in the porn industry who raped, beat, and forced her to take part in the movie, but rather, her own husband, Chuck Traynor, who had no other connection to the pornography business. Marchiano's autobiographical writings not only make clear that she experienced no abuse or force at the hands of participants in the porn industry; her writings also show that her career as a "porn star" gave her a welcome, if temporary, refuge from her husband's brutality. In *Ordeal*, Marchiano describes the sense of freedom she felt on the set of *Deep Throat*, and how she enjoyed the company of her co-star, Harry Keems. She wrote, "something was happening to me, something strange. No one was treating me like garbage ... We laughed a lot that first day of shooting ... And no one was asking me to do anything I didn't want to do." Evidently threatened by Marchiano's enjoyment of her participation in *Deep Throat*, her husband brutally beat her after that first day of shooting, throwing her against the wall and kicking her for hours.

Later, Strossen writes:

> The second reason Marchiano's experience does not provide proof of abusive working conditions within the porn industry is that she speaks only for herself. Therefore, even assuming for the sake of argument – directly contrary to what she herself has written – that Marchiano had been abused by members of the pornography industry, that still would provide no basis for concluding that other sex industry workers also suffered abuse. Nor does the fact that Marchiano's then-husband forced her to perform in *Deep Throat* support the contention that other pornography models or actresses are also performing under duress.[12]

Strossen offers a distorted and somewhat sanitized account of the life of Linda Marchiano. To begin with, given what we do know about this woman's life as a pornography "actress," to argue that she was used sexually solely because of an abusive husband (who was, according to Marchiano, also her pimp) is rather akin to arguing that women who are raped are not raped because rapists are sexual predators, but simply because they are in the wrong place at the wrong time.[13] In reading Marchiano's writings, one sees clearly that what happened to Linda Marchiano happened because there was an industry willing to let it happen, an industry that relied on it happening, an industry that was willing to exploit the abuse that she suffered at the hands of this man for the sake of its own and his economic gain. Chuck Traynor knew and understood the money to be gained from pornography and knew that the best way to attain it was to find a woman, already vulnerable and naïve, whom the porn industry could and did continue to prostitute.[14] While it is impossible to determine whether Traynor would have been a violent psychopath with or without porn, it *is* probable that he would have been less interested in capturing, torturing, and selling this woman had there not been an industry willing to profit from her abuse. To say, as does Strossen, that Traynor had no connection to the sex and porn industry is at odds with Ms. Marchiano's reports of the man's quite public relationships with industry kingpins, his knowledge of and ties to the sex tourism industry in South America and elsewhere,[15] the ease with which he was able to find and profit with men who filmed and distributed films that marketed bestiality and sexual torture, and his eventual use of Marchiano and other women in his own films.[16] Traynor had a product in Linda Marchiano that he trained and forced into submission. He knew exactly where and how to market his product and had little difficulty making and using the types of contacts one would need in order to do so. As Marchiano explains in her book, the man had a history of pimping women for profit, ran a sex club, and certainly did know and work with many in the sex industry. He was, one might argue, a lesser pimp who sold women such as Linda Marchiano to bigger pimps like the men who produced *Deep Throat*, and to better-known pornography producers, one of whom boasted with considerable pride in a conversation with Traynor of his "women with animals collection" of eight-millimetre pornographic movies.[17] According to Marchiano, these "animal films" showed women in sexual acts with "pigs, chickens, donkeys [and] horses."[18] Indeed, to the best of my knowledge, those *not* knowing something about the pornography industry and how it sells do not normally frequent the houses of industry kingpins for the purpose of discussing ways in which their wives can be used to have sex with animals. In this regard, Chuck Traynor was as much a part of the industry as those who produced the "animal sex flicks" that he and those he associated with found so sexually entertaining and which he was prepared to force on an unwilling Linda Marchiano.[19]

Similarly, to say, as does Strossen, that Linda Marchiano was not harmed by those in the industry itself would seem to ignore the fact that while she was being filmed or photographed, she quite literally had a gun held to her head, while those in the industry looked on and simply chose not to help her. No one intervened to save her. To which one must ask: does inaction *not* constitute action? And what of the actual physical assaults inflicted on her and filmed as pornography? Marchiano has described the film *Deep Throat* as the filming of her being raped. The assaults recorded are not fictional and should not be treated as such. Are her experiences not harmful enough to warrant concern and intervention?

Strossen seems to discount these harms because Marchiano later writes that she felt "liberated" while having sex with these men. To which one should probably ask: given the alternative, given that sex and life with Traynor equalled violent beatings, imprisonment, and sadism, how could forced sex with other men who were not beating her, even *with* a gun held to her head, be anything *but* liberating?[20] Put into its proper context, one should ask what, if anything, liberation even means to a woman whose only alternative to forced sex is death. Does the fact that no on-screen violence was actually seen during the filming of *Deep Throat* (and here I am assuming that Ms. Marchiano's critics simply overlook the fact that in other films Marchiano is being forced at gun-point to have sex with a dog – something which I would hope even Strossen would agree *is* violence – or threatened with her life unless she does film scenes in which she urinates on or is urinated on by others), and does the fact that Marchiano felt safer here than somewhere else mean that abuse was *not* a factor? Is Nadine Strossen, for example, advocating that battered women allow themselves to be used in pornography as some form of emancipation? To say, as Strossen does, that Linda Marchiano was not harmed because of the industry ignores the fact that the men she was filmed being violated by during the filming of *Deep Throat*, for example, had sex with her fully cognizant that she had just been beaten, her ribs were broken, she was covered in bruises, and that this might just be uncomfortable, if not excruciating. The same men also chose to completely ignore her screams for help while Traynor beat her and reminded her that she had no choice but to work for him, make money for him, serve him. While the men filmed with Marchiano on the set of *Deep Throat* were not physically beating her on the set of the film, they *did*, as Marchiano explains, nonetheless allow Traynor to do what he did in order to get her to comply with what they did to her. Rather than help her escape, once it was clear that she needed to, they simply continued to do what they were paid to do, without intervening to ensure that the woman who was the source of their paycheque was physically and mentally safe. Does *this* not count as abuse?

Perhaps most disturbing, to argue, as does Strossen, that abuse did not occur *because* of the industry again ignores the fact that this woman (and, as Ms. Marchiano notes, many others), battered and threatened with death (her own and that of those she loved), was filmed having sex with a dog – a film which was produced, marketed, and sold by an industry that, Strossen implies, cannot be held accountable for the likes of Chuck Traynor.[21] What Strossen and others ignore in order to justify what happens in and because of pornography is that Linda Marchiano was not involved in the industry by choice. Ms. Marchiano's point, made clear in her own voice, is that what it took to get her to do what was necessary to make pornography was abuse. How is the marketing of that abuse for profit consensual or empowering or liberating?

A line of reasoning similar to the one provided by Strossen is offered by Brian McNair, who, outlining the debate between those who, like Marchiano, have documented real abuse and those who claim to have benefited from working in and with the industry, writes:

> The evidence cited by the protagonists in this particular debate is, once again, largely anecdotal. On the performer-as-victim side of the fence, Linda Marchiano (formerly pornographic movie star Linda Lovelace) is frequently enlisted as an example of a woman who, by her own account, was enmeshed in an abusive relationship with the man who later introduced her to the pornographic film industry.
>
> Evidence for the opposing viewpoint is provided by women such as the pornographic film actress quoted in Delacoste and Alexander's collection of interviews, who finds performing in sexually explicit material satisfying on a number of levels: First, it provides a physically and psychically safe environment for me to live my exhibitionist fantasies. Secondly, it provides a surprisingly flexible and supportive arena for me to grow in as a *performer,* both sexually and non-sexually. Thirdly, it provides me with erotic material that I like to watch for my own pleasure. Finally, the medium allows me to explore the theme of celebrating a positive female sexuality – a sexuality heretofore denied us. In choosing my roles and characterizations carefully, I strive to show, always, women who thoroughly enjoy sex and are forceful, self-satisfying and guilt-free without also being neurotic, unhappy or somehow unfulfilled.[22]

McNair does not indicate which of the two worldviews he favours, stating that he is "unwilling to enter the debate about who among these conflicting voices is lying ... (since one or the other must be)."[23] Of course, *neither* need be lying. I have little reason to doubt the statements made by the woman quoted by Delacoste and Alexander. Nor, however, do I have any reason to question the abuse documented by Linda Marchiano. The point lost by McNair and others is that simply because one woman does not experience harm does not mean that another woman has not been harmed. Nor does the fact that one woman has not been harmed mean that another woman who has been should not be afforded legal protections and a safe forum within which to talk about her experiences without being accused of lying or misleading the public. To the extent that one woman *is* harmed in the name of sexual freedom and speech, those who support the industry because it benefits them arguably have a responsibility to ensure that steps are taken to guarantee that abuse and inequality *do* become a fiction. In this regard, it is probably fair to say that

Strossen's final assertion that Marchiano speaks only for herself is at best naïve. Women are hurt so that pornography can be made, and Marchiano's ordeal is not unique. She herself has written that "there are plenty of Chuck Traynors out there. And an endless supply of girls who are young, trusting and gullible. And it is certain that these people will, from time to time, come together. By the time they are pried apart, incredible damage can be done."[24]

To the extent that the material props up the types of systemic inequalities that allowed what happened to Linda Marchiano to happen in the first place, it seems important that those who do "enjoy" or "profit" from the production of material through which they personally are not hurt be held accountable. Thus, should their product promote other forms of discrimination on the basis of sex, and in so doing violate the sex equality principles outlined in *Butler*, then their source of "liberation" should be held legally accountable in order to prevent women such as Linda Marchiano from being subjected to violence and abuse and forced to produce pornography, and still others from being hurt as a result of its distribution and use.[25] To the extent that their materials do *not* promote these attitudes and behaviours of discrimination, and do not exploit unwilling or powerless people, no anti-pornography feminist committed to sex equality has ever argued that they should be stopped.[26]

Given what we do know about the production of heterosexual pornography, the question now arises as to whether or not those used to produce gay male pornography might also be susceptible to the harms documented by non-gay "actors."

Gay "Rights": Doesn't Joey Stefano Have Any?

In its submissions before the Supreme Court of Canada in *Little Sisters*, EGALE argued that unlike in the mass-market heterosexual pornography industry, "the publication of sexually explicit lesbian, gay and bisexual imagery is not a lucrative industry and economic profit is not the primary motivation for the production of this work."[27] Similarly, Little Sisters argued that the entire framework of production is different from that in place for the production and consumption of heterosexual pornography. Because of this, we are led to believe, gay pornography avoids the harms addressed in *Butler*.[28]

It would seem to me that the psychology of the people who produce pornography is irrelevant if what is produced results in harm. In any event, given the amount of money currently being spent by gay men on gay male pornography and the number of pornography videos, magazines, and books now being produced each year,[29] it takes a remarkable leap of faith to argue, as did EGALE in its submissions before the Supreme Court of Canada in *Little Sisters*, that the gay pornography industry is *not* an industry driven by profit. If it were not, then one would expect, among other things, that the materials distributed would be much cheaper than those presently available. As John Burger explains, one of the more noticeable things about the industry is the relatively low overhead for producing films and other products. "Actors earn anywhere from $200 to $500 per scene" with films "usually starring one or two actors in an average of two or three scenes, and feature an average of six other performers. The typical format of these videos consists of five scenes."[30] Burger continues:

> The budgets for these videos are remarkably low. Reportedly, the most expensive gay male porn film made to date is *Centurions of Rome.* This 1981 film was financed by a Brinks robbery (as the insurer of Brinks, Lloyds of London co-owns the film) and cost between $150,000 and $250,000, although sources differ on this. This cost range (for a 90-minute feature film) is roughly equal to the cost of a low-budget 30-second television commercial. By paying the crew under the table in cash, the producers of gay porn videos sidestep the film unions and their mandatory minimum wages, pension funds, as well as job title duties and regulations. The actors are often booked through model/ escort agencies. The agencies set the prices, receive the money, and subsequently pay the actors, retaining for themselves a percentage of the fee.[31]

Given the phenomenal number of videos alone being sold and the relatively low cost of producing these videos, it is evident that someone somewhere *is* driven by economic profit. More troubling, however, given the description of the types of gay pornography now sold worldwide, how it is produced, why it is produced, and what is produced, one must ask: would it really come as a surprise to discover that the gay pornography industry risks placing its "models" in situations that promote violence, cruelty, degradation, dehumanization, and exploitation and hence are violent, cruel, degrading, dehumanizing, and exploitative?[32] While deemed merely representational, hence "fictional," the "fantasy" offered in gay male pornography utilizes real people – a factor most pro-pornography advocates conveniently overlook.

Given the reaction to and condemnation of women such as Linda Marchiano who have tried to document and speak out about their experiences in the heterosexual pornography industry, it is not surprising that few gay men have been willing to investigate or talk about the use of men in the gay pornography industry. Indeed, given the extent to which the gay community so readily defends gay pornography as liberation, it is surprising that anyone is willing to discuss whether the industry, to create its product, relies on and uses those who are socially less empowered. The little information that has made its way to public speech, however, reveals an industry not foreign to the one described by Linda Marchiano and others.

While not every person who has been used to produce gay male pornography claims to have been harmed, and while it is arguably the case that not every producer of gay male pornography sets out to exploit those used to make his product, given the documented links between the production of heterosexual pornography and harm and given the experiences of some of the men who have been used to make gay male pornography, there is reason to believe that some pornography producers do harm, or at least turn a blind eye to the exploitation of the men they use. These men – the men sold as sex – matter, as do the men who take their place once they are no longer wanted or no longer exploitable through sex.[33]

One study, for example, reveals that some of the men used in gay male pornography are involved in it because they are psychologically and/or financially vulnerable. Many of these men were sexually, physically, or emotionally abused as children, often because they were gay. This, in turn, affected the way in which they saw themselves sexually as adults, with many viewing sexual inequality as the norm.[34] This becomes clear in the words of one young man, described as follows:

> *Jim Y.:* was raised by abusive, alcoholic parents. When Jim told his parents he was gay, at age 13, his father tried to kill him with a large kitchen knife. Jim left home at 17. At 19 he met Frank H., about ten years his senior, who was to become his lover. Frank was making a porno film at the time he met Jim, and convinced Jim to appear in it. Jim played a new arrival to the big city who engages in S&M, including bootlicking, bondage, beating with a belt, fisting, and implied murder. This film was the first film to show fisting and Jim says he is convinced that it created the gay interests in fisting as a sexual behaviour. The film also reflected the S&M relationship that Jim and Frank were to share for the next decade ... Jim has been seeing a psychiatrist for three years now. He has been trying to avoid S&M sex, and believes that his sexual behaviour was a way he sought out contact with his abusive father. He also recognizes that much sexual "fantasy" can be destructive; when asked where it comes from, he said, "Well, to some extent, from me; from my films, that is." About one month ago Jim was diagnosed with AIDS, and now fears that he has lost whatever chance he might have had to turn his life around.[35]

Still others left home because of their sexuality, often at a young age, resulting in a lower level of education that, in turn, left the sex industry as one of the few economic options open to them. Some, who, as young men, had seen pornography as the only source through which to interpret their own sexuality and who had defined themselves according to its terms, ultimately turned to the industry that reaffirmed this stereotype and promised them sexual validation.

This can end in catastrophe; many of these men are easily exploited by an industry ideally suited to manipulate those least likely to possess real life choices. For these young men, unfortunately, the industry becomes a trap and, literally, a dead end. Note, for example, the gradual destruction of the life of another young man:

> *Chris J.:* is 26 and has appeared in over one hundred gay films and numerous magazines. He "enjoys" heavy S&M ("all the queens in the leather bars are a bunch of pansies"), and is known for his "ravenous rectum." At a recent gay filmmakers awards show he was publicly whipped, led around the stage by a chain attached to a dog collar around his neck, and then penetrated by a large dildo; he says he loved it. He was recently arrested and charged with assault with a deadly weapon, after having tied up and beaten black and blue (with a belt) a famous porno star he had been friends with. Chris says he has become too well known in Los Angeles, and says he might leave town. He has studied martial arts and says he wants to become a mercenary ("I could go to South Africa and kill some niggers").[36]

It is a disturbing reflection of the state of gay male relations that so little is known about, and ultimately done to assist, many of the men held out as the images from whence gay male identity is derived. The description of gay male actors provided above, for example, while not exhaustive, presents a grim reality of the source of that identity – an identity in which men, severely traumatized for a wide range of reasons, are used sexually; an identity through which trauma, violence, and inequality are sexualized. Their experiences provide a starting point from which to begin a necessary unpacking of a self-serving façade that allows gay pornography supporters to deny some very real inequalities and the abuse resulting from them. What is clear from it and the work that follows is that the lives and experiences of these young men are very much like the realities of the pornography they are often used in.

These findings have recently been supported by the work of other men who, despite the inevitable pariah status attached to those who do question gay pornography, have been willing to expose an industry in which young men are seen as expendable and are ultimately used as such. Others, while not specifically criticizing the industry, have offered personal accounts which, when read in the right context, support the testimonies provided above. Ronnie Larsen, the director of the documentary *Shooting Making Porn* and the off-Broadway production of *Making Porn*, has worked with many of today's better-known gay porn "actors." His views of the industry paint a less than flattering picture. Discussing the recent suicide of 1990s porn icon Joey Stefano, Larsen explains that when he tried to direct such men on stage,

> [t]oo many of the stars pulled stunts after they'd settled into the roles. At the beginning it's very exciting to meet them, but to work with them was to see them as they are: immature and deeply disturbed –

men who desperately need psychotherapy ... By making my documentary I began to understand both their appeal and that so many of the
models are fucked up: [the late] Joey Stefano was not an anomaly –
it's amazing to me that there aren't more Joeys as drug use among
them is so rampant.[37]

Discussing the making of his documentary, during which he lived with many
of the men interviewed for months at a time, Larsen adds:

[Gay porn icon] Ryan Idol has cried on my couch that he didn't ever
want to make another porn video or turn another trick. Well, he's still
advertising in *Frontiers* as an "escort"! Everyone pretends the Industry
is such a big happy family – bullshit! They're miserable, unhappy
people. So many of the models say they don't like turning tricks, but
they continue to do it because they cannot see any other way to make
a living – they can't act and most come and go so quickly. Christ, it's
such a pathetic industry. I got sucked into believing the happy family
routine for a while, but so many are sick and need help. They aren't
paid all that well and what they make they blow on drugs.[38]

Larsen's experiences are validated by the description of the life of Nicholas
Iacona (Joey Stefano) in the biographical *Wonder Bread and Ecstasy: The Life
and Death of Joey Stefano*. Iacona, made famous through more than thirty-five
hard-core gay porn videos, ran away from home shortly after the death of his
father, at age fifteen. With little education to fall back on and "in search of the
American dream," Iacona soon found his way into the hands of porn producers quick to market his youth and good looks. The result, for him, could not
have been more tragic. Although Iacona eventually "danced an unforgettable
striptease in clubs across America and Europe, and hustled his way through
thousands of dollars paid to him by clients around the globe,"[39] all the fame
and contacts could not save this young man's life. From pornography, Iacona
entered prostitution, believing that the wealthy men who used him as "their
toy boy, as their trophy,"[40] would help him land roles in TV commercials and
big Hollywood blockbusters (none of which happened, of course). Refusing to
believe that "when he was told to turn over, it'd all stop there,"[41] Iacona,
naïve, vulnerable, and trusting, was swept up in an industry that only "loved
him for his body and sexual prowess, nothing more."[42]

In time, Iacona's star status faded as newer, younger men replaced him as
gay men's preferred sex object. Having done nothing with his life but "sell
sex," now finding that his "friends" in the industry had less time for him than
for the fresher, more popular, and now in demand boys, feeling like he'd been
taken advantage of, increasingly addicted to a drug habit that had robbed him

of any money he had managed to save, wishing that he had had nothing to do with the pornography industry in the first place, and now HIV-positive, Iacona, like many before him, fell into a state of despair from which he would not recover.[43] On 20 February 1994, at the age of twenty-six, he was found dead in a seedy Hollywood motel from an apparent drug overdose.

While Iacona did not suffer the types of on-film abuse experienced by women such as Linda Marchiano, it would be naïve to argue that what happened to this young man did not happen because of the porn industry, and that the industry did not benefit from his well-documented vulnerability. It would also be an injustice to deny that his experiences constitute abuse, inflicted and manipulated by that industry and the men who continue to fund it. Iacona sold the only thing he thought he had to sell to an industry all too willing to exploit his insecurities and lack of self-confidence. Once he was addicted to drugs and further marketed as a sex toy, this exploitation became easier, until the toy itself could be replaced with a newer model. Not able to leave the industry but less in demand, Iacona's life spiralled out of control. To label this as anything but abuse is to offer an unfairly restrictive definition of the word and the effects of inequality.

Unlike Stefano, but much like Marchiano, others *have* had their abuse documented on film – something some gay male activists and academics have denied. British legal academic Carl Stychin, for example, has written that there is no evidence that gay men are harmed during the production of gay male pornography. Apart from the fact that his analysis ignores the links between the lives of young men such as Iacona and the porn industry, Stychin's assertion that no one is hurt during the production of gay porn is troubling because it risks fictionalizing abuse. Stychin argues that statements attempting to document harm are unrealistic because, although he has no doubt "that the Hollywood film industry in general is highly exploitive of workers, it would be trite to suggest that the actors who portrayed Jews in the film *Schindler's List*, for example, were degraded in the way the characters they portrayed were within the narrative structure of the movie."[44]

To this, one need only respond that while it might be trite to make *this* argument, it is not trite to assume that the pornographic presentation of a young man being penetrated by a twelve-inch dildo might actually do some very real bodily damage to that young man or that the burning of a cigarette on human flesh, presented as a sexual stimulus, might actually result in a rather unpleasant burn and permanent scarring. Nor does it require too much insight to understand that the pornographic presentation of unsafe sex involves two real men engaging in an unsafe sexual practice and that the very real deaths of some of these people would have been avoided if, as Stychin claims, this presentation had been fictional. As Torres explains, within the context of the heterosexual pornography industry, the nature of adult motion picture production encourages unusual and unsafe working conditions. Producers have been known to force actors to do sexual acts that they would really rather not do. In most of the productions, producers do not test the performers for sexually transmitted diseases and do not require that performers practice safe sex. Additionally, some producers ignore the risks associated with allowing a performer, who may be infected with HIV, to perform in a film. In these situations, the performers are faced with the greatest risk of contracting AIDS.[45]

Similar dangers exist in the gay pornography industry. In his work on Joey Stefano, Charles Isherwood describes the industry's reluctance to reveal Stefano's HIV+ status to the public and to the men paired with Stefano in his films. Nor did the industry take precautions to ensure that condoms were used to protect Stefano in his early films. Nor would it appear that many in the industry have learned anything from the death of this young man and numerous others. As a recent article in *Frontiers Magazine* notes, the gay adult video industry leapt to the forefront of safer-sex promotion early in the AIDS crisis by introducing condoms into its pornographic videos – even incorporating their use into the storylines. It would appear, however, that the tide is turning and more and more unsafe sex is creeping back into gay porn videos. Richard Douglas, a leading director in the industry, justifies this re-emerging trend by arguing that

> being gay is about sex for gay men and it's about dick, and we've been denied that. While I may have some personal problems with it, pornography is only porn if it represents the culture it is a part of.[46]

> I don't give a damn about responsibility. This is business, and someone is going to do a video without condoms and get rich doing it, so it may as well be me.[47]

The concerns of those who do want to protect men from the many harms caused by the industry are further justified by the use of men and boys even more disempowered than Iacona; one need only note the increased use of young men from the former Soviet bloc to produce gay porn sold via the Internet. In the recent documentary *The Fall of Communism as Seen through Gay Porn*, we see first-hand the use of young Russian boys and men who, trying to survive in a devastated economy, find themselves trapped in prostitution and, exploited by pornographers, photographed or filmed for little if any money. A quick look at much of the pornography on the Internet and sold through less well-known pornographers (see examples marketing "soviet boys" and "young twinks" in Chapter 3) also makes it clear that less than safe sexual practices are being performed by and on young men with few life choices and who, as such, are probably less able to demand safety. The extent to which a lack of self-confidence can prevent or undermine safe sex is examined in Chapter 7. For now, it is probably accurate to argue that men wanting food and shelter are going to be less willing and not empowered enough to ensure safe sexual practices when filmed or photographed. Add to this the growing number of Web sites, magazines, and so on that now sell "homemade" porn (often of young men who are unaware that they are being filmed or that the pictures taken will be sold or seen by others) and one queries how "safety" of any sort can be guaranteed. Indeed, although the examination of porn "stars" such as Iacona (and Casey Donovan, discussed below) reveals considerable industry exploitation, it is important to keep in mind that these men were comparatively "empowered" by their celebrity status, in contrast to many of the young men now sold worldwide for sexual pleasure. Given the harm inflicted on these men, particularly once their celebrity status diminished, it is not hard to imagine the damage inflicted on others who might be even less "empowered."

Similarly, to return to the arguments made by Carl Stychin, if he is assuming that the slappings, whippings, forceful penetrations, unsafe sexual practices, and so on presented in gay porn are simply acting in much the same way as fake bullets are shot into the actors in *Schindler's List,* I would beg to differ. Given what we already know about the pornography industry as a whole, about the lives of those who work in it, and about the content of gay porn, I remain skeptical that many of the men who produce gay pornography are given any incentive to set up fictional scenarios of abuse when it is much easier (and much cheaper) simply to show the real thing – an option which will likely go unchecked as long as the "actors" used in the production of gay porn remain powerless and continue to die, and so long as gay men continue to purchase and demand materials which market, sexualize, and trivialize abuse.

This is a point again made clear in the biography of 1980s gay porn icon Cal Culver (Casey Donovan).[48] Like that of Iacona, Culver's life typifies the fall from favour and eventual self-destruction of too many of the men used to produce gay porn. Unlike that of Iacona, however, Culver's gradual transformation from "smiling, golden-haired, blue-eyed preppie" to "raging out of control sexual predator" was captured on film. Like many young gay men, Culver believed that he could use porn as a step toward a legitimate career in the mainstream media,[49] but his final days, as presented in his final movie *Fucked Up,* and well described by Roger Edmonson, were far otherwise:

> "I couldn't watch it," Cal's friend Jake Getty told me. "I started it, but Cal looked so spaced out, so lost, that I had to stop." Cal and his old friend, Clay Johns – identified in the film as John Clayton – are in Rage's *Fucked Up* together, and fucked up they are. Both men are ill at this point in time, and all taboos regarding drugs – whether as a result

of despair or dementia – are off. The film explores the extremes, its participants zonked out, pushing the limits of sexual experience over the edge.

"*Fucked Up* was the saddest thing I had ever seen," Rob Richards confided. "It was a horrible film. When I saw it I just couldn't believe it. Cal was so far gone, and he was being so used and abused. The whole thing was beyond abandoned. He was holding what appeared to be a big mayonnaise jar full of poppers or ethyl chloride – I'm sure there were other drugs in him at the time as well – sitting in the corner of a room. These faceless people arrive and push toys and fists up into him. He's drooling, and it is absolutely terrifying. I couldn't believe it when I saw it." It was ... a haunting study in self-destruct ... a pathetic footnote to a glittering career ... an unsettling record of the Golden Boy on a collision course with his own mortality.[50]

The daily reality of some of the men used in gay male pornography should, at a minimum, indicate that many in the industry are not completely committed to giving protection to the people used to generate a medium produced for profit. Many of these men are already susceptible to the effects of past emotional, physical, and sexual abuse. For a 1995 exposé on the porn industry, Australian writer Dale Reynolds interviewed a number of the leading men in gay porn films. Some of his findings support the testimonies that appear above. Specifically, on child sexual abuse, he writes:

One of the less pleasant things I learned in researching this article is that there's another thing which many of the models have in common: sexual molestation as children. Ray is a prime example of that horror. "I didn't know my father until I was nine years old and I went to live with him. He was a drug addict and when I was ten, he held a knife to my throat and told me he would show me what men and women did. I was raped so brutally that I had to go to the emergency ward of the hospital. The doctors ignored the evidence and sent me home, where he continued to rape me for three years, often trading me out to his friends in exchange for drugs. "I told my mother, but she felt powerless to help me. He lives in San Francisco now, but naturally I don't talk to him."[51]

These men are further endangered by some in the industry whose films do not guarantee safe sexual practices,[52] thereby promoting unsafe sex practices to those who purchase their product (see discussion in Chapter 7), and others who appear to do little to protect the very people who should be presenting positive and safe sexual practices. In addition, as the life of Joey Iacona shows, much of the industry is connected to the prostitution of these men[53] – resulting in the increased risk of exposure to HIV and the physical violence and exploitation commensurate with prostitution generally.

Conclusion

Scenarios of sexual violence and pain presented as pleasurable may in fact document real degradation that is neither pleasurable nor fiction. While it is easy to articulate a liberation theory that overlooks or ignores the reality of so-called fantasy, the use and abuse of young men in scenarios of degradation, dehumanization, and violence is being justified as integral to the sexual and political awareness of all gay men. The facts prove otherwise, for as LEAF argued in its factum before the Supreme Court of Canada in *Butler*, "if anything can violate a person's freedom and integrity more than direct sexual and physical abuse, it is the mass marketing of that abuse as sexual entertainment."[54]

At a minimum, the use of those who are most in need of community support for the sake of another's liberation reveals a level of insensitivity that few can be proud of. For gay men concerned with the politics of "community," the result is an almost complete abandonment of at least one subset of that community which, although very much in need of positive reaffirmation, is virtually discarded for the production of a medium that exploits some gay men – yet it is nonetheless somehow supposed to liberate us. It does not.

The argument has been made that the harms inflicted on these young men will be addressed when more gay men themselves are provided a greater role in the production of gay male pornography.[55] I remain unconvinced. The gay male pornography industry is driven by economic gain, heavily integrated into the non-gay reality of pornographic production generally, and relies on the use of young people, many of whom are socially disempowered. There is little reason to believe that gay men driven by profit incentive will be any more motivated to protect the people whose abuse makes them more likely to be in pornography and who, as vulnerable, are easily exploited in the name of increased revenue. Co-opted into mainstream consumerist society, the gay male entrepreneur has little need for community emancipation when money itself promises him personal liberation.[56] Even if efforts can be made to use less vulnerable "actors," the fact remains that the presentation of what is currently justified and defended as the source of gay male identity is what makes gay male pornography lucrative.

As Fung explains within the context of the use and resulting racial objectification of Asian men in gay male films produced by Asian men, "the race of the producer is no automatic guarantee of 'consciousness' about these issues or of a different product."[57] Racism, once eroticized, proves remarkably profitable. Similarly, the sexual identity of the pornographer is no guarantee that the resulting presentation will be any less harmful for those used to produce what makes gay pornography financially rewarding: inequality. Gay male pornography is profitable precisely because it presents what those who purchase it find pleasurable – sexual hierarchy. The use of men in scenarios of degradation and objectification – scenarios that, like those in heterosexual pornography, may actually require physical subordination – is necessary for the presentation of what this model of gay male identity is. If this identity politic results in profit – financial and sexual – then the elimination of those scenarios that result in the abuse of real people is unlikely to occur. The pornography market provides a profit motive for harming and exploiting the most vulnerable in our community, and the availability of expendable youth provides little incentive to protect these people when the alternative is reduced profit. As one young street prostitute explains the ruling ethos, "the established gay community will never really do anything for young, poor gays because poverty will force young gays to provide economical sex services. Let's face it. Who wants to have sex with an old troll?"[58]

5 Gay Male Pornography and Violence: Partner Abuse and Rape

My ex-lover used pornography. One of his first contacts with other men [was] in gay pornography theaters. He used pornographic magazines before I met him. He started wanting to look at pornography together. I believe that the pornography influenced his behavior. As our relationship progressed, it became violent. He threatened me with a knife, forced sex on me, and battered me on different occasions. The heterosexual pornography that I had been exposed to was one thing that convinced me that this kind of treatment was normal. The battering was one of the most profoundly destructive experiences of my life. Pornography has showed me that a man's love was violent and to be close to my ex-lover I had to accept his violence.

There is a lot of sexual violence in the gay community, and pornography condones it. I was with my ex-lover after he had been raped by a casual sex partner, and my ex said that rape was just a risk you had to take. I was with a friend after he had been violently raped by his boyfriend, and his boyfriend did not understand that violence and force was not supposed to be a part of sex. The objectification and the violent themes in pornography promote and increase these kinds of violence.[1]

> *Oral testimony of "Mr C.," testifying before the Minneapolis*
> *Hearings to include pornography as a civil rights violation*

Homosexual, Therefore Not Violent?

Even if we assume that no one *is* actually taken advantage of, physically or psychologically coerced into appearing in, or harmed during the production of gay male pornography (an assumption that would, based on the available evidence, be rather naïve), the question remains as to whether this suffices to address the harms-based analysis undertaken by feminist writers and researchers regarding heterosexual pornography. We know, for example, that the technology exists to create a digital pornography "star" and that a lot of pornography is entirely written or verbal. Does this eradicate harm? Similarly, even with respect to the use of "consensual" gay pornography actors (and, again, no one has ever claimed that there aren't any or that a few have not done quite well out of the industry), can it be stated that the behaviours and actions they promote cease to harm gay men generally and society's equality interest specifically, simply because they consent, or, in the case of verbal pornography, no one has to consent to being used? While I am not convinced that consent can be assumed, the question remains: does the identity sold in gay male pornography (in all its varied media) serve as a positive reaffirmation of gay male identity, or does it reinforce those already existing notions of acceptable male/female behaviour that ultimately result in harm? In focusing on the harms of consumption as opposed to those of production discussed in the previous chapter, this chapter examines that question. It argues that, although the social science research into the harms of heterosexual pornography has not been conducted on gay pornography specifically, an examination of what gay male pornography is, says, and encourages makes it clear that the harms of pornography are not eliminated within a same-sex setting. That is, there is no reason to assume that the research into the harms of heterosexual pornography, which is conclusive, does not apply to gay male pornography. Indeed, there is nothing about gay male pornography that saves it from this conclusion. Therefore, those who claim to be harmed by it should be allowed to prove this connection and take action against those responsible for the harms inflicted on them.

In its factum before the Supreme Court of Canada in the *Little Sisters* case, Little Sisters argued that "there is solid academic criticism of the equation of homosexual pornography with mainstream pornography. Erotica produced for a homosexual audience does not and cannot cause the kind of anti-social behaviour generally or through stereotyping and objectification of women and children that Parliament apprehended might be caused in heterosexual obscenity. While heterosexual obscenity is often misogynist that cannot be said of homosexual pornography."[2] This hypothesis warrants more analysis.

When one attempts to argue that there is a link between gay male pornography and violence, the first obstacle encountered is a considerable reluctance within the gay male community to acknowledge that some of the violence gay men experience is inflicted at the hands of other gay men. In *Glad Day Bookshop Inc.* v. *Canada (Deputy Minister of National Revenue, Customs and Excise)*,[3] for example, Kyle Raye, then a Toronto city counsellor and director at the Community Centre for Lesbians and Gay Men, was asked if the presentation of violent behaviour in gay male pornography might encourage some men to replicate this behaviour. Raye testified that he had never received complaints about violence between gay men nor had he received complaints about abusive sexual behaviour between gay males. Given that Toronto has the largest lesbian and gay male population in Canada and that, in the United States, gay male domestic abuse is the third largest health problem facing gay men,[4] Raye's opinion is questionable. More alarming, however, is the testimony of Barry Adams, a professor of sociology at the University of Windsor. In *Glad Day,* Adams testified that if a gay man wanted to avoid violence in a relationship he could do so by "not staying in the relationship," and that although there is coercive sex in the gay community, "there is underlying consent and it is sexual theatre."

These comments are not unusual. As rape education counsellor Michael Scarce explains, there is little appreciation or willingness to deal with the realities of intracommunity violence. Describing one media report on the topic, Scarce writes:

> As with sexual violence, not everyone sympathizes or recognizes the victimization of same-sex domestic violence. In the December 10, 1996, issue of the *Chicago Tribune,* columnist Mike Royko described his lack of concern for gay men who are battered by their partners because he believes men should have the power and privilege to simply walk away from an abusive relationship, regardless of the circumstances:
>
> It seems to me that if Bill lives with Joe and Joe makes a practice of pummeling Bill, then Bill would have the good sense to just pack a suitcase and get the heck out of there. It should be easier for a man to walk away from an abusive relationship than for a woman since men don't get pregnant and have babies.[5]

Royko continued by saying that if a battered partner chooses to stay with his partner, for any reason, "that is his choice and I respect it – so long as he is not my neighbour and doesn't start screaming for help or pound on my door at night."[6]

These assumptions, endemic within the gay male community, make the task of trying to draw a link between pornography and violence both frustrating and difficult. Add to this the fact that, to date, little research has been conducted on the effects of gay male pornography per se and one is left with little support from gay activists for the argument that harmful behaviour is encouraged by gay male pornography or that pornography promotes those practices, attitudes, and stereotypes that undermine social equality.

In attempting to get gay men to rethink their position, I should point out that, although no social science data exist on gay pornography specifically, if these gay male materials were heterosexual materials, and presented women with men rather than men with men, the evidence would be overwhelming. As noted in Chapter 2, studies prove that the result of exposure to heterosexual pornography is sexual abuse, the sexualization of violence, and a lack of respect for the integrity of the other presented as sexual stimulus and practice. To repeat, there is also considerable research indicating that the production and distribution of heterosexual pornography increases violence against women on an individual level and that, on the basis of sex, the gender hierarchies and stereotypes promoted in pornography undermine systemic equality on a social level.

In its factum in *Butler,* LEAF documented findings that of the many harmful, discriminatory effects of pornography, an increase in "the belief in male dominance in intimate relationships," "lower inhibitions on aggression by men," "the normalization of male aggression generally," domestic battery, and the embodiment of "society's most repressive and anti-egalitarian norms," are but a few of the harms resulting from the distribution of pornography.[7] The Court accepted these findings as evidence that pornography undermines society's interest in equality by encouraging anti-social and anti-egalitarian behaviour, mainly by men against women. The question for gay men is whether these findings are applicable to gay male pornography. That is, does the "gay" in gay male pornography make the pornography less pornographic in the harms-based equality analysis or is there something so qualitatively different about pictures of men violating other men that gay male pornography is harm-free and legally *Butler*-proof?

In arguments before the Supreme Court of Canada in support of Little Sisters, EGALE exempted same-sex pornography from the application of *Butler,* arguing that its test was intended to apply to heterosexual pornography only: "The specific materials at issue in *Butler* consisted of mainstream pornography produced for a heterosexual, predominantly male audience. In contrast, this case involves the systematic detention and seizure of sexually explicit homoerotic imagery and text, produced by and for lesbians, gays and bisexuals. The expression conveyed by the *Butler* videos echoed the dominant refrain on sexuality, while the expressions conveyed in the materials at issue in this case are those of dissenting minority voices."[8]

Similarly, Little Sisters argued that the Court in *Butler* "did not substantively or seriously consider gay and lesbian material."[9] Relying on the work of lesbian legal academic Brenda Cossman, EGALE also argued that the research undertaken to date on the harm of pornography was exclusively directed at heterosexual pornography: "It is an understanding of harm set in a heterosexual framework. The pornography is male heterosexual pornography, and its harm is that heterosexual men are likely to mistreat women. The feminist literature on which this understanding of harm is based has similarly operated within this heterosexual discursive framework."[10]

EGALE continued by arguing that the "*Butler* analysis of harmful effects of mainstream pornography is so embedded in a heterosexual context that it does nothing to elucidate the effects of lesbian, gay, and bisexual pornography" and that because gay pornography does not involve heterosexual representations, it "cannot eroticize a gendered power imbalance of male domination over women."[11]

The material before the Court in *Butler* was not limited to heterosexual sex acts – the videotapes at issue in that case included violent and degrading sexual acts between men. Same-sex material in *Butler* was not restricted to so-called lesbian sex produced specifically for heterosexual male audiences, as Little Sisters claimed.[12] Nor has the feminist anti-pornography/sex equality literature relied on by the courts ever drawn a distinction between non-gay and gay pornography when describing and analyzing the harms of pornography as the harms of sex inequality. Quite the opposite. In any event, even if *Butler* had not focused on same-sex pornography, and even if the research and writing undertaken on pornography thus far had focused on heterosexual pornography only, the question remains independently: is this analysis applicable to same-sex pornography? Again: does something about gay pornography ensure that it does *not* present issues of sex discrimination and gender inequality, and does not produce individual and systemic harm?

In 1985, the Special Committee on Pornography and Prostitution presented its report (the Fraser Report) to the Canadian minister of justice. On page 268 of the report, the committee observed that "sexually violent and degrading pornography is not limited in its focus to the abuse of women. There is some material, produced in which similar conduct is presented in a homosexual context."[13] The committee concluded that these materials offend the value of respect for human dignity of which Quigley J. spoke in *Keegstra,* and that the social harm to which the prohibition on pornography in the *Canadian Criminal Code* is directed is based on respect for human dignity in general and not restricted to human dignity in the heterosexual context.[14] Accepting this, the Canadian courts, prior to *Little Sisters,* recognized that lesbian and gay male pornography could harm and that the sexual orientation of the material was irrelevant.[15] In *Little Sisters,* on appeal to the British Columbia Court of Appeal, MacFarlane J.A. extended this analysis, arguing that harm was not reduced simply because the materials were shown to or used only by lesbians and gay men. Specifically, applying the decision of Wilson J. of the Supreme Court of Canada in *Towne Cinema Theatres,*[16] His Honour reasoned that "it is not ... open to the courts ... to characterize a movie as obscene if shown to one constituency but not if shown to another."[17] This argument was also raised by the Attorney General of Canada in *Little Sisters,* who argued that MacFarlane JA was correct when he said:

> [i]f the appellants' argument is that Parliament had no reasoned ba
> sis for apprehending harm because no harm results from the receipt
> and use by the gay/lesbian community of obscene material, then I
> must reject it. Harm is not to be determined by the standard of the
> gay/lesbian community but by application of a general community

standard. The question is not whether harm will be caused to the gay and lesbian community by the importation of obscene material, but whether harm to society generally may be caused by importation and proliferation of such material. The objective of the legislation is not to prohibit non-obscene gay and lesbian literature, but to prohibit importation of obscene material as defined in s. 163(8) of the *Criminal Code*.[18]

To some extent, the Attorney General's support of these comments in *Little Sisters* risks implying that in some circumstances gay pornography can be harmless for gay men themselves but nonetheless harmful to society as a whole. With respect I find this reasoning somewhat illogical. Given what we know about the links between homophobia and sex discrimination, it is unlikely that, to the extent gay pornography can be shown to be harm-free (i.e., to the extent that it does not rely on those stereotypes that violate "egalitarianism, non-violence, consensualism and mutuality"), it is difficult to see how it might in turn violate the broader sex equality perspective outlined in *Butler*. In other words, to apply the sex equality analysis test adopted in *Butler*, if pornography doesn't harm gay men, it is unlikely to harm women and vice versa. Conversely, if it does harm gay men, it will also harm women because the harms in both situations are gendered and do not apply disparately.

This line of reasoning is also problematic because of the risk it poses for ignoring the very real dangers to gay men that might result from gay male pornography – harms that feed into the types of broader systemic sexual inequalities referred to above. Hence, it is futile to attempt to address the wider social harms of pornography unless we recognize and address the extent to which the attitudes and inequalities promoted in gay pornography harm gay men and, in so doing, *then* serve to reinforce the biases and inherent gender hierarchies that result in the systemic inequality referred to in *Butler* through which *both* gay men and all women are harmed.

There are other aspects of the Attorney General's submissions in *Little Sisters* that are also problematic. For instance, in addressing the claim that no proof exists that gay male pornography is harmful, the Attorney General stated that

the argument of the appellants that no causal link has been demonstrated between homosexual erotica and harm, and that there is no evidentiary foundation to support Parliament's view that harm may result from the proliferation of obscene matter, must fail ... *Butler* holds, at pp. 501-502, that a causal link may be impossible to establish and that harm may be presumed. There are references throughout the reasons of Sopinka J. in *Butler* to difficulties in proof, and to the controversial opinions held by those trained in the social sciences. In the end, the evidence is inconclusive but conclusive evidence from social scientists is not required.[19]

This claim, that there is no causal connection between harm and pornography, merits clarification. While there is of yet no social science data on the links between gay male pornography per se and harm, there is irrefutable evidence to this effect with respect to heterosexual pornography. This is an important point and one that should not be overlooked. It is important because it raises the question of whether gay male pornography can be proven harmful by way of analogy. In *Little Sisters*, EGALE agued that an analogy could not be drawn because of the way in which same-sex pornography is used by gay men and lesbians, the way it is produced and why, and the different socialization processes that occur prior to and when gay men and lesbian women use pornography.

This rejection of any analogy-based argument is interesting given that gay men have long held that an analogy should be drawn between, for example, the harms of racial hate speech and anti-gay hate speech. Although there is of yet no scientific proof that racist hate speech causes harm, gay men have argued that when the courts recognize it as harmful, an analogy should be drawn between it and anti-gay hate speech, despite the fact that no "absolute" proof of harm exists for either.

In the pornography context, the analogy would seem to be even stronger given that heterosexual pornography *has* been proven harmful. This is a point made clear by those who have conducted research on the harms of heterosexual pornography. These researchers have argued that although harms-based research has thus far relied on the effects of heterosexual pornography, the reality of gay men generally (already affected by pervasive homophobia and resulting self-hate), once influenced by what gay pornography says about appropriate gay male sexual behaviour, suggests that these findings are equally applicable within the context of gay male pornography. As Dr. Neil Malamuth, an expert on the links between pornography and those behaviours that cause injury, has explained,

> there may be similar processes operating regardless of the sexual orientation of the material. I therefore suggest that it may be appropriate to generalize from this research to the specific content in question, even though there are some differences in content. In keeping with considerable research I am suggesting that processes of influence, attitude change, normative effects, consequences of arousal, etc. do not differ fundamentally as a function of a person's sexual preference. Therefore, in many areas, similar theoretical models may be applied to both heterosexuals and gays. Furthermore, there are many similarities among gay and straight people in motives for various

behaviours, including sexual activity and in problems of sexual and non-sexual coercion.[20]

In *Little Sisters*, the trial judge, accepting this argument, concluded that there was sufficient evidence to support Parliament's reasoned apprehension that homosexual pornography could cause the types of harms at issue in *Butler*. The Supreme Court of Canada affirmed this finding. The remainder of this chapter aims to respond to those who continue to argue that no such finding is merited based on the evidence available to the Court.

In undertaking such an analysis, it is important to note that Malamuth and others are not suggesting that the result of exposure to gay male pornography is exactly the same as the result of exposure to heterosexual pornography. They are just unwilling to conclude, because evidence is lacking or on the basis of existing evidence, that no harm is there – quite the contrary. Specifically, it is not unreasonable to assume that scenarios of violence and degradation might lead to increased violence against real people. While the resulting harms are not exactly the same (because gay men are not in the same position that women are in socially), an analogy can nonetheless be drawn – an analogy that says that certain things cause certain behaviours and that these behaviours result in harm inflicted on real people. If masculinity is the defining and preferred construct in gay male pornography, does this not simply reinforce those male/female stereotypes that result in systemic inequality? Is this not particularly problematic when used by gay men – men who are already encouraged, socially, to buy into these stereotypes? If the presentation of what is acceptable male behaviour in heterosexual pornography is a source of male aggression against women, can it not be readily inferred that some gay men, already subject to the rejection resulting from being socially defined as non-masculine, might also be negatively affected by a medium that encourages the use of male power over others, with the end result being rape, domestic violence, and other forms of male hostility and aggression against others?

Gay Male Rape

One of the arguments advanced against the production and distribution of heterosexual pornography is that it makes men more tolerant of sex as violence, resulting in sexual assault and abuse against women. Pornography then, far from being just theory, becomes a practice. As the brief analysis of the attitudes of and about men who rape men and who are raped by men below indicates, the risk of harm resulting from gay male pornography, like the harms that result from heterosexual pornography, is real, especially given what gender inequality, now sexualized, has come to mean socially and the effect of sex role stereotypes on gay men in particular. Specifically, if we look at what rape is, what it is about, and what it says about male aggression generally, it does not require much to at least infer that any expressive medium that eroticizes male sexuality as dominance, inequality, abuse, and hierarchy might result in physical and psychological harm to others.

In his recent insightful book on male rape, Michael Scarce explains that "although it remains uncertain, evidence suggests that gay men are more likely to be raped than straight men. Despite the fact that heterosexual men far outnumber gay men in sheer masses, gay men seem to be more at risk, on average, than their heterosexual counterparts."[21] In a 1989 study by psychologist Caroline Waterman at the University of Albany, 12 percent of 34 men in gay relationships "reported being victims of forced sex by their current or most recent partner."[22] Similarly, in a 1990 study, researchers found that gay college students reported significantly higher lifetime prevalence of sexual victimization than did heterosexual men participating in the same study.[23] Finally, in a study of 930 gay men living in England and Wales, 27.6 percent reported that they had been sexually assaulted at some point in their lives.[24]

It is clear then that rape is a gay male issue, one that must be taken seriously. While to some this might seem a restatement of the obvious, what becomes apparent from a reading of the testimonies offered in Scarce's book is that, like the abuse inflicted on Joseph Oncale, the horrors experienced by some gay men risk being dismissed as sexual theatre. This risk increases so long as gay men sexualize inequality and powerlessness. By sexualizing masculinity and femininity through pornography, gay men do exactly this by making the feminine/masculine interaction sexy to gay men. Consuming pornography is done sexually, experienced sexually, *as* sexuality, the practices of which are identical to the top/bottom sexuality of male dominance. It is the sexuality of male dominance that gay male pornography pushes and eroticizes. The result is male dominance in action with all the harms, including rape, that flow from it and sustain it. In his work, for example, Scarce provides an account of one man, "Darren," who was abducted by two men in the car park outside his gym. The men held a gun to Darren's head and forced him into their van, handcuffed him, and drove him to a house, where they proceeded to sexually humiliate, abuse, and ultimately rape him. His ordeal says much about power, abuse, and the effect of gender once sexualized in his life and in the lives of his attackers. That he continues to survive is miraculous. That he is willing to talk about it in order to assist others shows an inner strength perhaps known only by those who have survived similar abuse. As such, his words deserve repeating, and all gay men would do well to think critically about the torturous events he describes:

> They took me down to the basement, and they had a platform in the center of the room. They made me stand up on it, my hands still cuffed behind me. They walked around and looked at me and told me they were going to uncuff my hands. At this point they both had guns, and one of the guys uncuffed my hands. They told me to pull off my

gym shorts and I did. They made me pull my T-shirt back behind my neck. All I had on was gym shoes, socks, and a jock strap. They made me get into different poses and positions for them for a long time. They held the guns on me the whole time. I was really scared because I was afraid the guns might even go off accidentally. I kept thinking I didn't know what they were going to do to me, that they might cut me up or mutilate me. They were touching themselves with one hand, masturbating while they were watching me.

One of the guys started talking about how he was going to fuck my butt. They put me over a wooden sawhorse and made me lie across it. They pulled my jockstrap off and then tied my hands and legs to it so I was over it. Then they both took turns raping me. That went on for a long, long time, an hour and a half or so.

They seemed angry when they were fucking me because they did it so hard, with so much force[.] Earlier when they were using the switch on me, it was like they were trying to get every piece of anger or rage they had out on me. The rest of the time they were more sarcastic or condescending, more trying to humiliate or degrade me than angry.[25]

Darren's experience is not pornography. But, like the ordeal described by Joseph Oncale, it could be. From an equality perspective, if this description of a rape appeared in a gay male pornography magazine, and was sold and used as sexual practice, it would be pornography, particularly as it encourages, by sexualizing, sexual assault. And to the extent that someone uses it and then acts it out, his victims should be allowed to take action against those who published it as gay male pornography and sexuality, as well as against he who raped them.

Indeed, if the above passages had appeared in Chapter 3 of this book, the reader could be forgiven for mistaking Darren's horror for the "pleasure" presented as sexuality and liberation in quite a few of the exhibits defended in the *Little Sisters* trial: a young, attractive, physically fit male is abducted in a car park. His captors, threatening to kill him, and laughing at his fear, drive him to their "rape house." They handcuff him, make him perform, and masturbate while watching him. Stripping him naked, they objectify his body, sexualize his fear, and act out their most vivid pornographic fantasies. Handcuffed, the young man is posed on a platform, whipped with switches, then tied to a sawhorse, where he is brutally raped and beaten with a paddle. Throughout it all, degraded and ridiculed, he is made to service men who, while simultaneously sexualizing and condemning his sexuality, find validation in the abuse inflicted by real men needing to reaffirm their masculinity through violence, humiliation, and the stripping away of another man's manhood.

Darren's experience, like that of many men who have been raped, says a great deal about the dangers inherent in a society that sexualizes inequality.

What his story epitomizes is misogyny gone mad. Feminizing him in order to condemn him and use him as an unequal, while reasserting their own masculinity through the acting out of sexualized violence, these men do sexually what male dominance requires in order to survive. By degrading Darren, these men, through violence, dehumanization, and rape, successfully put Darren back in his place. This, in turn, empowers them as men. Stripping him of his manhood, they prop up their own. Their actions typify homophobia and self-hate in action – sexism made sexy.

These conclusions are further supported by the work of those who have detailed the factors that motivate rapists. In a 1980 study on men who rape men, for example, Groth and Burgess outline these motivating factors for men convicted of raping other men:[26]

1　Conquest and control. All assaults served as an expression of power and mastery on the part of the offender;

2　Revenge and retaliation. In some cases of male rape, the offence is activated by the assailant's anger towards his victim and is regarded by him as some form of retaliation;

3　Sadism and degradation. For some assailants, aggression itself becomes eroticized, and they find excitement in the sexual abuse and degradation of their victim;

4　Conflict and counteraction. Another component in some male rapes is the assailant's attempt to punish the victim as a way of dealing with his unresolved and conflicting sexual interests.[27]

In the same study, the authors describe the attitude of one man toward his victim: "I had the guy so frightened I could have made him do anything I wanted. I didn't have an erection. I wasn't really interested in sex. I felt powerful, and hurting him excited me. Making him suck me was more to degrade him than for my physical satisfaction."[28]

Similarly, in analyzing the rape of men by men in prisons, Susan Brownmiller notes that to talk of rape as violence only, without acknowledging the extent to which that violence is gendered, risks overlooking the extent to which the "sex" in the expression "sex crime" is socially constructed and enforced by sexism and the homophobic desire for male supremacy. Within the context of gay male pornography, any analysis that omits gender also risks valorizing the violence that we then risk sexualizing and thus normalizing. Brownmiller notes, for example, that prison rape can be seen as "an acting out of power roles within an all male, authoritarian environment in which the weaker, younger inmate ... is forced to play the role that in the outside world is assigned to women."[29] As MacKinnon elsewhere explains, "this lowers the victim's status, making him inferior as a man by social standards. For a man to be sexually attacked, by placing him in a woman's role, demeans his masculinity; he loses it so to speak. What he loses, he loses through gender, as a man."[30] To this, one would add only that for a man to sexually attack, by confirming his role as a real man, reaffirms his masculinity. What he maintains or gains, he gains through gender, as a man. Hence, when a man sexually abuses another man, his actions are gender-based, thus sexual. And so male domination of some men over other men is part of the social system of gender whereby men dominate women and through which, as noted in Chapter 1, straight men dominate gay men. Hence, male rape, like anti-gay violence generally, is also a weapon of sexism, finding its source in the social institutions that prop up masculinity and, in so doing, suppress any sexual expression that threatens it. As McMullen concludes,

> [t]he general attitudes inherent in this rapist's words remind me so much of various school bullies from my own childhood. How males see themselves as male, and how that perception is enabled in the family, schools and other institutions, is central to any understanding of male rape. Male upon male bullying in schools is all too often positively sanctioned and treated by both parents and teachers as normal behavior. It is, of course, not right for one person to bully another. How often one hears the unqualified male-propelled phrase "boys will be boys" used to justify such bullying. Undefined and therefore confused notions of what it means to be a masculine, powerful, dominant man echo through our culture like football chants, arbitrary and self-congratulatory.[31]

Some of the work outlined above is not specific to gay men who rape gay men. This does not, however, make their risk of being raped any less real. Indeed, given these findings, gay men might well discourage, rather than sexualize, the harms documented. Unfortunately, gay men are not discouraging them. And so I ask: in examining what gay male pornography is, should we not at least acknowledge that harm is possible, given that this medium is intended for men who, as gay men, are socially feminized, told they are inferior, and, as such, likely to take quite seriously the message conveyed in a medium that fuses dominance with sexuality, that promotes male empowerment by dictating that power is to be found in a sexuality in which he who dominates is powerful, and he who does not, is not? Should we not be concerned that gay male pornography represents sexuality generally and it is *this* sexuality, the sexuality of male dominance, that is at the root of all that is anti-woman and anti-gay, but pro-male? Gay male pornography encourages this hierarchy, from which harm seems inevitable. Consider, for example, the following images from two of the gay male pornography exhibits in issue in the *Little Sisters* case.

In a magazine, a young office worker, dressed in suit and tie, leaves his office and enters his car. From behind he feels a knife. In his rear-view mirror he sees two men, both dressed in leather, army boots, and studded jackets. He is urinated on, raped orally and anally, but described throughout as enjoying it and anxious for more. The story reads:

> Hands on my waist he rammed, slamming the unlubricated head and the whole dry shaft deep inside me. It hurt like hell. I moaned ... in agony. It was tearing me apart like a chisel in the crack of a stone. I felt myself splitting into two halves and I could do nothing to stop it and I felt my cock stiffen in response. He was ramming into me now like a man possessed, sliding in and out without attention to my screams of pain. It felt like a goddamned log, bark and all, being slid up my crack. I heard his friend screaming, "fuck him, fuck the hell out of him" and I loved it.[32]

In another magazine, a "slave training manual" teaches the reader the proper etiquette for training a slave on how to use the phone:

> Whenever he phones his Master, the slave should be naked, kneeling and wearing tit clamps. When phoned by his Master, the slave should always immediately drop to his knees and continue the call, looking downwards and with his spare hand behind his back. Alternatively, the slave can be taught that when his Master phones, the slave should always ring off, strip naked except for tit ring and then phone his Master back from a kneeling position of course. The Master should always stand up when making telephone calls to his slave. A curious fact acknowledged by business psychologists is that standing up while conducting a phone conversation increases the apparent authority of the speaker, particularly if the receiver is not standing up. Conversely, kneeling will increase the apparent servility of the speaker. When one party stands and the other kneels, the Master servant relationship is powerfully enforced.[33]

As the activist group Men against Rape and Pornography explains, what the above essentially provides is a user's manual on how to get and keep power through sex, through sexuality – a message that, given the level of anti-gay violence within the community, can only hinder the call for equality:

> Although unrecognized and hidden well within our community, rape is very common. Typically, as with male-female rape, the rape is likely to happen on a date or other situation where the victim and rapist

already know each other. One man is at another man's apartment and he is pressured or forced to "have sex." This is rape. One man tries to talk his partner into trying a new position he has seen in porn. The partner says no because of the pain; the first man continues anyway against his partner's will. This is rape. One man insists on tying another man to the bedpost and says that he needs to do this in order to really "get off." He saw this done to someone else in a video. This is rape. It is about power, domination, force, and control over another person, which has been sexualized.[34]

Building on this analysis, it is also clear that a number of myths about male rape are enforced through the sex that is pornography. These myths, once sexualized, encourage it and undermine attempts to arrest it. Central in this regard is the myth that "no" means "yes," particularly if it is a gay man who says no, because, according to the myth now made sexy through pornography, gay men enjoy rape. For us, according to this stereotype, rape *is* sex, so all sex is consensual and enjoyable.[35] Another myth is that which assumes men are entitled to sex with their partners whenever they want, even if their partners don't. Any guilt attached to this is soon laid to rest by the myth that if your partner ejaculates or at least appears to be sexually aroused while you assault him, it isn't really rape, because he enjoyed and wanted it anyway.[36]

If we look at what gay male pornography says and compare this with how rapists and rape victims are believed and supposed to feel, what we see is that gay male pornography encourages and is a sexuality that promises the gay male the power he so desperately wants but that society has denied him, and that it is a form of power that very much depends on the violent degradation of someone else. This degradation, sexualized and made real though rape, is what makes pornography sexy and what makes rape a consequence of the materials gay rights advocates would have us defend as non-harmful. Gay male pornography also teaches the rapist that other men enjoy the violation through which he can seek empowerment – that he will find pleasure in an act of violence committed against another. Rape, normalized though sex, becomes gay sex and in so doing ensures that gay sex does little more than prop up the sexual hierarchies that make homophobia and sexism sexy and the cornerstone of inequality on the basis of sex. Finally, gay male pornography, produced by and sold to a community in which sexual violence is common, continues to promote materials that tell those who have been raped that they should enjoy and want this abuse. When rape equals sex, equals gay male identity, equality (both within the gay community and society generally) finds that it has no role.

Gay Male Domestic Violence

Similar concerns arise when we analyze the harms resulting from gay male domestic violence. In a study of 105 women staying in battered women's shelters in Ontario, 25 percent of the women reported being forced to perform acts their partners had seen in pornography.[37] While similar statistics have not been recorded within the gay male context (in part because no one has yet seen fit to offer safe shelters for male victims of violence, making it rather difficult for these men to talk safely about their experiences), we do know that there exists a massive consumption rate of gay pornography in our community.

Worldwide, sales of gay pornography represent a disproportionately high percentage of the pornography market.[38] In an informal US survey conducted in 1979, half of the 1,038 gay men surveyed stated that they used pornography for masturbation. In 1997, more than half of the gay men who participated in a *Frontiers Magazine* survey stated that they used pornography videos as a prelude to having sex.[39] These surveys did not take account of the amount of pornography being accessed on the Internet – an amount that cannot be discounted. It is believed that pornography sales have grown during the last twenty-five years from approximately US$2 billion in total annual revenue to at least US$10 billion, with some arguing that it may now be as high as US$20 billion. Of that total, adult Web sites contribute an estimated US$1 to US$2 billion a year.[40] There is little reason to believe, applying the surveys thus far done of gay male pornography use, that, of this amount, gay male use of pornography available on the Internet is not as significant as that of heterosexual men.

Examined within the context of gay male domestic violence, these figures are alarming. A 1991 study on gay male domestic violence reported that there are 350,000 to 650,000 victims of gay male domestic violence in the United States each year.[41] That makes gay male domestic violence the third largest health problem facing gay men in the United States today.[42] What is most revealing for an analysis of gay male pornography, however, is the study's findings about the type of man who batters, how he perceives himself, and why. The conclusions reached say a great deal about any medium that reinforces the idea that "male" equals masculine, equals dominant, while non-masculine equals feminized, equals subordinate.

Gay men who batter and abuse their partners have specific ideas about masculinity and what it means to be "male." This is in part a reaction to a complete lack of positive gay role models, a homophobic environment in which being gay means being "non-masculine," and the internalization of social rejection and self-hate. Gay men, growing up in a world with little or no positive reinforcement, are inundated with a value system that equates masculinity (as the determiner of appropriate male behaviour) with aggression, control, and frequently violence. As Island and Letellier explain,

> Hollywood, television, sports, the military, advertising, music, and visible male heroes and leaders are all guilty of making this connection ...

Negative ideas about masculinity popular in America include acting tough at all times, not showing tender feelings at all. The lean, mean super cool, stoic cowboy is a perfect example of this view of masculinity. Another particularly obnoxious view teaches men to get their way by flexing muscles, drinking to excess, getting angry and hitting people. Being masculine means to intimidate, to dominate, and to do what they damn well want to, no matter what the consequences to themselves and to other people. Being masculine is their attempt to control others so that they are sure that no one controls them, because being influenced by others is scarily unmasculine.[43]

Nowhere is this more evident than in the pornography used by these men. Made sexy, masculinity becomes a turn on. Gay male pornography consists of "values" such as strength, power, lack of tenderness, vulnerability of the other, control, and non-mutuality. A re-examination of the masculine ideal held by those men who psychologically abuse, rape, beat, and sometimes kill their partners reveals that their practices and value systems are exactly the same. This means, quite literally, that gay male pornography equals, promotes, and sexualizes *this* view of masculinity – the same view that daily results in gay men abusing and killing the men who love them. While no research has been done to determine if gay men who abuse other gay men use gay male pornography, there is no evidence that they do not. To my mind, the fact that gay male pornography does promote through sex the macho as value means that this message, once interpreted by men who may not fit the desired norm but who are told and feel that they can and should through sex, has the potential to cause considerable harm.

For some gay men, overcompensation for their sense of non-worth becomes inevitable. Applying what they believe will provide control, power, and what they hope will amount to social acceptance, those who ultimately do batter become one with the value system they equate with masculinity – something society thinks is more socially "male," hence appropriate. "As real-live puppets, they perform a role, read a script, and mechanically act-out whatever their ideas are about masculinity."[44] The result, for some, is an effort to be the masculine prototype. These men interpret assertiveness to mean aggression and so ignore the rights and feelings of others, think of strength as a licence to be sexually violent or intimidating, see power as a licence to terrorize, and view mutuality as a threat to these privileges.[45] They follow a prescription, a recipe for masculinity now made sexy and normal through pornography, and, after beating their partners, excuse their behaviour by claiming that their actions are sexually acceptable.

While much of the above also applies to heterosexual men, the effects of this "masculinity as norm" myth for the gay male already affected by deeply embedded stereotypes are particularly significant. Indeed, while one might think that it is only those who already conform to the masculine prototype who beat their partners, studies reveal the opposite. Many gay male domestic batterers do "not fit the stereotypical super-macho man."[46] Rather, they suffer from what can only be termed "failed macho syndrome."[47] Socially rejected for their failure to conform, they feel that they do not reach the masculine ideal of "dominance and coolness."[48] In an effort to reach this desired "norm," that which society has told them they are not, they attempt to control other people, often though sex.

These findings say a great deal about the power of systemic homophobia as a social force aimed at limiting same-sex sexual activity. Gay men, to the extent that they threaten to undermine masculine/feminine polarity, are terrorized so as to diffuse this threat. Ridiculed as feminine, defined as socially inferior to "real" men, gay men are silenced so as to ensure that they do not reveal their sexual orientation. Those who do are systematically attacked. Left with few options, the result for many is fear, confusion, and self-hate. They are told that they can reject the masculine norm and be further harassed, or they can attempt to become it (and, in so doing, hide any distinct, non-misogynistic gay male identity), thus making themselves (as gay) invisible. Unfortunately, the pervasiveness of anti-gay male violence and discrimination means that many gay men may overcompensate through sex and attempt to adhere to those sexual "values" that they believe will make them less visible, more "male." As Island and Letellier's findings indicate, this overcompensation can result in some particularly destructive behaviours, causing physical and emotional harm to others. They also ensure that male dominance, now sexualized, hence normalized, remains in place.

Conclusion

To date, our community has shown an apparent unwillingness to take seriously the very real harms of intracommunity rape and violence. There are undoubtedly a number of reasons for this. The question I have attempted to pose in this chapter, however, is whether, to some extent, our inaction can be explained by the pornography many now defend as gay male identity and liberation. The facts seem to support this assertion. Indeed, we have become so obsessed with defending and becoming pornography that the most serious of subjects now find themselves sexualized, trivialized, or, worse (as in the case of anti-gay violence), glorified as a source of sexual empowerment. This is a point noted by Edisol Wayne Dotson, who critiques the article "Battered Husbands: Domestic Violence in Gay Relationships," which appeared in a 1991 edition of *Genre Magazine*. As Dotson explains, the magazine's cover story

> features a cover photograph of a man who is presumably naked ... and posed in a way that suggests he is cowering from a would-be attacker. The photographs used to illustrate the article are of men in their

underwear who are presented more as sexual fantasies than as victims of abuse or the abuser. Although both men appear wearing only a pair of underwear, one of the men is photographed from behind to draw attention to his well-shaped buttocks ... the underwear is drawn up between the buttocks and immediately brings the reader's attention to the man or rather the buttocks and the sex they represent. The text and substance of domestic violence in gay male relationships becomes secondary.[49]

For many pro-pornography advocates, gay male pornography is harm-free. To these people, I ask, quite simply, whether it is unreasonable to assume that materials that encourage a masculinity through which male sexuality is aggression, violence, and degradation of others, once used by men who already feel inadequate and who have little or no incentive to feel otherwise, might encourage these men to become the very thing society tells them they are not but should be (i.e., more "male," sexually and socially). While disturbing and easy to ignore, the consequences of male rape and gay male domestic abuse remain too real and too serious for us simply to assume that pornography plays no role in the situation and that, ultimately, its effect is non-harmful.

6 Gay Male Pornography: An Issue of Sex Discrimination

> Though the neo-Nazi adorations ... are more sinister than the innocuous ideals of the weight-lifting room, they are equally mindless. The offence is not aesthetic; it is entirely political. The homosexuals who adopt images of masculinity, conveying their desire for power and their belief in its beauty, are in fact eroticizing the very values that have tyrannized their own lives ... The perversity of imitating their own oppressors guarantees that such blindness will work itself out as self-contempt.[1]
>
> *Seymour Kleinberg*

Degrading/Dehumanizing/Unequal on the Basis of Sex

What of those materials in which violence is not sexualized? Can non-violent materials also cause harm? In *Butler*, LEAF argued that while the sexualization of violence obviously poses significant risks of physical and psychological harm, non-violent materials are also harmful because, like violent materials, they too result in and support a system of gender inequality – a system that, to again quote the Supreme Court of Canada, reinforces "male-female stereotypes to the detriment of both sexes."[2]

There are some in the gay male community who would argue that any harms that might arise from the presentation of violence are undermined within the context of gay male pornography because it is just that: gay male. Still others, while agreeing that violence is not to be promoted or encouraged, would baulk at the suggestion that non-violent materials might cause harm.

To my mind, both positions misunderstand or are at least unwilling to acknowledge what makes pornography harmful at its core: inequality on the basis of sex. Whether violent or non-violent, any presentation of gender that sexualizes hierarchy risks solidifying those social biases that result in discrimination and the harms, both violent and non-violent, of inequality.[3] In *Butler*, the Supreme Court of Canada did recognize the harm inherent in these presentations, arguing that no justification could be made for materials that encourage systemic gender inequality. The question posed by *Little Sisters* is whether gay male pornography is sufficiently different to avoid the harm arising from the distribution and use of heterosexual pornography. That is, can it be said that same-sex pornography, produced for and used by a gay male audience, is not an issue of sex discrimination and thus not a threat to society's equality interest?

The materials I review in Chapter 3 are indicative of the types of materials defended by Little Sisters, those who intervened on its behalf, and a not insignificant number of lesbian and gay male academics and activists.[4] A critical examination of these and other gay male pornographic materials, thus far missing from much of the work undertaken on pornography, indicates that the harms of sex inequality are not undermined by pornographic materials that replace women with men, but are rather promoted by them. As such, they are caught by the Supreme Court of Canada's concern to limit the distribution of materials that, because they are degrading and dehumanizing, violate society's sex equality interest. This chapter, building on the work outlined in Chapter 5, argues that materials need not be violent in order to be an issue of sex discrimination, hence harmful.

Men Instead of Women: Biological Essentialism as Gay Male Scapegoat

As stated, some gay activists have argued that even if straight pornography is harmful, any perceived inequality evident in gay male pornography is rendered non-harmful, indeed subversive, because in it, unlike in heterosexual pornography, women are not sexually exploited. That is, men are presented with men, not men with women, and the sexuality presented is used and experienced by gay men, not straight men. This was a central argument throughout much of the *Little Sisters* proceedings and is best represented by the testimonies and evidence relied on by Little Sisters and EGALE. Little Sisters, for example, cited the work of Thomas Waugh, who acted as an expert witness for the store, restating his earlier writings in which he distinguished gay pornography from straight pornography on the basis that "gay men fuck and suck and are fucked and sucked, etc., in a wide range of combinations and roles not determined by gender."[5] Waugh writes: "To be sure, gender is the ultimate determining factor of power relations within and around heterosexual eroticism rigidly prescribing roles for men as producer, consumer and inserter, and for women as model, commodity and insertee. But the absence of gender as a determining factor distinguishes gay eroticism from straight eroticism, and this is crucial, politically and morally as well as aesthetically."[6]

In a similar vein, Canadian sociologist Gary Kinsman, cited by EGALE as a leading authority, stated at trial that with respect to the Court's concern for "degrading" and "dehumanizing" materials, "[these] terms ... have been generated from an analysis of some of the problems that are presented within heterosexual pornography made for men and if we look at gay sexuality and gay sex representations it's organized in quite a different way. So that those relationships of gender inequality, gender power relations, are not a central defining feature of gay male pornography."[7]

Finally, it is again worth noting the testimony of Thomas Waugh before the British Columbia Supreme Court, who argued that

> [g]ay male materials are produced by gay men for gay men and show performances by gay men that have centrality within the gay male community. There are no divisions between who is depicted and who consumes. I think the argument that feminists always make about heterosexual material about women being silenced by heterosexual pornography is very true and this silencing of the woman as object has no equivalent in gay pornography systems. This community based production system, ensures that the gay men have a voice, are active participants in this cultural material.[8]

Apart from the fact that the experiences of some of the men used to make gay pornography fail to support the claim that "silencing" does not occur because gay men have more say in what gets produced and how, arguments like those above imply that, because men in gay male pornography can and do assume the submissive role normally afforded women, the whole idea of male dominance is undermined because it becomes evident that men too can be and are dominated within gay male sexual relationships. This line of reasoning is not sustainable. Arguments that focus predominantly on the use of men in gay male pornography risk claiming that what makes heterosexual pornography harmful is the use of biological females by biological males and that it is this biological polarity that makes women unsafe and unequal. This is misleading, as well as sexist and homophobic: sexist because it implies that harm to men isn't harm, and homophobic because it implies that harm isn't harm if it is done to gay men. Gay male pornography does not eliminate harm simply because it doesn't involve women. At a basic level, this argument assumes that there is something about men hurting and violating men that makes the resulting assault non-harmful, normal, and acceptable – an assumption that only reinforces already dominant assumptions about acceptable male behaviour and male aggression generally. Sexualized violence *is* violence, and the biological capabilities of the person who harms or who is harmed are irrelevant.[9] Moreover, any analysis that rests on biology is dangerously naïve. Power does not depend on the biology of those who assert it. Straight pornography is harmful not simply because it presents a biological male violating a biological female, but because of the model of behaviour offered the biological male and presented/sexualized as normal male gender behaviour. The mere absence of biological "opposites" does little to undermine the very real harms of rape, abuse, assault, harassment, and discrimination resulting from materials in which "male" equals masculine, equals dominant, equals preferable. That a biological male can also be a "bottom" is in many ways irrelevant if, in order to be that bottom, he is required to assume those characteristics that ensure that those who are "men," socially defined, remain on top.

The coupling of two biological males does nothing to destabilize sexual and social power inequalities divided along gender lines if those behaviours – central to the preservation of gender hierarchy (cruelty, violence, aggression, homophobia, sexism, racism, and ultimately compulsory heterosexuality through which heterosexual male dominance is preserved) – are not themselves removed from the presentation of sexuality as power-based. Because gay male pornography sexualizes gender stereotypes and the inequalities inherent in them, it reinforces those behaviours and characteristics that ensure heterosexuality remains the norm and is compulsory because it does little to advance a model of gay identity that subverts those socially prescribed gender roles that ensure and enforce heterosexual male privilege.

Objectifying Ourselves: Must Self-Hate Be Our Source of Arousal?

The argument has also been made that because gay male pornography presents gay male sexual activity and because it is received and used by gay men, this makes it impossible to construe the victimized person as a victim since he, like the viewer, is also male. That is, as Philip Galanes explains, because the "other" is a reflection of the self, the dehumanization of that other is alleviated by the fact that when the viewer objectifies another man, "he implicates himself as a biological mirror"[10] of the man he is using for his own sexual gratification. He therefore knows that he can be that person and may, in fact, want to be him. As gay male historian Michael Bronski argues,

> although the viewer, sexually aroused, lusts after the object, it is equally true that he may also want to *be* that object. This element of identification *with* as well as *for* the sexual object is what distinguishes gay porn and straight porn. This is perfectly illustrated in the 1976 film *Heavy Equipment*. In an old magic book, a meek young clerk finds a formula which will transform his physical appearance. Looking through porn magazines, he finds a picture he likes, mixes his elixir, and, reciting the incantations, becomes the magazine image. The fact that identification exists simultaneously with objectification transforms the power relationships which some have presumed to be inherent in the viewing of sexual images.[11]

Gay male pornography, like straight pornography, offers the viewer two objects. In straight pornography, however, while the male viewer may frequently lust after and envy the male dominant and want to be all that that object says he (as a man) should be, he rarely, if ever, desires to be the female object. In gay male pornography, the gay male viewer can either objectify the masculinized top and want to be him or he can objectify his non-masculinized victim and want to be him. Hence, proponents claim, the power dynamics in gay male pornography are qualitatively different.[12]

Within the context of a pornographic medium in which mutuality and compatibility rarely exist, one needs to ask what it says about gay men generally that they might want to be the objects presented as sexual stimuli in gay male pornography. That is, what does it say about being gay that one's "chosen" identity is, as Galanes notes, the victim of an aggressive, domineering prison officer, Nazi, Klansman, violent "father figure, or ostensibly straight male"? Why is the "option" of being a weak, loathed, and despised little poofter found worshipping a muscular, straight-acting dominant so subversive and empowering? Does being an object at the hands of an aggressive subject not merely reinforce gay men's already strong sense of self-hate? Does the "desire" to be inferior have anything to do with the fact that, in our society, to be "fucked" means to be a woman and because gay men do, after all, like being fucked (or so they are told), they must *be* a woman sexually? If so, what does it say about gay men that in order to be sexually aroused, they must enjoy and permit the degradation thrust on them as children? Why must self-hate now be the source of sexual arousal? Why must sexuality always be defined by punishment? And if the "object" of the gay man's desires is an aggressor (who in real life is his oppressor), what does this ultimately do to gay male identity? What does it mean to mimic our enemies simply because we have the "option" of doing so?[13]

In sum, in that the choice offered by gay male pornography is to be that which society has told you you already are (i.e., weak, feminized, hence "female") or to become that which society has told you you are not (i.e., masculinity linked with aggression, hence "male"), so that you too can "pass," then surely, if liberation is your goal, you might want to ask how this "choice" undermines those power hierarchies that result in homophobia in the first place.

Playing Top and Bottom: Equality Disguised as Reciprocal Abuse?

Gay historian John Burger argues that the inequalities evident in straight pornography are undermined in gay pornography because the men in gay pornography, and gay men generally, have the "option" of participating in a role reversal not normally given women – that is, they can "take turns" being top and bottom. As a result, they further challenge the idea that gender roles are fixed or immutable and thereby question the assumption that men must always be on top. According to Burger, "[i]n male homosexual sex, gay men wield 'power' over other men (instead of women) at the same time as they allow themselves to be rendered 'powerless' by men (like women are supposed to be in the orthodox world of sexuality). The gender power system breaks down in homosexual sex. Gay men embody both masculine and feminine traits, thereby disproving the constructed quality of absolute gender and gender roles. Orthodox sexuality's untruths are made visible, and when this occurs, new truths can be constructed and substituted."[14]

This was also a point raised by EGALE, which, in its factum before the Supreme Court of Canada in *Little Sisters,* argued that "the presumption that homoerotic materials cause the type of social harm identified in *Butler* is contrary to logical reasoning. Indeed, the academic literature suggests that sexually explicit homoerotic materials have liberating effects that *benefit* women in general, as well as lesbians, gays and bisexuals. By subverting dominant constructs of masculinity and femininity, homoerotic imagery and text challenge the sexism that is believed to be endorsed and reinforced by mainstream heterosexual pornography."[15] In making this point, EGALE seems to rely predominantly on the work of legal academic Carl Stychin, who argues that gay male pornography subverts the power and gender hierarchies present in heterosexual pornography because "the ability of gay men to assume both dominant and submissive roles establishes fantasy as open and boundaryless."[16] In other words, the fact that one dehumanized "other" can become the aggressor and then dehumanize the one who has just dehumanized him, and because the viewer can (biologically) be both, this undermines that gender hierarchy in which men must always be the oppressor/top/penetrator/"male."

If we look at what gay male pornography actually is, what it says, what it makes into sex, and what it promotes, I read Stychin's analysis to imply that the reason gay men are not hurt by gay male pornography is that although they may be presented as abused or subordinate, they always have the option of "turning the tables." If they abuse, they can always be abused themselves; there is reciprocity. Proponents of gay pornography appear to advocate an equality of mutual abuse in which gay men are empowered by a model of equality that liberates by admitting that while I might assume the status of a weak, submissive, subservient "bottom" at the hands of a descriptively more masculine "top" one night or for one turn, any resulting disempowerment is harmless because I have the option of becoming that top, thereby abusing my abuser or his surrogate.

In this regard, Stychin relies on those who argue that gay pornography has liberatory potential because it exposes the artificial nature of gender by challenging the notion that gendered hierarchies are fixed, immutable, "real." He writes:

> Because gay men exhibit behaviour that does not conform to the dominant culture's understanding of gender, the concepts of gender and subjectivity begin to unravel. This failure to conform to the cultural

construction of gender fragments the coherence of the concepts of male and female. Once gender is deconstructed and reduced to performance, that performance is evaluated for its potential to interrupt and fragment the social construct of gender. If performance reveals the artificiality of gender, it also undermines hierarchical gendered arrangements. Gay male pornography then should not be understood to reinforce objectification. Rather, it redefines the sexual subject and reveals new possibilities.[17]

Stychin's work relies on and builds on the writings of lesbian author Judith Butler, who argues that gender is little more than "drag," something artificial, a "performance," a concept to play with.[18] Butler's ideas are effectively explained by lesbian feminist writer Sheila Jeffreys:

> The revolutionary potential of drag and role-playing, Butler asserts, lies in the ability of such practices to illuminate the fact that gender is socially constructed. They reveal that gender has no essence or ideal form but is all just drag whether put on by feminine heterosexual women or masculine, heterosexual men or role-playing lesbians or male gay drag artists or clones ...
>   Gender, in as much as it comprises only gestures, costume and appearance, can indeed be seen as drag, or as Butler also calls it "performance." The "performance" is supposed to show up the fact that there is no "inner sex or essence or psychic gender core."

Stychin applies this concept to gay male pornography, arguing that, because it shows the artificiality of gender, it undermines the divisive power and destabilizes the heteropatriarchy. At its most basic, the problem with such analysis is that it is completely removed from the reality of the power relations under which gay men and women actually live. This is a point best made by Jeffreys who, responding to Judith Butler's claim that "gender is drag" asks, "if this is to be a revolutionary strategy then how would it effect change?" Jeffreys' response is that it cannot. Dismissing the argument that gender is just an idea, rather than something concrete and oppressive, Jeffreys writes:

> Male supremacy does not carry on just because people don't realise gender is socially constructed, because of an unfortunate misapprehension that we must somehow learn how to shift. It carries on because men's interests are served thereby. There is no reason why men should give up all the real advantages, economic, sexual, emotional, that male supremacy offers them because they see that men can wear skirts. Similarly the oppression of women does not just consist of having to wear makeup. Seeing a man in a skirt or a woman wearing a tie

will not be sufficient to extricate a woman from a heterosexual relationship when she will suffer socially, financially and quite likely physically, in some cases with the loss of her life, if she decides to slough off
her oppression.[19]

If we apply Jeffreys' analysis, it is evident that Stychin's fascination with the
subversive potential of gay pornography ignores the reality of gay men's lives,
their social marginalization, and the desire, now sexually promoted and promised in pornography, to get and benefit from male dominance. If gay men and
men generally were willing to give up male privilege, then *maybe* playing with
gender would work. But they are not. Accordingly, many gay men seem obsessed with getting and taking advantage of that which their straight counterparts have had all along, including pornography. For many, gender and male
privilege promise a great deal in a world in which being a man still means
something. Therefore, any medium that promises validation through gender
conformity tends to lose its subversive potential and, on the contrary, ensures
that those constructs that constitute and construct male supremacy, that make
it what it is, remain in place. For many gay men, pornography is not a game. It
offers them something very real: power – over men, as men. There is nothing
particularly challenging about this bit of "theatre," regardless of the biological
attributes of those who "perform" it.

What this focus on role play and role reversal as a means of undermining
gender hierarchies overlooks is that the pleasure found remains the pleasure
derived from dominance and submission. Although these roles can be reversed,
they are still clearly defined roles. There is always a top and there is always a
bottom, articulated along gender lines so as to differentiate between those
with and those without power. Hierarchy – inequality – thus remains central
to the sex act. While there is mutuality, it is in the "pleasure" found in shared
degradation – the pleasure derived from controlling or being controlled by
someone else. Mutual abuse does not eradicate abuse. It doubles it and risks
trivializing it through sex. As Galanes explains,

> [t]o play at degradation of others, to take turns at it – even when the
> other is a supposed "mirror image" of the self, as the defenders of gay
> pornography would have it – is to affirm that abuse of others is toler-
> able. To make a game of oppression, to sexualize it for one's pleasure, is
> to mock the people who suffer degradation in a daily way, for whom
> there is no chance at the supposed equalizing opportunity to degrade in
> return, and, for whom the question of consent is not a question, at all.[20]

Thus, gay male pornography, defended as equality, is far from it. Rather, it
ensures an odd form of mutuality that very much depends on the gendered

power system found in "orthodox" sex. What remains is an undeniable, indeed undenied, power dynamic found in sexualized inequality. The result may be mutuality, but shared degradation does nothing to ensure equality for those who do not exist in a fantasy world. To sexualize abuse and promote male aggression is to ignore those who do not want to be inferior, and the reality in which they are kept inferior, and to assert that abuse is both unproblematic and sexually stimulating for both parties – making it not abuse at all. While some gay men may "choose" to be the objects of eroticized violence, degradation, beatings, and verbal abuse, as presented in gay male pornography (and one should query why), not everyone has or wants this "choice." Any liberation theory that embraces dehumanization as a means of ensuring equality is both frightening and politically questionable.

Penetration as Affirmation: But Must I First Be Punished for It?

Some gay men argue that they find validation in the pornographic representation of dominance and submission because it reaffirms that they can be sexually penetrated and should not feel ashamed of the pleasure found in anal and oral intercourse. Professor Jeffrey Sherman, for example, notes that young gay men need to see explicit, unashamed sexual imagery – one assumes he means anal and oral penetration, given his disapproval elsewhere in his work of gay male sexual imagery that shows men embracing, kissing, and holding hands only[21] – to overcome the immense stigma and social disapproval attached to gay sex: "The struggling gay adolescent or young gay man requires sexual images, not images of locker room buddy-buddy bonding. Only sexual images possess the liberatory power to counteract society's heterocentrism and homophobia and offer young gay men models of affirming and unashamed sex between men. Without such models, a gay man may never take those crucial first steps towards self-acknowledgment and liberation."[22]

While I am not convinced that the act of penetration is that which defines gay male sex, I might be less quick to reject the argument that gay men need to see it if the pleasure promised in being penetrated did not require that the person who is penetrated assume the status of someone being demeaned for his failure or inability to be a gendered equal; that is, the status of someone who socially is deemed worthy only of abuse and insult.[23]

Gay male pornography tells us that we should find validation in submission laced with humiliation. It is not uncommon, for example, for gay male pornography magazines and other pornographic mediums to sexualize childhood abuse. In the January 1995 edition of *Manscape Magazine*, a gay man purports to recount his first sexual experience with his father. This is a lesson that, according to the writer, apparently served to teach him the importance of obedience and the pleasure to be found in pain and submission. Note the following excerpts from his letter to the editor:

The first session I remember with Dad was wild. He told me to go
down to the basement and wait for him. He came down in ten minutes
and told me to strip totally naked. I cringed at the thought of this – I
was a little slow for his tastes – and he slapped my face. I was stunned
but quickly tore off the shirt and jeans and underwear as I was told.
Dad started to lecture me about being obedient and that he was going
to make a man out of me because I was nothing but a pussy ...

All of a sudden he started to slap my ass with the flat of his hand. I
guess I whimpered because he called me a "girl" and a "baby" and I
cried bitterly ...

Then it happened. I have no idea why, but I got a hard on which I
could not hide ...

This made him hit me harder and I was getting a little high from it
all. The shit hit the fan when Daddy's little faggot shot a massive load
of cum all over the workbench.[24]

In detailing this experience, the author queries why he got a hard on from
being abused. Given what gay men are told about sex and sexuality by other
gay men through pornography, the answer would seem self-evident. To those
who do find this to be a sexual turn on and validating, I would ask what it says
about being gay that our chosen identity must be determined by a hyper-
masculine, ostensibly straight male. Through pornography, we are told that
sexual pleasure (and the empowerment allegedly promised by it) can be found
only in the form of abuse presented as compensation for some perceived gender inadequacy. Sexual pleasure is to be found in the form of a role play that
does little more than mimic the punishment and physical battery many of us
experienced as children at the hands of those wanting to punish us for not
being "man enough." This abuse and pain, in turn, can be forgotten simply by
reliving it through sex.

Gay author Seymour Kleinberg writes that "the homosexual whose erotic
feelings are enhanced by the illusion that his partner holds him in contempt,
who is thrilled when told his ass or mouth is just like a cunt, is involved in a
complicated self-deception."[25] One might have hoped that gay men, living in a
society in which anti-gay violence is rampant, had had quite enough abuse for
one lifetime. Are we now to believe that our sexual identities depend on and
require it? And to those who choose to abuse, rather than be abused, I ask,
what does it mean for gay male liberation that power is found only in the
ability to emulate those sexual and social behaviours that, once accepted, ensure that sexual power is offered only to those who reject equality? And what
does it mean for gay male liberation that those who do reject equality do little
more than reinforce the very foundations of compulsory heterosexuality and
the harm, including homophobic harm, that results from the conqueror-
victim paradigm on which it is built? Kleinberg explains that "to play with

powerlessness is to deny it, and worse, to immune oneself from sympathy for those who are truly helpless prisoners."[26] Given what we know about male rape and the alarming reality of gay male domestic abuse in our community, one might have hoped that gay men would denounce, rather than promote, any expressive medium that ranks self-gratification ahead of mutual compassion, integrity, and physical safety.

I also query whether the pleasure and affirmation allegedly found in being the bottom to a masculine top and the ability or willingness to take turns being that bottom is as readily promoted in gay pornography as advocates would have us believe. For although we all acknowledge that there is always a bottom in gay pornography, the real power promised by gay pornography, the real focus of all that is deemed to be sexually stimulating, is found in the hands of those who are presented on top and who, as such, assume the status of "real" men. As Richard Dyer explains, "[a]lthough the pleasure of anal sex (that is, of being anally fucked) is represented, the narrative is never organized around the desire to be fucked, but around the desire to ejaculate (whether or not flowing from anal intercourse). Thus although at a level of public representation gay men may be thought of as deviant and disruptive of masculine norms because we assert the pleasure of being fucked and the eroticism of the anus, in our pornography, this takes a back seat."[27]

This is a view shared by author Marc Simpson, who explains within the context of gay male pornography "star" Jeff Stryker that "the portrayal of anal sex seems to have become even more constructed as 'the desire to the goal of visual climax' – the desire, that is, of the fucker, who in the person of Jeff Stryker is one who never experiences the pleasure of anal sex in any other position except that of the fucker. In other words, Stryker's screen persona in gay video porn seems to deny his own anality and just endorses the pleasure a 'stud' can get in plugging any hole."[28]

John Stoltenberg, expanding on this analysis, notes that not only is penetration central but aggression, control, and dominance are also prominent. This is particularly troubling in that these traits, sexualized in pornography, signify male identity generally:

> [A]ll that is shown in gay male sex films is presented as conspicuously male, of course ... [g]ay male sex films characteristically depict the male body as sex object, but insofar as they also display the male body functioning prominently as sexual subject, gay male sex films present a distillation of what nearly all men believe enviable sex in an anatomically male body might be like if they were ever to have endless quantities of it themselves. As artefacts of a heterosexist culture that is rigidly polarized by gender, gay male sex films exhibit the apotheosis of male sexual functioning as imagined by men, who, not unlike straight men, dread the taint of feminization.[29]

Stoltenberg's argument is best supported by the status of the gay male "folk hero," the gay pornography celebrity. Straight-acting, muscular, well endowed, and quick to note his preferred position (on top), he is the glorified norm. When the gay male super stud does take bottom status, hence assuming a role reversal, its significance is not lost on the viewer. While Stryker, the ultimate top, is (at least physically) capable of adopting the role of a submissive bottom, when he does so, he becomes descriptively less relevant, less powerful. He is stripped of the male power derived from eroticized masculinity, assuming the role of someone whose manhood is weakened. The message sent is clear: while gay men have the option of being both top and bottom, the fact remains that there is always a top and *he* is very much the focus and idealized masculine norm. As that top, he alone is given liberty to refer to those beneath him as "girlie," "whores," "bitches," and "sluts" – "female."[30] Because he is overtly masculinized, he ensures that those beneath him are in turn emasculated (read "feminized"). Because gay male pornography focuses on the party who ultimately penetrates, and because in gay pornography the characteristics of the more aggressive, more masculine, more male penetrator are always valorized, this offers much support to the argument that in order to "fuck," you need to be superior, and that in order to be "fucked," you need to be sexually accessible, inferior, and socially less relevant. The gay male pornography "star," typified by men such as Stryker (who, after a brief stint in the heterosexual pornography market, has regained his preferred status as a top man in his gay male pornography films – now refusing to be penetrated by others or to publicly identify himself as a gay male),[31] again offers the gay male two choices: as a gay man, he can be like him or the one who replaces him (read masculine) and be empowered, or he can be the one who is taken by him (read inferior) and, as such, assume the status of those who, in gay male pornography as in real life, *are* degraded and expendable. Either way, he is invited to participate in a sexual, social, and always gendered hierarchy.

The above should not be seen as implying that there is no objectification or sexualization of the feminized other in gay male pornography. As Fung has explained within the context of gay male pornography featuring Asian men, objectification of the Asian stereotype is central to the power dynamics presented. As Fung also notes, however, the central focus is nonetheless on the role of the white dominator (who, not surprisingly, is usually also the more aggressive, more idealized of the two), and it is this focus on the subject that makes the still visible objectification of the non-white male even more objectifying and more socially damaging.[32] If we extend Fung's analysis, the focus in all gay male pornography is not just the white over non-white male but also the more male over the feminized, less male partner, who becomes, as a result, "female." Because gay male pornography focuses on the party who ultimately penetrates, and because in gay male pornography the characteristics of the more aggressive, more masculine, more male penetrator are what are always glorified, this focus makes the objectification of the non-focus more harmful. The objectified other, because he is stripped of eroticized power, becomes descriptively less relevant, hence, descriptively less male. While your anatomy may allow you to take turns at being the person who ultimately penetrates, the fact remains that to do so, you must assume certain acts, practices, and attitudes – all of which are the very source of inequality and non-mutuality. "Role reversal" may occur in gay male pornography, but there are always roles, and because one of them equals male aggression and hyper-masculinity, this behaviour remains definitive and normalized.

In a somewhat more troubling commitment to the notion that "fucking" must be seen by as many people as possible, Leo Bersani, in "Is the Rectum a Grave?" calls for more anal sex between gay men and more representations (one can assume through pornography) of gay male sex (which he defines as passive anal sex). Seeing the rectum, once violated, as the grave in which "the masculine ideal of proud subjectivity can be buried," Bersani asks that we now promote what male supremacy finds so unnerving about gay male sex – anal penetration: "If, as Jeffrey Weeks puts it, gay men 'gnaw at the roots of a male heterosexual identity,' it is not because of the parodistic distance that they take from that identity, but rather because, from within their nearly mad identification with it, they never cease to feel the appeal of its being violated."[33]

Although I may be oversimplifying his complex and disturbing analysis of the apparently subversive potential of gay male sexuality (defined here as passive anal intercourse), Bersani seems to be suggesting in this work that gay men play with powerlessness in order to undermine power. We should, in other words, use power, glorify it, in order to destroy it – something achieved by embracing the idea of violation, of self-sacrifice: "Gay men's 'obsession' with sex, far from being denied, should be celebrated – not because of its communal virtues, not because of its subversive potential for parodies of machismo, not because it offers a model of genuine pluralism to a society that at once celebrates and punishes pluralism, but rather because it never stops re-presenting the internalizing phallic male as an infinitely loved object of sacrifice. Male homosexuality advertises the risk of the sexual itself as the risk of self-dismissal."[34]

In referring to the dismissal of the self, Bersani refers here to the "self that swells with excitement at the idea of being on top, the self that makes of the inevitable play of thrusts and relinquishments in sex an argument for the natural authority of one sex over the other."[35] Bersani argues that it is only during sex, during sexual pleasure, that "the self is momentarily disturbed by sensations or affective processes beyond those connected with psychic organization."[36] Hence, sexuality as presently constituted (i.e., through a system of dominance and submission) can ultimately lead to a "destruction of the self" because it places the participant (here, the male participant who is penetrated) in a position of powerlessness through which the self is let go of and ultimately annihilated. The naturalness of sexual hierarchy is thus defeated because one is left with the "seductive and intolerable image of a grown man, legs high in the air, unable to refuse the suicidal ecstasy of being a grown woman."[37]

Bersani's analysis of sex as disruptive of present power imbalances leads him ultimately to reject the anti-pornography work of MacKinnon and Dworkin, for although their view of sexuality as violence and inequality is, he acknowledges, correct,[38] this, he argues, is the very reason we should praise the pornographic presentation of the sexuality they condemn:

> Dworkin and MacKinnon have given us the reasons why pornography must be multiplied and not abandoned, and, more profoundly, the reasons for defending, for cherishing the very sex they find so hateful. Their indictment of sex – their refusal to prettify it, to romanticize it, to maintain that fucking has anything to do with community or love – has had the immensely desirable effect of publicizing, of lucidly laying out for us, the inestimable value of sex as – at least in certain of its ineradicable aspects – anticommunal, antiegalitarian, antinurturing, antiloving.[39]

Hence, gay men should celebrate the sexuality rejected by writers who seek equality because, as Rambuss explains within the context of Bersani's work, sex as we presently know it in our society and as we see it in pornography "isn't a good thing because one acquires a sense of an integrated self from it; rather, the experience of sex [which Bersani correlates with passive anal sex] is a good thing because its shattering power prevents us from unbatingly maintaining our subjectivities."[40]

To be penetrated, then, is to abdicate power, to send masculinity to its grave – a grave best embodied by the rectum, the site through which the male self is defeated and disempowered. Given this, more men must be seen to be sexually violated, seen to participate in a state of powerlessness and the loss of self-control through which the self and ultimately male power can be finally discarded – a violation evident in the penetration sexualized in pornography.

While there are many problems with the arguments advanced by Bersani (the least of which is that, when taken to their extreme, they rather stand out as a justification for male-on-male rape), within the context of the discussion outlined thus far, it is clear that his work, like that of many of the writers mentioned above, ignores the significance of the person who is not anally penetrated but who instead penetrates and who, in so doing, does very little to subvert male power. The annihilation of self presented here as the victory that gay pornography and sex accomplish is precisely what femininity accomplishes, and to the extent that a man can be denied male power and have his identity as a man threatened simply by being penetrated, the question needs to be asked whether subversion is actuated insofar as the person who penetrates holds onto or reclaims his masculinity simply by emasculating (feminizing) another through male dominance. Even when role reversal remains an option, gender-specific roles are nonetheless evident, with the right to be male still found in the right to penetrate – a right which, within the context of pornography, equals the right to dominate.

Although gay men can embrace violation (and do), violation remains central to the sexual act and remains an act of control exercised by one who has not lost power and whose self-identity is determined by his masculinity, found only at the expense of someone else's. Masculinity remains in place, the self still empowered through the hierarchical ridicule of another, gender anything but subverted. The argument that to be penetrated equates to a loss of power is not a radical restatement of what we already know about sexuality. Feminists have been saying the same thing for some time now. Similarly, to turn the argument on its head by calling for more of the same is anything but original. Pornographers have been doing it for some time as well. What is troubling about Bersani's need to embrace the "annihilation of the self," however, is that the annihilation he risks encouraging is the type of annihilation that happens every day to real people at the hands of men too quick to find empowerment through the sexual violation of other men for whom powerlessness is anything but a game.

Equally troubling in Bersani's analysis of the liberatory potential of sexualized violence is his almost complete omission of any discussion of the role of women within the framework he promotes. That is, even if men might be liberated by powerlessness, how is it that women, who *are* socially disempowered, will benefit from a sexuality that simply props up the sexualized role play that resulted in their unequal status in the first place? Are they to assume that eventually all men will succumb to the liberation found in penetration and that equality will thus prevail for both male and female? Or – and one can be forgiven for thinking that this outcome is more likely – will they simply continue to suffer under a system in which those men who have had their masculinity stripped back regain it through the continued sexist exploitation of female inequality? And, to the extent that this remains the case, will masculinity ever be undermined? I think not, for so long as gay men (and indeed all men generally) have the option of *being* men by penetrating the person made inferior through the sexualized inequality attached to penetration (an option promoted, encouraged, and actualized by the pornography Bersani himself applauds), equality will remain distant.

Despite his acceptance of the social power of pornographic presentations of inequality, Bersani nonetheless celebrates their continued distribution because, he argues, it is only through the sexuality they promote that the subversive potential of anal penetration, resulting in powerlessness, ultimately resulting in the death of masculinity, can be realized. This, I am sure, is of no comfort to the millions of women, and those gay men, who will continue to suffer the harms that result from sexualized violence until Bersani's project is eventually achieved. Nor am I convinced that the mere pornographic presentation of anal intercourse will emasculate male privilege if, in the process of "annihilating one man's self-identity," another man reaffirms or strengthens his. In the end, Bersani's radicalism finds support in the same power play that justifies rape, domestic violence, misogyny, and homophobia. And to the extent that gay men sexualize *that* for self-gratification, they do little more than buy into a model of self-identity that is far from a threat to sexuality as we know it.

Playing with Masculinity: But Do You Defeat Your Enemy by *Becoming* Him?

Carl Stychin, while agreeing that gay male pornography does appropriate masculinity and all that that entails, nonetheless asserts that because it is appropriated into a new unauthorized context, "the representation of that masculinity appropriates a new unauthorized signification." He continues: "The feminist critique fails to recognize the marginalization of gay men. This marginalization affects the viewer's perception of the pornographic signifier and the differing context changes the signifier's very meaning. The signifier assumes a new meaning because it is received at the fringes of dominant culture. In other words, if the viewer's context defines the meaning of an image, then the dominance and significance of pornography assume a different signification when received by marginalized gay men."[41]

To the extent that masculinity has always been the possession of the straight male, this analysis is correct. To the extent that gay men see the appropriation of this masculinity as a mere parody and not as a reflection and reinforcement of straight male privilege that they have been denied, however, this analysis goes astray. In particular, it underestimates the power of those social forces that make gay men marginalized in the first place. In the realm of reality as opposed to "fantasy," a world in which gay men are chastised for their perceived femininity, the result for some gay men of promoted masculinity is shame for any apparent non-maleness. Any pornographic medium that promotes the masculine as power, when used by those who have no alternative value system and who have always been told that because they are non-masculine, they are less male, is likely to exacerbate feelings of inadequacy – whether or not they choose to be top or bottom.

It is the *reality* of gay men's lives generally – *precisely* their social marginalization – that makes gay male pornography the homophobic threat that it is. The purpose of homophobia is to ensure that gay men are bullied into rejecting any sexual expression that undermines male power. As noted in Chapter 1, insofar that male supremacy depends on gender inequality, gay men, because they have the potential to develop relationships that do not rely on a male-female hierarchy, threaten male supremacy. As Pharr explains, "misogyny gets transferred to gay men with a vengeance and is increased by the fear that their sexual identity will bring down the entire system of male dominance and compulsory heterosexuality."[42] Homophobia, which finds expression in gay bashing, employment discrimination, and familial and social ostracization, reminds all men that if they "break ranks with males through bonding and affection outside the arenas of war and sports," they will be perceived as not being "real men," that is, as being identified with women, "the weaker sex that must be dominated and that over the years has been the subject of male hatred and abuse."[43] The gay male, socially feminized, internalizes this misogyny and seeks to mimic those behaviours and characteristics that will, he hopes, allow him to "pass" for the man he is supposed to be, and receive the value of the male status. Masculinity, for those gay men who have been penalized for failing to meet its criteria and who are told that they are "weak, effeminate and maladjusted,"[44] promises privilege and a safety net with which to find social acceptance and status, rather than a means by which to really parody and subvert oppressive gender categories.

This assumed safety net is exactly what makes gay pornography the threat to equality that it is. It tells the gay male that sexual relationships must be hierarchical and that male power is at the top of that hierarchy. Gay pornography promises the gay male a false security that he too can gain more power if he can become that which epitomizes male power – masculinity taken to its extreme. Unfortunately, the power promised is a façade and does a great deal to further maintain male dominance – the source of all that is anti-gay and anti-woman.

For gay men, mimicry and assimilation ensure that those who are "visible" become the victims of greater physical and emotional abuse and discrimination. Because they continue to challenge the "normality" of gender polarity and in the process undermine male supremacy, these men will be brutally silenced.[45] This reinforces the idea that gay men can either fail to conform to masculine mimicry and be the feminized other they have always been told they are (and hence be further abused), or they can copy it. Copying it, however, will not render its effect any less damaging. As Kleinberg explains, mimicking your enemy just because you can get away with it does not save you from the wrath or violence of that enemy. It ensures only that the internalization of social rejection becomes self-contempt for all that is socially perceived as non-masculine. Hence, gay men who choose concealment and who embrace and encourage that masculinity so central to male dominance do little more than sexualize their own oppression – making a fetish of that which ultimately silences them.[46] A similar point is raised by Leo Bersani, who writes: "[I]f licking someone's leather boots turns you (and him) on, neither of you is making a statement subversive of macho masculinity. Parody is an erotic turn-off ... The dead seriousness of the gay commitment to machismo ... means that gay men run the risk of idealising and feeling inferior to certain representations of masculinity on the basis of which they are judged and condemned."[47]

The question must also be asked: who do those who choose to "change status" think they are deceiving? Politically, their silence ensures that gay "rights" will be a long time coming. Masculinity, once glorified, constructs a closet from which there is no escape. In addition, one must ask whether, apart from the damage caused by hiding, they really think they *can* hide. Eventually the values they worship will turn on them and result in the abuse some of us are trying so hard to eliminate.[48] And then they too can be the bottom, socially defined.

Becoming "a man" does nothing for gay male liberation. It does, however, do a lot for male supremacy. It ensures that the rejection of male dominance, necessary for gay male liberation, will be more difficult and that those of us who do choose to do so will face more hostility from both straight men and those in our community who have sold out. It ensures that the "grovelling faggot," aware that he can never be the man he is supposed to be, will be just what gay male pornography and society says he should be: the object of scorn and male aggression. It ensures that the closeted youth already attacked for being different will stay closeted, afraid to express any "difference" that might reveal his secret and make him the target of more hatred. And while the pornographic reality, cloaked as fantasy, might promise him vindication because he too can be the "top," the struggle to become that top will only reinforce the social hierarchy straight men have supported all along. The result is gay male silence and subordination, male superiority, and female inferiority.

Racialized Bodies: A Prerequisite for Patriarchy?
This obsession with reclaiming a lost or denied masculinity is also evident in those pornographic materials that sexualize racial difference. As LEAF itself demonstrated in its submissions before the Supreme Court of Canada in *Butler* in 1991, pornography is not only a practice of discrimination which disadvantages people and treats them as second-class citizens on the basis of sex but it also uses race and age to discriminate through gender.[49] Nine years later, in the case of *Little Sisters*, nothing has changed, other than LEAF's own position on this argument. This is evident throughout many of the materials defended in *Little Sisters*. In the drawings of *Tom of Finland*, for example, African-American men are shown either as predators (e.g., one white man is depicted being assaulted by four black men) or as being exploited by groups of white men (e.g., a black man being whipped with a belt by two white men).[50] In the same collection, we see a black man being held down on the hood of his car by two white police officers. Both officers are holding their penises, preparing to rape him. Racial inequality appears to be the norm throughout these publications, and much of what is sexualized relies heavily on racial stereotype. Similarly, in the book *Sex Stop*, we are offered the stereotypical description of the older black male finding validation as a slave at the hands of a white youth.[51] Conversely, in *Martie: Black Summer, White Heat*, the black male

is presented as a violent sexual predator.[52] Finally, in *Oriental Guys,* the Asian male is presented as submissive and sexually subordinate to all white men.[53]

These examples, like much of the pornography used by gay men, say a lot about those gay men in our community who do not benefit from the privilege attached to white skin. Specifically, they are not to be treated as equals. These materials also say a great deal about the connection between race and gender. It is often alleged by those most critical of sex equality theorists that those who attempt to define systemic inequality as an issue of sexual subordination fail to paint an accurate picture of the ways in which subordination differs from one person to another. More specifically, radical feminist theorists have been accused of failing to take seriously the harms of racial inequality when discussing the role of gender hierarchies in defining and describing the social status of those who are female, with many arguing that to talk of gender is to implicitly ignore race.[54] A rereading of the work of anti-pornography feminists on this point reveals that no such exclusion or omission exists.

To talk of and demand sexual equality in a society in which gender is hierarchical does not imply that one dismisses the role of racism in maintaining systemic inequality. Quite the contrary. bell hooks, for example, has argued that racialized bodies are both a turn on and a prerequisite for patriarchy,[55] and both Andrea Dworkin and Catharine MacKinnon have previously advanced similar arguments. MacKinnon writes that within the context of heterosexual pornography, "[e]ach specifically victimized and vulnerable group of women, each tabooed target group – Black women, Asian women, Latin women, Jewish women, pregnant women, disabled women, retarded women, poor women, old women, fat women, women in women's jobs, prostitutes, little girls – distinguishes pornographers' genres and subthemes, classified according to customer's favourite degradation."[56]

What is clear from the work of these and many other women is that within the context of the radical feminist anti-pornography struggle, to focus on the systemic harms of sex inequality and all that it stands for is also to focus on the harms of racial inequality. The two cannot be severed, and no one has argued that they should be.

As early as 1978, for example, Andrea Dworkin described in powerful detail the sexual stereotyping of the racially degraded male:

> Either he is the rapist, the sexual animal with intense virility and a huge potent member; or he is desexualized in the sense of being demasculinized – he is considered castrated (unmanned) or he is associated with demeaning (feminizing) and demeaned (not martial) homosexuality. It is the relationship of the dominant class to masculinity that determines whether males of the racially despised group are linked with rape or with castration/homosexuality. If the dominant group insists that the racially despised male is a rapist, it means that

the dominant males are effeminate by contrast; it is they who are tinged by homosexuality in that they are less manly. They will climb the masculinity ladder by killing or maiming those they see as racially inferior but sexually superior.[57]

Dworkin further explains that, in the United States, the black male was not widely characterized as a rapist until after the abolition of slavery. While he was still a slave, his position as the property of a white male owner ensured that he remained "unmanned." "His degradation was as a symbolically castrated man; a mule, a beast of burden."[58] The end of slavery symbolized a potential threat to the white man's masculinity – the former slave reminding him of his lost manhood, his humiliation at losing power over a socially castrated/feminized subordinate: "rape has been traditionally viewed as a crime of theft: a woman stolen from a man to whom she rightfully belongs ... The Black rapist was accused of a crime of theft, only what he stole was not the white woman; he stole the master's masculinity. The crime had nothing to do with women – it almost never does. The white men, unmanned, were accusing the Black man of having raped them."[59]

When we look at the materials at issue in *Little Sisters*, it is apparent that much of what has been defended risks replicating and enforcing the racist ideology described by Dworkin. Given the links between this ideology and that system of sexual inequality in which homosexuality equals subordination, it would seem to me to be both offensive and naïve to assume that this obsession with role play will not have repercussions for both those black gay men who see it (a point I return to in Chapter 8) and for those of us who are not black but who are now expected to defend racism as part of a larger gay male liberation platform.

The politic presented in gay pornography is one in which some black men long to be slaves, while others are presented as men to be feared and ultimately loathed as a result of their ability to emasculate the rest through rape. The question I want to ask here is, is not the idea that someone might *want* to be a slave simply patterned on those racist and sexist notions that it is right to dominate certain individuals or groups because they want or deserve to be dominated or because domination is the only way to keep them in check? Similarly, doesn't the idea that someone is to be labelled a rapist simply because of the colour of his skin buy into the same agenda that straight men use against gay men who they fear might, simply by having sex with them or by refusing to participate in the misogynistic exploitation of women, disempower them by robbing them of their masculinity (i.e., isn't it racist)? My concern here is that by playing with the racial stereotypes first created and used by the white straight male in an attempt to regain *his* lost masculinity, gay men are now telling each other to loathe and fear the black male for his ability to do the same to *us*. If so, what might this achieve socially, other than promoting racism, ensuring that white gay men go out of their way to prove themselves by emasculating the black male in all other walks of life?

My fear in this regard is that by promising empowerment through racial subordination we risk excluding the black male from participation in what should be a community of support, while simultaneously propping up those gender norms that link the straight male's justification for the killing of black men with his public denunciation of male-male sex relations as a perversion. Masculinity remains central to both inequalities, and gay men risk a great deal by sexualizing them in the name of freedom. Sexualized racial stereotypes are not simply bedroom turn ons. Linked as they are to sexism and homophobia, they go a long way toward ensuring that the breakdown of the disparities needed to achieve sex equality will be a long time coming.

This fusion of race and gender and the codification of racially based sexual desire is also evident in those materials in which Asian men are sexualized, again primarily for the benefit of non-Asian men. Feminization is central to the presentation of gay Asian men within gay male pornography, such that it combines with race to support the entrenched marginalization of non-white men through a process of sexual disempowerment. This is best evidenced in magazines such as *Oriental Guys,* defended throughout the *Little Sisters* proceedings. With a monthly distribution in the thousands, the effect of this and other such magazines on gay men's perceptions of themselves and other men should not be underestimated. The cover of each *Oriental Guys* edition promises the reader "positive images of Asian men." The contents speak otherwise. Simon Obendorf, a young Australian gay male, describes "Hitchhiker Kidnapped?" a twenty-page photo spread of a young Asian man (named Gary), found in a 1997 edition of the magazine:

> The photo spread, and accompanying text, introduce the consumer to Gary, purportedly a member of some military organisation, indicated by his camouflage shorts and bandanna. He is initially presented beside a road, attempting to thumb a ride from passers by. He is bare chested, with a well-defined physique, and appears to be in his early or mid twenties. As the pages of images unfold, Gary is blindfolded, bound and thrust into a car by an unknown and unseen assailant. Indeed, in all the images that follow, one is never shown the person who is performing actions upon Gary's body, the intention presumably being to invite the spectator/consumer to imagine himself in the position of dominator. As the fantasy continues, Gary is collared, leashed and led to some undisclosed (but nonetheless exotic and Oriental) jungle location where he is undressed, handcuffed and bound into various poses of submission. His clothing is gradually removed, revealing his erect penis. His face, when shown, reveals changes in expression from pain and surprise in the first few photographs, to pleading and submission

in the middle photographs, finally ending in an expression of ecstasy. As this change occurs, Gary is seen variously thrust into a large "Asian" earthenware pot, with a leather belt draped across his bound body, and finally trussed firmly with rope and with nipple clamps attached to his erect nipples. It is by this stage that Gary is seen to be exulting in his degradation and forced submission.[60]

Obendorf's description of the sexuality offered the Asian gay male in *Oriental Guys* and magazines like it supports the conclusions made years earlier by gay Asian-Canadian writer Richard Fung in his work "Looking for My Penis: The Eroticized Asian in Gay Video Porn." Describing the film *Below the Belt*, which features Sum Yung Mahn, Fung writes that, as in almost all the gay pornography which uses Asian men, the sexual pleasure promised is a sexual pleasure experienced only by white men. More troubling is that it is to be found only as a result of the humiliation and pain inflicted on Asian gay men:

> Greg fucks Sum Yung Mahn, who is always face down. The scene constructs anal intercourse for the Asian (male) as an act of submission, not of pleasure ... To a greater extent than most other gay porn tapes, *Below the Belt* is directly about power. The hierarchical dojo setting is milked for its evocation of dominance and submission. With the exception of one very romantic sequence midway through the tape, most of the actors stick to their defined role of top or bottom. Sex, especially anal sex, as punishment is a recurrent image ... What is significant, however, is how race figures into the equation. In a tape that appropriates emblems of Asian power (karate), the only place for a real Asian actor is as a caricature of passivity.[61]

Not surprisingly, the stereotypes sexualized in gay pornography are now mainstreamed into and accepted by many gay men as fact.[62] This in turn creates a sexualized hierarchy among gay men that again equates racial difference with gender inferiority. As Tony Ayres, a young Australasian man explains,

> [b]ecause the majority of gay Asian men in Australia are slimmer and smaller than their Caucasian counterparts, they are stereotyped as feminine or "boyish." However, in a culture that worships Tom of Finland, being feminine is neither respected or valued ... I've often been told that I'm tall "for an Asian." It doesn't matter if we're from the north of China or the south of Vietnam, irrespective of body type, size, age or weight, Caucasians have a preconception of what an "Asian" looks like. It's this preconception that puts us near the bottom of their sexual hierarchy.[63]

Richard Fung, aware of the inequalities evident in gay pornography, and while agreeing with the personal accounts provided by men such as Ayres, nonetheless assumes a pro-pornography position in arguing for the continued production of gay pornography. Not wanting to be seen as anti-sex, he writes:

> As with the vast majority of North American tapes featuring Asians, the problem is not the representation of anal pleasure per se, but rather that the narratives privilege the penis while always assigning the Asian the role of bottom; Asian and anus are conflated. In the case of Sum Yung Mahn, being fucked may well be his personal sexual preference. But the fact remains that there are very few occasions in North American video porn in which an Asian fucks a white male. So few, in fact, that International Wavelength promotes the tape *Studio X* (1986) with the blurb "Sum Yung Mahn makes history as the first Asian who fucks a non-Asian."[64]

If we follow Fung's reasoning to its logical conclusion, it is arguable that one "solution" to the problems he identifies is to produce and market pornographic videos that show "an Asian male fucking a white male." The question remains, however, whether this will eradicate the inequalities he wants rejected. That is, to the extent that the Asian male can now assume the role of the dominant male who, as such, has the right to find empowerment through sexual conquest, will this subvert the expectation that many gay men have that sexuality must be hierarchical to be pleasurable? It seems unlikely. As Ayres again explains, the risk with such an argument is that it may only entrench these inequalities while creating newer, equally divisive divisions among Asian men themselves. Describing the push among many Asian men to reject the feminine stereotype thrust on them, Ayres writes:

> The influx of Asian migration through the mid to late-80s has led to an increased presence of gay Asian men today. A new generation of young men are going to the gym, bulking up, doing drugs and dance parties, finding a place for themselves. It's not that the dominant paradigm of the desirable body has expanded, but that there are now Asians who fit into this paradigm. This is still buying into the cult of youth and beauty which dominates the gay scene. It does nothing to make ordinary Joes like myself feel any more secure about our place.[65]

If, applying Fung's analysis, we *do* produce pornography that supports the idea that Asian men can gain empowerment through hyper-masculinity found though "fucking," through the presentation of an identity model in which "sex, especially anal sex, as punishment is a recurrent image," will this result in equality or will it simply ensure that those who cannot or who choose not to conform will remain racially and thus sexually inferior? Fung argues that pornography is needed because it is all that Asian men have.[66] He admits, though, that the pornography available is anything but rewarding for the Asian male who views it.[67] His proposed solution is a new kind of pornography. One that *is* liberating. What he fails to offer is some indication of how one might construct a liberation strategy from a medium in which sexual hierarchy remains central to the act – a medium that finds its cultural popularity in the fact that as gay men we are taught to respond erotically to the sexual presentation of dominance and submission. If, as it would appear, Fung is asking Asian men to find self-empowerment by simply swapping roles, he needs to question how equality can be achieved insofar as the same sexual hierarchy, reinforced through a gendered role play, remains intact. To again quote gay historian Seymour Kleinberg, one does not defeat one's enemy by simply becoming him.[68] If equality is Fung's goal, and it undoubtedly is, then hierarchy cannot be sold as sexuality. If the Asian male is now asked to find strength only through the emasculation of another, and in particular, those white men who have been the source of his own debasement, can we expect equality if the same white male is later promised validation and salvation though the subordination of Asian men elsewhere? We may find that, stripped of his manhood by someone he himself has been taught to exploit, the now "unmanned" white male will seek empowerment by again exploiting those racial inequalities already pervasive in our community – inequalities *his* pornography encourages. The end result can only be further discrimination, further resentment, further division along the lines of race and gender, further inequality.

I should not be seen as suggesting that a sexuality in which inequality does *not* exist cannot be created or envisioned. Rather, what I am saying is that it will not be achieved so long as pornography, which requires inequality, is the source of that objective. As Australian academic Carl Gopal writes:

> If the lobby is going to scream about human rights, it had better take a good look at the stark racism and class prejudice within its own backyard. Working-class men are not just "rough trade"; Asian men are not just "rice queens"; gay men and lesbians have far from equal power in gay society and the power games in sexual politics, eulogizing cultural and economic exploitation, are entrenched in gay pornography. To stop being a victim, one must stop victimizing others, and until the gay community does this, its mandate to rule will always be dependent on mainstream hierarchies. The gay lobby has [not] won the fight ... but I believe that it must continue its commitment to human rights ... and progressive and caring social policies for *all* its members, lest it should collapse under its own hypocrisy.[69]

Gopal's call for a rejection of all mainstream hierarchies is particularly significant at a time when those gay men who are not white continue to struggle for a voice within a community in which racism is both common and promoted as sexually acceptable. The challenge for all gay men is to create those safe spaces in which all of us can flourish – politically, sexually, and otherwise. Gay male pornography does not create this space. Self-empowerment must remain central to any human-rights-based agenda. Sexual empowerment will not be achieved by buying into a sex-based system of inequality that segregates according to the white male's construction of sexual availability.

Conclusion

At its core, gay male pornography is, quite simply, homophobic. Much, if not all its content presents an image of male sexuality and power that shows and reinforces attitudes and behaviours about what it takes to be a "real man." Its message, that gay men should reject any expression of male-male sexuality that is equal and non-hierarchical, has implications that reach far beyond the gay male community. For women, the acceptance of a sexuality premised on male-female polarity is but one more tool with which to preserve that gender hierarchy necessary for social inequality. As such, gay male pornography also amounts to a practice of sex discrimination.

Gay male pornography does what the homophobe has done quite successfully for some time. Specifically, it works to maintain gender roles by encouraging gay men to adopt an identity that valorizes male dominance and by stating unequivocally that those who choose not to adopt this identity have no value, no power. It embodies the essence of sexual *in*equality by promoting all that is pro-male dominance, hence anti-woman and of necessity anti-gay. It ensures that those models of sexual behaviour that might undermine sex inequality are suppressed and that women and those men who *do* fail to conform remain unequal. Ultimately, this does nothing to affirm personal liberties and freedoms. It does, however, do a great deal to ensure the survival of a system of gender inequality that is degrading and dehumanizing and that reinforces, by sexualizing, the power dynamics that ensure systematic inequality.

In sum, to again paraphrase the Supreme Court of Canada's decision in *Butler*, gay male pornography, like heterosexual pornography, reinforces "male-female stereotypes to the detriment of both sexes [and] attempts to make degradation, humiliation, victimization, and violence in human relationships appear normal and acceptable." In doing so, it violates values of "egalitarianism, non-violence, consensualism and mutuality" – principles basic to equality and non-discrimination – and does nothing for those communities still very much in need of political liberation. As such, far from being exempt from the analysis offered in *Butler*, gay pornography is and should be caught by it.

To the extent that sex inequality hinders legitimate minority expression, and homophobia is a means of ensuring that sexism prevails, gay men and women can and must form alliances as persons committed to social justice. However, insofar as gay men support a practice that contributes to the real abuse of real people, that normalizes male sexual aggression, and that encourages the subordination of one individual to the domination of a descriptively, more stereotypically, "male" other – in sum, a practice that is itself homophobic – gay men do little to ensure that alliances will occur. As one woman has so aptly explained, "if liberation is your goal, then you must work with other oppressed peoples in defining both the oppression and the vision of a free, liberated society. Allies are essential, especially to a minority struggle like gay liberation. Feminists can be allies in your struggle – but you don't get political women standing with you when you consistently take a position that is dangerous to us."[70]

In the name of liberation, many gay men have ignored the claim that pornography does real damage. Seen more as an issue of sexual freedom, gay male pornography has been defended as a base from which to challenge and subvert compulsory heterosexuality and develop gay male identity. Closer re-examination reveals that there is little, if anything, liberating about a medium that encourages aggression as a sexual practice, promotes physical harm as erotic and identity defining, and reinforces an already entrenched system of sex discrimination on the basis of sexuality and gender.

Gay men must construct a platform from which to re-examine what gay male identity is and the models from whence that identity is derived. If liberation is our goal and subversion our objective, gay male expression must be protected. As persons committed to the dissolution of injustice, we owe it to ourselves and other oppressed individuals to ensure that the mediums through which we gain the voices with which to dismantle injustice do not reinforce those power dynamics that have always made real liberation and equality – ours included – unattainable.

7 "Protecting" Gay Youth: Why Self-Loathing Is Not a Path to Safety

Silence is where the hate grows that killed my son.[1]

Gabi Clayton, mother of Bill Clayton,
aged 17, found dead from suicide

Anyone dealing with the prospect of "coming out" faces a range of feelings – from confusion to distress, to despair. Sadly, many in the gay community fail to acknowledge the angst faced by young gay men in particular. The following review of a British teleseries demonstrates this:

> TWO OF US (SBS, 12:30PM) sees two 17 year old guys confused about what to do with their feelings for each other. Being something of a sage when it comes to relationships, much like Yoda but taller and without Frank Oz's hand up my butt, I have a quick remedy for the situation: trot down to a video store, rent anything with the words a) male b) bonkfest c) Jeff d) Stryker in the title, take it home and copy everything exactly. Adios, confusion.[2]

In 1996, *The Two of Us* was shown on SBS Australian television, as well as on stations throughout Canada and the United States. The series, which traces the life of two young gay adolescents, might best be described as a program that encourages some level of self-acknowledgment and self-acceptance by presenting, among other things, publicly accessible images of two young men "holding hands, hugging and kissing and running through meadows in slow motion."[3] The series does not feature gay pornography icon Jeff Stryker. This fact alone is – if we are to believe the words of the film critic quoted above (writing in the weekly gay newspaper in Perth, Western Australia, but whose "advice" is, I am sure, relevant elsewhere) – reason enough to dismiss the show as boring, out of touch, and not worth watching.

Research concerned with the problems facing gay youth today highlights two reoccurring elements that require immediate attention on the part of educators and social activists. The first is an alarming suicide rate among lesbian and gay adolescents.[4] The second is what has been referred to as a second wave of HIV/AIDS transmission among young gay men between the ages of fourteen and twenty-five.[5] These facts, and others, point to a generation of young gay men very much in need of self-acknowledgment and self-acceptance.

While the views expressed by the journalist quoted above might be seen as tongue-in-cheek, it is nonetheless troubling that the message conveyed by him is apparently all too readily supported by people who profess to care about, and who claim to speak on behalf of, gay youth. This attitude is particularly evident when examining the arguments of those who intervened on behalf of Little Sisters in its litigation before the Supreme Court of Canada. While it is undoubtedly the case that many of these groups are committed to ensuring the survival of a generation of young men too quick to abandon their futures, when one examines them within the context of the materials defended in this case, one is left wondering how they intend to provide the safe environment needed to develop the self-confidence, self-respect, and respect for others that will, or so one would hope, decrease the levels of anxiety and confusion that are quite literally building a wall of silence around our community, resulting in the death of far too many of us.

Here I respond to the claims made by these groups and others that the gay male pornography defended in *Little Sisters* promotes safety. I hope to demonstrate through analysis of the struggle over identity and acceptance (both by their peers and society at large) confronted by young gay men today that the ideals conveyed in what pro-pornography activists label "safe sex" and "educational" materials are anything but safe. Overall, I argue that while gay men are entitled to, and should, question legal efforts to regulate same-sex sexual images and representations that *are* life-affirming, they should not do so without first examining whether the materials they seek to protect actually empower gay men to respect and protect themselves and others, or whether they simply reinforce the types of cultural stereotypes and inequalities that trigger self-loathing and self-deprecation.

Gay Youth and the Need for Safe Sexuality Education

Gay youth counsellor Kevin Jennings explains that in a society in which homophobic violence and gender inequality remain rampant, being a gay or lesbian youth is less than easy. What makes gay and lesbian youth different from other minority and disenfranchised groups is that they do not, for the most part, grow up with people like themselves.[6] Their isolation becomes more encompassing, for a homophobic social environment can be duplicated in the home. As Jennings notes, lesbian and gay youth are predominantly the product of heterosexual families and come from communities where lesbian and gay adults are rarely visible. They attend schools with (usually) no openly gay staff and belong to peer groups in which "fag" is the favoured insult and "that's so gay" is a common term of abuse.[7]

According to Professor James Sears of the University of South Carolina, the average student realizes his or her sexual orientation at the age of thirteen.[8] For heterosexual adolescents, there are many avenues of support through which they can overcome, or at least discuss, developmental or peer pressure difficulties that inevitably accompany adolescence. By contrast, gay youth rarely feel able to ask their families, friends, schools, or communities to help them out, fearing the possible and often likely negative response they would receive.[9] This is supported by research conducted by the London Gay Teenage Group, which found that 25 percent of young gay men and lesbians in London felt isolated, 21 percent suffered verbal abuse, 12 percent were physically assaulted, and one in five young gay men and lesbians attempted suicide because of anguish, loneliness, or despair.[10] Still others have concluded that young gay men account for seven out of every ten suicides.[11] Isolation thus becomes intrinsic to the existence of a large number of lesbian and gay adolescents, and this feeling of isolation is often accompanied by self-hate and confusion as to their future.[12]

Like many of its counterparts worldwide, the Western Australia Health Department recently released a report aimed at reducing the increase in youth suicide, entitled *Making A Difference: Youth Suicide Prevention Manual*.[13] The report's findings indicate that young gay, lesbian, and bisexual people often live in hostile and condemning environments, with verbal and physical assaults both evident and rampant.[14] There is a lack of positive role models and information about homosexuality, with little opportunity for gay youth to recognize, take pride, and act on their sexual identity. This affects their self-esteem, leaving them isolated and vulnerable, internalizing self-hatred or denying their sexuality. This in turn may lead to a situation where their sexual activity takes place anonymously (such as at "beats") or gay and lesbian bars and nightclubs. This increases their sense of isolation, and exposes them to the risks of access to alcohol and other drugs, and the chance to engage in opportunistic sex work.[15]

Research undertaken in the United States exposes similar difficulties and dangers faced by lesbian and gay youth in that country. These include violence resulting from hate crimes, with one survey conducted by the National Gay and Lesbian Task Force reporting that 45 percent of gay men and 25 percent of lesbians had been harassed or attacked in high school because they were believed to be lesbian or gay. Added to this is persistent verbal abuse, with comments such as "fag," "dyke," and "that's so gay" used so regularly in high schools (sometimes by teachers) that few even notice such vilification being out of the ordinary.[16] One survey conducted by the Massachusetts Governor's Commission on Gay and Lesbian Youth found that 97 percent of students at one suburban high school had heard homophobic language used in school. The result is often homelessness, a outcome made even more likely by families that react negatively when they discover that their child is lesbian or gay.[17] A University of Minnesota study found that 26 percent of young gay men reported being forced to leave home because of conflict over their being gay. Still others resort to substance abuse; the same study found that 58 percent of the young gay men surveyed could be classified as having a drug or alcohol abuse disorder.[18] Not surprisingly, many of these young men drop out of school to escape the harassment, violence, and alienation they face as students.[19]

All of the above create an environment in which suicide becomes a tangible option for young lesbians and gay men. As Jennings notes, according to the United States Department of Health and Human Services, gay and lesbian youth are two to three times more likely to attempt suicide than heterosexual youth (with 500,000 suicide attempts in the United States annually).[20] Up to 30 percent of successful teen suicides each year are by lesbian or gay teens (1,500 out of a total of 5,000 deaths). Extrapolating from the department's statistics reveals that, in the United States, a gay or lesbian youth tries to kill himself or herself every thirty-five minutes, and that a gay or lesbian youth succeeds in killing himself or herself every six hours.[21]

What one sees from a reading of the above is a significant relationship between homophobia and low self-esteem,[22] resulting from the "painful experience of being different,"[23] of being considered a lower order of humanity. As Martin and Hetrick explain, the gay youth, raised in a society in which gay equals deviant, may come to accept that gay men "are predatory, unsuitable for the hard professions, unable to form mature non-erotic relationships, inimical to the survival of the race, criminal seducers, haters of the opposite sex, immature and the victims of pathological development, sexually disordered, the cause of crime in the streets and the cause of AIDS."[24] The result can be catastrophic. For the gay youth, the psychological, emotional, and social consequences of these messages will result in the types of coping mechanisms found in all stigmatized groups, such as "denial of group membership, withdrawal and passivity, identification with the dominant group with resulting self hate (and) aggression against one's own group."[25] As Martin and Hetrick note, the sense of worthlessness that arises should not be unexpected:

> In a society in which a leading newspaper, the *New York Times*, can publish an essay that seriously recommends that homosexuals be tattooed on the buttocks as a precautionary identifying measure, without an opposing view published at the same time, and where a father may indicate that the worst possible thing that could happen to his child is homosexuality, it is not surprising that the homosexual adolescent develops ... self-hatred ... Sexual desire, a central aspect of the

adolescent's self, becomes for the homosexual adolescent a threat to everything toward which he has been socialized.[26]

It is not surprising, given the above, that many young gay men choose not to reveal their insecurities and concern to their families and those whom they might normally turn to for support. As MacDonald explains, many young gay men simply become "half-members of the family unit: afraid and alienated, unable to ever be totally open and spontaneous, to trust or be trusted, to develop a fully socialized sense of self or self-affirmation. This sad stunting of human potential breeds stress for gay people and their families alike – stress characterized by secrecy, ignorance, helplessness and distance."[27]

And what of the long term? What happens to those who internalize the stereotypes through which we are told to form an identity? For many, the stereotypes attached to being gay mean that they are stigmatized, hence less worthy of respect and dignity:

> What is internalized for a young man who has identified himself as homosexual? Once there is a mutual acknowledgment between a young man and the members of his social world that he is homosexual, he faces implicit condemnation and increasing stigmatization. A hostile and rejecting world unfolds for homosexuals in which the objective understanding they have of homosexuality as unnatural, abnormal, and despised becomes a statement of self-definition. These interactions are particularly influential because they take place within the major socializing contexts for humans, that is family and peers.[28]

As Savin-Williams notes, for some, the only response is to run away or get involved in prostitution and other crimes, "because they are unable to cope with the obligatory deception, isolation and alienation."[29] Some find solace on the streets, where they are able to encounter an identity model that "corresponds to the cultural image of the male homosexual." Others, sexually abused as children, normalize this abuse, and, thinking that violence is sex, turn to the types of abuse that first shaped their sexual identity, believing that this is what it means to be gay:

> Cultural myths regarding the etiology of homosexuality influence how one interprets the experience of sexual victimization. A cultural myth that is available to all boys, regardless of how fixed their sexual orientation may be, is that a homosexual experience may result in "becoming" a homosexual. This myth is available as a potential source for interpreting experiences and shaping both self-understanding and social identity. Due to the stigma associated with homosexuality, males

who have been sexually abused seldom report the abuse. Consequently, they seldom receive the help they need to resolve the incident. But most importantly, the sexually abused possess knowledge and experience other delinquents may not have. They know there is a market for certain kinds of sexual activity.[30]

Some believe that doing "tricks" is the only way to meet other gay people. Still others turn to prostitution because this is where society has told them they belong. As one study of young gay prostitutes reveals, prostitution provides an identity that corresponds with the cultural image of the male homosexual – a "distorted and exaggerated sexuality, of promiscuity, and deviance" – with male prostitutes literally practising what they believe to be appropriate gay male sexual behaviour. "As prostitutes, they enact the myths ... [reflecting] the images of stigma they had learned." Any elation at finding a community and identity, however, is short-lived; these young men soon find "themselves coping with the added stigma of prostitution."[31] For many, the result is a world of drug dependency,[32] sexual abuse, AIDS, and, for some, suicide – a social phenomenon all too readily produced by the cultural constructions of sex and gender.[33]

While not all young men reacting to the stigma of being gay become prostitutes, many do take considerable steps to avoid the stigma attached to being gay – steps that result in considerable harm. As sex counsellor Richard Troiden explains, these can range from inhibiting behaviours or interests they have learned to associate with homosexuality, limiting exposure to the opposite sex to prevent peers or family from learning about their relative lack of heterosexual responsiveness, assuming anti-homosexual postures, engaging in heterosexual immersion, and pursuing escapism in the form of drugs and alcohol.[34]

I have argued throughout this book that one of the main effects of homophobia is to encourage gay men to hide any sexual identity that threatens gender male privilege. It would appear that the strategy of homophobia has thus far proven remarkably effective. Given this, it is not surprising that young gay men have also been quick to "assume anti-homosexual postures" or to attempt to "pass" as straight men in order to avoid the stigma attached to gay identity. While this strategy has much broader systemic effects, within the context of safe sex and youth suicide prevention strategies, it is clear that attempts to hide sometimes inflict a deeper personal toll on the young. As Troiden explains, passing as a heterosexual is probably the most common stigma-evasion strategy and can lead to considerable emotional despair.[35] As Berger notes, it can hinder the formation of a positive social support network for gay youth, as it tends to isolate gay youth from those most able to offer them the support they need. It impedes the formation of intimate relationships, as these young men fear that these relationships will reveal their true identity.[36] Finally, the gay youth who does attempt to "pass," thus risking social isolation, may in fact be the least likely to receive the types of affirmation needed to avoid those sexual, social, and interpersonal practices that increase the risk of emotional and physical harm:

> The teenage gay male ... may soon learn that he can make "contact" in certain neighbourhoods, bookstores, movies, and parks. Unfortunately, this contact is usually only sexual in nature ... His obsessive concern with his sexual orientation, which results from his fear of disclosure, is transformed into an obsessive concern for sexual behavior. The casual sexual contact also helps to maintain hiding, as it becomes a means to compartmentalize his life and to separate sexual behavior from all other aspects of his life. The setting, the danger, and the type of individuals who exploit young people in this way all tend to reinforce the belief that a homosexual orientation is all that society has said it is: sick, deviant, despicable. The negative self-image is intensified. In addition, he grows to view his partners and by extension all homosexual people in the same way.[37]

Given the amount of effort young gay men are putting into "passing," into "hiding" who they are, it should not surprise us that other debilitating effects, also linked to low self-esteem, are now rampant. If, as seems to be the case, escapism is required to survive, then, for those who do actually survive, external quick fixes that promise escape will also find an increasingly eager market desperate to consume anything that offers a coping mechanism. The results, however, are anything but life enhancing. Alcoholism in the gay community, for example, has now reached the stage of being pandemic,[38] as has the use of illegal drugs.[39] Far too much extremely important work has been done in this area to do it justice here; however, much of the research undertaken concludes that not accepting being gay as a positive self-attribute goes a considerable way toward explaining the high incidence of alcoholism among gay men. Alcohol, like most drugs, serves as a denial and coping mechanism for gay men's often internalized homophobia.[40] As one young man explains,

> I used alcohol as an anesthesia around unresolved conflicts. I just denied and refused to deal with a whole lot of issues, not the least of which was my sexuality. And I would drink to make the pain go away. I was just so torn up and in turmoil that alcohol was the only thing that would make the pain go away. Plus, when I drank, I reached a certain point that I allowed myself to act out my homosexuality which I didn't do in sober states. So I would drink to a certain level and then I would get in the car and go to the baths, or the bars, or whatever.[41]

In other words, in an attempt to avoid confronting their homoerotic feelings, some gay men will abuse both drugs and alcohol. As Troiden explains,
"getting high on drugs provides temporary relief from feelings of identity confusion and may be used to justify sexual feelings and behaviours ordinarily
viewed as unacceptable."[42] Gabriel Rotello notes similar findings in his
groundbreaking work on gay men and AIDS, *Sexual Ecology*. In particular, Rotello
notes that many young gay men are increasing their drug use in an attempt to
lose the inhibitions that inevitably result in a society in which gay sex is stigmatized. The outcome, unfortunately, is an increase in the types of unsafe
sexual behaviours that can only result in a community in which self-respect
and respect for others assumes a back seat. Rotello notes that up to 60 percent
of those who have unsafe sex are either drunk or high at the time. While
education strategies to combat alcohol and drug dependency can and have
been implemented, these strategies can do little to combat the more frightening finding that some gay men deliberately use drugs in order to engage in the
kinds of sexual activity they might not engage in were they sober. As Rotello
notes, "They get intoxicated precisely because they want to have unsafe sex
[and] are unable to have it when sober. Only when they are drunk or stoned
are they able to lose their inhibitions, forget about AIDS, and have the sex
they dream of."[43]

Rotello's concerns should not be dismissed. Indeed, we might do well to
make his work mandatory high school reading for all gay youth and those who
educate them. Gay men, especially young men, continue to be the most vulnerable to HIV infection. Indeed, in Canada, the average age of infection
among gay men has fallen dramatically, from 29.6 years between 1975-84 to
24.5 years between 1985-90.[44]

Although Rotello's comments in this instance refer to the links between
HIV/AIDS and substance abuse, his message has much wider implications for
those concerned about the health of a community lacking self-confidence and
in which self-inflicted harm is a daily reality. While it is true that many do
ultimately choose death over anguish, it is also true that others simply fail
to take those precautions that ensure that death and suffering through
HIV/AIDS will not be forthcoming. The two, youth suicide and HIV/AIDS
transmission, are not unrelated.[45] Both find their roots in shame and non-
acceptance, for as Rotello again notes, "shame, after all, is the force that society has traditionally used to try to prevent gay people from being gay in the
first place. One of the primary evils of homophobia is the way it has instilled
a sense of shame in gay men and lesbians around the most basic sense of self
and identity."[46] Rotello further notes that the need to address this fact is particularly evident when dealing with gay youth as "one of the central goals of
gay liberation has been to create a social atmosphere in which young homosexuals can grow up without shame, free to express themselves and their sexuality as openly as heterosexual young people do."[47]

Unfortunately, many gay youth today do not feel free to express themselves. Those who do often do so in ways that have the potential to harm themselves or others. This is a point I will return to shortly. First, however, given what we know about homophobia, it bears asking what we need to do to stop this trend. Once this question has been answered, we can then ask whether, as a community, gay men are themselves doing enough. As one youth worker willing to question the efforts of the gay male community to offer support and guidance explains, the impact of misinformation, vilification, and homophobia affects everyone, regardless of sexuality. The question we need to ask is whether we ourselves are denying young people the opportunity to feel good about themselves.[48]

A reading of much of the literature on gay youth indicates that the self-esteem of young people must underlie any comprehensive health (both mental and physical) education approach. AIDS/Health Educator/Consultant to the Massachusetts Department of Education, Kevin Cranston notes, self-esteem is considered the linchpin in the ability to use the content of health education.[49] Young people cannot be expected to self-preserve or choose healthy behaviours (whether it be good nutrition, seatbelts, or safer sexual practices) if they do not possess a strong sense of personal worth. If we do not offer young gay men positive role models and instil in them a sense of self-worth that merits preservation, we do little to encourage them to protect themselves, for we merely reinforce the belief that they are socially devalued, and not worthy of the protection offered by safe sexual practices.

Similarly, we need to ensure that safe-sex education programs deal with the realities of same-sex sexual activity so that young gay men are made aware of what is and what is not safe sexual activity. This requires an at times blunt and explicit description of what gay sex is and how best to ensure that any sexual activity engaged in is in fact safe. Given that most high schools have adopted sex education curricula, the responsibility to do so should and must rest on those charged with developing and implementing these programs. Safe-sex education is not just about wearing condoms (a point I will return to shortly). Young gay men must also be taught that self-loathing and shame are not normal or acceptable. Teaching self-confidence will assist in saving lives by indicating to gay youth, and students in general, that homosexuality is not a taboo subject, that homosexuals are not socially deviant (hence worthy of abuse and ridicule), and that heterosexuality is not the only sexual orientation worthy of respect, support, and basic human rights protections. Until this occurs, young gay men (indeed, all gay men) will not be in a position to make the types of choices needed to ensure personal safety. As Cranston again argues:

> Beyond a fundamental love of self, young people need to learn a set
> of personal skills around all health issues that enable them to make
> choices that preserve their well being. Among these are skills in

decision-making, communication, relationship building, and the negotiation/refusal of behaviors. While these capabilities have relevance to a number of health concerns, they are crucial to the prevention of HIV and other sexually transmitted diseases. The capacity to choose safer sex, for example, requires that a young person be effective in expressing personal needs, deciding on an acceptable level of risk, maintaining an intimate relationship, and discussing the options of sexual expression with a partner.

High self-esteem and competency in certain personal skills combine to create a sense of self-efficacy, the belief that one possesses the ability to use the learned skills in defence of personal well being. Self-efficacy emerges in much of the research into adolescent HIV prevention as a crucial component in the successful adoption of risk reducing practices.[50]

Cranston and others argue that this process must begin within schools and cannot be left entirely to the gay community. This is not to say that the gay community does not have a role. Nor does it deny that many schools simply do not do that which they *should* do. The goal, Cranston argues, must be personal and collective empowerment, a supportive environment in which young gay people can enter into a critical dialogue about their lives in the presence of both HIV and heterosexism.[51] Students need this, and both educators and gay activists committed to it have a responsibility to provide it.

Is Pornography the Answer?

Many gay advocates argued during the *Little Sisters* case that pornography is what it takes to save gay youth from self-destruction. At trial, the Canadian AIDS Society (CAS) quite accurately noted the need for safe-sex educational materials aimed at promoting self-esteem and preservation. Arguing that healthy sexual identity fosters responsible sexual behaviour and the practice of "safer sex," essential to curbing the transmission of HIV/AIDS,[52] CAS called for the distribution of materials that are sexually explicit, frank, and direct: "[a]ltering human sexual behaviour, the object of AIDS education, is a daunting task. Simply put, safer sex education is impossible without talking about sex. Clinical depictions of safer sex are simply not as effective as materials with erotic content or with an erotic subtext."[53]

Similar arguments were advanced by EGALE, which, promoting the link between positive presentations of sexuality and the reduction of self-inflicted harms and HIV transmission, argued that the "unequivocal message conveyed by mainstream cultural representations is that heterosexuality is the (almost universal) norm, and our lesbian, gay, and bisexual sexualities are unnatural, deviant, and perverse."[54]

In this regard, EGALE relied on the testimony of Thomas Waugh, who stated that "the gay community is a stigmatized and abused community" within which young gay people are taught to feel shame about their bodies and sexuality.[55] The solution to the isolation caused from this stigma is, according to EGALE, "sexually explicit lesbian, gay, and bisexual materials," because they "challenge the dominant cultural discourse" and provide "affirmation and validation of our sexual identities by normalizing and celebrating homo- and bi-sexual practices, which mainstream culture either ignores or condemns."[56]

In a similar vein, LEAF, relying on findings that suicide attempts appear to be two to fourteen times higher among lesbian, gay, and bisexual youth than among heterosexual youth, argued that the suppression of lesbian and gay materials fosters the oppression of lesbians and gay men through invisibility and denigration.[57] Arguing that these materials perform a critical role in developing and nurturing lesbian, gay, bisexual, and transgendered communities and cultures, LEAF argued that to overcome social isolation, lesbians and gay men set out to learn about a new culture and to find more accepting communities.[58] Sexually explicit materials, according to LEAF, serve as a compass, pointing lost lesbians and gay men in the right direction, particularly when it comes to learning about safe-sex sexual practices: "[m]aterials about safer sex practices, sexual health and HIV must present information in a format appropriate for the intended audience. The format must be sensitive, amongst other things to the literacy level, sexual orientation, occupation, language, abilities, and age of that audience. Prohibiting access to this information endangers health."[59]

There is little reason to disagree with these arguments concerning the education of gay youth about sexuality and identity. In isolation, the points raised regarding the need for education about safe sex and positive sexual attitudes are supported by all those working in the field of youth health education; it is hard to imagine anyone in this field of study taking issue with them. It is their context and purpose that become problematic.

All these statements are made within the context of a court case aimed at ensuring the production and distribution of lesbian and gay male pornography. The arguments of sex education thus have the effect of defending the materials outlined in Chapter 3, materials with titles such as "I Was a Substitute Vagina," "Conservatives in South Dakota Call Youth Faggot Whilst Raping Him," "I Slapped Him Until He Came," and "Pass Me Another Young Boy: This One Is Split." In this setting, the arguments become harder to justify. CAS, for example, pointed out – correctly – that schools are not doing what they must to promote positive and life-affirming gay sexualities. This, the group argued, means that

> [h]omosexuals, especially young gay men, are more likely to turn to sexually stimulating material available at well known commercial outlets like Little Sisters to become informed about their sexuality and health;[60]

> The deleterious effects of the seizure and ban of material designed
> to educate gay men about "safer sex" are significant. Because many
> gay men do not access mainstream materials on the prevention of
> HIV or AIDS, the materials at issue in the within appeal are one of the
> few tools available to educate gay men on "safer sex" practices.[61]

This is true to some extent, but rather than query whether these materials *do* achieve what the group argued they should, CAS simply stated that the materials sold in these stores must be protected, implying, one is left to believe, that these materials represent the types of educational materials they would have distributed in schools were schools more willing to tackle homophobia head on. This is evident in CAS's assertion that pornography is important to self-worth and that self-worth is the key to safe-sex sexual practices.[62] Justifying pornography as a source of effective AIDS education, the group concluded, quoting from the Yale AIDS Law Project, that "when the only known means of curbing an epidemic is education, but effective educational materials offend some members of the public, how should the interests of the public's sensibility and the public's health be balanced? When the cost of not offending someone is someone else's death, the answer to the question should be clear."[63]

In a similar line of reasoning, EGALE again relied on the testimony of Waugh and lesbian activists Becki Ross and Chris Bearchell in defending the sale and distribution of gay pornography as examples of the kind of safe-sex materials needed to promote self-awareness and empowerment. Waugh argued that, through pornography, young gay men "learn to discover that there are other people out there like them. They learn to acquire feelings of self-worth and dignity and belonging to a larger community."[64] Ross, in turn, stated that lesbian-specific materials validate lesbian sexuality as healthy, as meaningful, and as empowering because they provide lesbian readers or viewers with an avenue for self-affirmation.[65] To this Bearchell added that pornography provides young women with affirmation for their desires, helping them discover that sex between women can be enjoyable as well as possible. This, we are told, allows these young women to "reach out to others with similar experiences and to find a place to belong and a way to contribute to [their] world."[66]

EGALE continued by arguing that sexually explicit lesbian, gay, and bisexual materials also empower us in other ways. For example, "they make a valuable contribution to the historical and contemporary documentation of lesbian, gay, and bisexual existence and experience. In that respect, they are critical to the formation, evolution, and continued vitality of our communities."[67] Here, EGALE relied on the work of Karen Mitstysyn, who has written that "anyone who comes out [as lesbian, gay, or bisexual] knows the need usually to read literature and find out about one's history or identity."[68]

Finally, EGALE attempted to build a bridge between positive sexual identities and safe sex by arguing that "explicit lesbian, gay, and bisexual materials also serve as an important source of information used to promote healthy and safe sexual practices within our communities. In that respect, they perform a crucial educative function that is not fulfilled by mainstream pornographic materials, which are directed at heterosexual audiences and are therefore largely irrelevant to us." In this context, the group again relied on the work of Chris Bearchell, who wrote: "The health of individual lesbians and gay men and of our community itself – and the success of the overall battle against AIDS – are seriously threatened by efforts to restrict or eliminate those aspects of lesbian and gay culture and community which foster sexual knowledge, discussion, representation and safe sexual behaviour."[69]

Although Ross and Bearchell refer here and above to lesbian content only, their arguments are equally applicable to young gay men; similar arguments have been made by gay men attempting to justify the sale of gay male pornography. The same can be said of arguments raised by LEAF, who, in defending the materials on trial in this case, argued: "The creation and distribution of materials about lesbian sexuality affirm this sexuality by presenting it as healthy and meaningful. Such materials are about self-exploration and creating cultural communities. Lesbian materials also attempt to counter dominant heterosexist misrepresentations of lesbian sexuality as perverse and deviant."[70]

Finally, relying on the work of author Nino Ricci, LEAF attempted to convince the Court that the pornography in question must be seen as a positive source of validation and affirmation: "[v]alidation literature ... [is] a literature which serves to say we are here, this is what we are ... they are establishing the right of a community to speak ... about a reality that is often not documented in mainstream sources, that is often reviled or stigmatized. And therefore ... these works perform the work that literature and art often performs."[71]

One wonders whether these groups have looked at the materials they are defending, to see what they convey about safety and respect. If many of the materials defended in *Little Sisters* embody the identity championed by pro-pornography and pro-gay advocates, as these groups say they do, the "safe sex" they uphold is a sexuality of inequality and it is far from safe. The question is, what impact do such materials have on those who, for the reasons discussed thus far, are already disenfranchised and socially and sexually disempowered?

If I Said You Had a Beautiful Body Would You Hold It against Me?
Sacrificing Safety for Sexual Acceptance
Doubtless some who advocated eliminating Canada's anti-pornography laws in *Little Sisters* did not specifically intend their call for safe-sex materials to include all the materials that would be permitted to circulate if their side won.

But their arguments did *not* – and rarely do – draw distinctions between such materials and what they do defend. Nor do those who rely on their efforts and analysis when defending this same pornography. As Roger Myrick explains, gay community-based safe-sex education strategies show men engaged in various sexually explicit activities in which condoms are used.[72] The men shown in these materials are supposed to be representative of the gay community generally. As such, these materials frequently present men dressed in leather or cowboy attire, and show various sexual activities, including sado-masochism, water sports, and phone sex. This, we are told, allows gay communities to "construct erotic messages that speak to their desires and correspond to their various relationships to the world."[73]

Given what we already know about the content of gay pornography and what that content does, the question that needs to be asked here is whether the fact that a condom is actually shown or discussed (and recall that often it isn't) is enough to ensure that the sexual acts and relationships referred to by Myrick and defended throughout the *Little Sisters* trial are "safe" once used by gay men.

In a courageous 1994 *Harvard Civil Rights, Civil Liberties Law Review* article, law professor David Chambers discusses and criticizes the gay movement's safe-sex strategy, which he labels "the code of the condom."[74] According to this code, the dangers of unsafe sex lie only in unsafe anal sex. Hence, campaigns for safer sex focus almost exclusively on the use of condoms during anal intercourse. The core rule we are told is that "anal sex is fine, but always use a condom." Chambers expresses concern with this strategy, noting the reliability problems associated with condoms generally and the dangers of unsafe oral sex (something not readily incorporated into the condom code). Even more importantly, Chambers queries whether the condom code as it now stands can really save lives if the messages conveyed do not also address the emotional baggage, shame, and self-loathing often carried by men who have sex with men. That is, is it enough to insist on the use of a condom during anal sex without also addressing the social stigma under which these men live? Put more bluntly, can condoms work if some gay men do not feel they merit protection in the first place? Chambers writes:

> If research about stigma and self-labeling in other contexts applies here, some of these men, already struggling with heterosexual society's judgment that they are immoral because of who they are, may well redefine (or reconfirm) themselves as the sort of person who does bad or stupid things. These men become more likely to engage in unprotected sex in the future. Moreover, their feelings of shame may keep them silent about the risks they take, when they should talk to others for counseling and renewed resolve.[75]

Chambers offers a number of alternatives to the code as it now stands. One is to encourage gay men to avoid anal sex. The fortitude it takes even to suggest such a radical alternative should not be underestimated.[76] Gay men have attached a great deal of significance to the act of fucking and are not likely to respond positively or warmly to the suggestion that gay sex without it can still be gay sex.

I am not convinced that gay men will give up anal sex. Nor am I convinced that gay men are in any great rush to reduce the number of men they have sex with. The further questions that need to be asked then are, how do we encourage gay men to use a condom when they do have sex, and, more importantly, is there a way to get them to think about what it means to have sex with each other that reduces the more dangerous sexual activities? Chambers concludes by asking that we find new ways to deliver our current messages more effectively and to think afresh about what our messages should be.[77] I want here to accept this challenge by suggesting that, rather than simply telling gay men not to have anal sex, we need first to reconstruct the entire notion of what it takes to have sex with men – who is entitled to it and what it means. In this regard, I want to build on the work of Gabriel Rotello, who argues that what we need is a gay sexuality not premised on the ideal of sexual conquest:

> In many ways the prevailing gay urban ethos seems just as overwhelmingly sex-oriented in the 1990s as it was in the clone culture of the 1970s. Although there are now gay churches and community centres and sports clubs, the central gay institutions in large cities remain bars and discos, and much of the urban social scene continues to confer status and self-respect primarily on the basis of looks, muscles, and sexual conquest. This seems so deeply embedded at the heart of the gay male world that virtually all of [the] behaviors that need to be modified if we are to build a sustainable culture instead continue to be hailed by some leaders as the essence of gay life.[78]

What I aim to argue throughout the remainder of this chapter is that to the extent that we use pornography to learn about sex and to the extent our present safe-sex and youth-oriented campaigns rely on the sex pornography sells and causes in order to educate about safety, we cannot expect condoms, seen as *the* means of protection, to work. Nor can we expect young gay men to take those steps necessary to even begin to question the types of sexual and personal behaviours they presently engage in and that are, quite literally, killing them.

Safe Sex as Gay Sex: The Condom as Stigma

As noted, there is a move among some gay pornography producers to create films in which the actors do not use condoms. Other producers attempt to disguise the condoms being used, thus offering the viewer a sexual act in which the condom is barely visible. What these producers are promoting is a practice referred to as "barebacking," or unprotected anal sex. As West Australian journalist David Menadue explains, the term was initially used by pornography "star" Scott O'Hara, who, in his magazine *Steam*, a journal about sex in public places, wrote, "I'm tired of using a condom and I won't ... and I don't feel the need to encourage negatives to stay negative."[79]

Although the practice of deliberately and knowingly having sex without a condom initially occurred only between HIV-positive men, it is now apparent that it has taken on far greater significance in the lives of many gay men, becoming instead something seen as subversive, daring, and sexually liberating. A read of a number of the newer barebacking Web sites from the United States, for example, reveals that what appeals to these men is the element of danger involved in unsafe sex. Because it is dangerous, it is more sexy, more of a turn on: "I'm negative and I want to play Russian Roulette with poz cum. The thought of getting infected has me rock hard. I like lots of danger sex, like letting strangers tie me up and blindfold me and fuck me bareback, so I don't know anything about the guys fucking me. Make arrangements to meet me on a street corner or a park where you'll find me blindfolded and lead me to your van to use me. Anyone want to give me a gift?"[80]

Dangerous sex is experienced as more sexy: when you risk death, you heighten arousal. Safe sex, under this model, does not eroticize danger and harm: it is not sexy. Gay sex, then, to be sexy, must equate with dangerous sex. For as Menadue notes, while it is clear that some of these men are generally just opposed to the "AIDS establishment" in the United States, describing mandatory condom use as too limiting to the point of being oppressive, it is also clear that others simply see safer sex as boring and not really gay sex.[81] As one writer explains, "I was so afraid of becoming positive for such a long time and once it happened I felt relief. I also decided I didn't want to spend my whole life going without the sex I love the most."[82]

These attitudes, now enforced in pornography, say a lot about what gay sex means today. What one sees in gay pornography and in the statements of those who like what it says is a sexual model that copies the power inequalities present in straight sex – sex through which (male) power is gained by controlling and dominating those around you. Given that the gay sex presented in gay pornography attempts to look, quite successfully, a lot like the sex that straight men have in straight pornography, and given that, socially, the act of penetration determines who controls who, and who, as a result, gets male power, and given that all pornography focuses on the right of the masculine top to penetrate the disempowered bottom, be this a woman or a less aggressive man who as such is socially feminized, deemed less male, and rendered socially less significant, it is not surprising that gay pornography continues to present unprotected penetrative sex – that is, penetration in which the condom is either not used or, for the purposes of pornography, carefully concealed. Safe sex has come to be regarded as gay sex (hence less "male"). It is less male because it is less dominant, not as dangerous, not as life-threatening, not as sexually stimulating. Thus, gay sex that rejects safe sexual presentations becomes descriptively less gay, socially more "male" – the real identity sold in gay male pornography. Its result is such that "safe sex" in the current sexual paradigm becomes an oxymoron.

Returning to the writer quoted above, it is apparent that if the "sex we love the most" remains the sex seen in pornography, those of us who do care about protection and self-preservation have our work cut out for us. Given what the sex in gay pornography has come to represent, it is clear that in many ways safe sex stands to emasculate the pornographic symbol. For safe sex to work, one needs to accept that both parties have rights and that both are sexual equals. Both parties merit protection and both have the right to a recognized human existence. In a sense, safe sex represents a form of sexual negotiation imposing limits on sexual conduct – negotiation that presupposes relatively equal parties. More importantly, however, it recognizes that there are limits on what you can do to someone else through sex and what they, in turn, can do to you.

Gay author Michelangelo Signorile writes that this notion of equality fell out of the equation soon after AIDS became a reality for gay men and all men generally, with AIDS exacerbating gay men's insecurities about masculinity and eventually cementing rigid gender roles defined though sex:

> Now the sexual "bottom" was the focus of negative attention. In much of the public's eyes – and certainly in the eyes of many gay men – it was the submissive "feminine" role in homosexual sex that led to disease. Being healthy was now associated with taking the "manly" role in sex, the top – or at least pretending to. The term "straight-acting," a term to signify masculinity, became more popular than ever in the personals of gay publications and throughout gay cyberspace and was seemingly accepted – or at least reluctantly so – by much of the community.[83]

Given this, and given that gay pornography presents a sexuality in which "real" men can do what they want sexually, when they want, and to whom, it is not surprising that the condom itself, an "appliance" that imposes a limit on this right, becomes gendered and is not promoted. Much like straight sex, sex in which women are made responsible for protecting themselves physically with contraceptive techniques and devices that can cause irreparable harm and sometimes death, and in which men are deemed to have no responsibility whatsoever for the safety and comfort of their partners, gay sex, as presented in gay pornography, teaches gay men that real men do as they please, while fags, because they are feminized, simply hope for the best. This option is particularly troubling since many of the men in gay pornography are offered no voice with which to insist on safe sex and are instead told that they should simply find gratification underneath the weight of a real man who wants to use them – to death, in some instances.

Gay male pornography, in common with all pornography, treats those it uses as objects that deserve only to be used and ultimately discarded. Its message is that inequality – between the user and the used, the subject and the object, the inserter and the insertee – is the norm. The dominant male it glorifies is invariably straight-acting, and the person upon whom he acts is not. Even when only one figure is shown, the problem arises, as the figure presented is invariably the idealized masculine norm – an ideal now permeating popular gay male culture such that it has, in many ways, become a pornographic culture devoid of those qualities on which true equality must be built – or a body which, once exploited, allows the viewer to become the masculine icon he longs to be. Given that for so many gay men gay pornography *is* gay male, it is not surprising that the messages gay men use to educate each other about safe sex tend to mimic and rely on the body imagery and sexual identity sexualized in gay pornography.

HIV/AIDS education aimed at the gay male community almost invariably relies on the use of young white men who are hyper-fit, hyper-masculine, and hyper-"male." A recent flyer circulated by the West Australian AIDS Council, for example, features the muscled torso of a young man posing in a pair of tight-fitting Calvin Klein underwear, the outline of his semi-erect penis clearly visible. The flyer was intended to encourage gay men to attend a series of workshops on safe sexual practices. It is typical of the materials used today to teach gay men about safe sex. Similar flyers can probably be found in most HIV/AIDS organizations elsewhere in Australia and throughout Canada and the United States.

The efficacy of this image as a method of teaching gay men about HIV transmission and AIDS needs to be questioned. Analysis of the messages it and others like it convey says a great deal about how gay men are supposed to look, act, and feel about their sexual identity. This is particularly evident if we examine what safe sex is and what safe sex requires.

Safe sex is often referred to by safe-sex advocates as a process of negotiation. Building on this, I propose the following theory of safe sexual practices:

1 Safe sex requires negotiation between those having sex.
2 Such negotiation requires that the parties treat themselves and each other as valued human beings, deserving of equality, reciprocity, and respect.
3 Self-esteem is critical and required before we can respect ourselves and others and ultimately engage as equals with others.

4 Equality lies at the heart of self-esteem.
5 You have to want to be safe. Safe sexual practices thus have to be arousing sexually if they are to find acceptance.
6 Equality then must be made sexy.

The question that needs to be asked is whether the messages gay men are presently conveying to each other about same-sex sexual activity support the type of equality-based relationships with others needed to ensure negotiation among equals, safe sexual practices, self-preservation, and the preservation of others. Or, is the sexuality of pornography consistent with safe sex?

In the West Australian AIDS Council flyer, we cannot tell "who" this young man is (we are presented only with a muscular, white torso). We are thus left to ask "what" he is. He – what we see of him – is only part of a person. He is incomplete and anonymous, with no identity other than his body. He is presented as an object, not as a whole person. In a world in which gay men are forced (sometimes violently) to hide their real identities, this image invites us to treat others as objectified parts of bodies, as "things" devoid of human identity.

This is problematic for a number of reasons. To begin with, it is only when someone is recognized as a subject, rather than a thing, that we usually feel obliged to think about who he is, what we are doing to him, and to care about what the consequences of our actions are for him. More importantly, it is only when we have the subject in mind that negotiation even begins to be relevant – assuming, of course, that you recognize him as one. The image also presents what many in the gay male community today perceive to be the physical ideal. The flyer could easily be taken from any number of "soft" gay male pornographic magazines presently available throughout Australia. As noted, many in the gay male community believe gay pornography is central to the development and formation of gay male identity.

As outlined in previous chapters, gay male pornography invites the man who uses it to participate in a sexual dynamic premised on sexual inequality. With titles such as "Beat Me Till I Come," "Stud Daddy," and "I Was a Substitute Vagina," it sends a clear message about what the idealized gay male is in today's society: young, muscular, "good looking," preferably white, definitely able-bodied. In all these materials, it is the white, physically more powerful, more dominant, ostensibly straight male who is rewarded with role model status. The result is a sexuality that is rarely mutual and based on compassion or respect for others – in sum, an identity politics that mimics a model of behaviour which is more concerned with the use and abuse of others found in the form of sexual hierarchy than with liberation from that hierarchy. Negotiation, of any sort, is not an issue here.

Given that pornography is now, for many gay men, a sexual practice, this raises issues that require immediate attention. Gay men assert that we are not to blame for AIDS. We cannot, however, state with the same certainty that we offer each other any incentive to care about ourselves, to look to the future, and to recognize that our lives are worth preserving. We tell each other that to be gay is to live, through sex, for the moment – to use it while you have it and to make sure that if you don't have it, you work hard to get it. Because we are encouraged to participate in a sexual game devoid of caring and compassion, both for ourselves and others, a game that focuses only on controlling or being controlled sexually, we define our personal integrity through our sexual encounters – by how often we get sex and with whom. For many, the power of sex, of stimulation and arousal found in "getting off" with or as a "real" man, far outweighs any need for mutual preservation. If you believe that you have no right to question, that you should get turned on when a real man uses you sexually, or that to be a real man you need to eroticize the sexual conquest of a sexual inferior, mutual respect and safety take a back seat – with often catastrophic results. Inequality is made sexy, unsafe sex the norm.

This problem is part of a broader problem of identification. Even when we do "come out," our sexuality remains anonymous. We fail to own it. It is not a part of us but, rather, something we treat as separate from our individuality. When we sexually interact with others, we see ourselves as operating on a sexual basis only. We don't interact as individuals. Sex becomes anonymous, through which objectification is permitted and made sexy in this model. Why, then, worry about someone you see only in sexual terms? Indeed, why ask that they care about you?

Legal academic Carl Stychin has argued that "rather than focusing on sexual practices and representations, as gay men we need to examine how we treat our employees, students, co-workers and friends, as well as our sexual partners in our everyday lives and the extent to which our dealings undermine (or reinforce) systems of gender, racial and sexual oppression."[84] This is not an either-or matter. To the extent that Stychin's analysis calls on us to examine how we treat each other, I agree, although I would add that we also need to reflect on how we treat ourselves. I fail to see, however, how gay men can do so without *also* examining, questioning, and ultimately rejecting the reasons why we treat people as we do. That is, how can we even begin to figure out why gay men are the way we are and why and how our actions *do* reinforce oppressive gender, racial, and sexual constructs, without first focusing on our sexual and interpersonal practices and the means by which we are taught the tools of oppression? In essence, Stychin's analysis assumes that gay male pornography does *not* impact our everyday lives, and that one can simply examine the lives and actions of gay men without also examining why we act the way we do.

Whether it be within the confines of the gay bar, gym, bathhouse, cruising park, or even on the street, gay male identity today is concerned less with compassion and any commitment to others than with self-gratification and the satisfaction of knowing that gay men can also reap the benefits afforded "real" men so long as they are willing and able to become these men.[85] I have often heard gay men boast that they have redefined manhood by cloning their oppressors, such that it is now difficult to distinguish between straight and gay. This is not a redefinition. It is mimicry and assimilation leading to gay male invisibility, the closet, and subordination. Pro-pornography advocates admit that gay pornography acts as a learning tool in a society in which homosexuality remains taboo and in which learning tools are rare.[86] Perhaps, but is this a lesson worth learning? Given what gay male pornography says about appropriate gay male behaviour and identity generally, should we not be concerned about its role in a community in which gay men have excelled at becoming, or want desperately to become, the men society has told them they should have been all along?

The gay male entering a gay bar or seeking physical, sexual contact in gay zones such as a bathhouse is confronted with a community quick to define his status, his role in that sexual "game" we call cruising. Cruising, objectifying others or waiting to be objectified, relies heavily on the type of role play and model of behaviour offered in gay pornography. Specifically, gay men in bars cease to be people. They are denied a human identity and are instead offered a predetermined sexual identity void of humanity. They become the chests, buttocks, and bulging biceps meant to turn others on, and if they fail to meet the sexual standard, they simply cease to exist. The result for many is a concerted effort to become the embodiment of physical perfection. They follow a recipe for success in which masculinity is the main ingredient[87] and soon define, and are defined, according to what they think their bodies are going to do *to* others or *for* others.

This point is made all too clear in Signorile's brilliant overview of contemporary trends in the gay male community and, in particular, its commitment to what he refers to as "body fascism," which he describes as

> the setting of a rigid set of standards of physical beauty that pressures everyone within a particular group to conform to them. Any person who doesn't meet those very specific standards is deemed physically unattractive and sexually undesirable ... In this sense it is not unlike racism or sexism or homophobia itself. In this worst-case scenario, the only way one can become valued *as a person* is if one conforms to the set of standards – if one is lucky enough, from a genetic perspective, to be able to do so.[88]

To this I would add only that the basis of body fascism is homophobia, racism, and sexism in that what it does is penalize, through rejection, those who do not conform to the standards that ensure heterosexual male dominance. As

Rotello notes, gay culture "has developed a powerful, even merciless system of rewards and penalties based on body image."[89] Conformity is sexualized under this model, gay male invisibility and inequality the end result.

Conformity, in the form of hyper-masculinity, promises the gay male the self-confidence lacking in so many of us. But what of those who do not conform? This need to blend, and to be all that a community obsessed with manliness says a man should be, can, it is clear, result in incredible self-loathing, low self-esteem, and self-hate. The standard set is not easily met nor easily maintained. As writer Will Harris explains, "porn videos – with [their] tired images and stereotypes of perfect pumped up blondes and smooth dark men with large penises – can only compound feelings of poor self-image."[90] Dr. Richard Quinn, a Sydney-based physician, agrees. He argues that "[p]eople can develop serious psychological problems from images presented to them, and images in porn videos contribute to this. So many gays feel they haven't got anything to offer because they can't live up to the expectations that are thrown at them on how they should look. They feel that because they don't have that certain look, nobody wants them."[91]

For many gay men – men who have been denied participation in a society quick to suppress their self-expression and individual development – the sexual representations the gay male community offers as identity also result in an overwhelming sense of non-belonging. As journalist Dave Ford, writing for the *San Francisco Bay Times,* explains, "[w]hen Sexland spills over into the real world – at clubs, say, or at the gym, or in the Castro – I once again feel an outsider, same as I did when I was the only queer boy (that I knew of) in a straight high school class. I feel excluded by my community, or a piece of it; on bad days, my self-image nose-dives."[92]

Should it surprise us then that this too, when combined with the effects of homophobic rejection generally, has already taken its toll on our community and the community at large? The spectre of AIDS has shown us that we can care and we must care. We have not, however, carried this over into our sexual relationships, and, perhaps ironically, this has only worsened the reality of AIDS in our community. This is evident in the words of one of the gay men interviewed by Signorile. A twenty-seven-year-old Miami nurse who, at five foot nine and 220 pounds, describes himself as "tubby," Larry finds that he is willing to have unsafe sex if it means going home with someone better looking than himself: "I've allowed men to fuck me without condoms on more occasions than I can count, quite honestly ... I can't believe he'd even consider having sex with me. And when he does, it's anything goes. I just don't think about it. I'm too caught up in it. And he is too, because he doesn't think about it either."[93]

Signorile argues that these perceptions put gay men at risk by lowering their self-esteem, by making unsafe sex sexy and normal. Describing an encounter with a friend in a gym with whom he is having a discussion about safe sex,

Signorile quotes his friend as saying, in reference to a "hunky guy doing crunches on the floor," that "[I]f I were drunk, I'd probably allow him to fuck me without rubbers ... What worries me is that I feel so beneath guys like that, I'd allow them to do *anything*."[94]

While it is, of course, true that pornography alone cannot be held accountable for the insecurity – the hierarchy – so evident in the words of these men and the sexual stereotypes they embody, it is also true that pornography cannot be excluded as a source of these feelings either or the actions resulting from them. One American pornography "star" is on record as stating that "people who have problems about their appearance or weight shouldn't blame pornography videos or magazines for their problems."[95] Really? If, as those appearing before the Supreme Court of Canada in *Little Sisters* assert, gay pornography is the sole sexual outlet for many gay men, why should it surprise us that for many, gay pornography videos and magazines – with their presentation of "pumped up blondes and smooth dark men with large penises" – powerfully reinforce already socially enforced feelings of poor self-image? Of course, the argument can be made that gay men do not have to use gay pornography. They can instead find validation elsewhere. But where exactly? The bars and dance clubs? The same bars that promote the message so actively championed in gay pornography, and which again remind gay men that they fail to meet the expectations of an image-conscious scene obsessed with muscle and beauty? If not there, where? Should they avoid being judged and sneered at by others and instead resort to that "sole outlet" of positive imagery where the only ones sneering at and judging them are themselves?

This, of course, also offers a response to those who would argue that the private enjoyment of erotica provides an opportunity to practise the "safest sex" possible for individuals because you simply masturbate to it, rather than have bodily contact with a human being (the catharsis hypothesis). To this one need only ask, where is the safety in self-deprecation or in the use of materials that encourage you to treat yourself and those around you with contempt and discrimination, as unequals?

The choices offered are far from appealing or equality promoting. Criticism, from others or self-inflicted, takes its toll. For many, it results in the silence found in disempowerment – empowerment being the very thing needed by a minority community in search of equality. Aware that they cannot participate, many gay men often simply refuse to do so, thus limiting the public strength found in numbers, and ensure in turn that the mass visibility needed to effect change never emerges.

Ethnic Gay Youth
The dynamic just analyzed would seem to be particularly destructive for ethnic gay youth. As is best evidenced by the pornography introduced at trial during the *Little Sisters* case, our community's track record of inclusion and

diversity is less than impressive. If, as some safe-sex advocates and youth workers would have us believe, we need pornography because it is the only way for young gay men to develop the sense of worth needed to address youth suicide and prevent the transmission of HIV/AIDS, one is left to ponder how this argument applies to those young men who are not white. How, specifically, does a young black male find acceptance in a community that fights for the right to market the magazine *Sex Stop,* in which an adult black man is quoted as saying to a young white boy, "[W]ould you like a slave like me, boy?" Similarly, how should a young Asian male react to a magazine such as *Oriental Guys,* which, sexualizing his race, feminizes him for the purpose of someone else's sexual arousal?

According to psychologists Bob Tremble, Margaret Schneider, and Carol Appathurai, an unspoken myth exists that the homosexual community, as a culture of people who know oppression, is tolerant and accepting of differences. Unfortunately, the experiences of ethnic gay men reveal the opposite.[96] This was perhaps most blatantly demonstrated in the mid-1980s, following the publication of a "wanted" ad in the Toronto gay newspaper the *Body Politic:*

> BLACK MALE WANTED
> HANDSOME, SUCCESSFUL, GAY WHITE MALE, would like young, well-built BLACK MALE for houseboy. Ideal for student or young business-man. Some traveling and affection required. Reply with letter, phone, photo.

Prior to the publication of the ad, a black male on the editorial board of the *Body Politic* asked that it be pulled. It was not. Shortly thereafter, the newspaper was inundated with letters from gay men in the community, defending or criticizing the paper for allowing the ad to run. A number of men, predominantly white, attempted to justify its content as mere fantasy and sexual desire. Others adopted the libertarian and not unrelated stance that all speech is good speech if it helps clear the air. One of the paper's editors, Gerald Hannon, expressed "shame" that the paper would even think of "censoring" the ad, arguing that it was important to validate the writer's sexual desires, thereby allowing him to know that male-male sexual desire is okay. In a similar vein, gay activist Ken Poppart wrote that, to his mind, gay liberation is about sex, and when people start censoring classified ads for political reasons, his immediate reaction is to feel threatened.[97]

The responses from both Asian and black men, the men most silenced by Hannon's ode to freedom, as well as the words of white men unwilling to build their sexual fantasies on the backs of men of colour, say much about empowerment and validation. Always eloquent and to the point, gay Asian-Canadian writer Richard Fung, for example, responded:

> Things aren't always what they seem. At first glance, the emancipation of desire appears to be a very straight forward goal [but] to champion the cause of uninhibited desire without addressing the impact of racism and sexism in the sexual arena is to call for the entrenchment of white male privilege ... Last year I responded to an article in *TBP* which said something like "we as lesbians and gays understand homophobia, but we don't understand racism." I replied that some of us do because some of us are not white ... Non-white lesbians and gay men are just not seen as totally gay. We are outsiders, our interests are appendices.[98]

Another writer explained that the issue is not one of sexuality versus racism; the two should not be separated:

> As a magazine for gay liberation, our responsibility is not so much towards the expression of the sexual desire of any individual or group of individuals. Our responsibility is primarily towards the task of building a gay community, defending it, developing it and helping the gay movement mature and become a social force powerful enough to guarantee *all* gay people the respect and the justice that we deserve as human beings. While the exploration of our sexualities is an important part of that community development, it does not follow that anyone's desire is somehow inviolable. We do not support the desire which fulfils itself in the practice of rape, no matter how much a turn on rape may be for rapists. There are clearly acceptable and unacceptable expressions of desire. Its effects on the lives and rights of others are a clear limitation.[99]

I have argued earlier that sexual expression must be addressed to the extent that it encourages some to act out against others. In a similar way, it merits arguing that in this context, limitations must be placed on those forms of sexual expression that, when interpreted by those who do not conform, can result only in confusion and self-inflicted harm. This is particularly relevant for gay ethnic youth, for, as Tremble, Schneider, and Appathurai again explain within the context of their work with Toronto's ethnic communities, the ethnic youth, particularly from a visible minority, faces double discrimination – race discrimination from those outside his cultural community who are white and sexuality discrimination from those within it who are straight. As one gay Chinese adolescent from Hong Kong stated, "I am a double minority. Caucasian gays don't like gay Chinese, and the Chinese don't like gays. It would be easier to be white. It would be easier to be straight. It's hard to be both." Add to this, discrimination within the gay community itself against those who are not white, and what one gets is a population of young men with "inadequate coping techniques, poor self-concept and stereotyped behaviour."[100]

Today's reality seems to be that we have learned little from the debates of the past. Indeed, the debate is ongoing. The *Body Politic* ad mentioned above could have appeared in any one of the magazines outlined in Chapter 3. Many of these magazines sexualize black men for their supposed ability to dominate; others seek out Asian youth for their ability to submit. All require and lust after inequality, both racial and sexual. In 1992, for example, the gay magazine *Campaign* put a young Asian male on its cover. This was a first and, if the reaction of its readers is any indication, it may be the last. A month after its publication, a reader wrote to the editor, complaining about the use of an Asian male:

> How come there are thousands of gay men coming out from Asian countries? Who lets them in when there are thousands of American, German, Irish, Hungarian and Italian queens who could immigrate getting knocked off? ... It is OK to go to bed (for one night) with a coloured person but to have an everlasting love affair is out of the question. So you are kidding yourself when you feature an Asian on the cover and try to be multiracial. There are only a few white men interested in the small Asian dick. You can show me a small dick and show me a big black one and it is more important to go off with the big black one than the small Asian one.[101]

The appalling racism this letter justifies, and its sexualization, is indicative of a community in which inequality is made acceptable, sexy, through sex. For the gay youth, attitudes of this sort, propped up by pornography and then mainstreamed into gay male culture, send a clear message: you are an outcast, hated, unequal. The consequences of these messages are well documented and were squarely addressed by the Supreme Court of Canada in its decision in *Keegstra*, in which the Court sought to address the harms of racist hate speech. Indeed, one might query whether in Canada this letter could constitute hate speech, actionable under both the *Canadian Criminal Code* and the various provincial human rights statutes, if it could be proven to undermine the equality rights of Asian men. Recall that in *Keegstra*, the Court noted that one of the harms of racial vilification is its ability to humiliate and degrade those targeted by it, thereby making them unable to participate as full members of society. Could it not be argued that letters such as the above do just this? In this regard, it is worth quoting the words of another young man who, responding to the claims of sexual fantasy articulated by those quick to defend the *Body Politic* ad, argued that "although we demand the freedom to play with the symbols of social power, our goal is to overcome the abuse of that power in the real world. The ad does not ask for someone to pretend to be black. The racial difference required is real. The power difference required is real. The ad calls for a real relationship based on historical stereotypes."[102]

In agreeing, I would add only that all the pornography discussed thus far does what he and others find so objectionable. The sexuality it asks us to support does not ask that we pretend to be disempowered. The inequality required is real, its consequences not a fiction. Gay male pornography, like all pornography, calls for real relationships based on those historical stereotypes that harm all gay men and those who suffer as a result of our desire to buy into the racial, gender, and sexual inequality it eroticizes. As *Body Politic* writer Tim McCaskell notes, we *have* allowed for the sexualization of rape and inequality, and therefore, I fear, we send a particularly damaging message to those men most in need of courage and a community of support.

Conformity as Invisibility/Mimicry as Self-Hate
Of course, the question also has to be asked, and what of those who do fit in, who find validation in assimilation through masculine mimicry? What of those who become what our community and its models of masculine behaviour say they should be? Will they alone ensure gay male liberation? I think not. Mimicry ensures only that those who cannot or who choose not to conform – and who, as a result, continue to threaten heterosexual male privilege – become the victims of greater physical and emotional abuse and discrimination. Because they continue to challenge the normality of gender polarity and in the process undermine male supremacy, these "non-conformists" will remain the objects of brutal suppression. This in turn reinforces the idea that gay men can either fail to conform to male standards and be the feminized other that society has always told them they are (and thus be further abused) or they can copy them. Copying male standards, however, will not make their effect less harmful. For many, mimicry will result in self-hate. As researchers Lynette Lewis and Michael Ross explain within the context of their study on young gay men who attempt to emulate the "straight acting," "hyper-butch" role model[103] now presented as the preferred identity for gay dance club patrons,

> [t]he two gay identity symbols (effeminate and "straighter-than-straight") may lead [to] self-hatred, internalized homophobia, self-destructive behaviour (including risky sexual and drug-related behaviour) ... This identity transformation may have increased levels of anxiety, stress and inter-group alienation, rather than reduced them ... Evans describes the new compulsive bodybuilding trend among gay men as internalized homophobic values ... and so intense is their self-depreciation that they have fallen in love with the image of their worst homophobic oppressors.[104]

By encouraging gay men (indeed all men, given that hyper-masculinity isn't "natural" for anyone) to "change status" in order to become exactly what society says men should be, and by constructing an entire community identity around this model of behaviour, gay men have done little more than create a liberation strategy based on assimilation and, more significantly, on the invisibility that results from assimilation.[105] In the end, the only victors in this game of hide-and-seek are those most served by homophobia and sex discrimination – those straight men for whom gay male invisibility and female subordination are a must. The losers are those most in need of our support and encouragement. Lewis and Ross note that young gay men today are "prepared to risk their lives, rather than risk losing their self-delusions as personified in the 'straighter than straight'"[106] image now sexualized as gay identity. Others, unable to conform, simply accept that life is not worth living. Chastised by non-gays and gays alike, self-preservation seems less and less appealing. Unable or unwilling to buy into a gym culture which offers little more than "an opportunity to attain authority over their own bodies and then, eventually, over others,"[107] many choose to opt out – literally.

Conclusion

> 'Faggot! Pooftah! Fairy!' They kept yelling it at me as I left the
> schoolyard. When some stones flew in my direction – one hit my head –
> I started to run. Earlier that week I had received an anonymous death
> threat by e-mail on the school's computer system, which said someone
> would bring a gun to class and shoot me. I guess my enemies were
> extra mad because I took a copy of it to the [principal].[108]

Chris Grant was seventeen when the events he describes above occurred. They happened because he needed to talk about what it means to be gay and risked confiding in friends. As he explains, "I'd been living with it in my head for years; it reached the point where I needed to tell a couple of friends." Unfortunately, his friends were unwilling or unable to help him. "Most of my friends deserted me once word got out: they found that if they continued to socialise with me, they got abused as well,"[109] he says.

Anyone who has grown up gay, who has risked telling anyone, or who simply does not fit the model of masculinity offered to young boys knows that events such as the above, resulting in considerable pain and humiliation, are not infrequent. Indeed, they are commonplace. As any high school counsellor will tell you, Chris's story is all too familiar: "daily assaults of teasing, bumps and shoves in the corridor, being spat on, steely-eyed glares, which often graduate to kicks, punches, beatings even death threats."[110] This is the reality for today's gay youth, and while some "survive" it, many do not.

It was within the context of this reality that the *Little Sisters* trial assumed considerable significance. Held up by activists and academics alike as a decision that would determine the right of gay men to distribute the types of life-affirming materials that would give Chris Grant the support and self-confidence he needed to survive the insecurities our society dumps on us, *Little Sisters*, we were told, would either save or further ostracize our gay youth, depending on the Court's willingness to embrace pornography as liberation.

If we look at what happens to young men such as Chris Grant within a broader social context – a context in which gender conformity or non-conformity determines one's status and peer group placing – the question needs to be asked whether the materials defended in *Little Sisters* as pro-gay, pro-youth, and pro-equality can do anything to ensure that gay youth do not hide, inflict self-harm, or mimic a sexuality that asks only that they cease to care about their futures. Much time and effort has been spent by gay activists arguing that the gay adolescent needs to know about gay sex. I agree. But what if the sex we offer them does little more than reinforce the notion that some of us *are* "faggots," some of us *are* "pooftahs," and some of us *are* "fairies"? *Little Sisters* was a case about pornography, and while youth support workers can and do argue about the need for safe-sex education, anti-homophobia strategies, government support, and equal rights, *this* case, a case these same people were quick to hold up as crucial to the struggle for rights, required the defence of materials which are *not* about breaking down gender barriers, ensuring safety, self-preservation, and community support.

Undoubtedly, much will be achieved by ensuring that men such as Chris Grant are able to access sexuality information and materials that combat the guilt and shame thrust on him as a boy. Indeed, materials that do so would probably go some way in saving his life. But to link affirmation with the pornography defended in *Little Sisters* is to link equality with the types of abuse that result from the harms of rigid, polarized, socially enforced gender stereotypes. And to do so, I would argue, is to risk ridiculing everything gay liberation should stand for. What happened to Chris Grant would not have happened in a world in which young boys are not taught to loathe and quash sexual equality. But they *are*, and no amount of pornography, gay or straight, will combat this fact of life.

If we are truly committed to protecting our youth, to ensuring that they are able to develop the confidence and self-esteem needed to facilitate their survival, it is clear that multiple, often overlapping education strategies need to be developed, protected, and promoted. While it is clearly beyond the scope of this book to provide a comprehensive strategy, if one thing is clear from the arguments presented thus far, it is that any education campaign must have at its core the eradication of gender as an expectation.[111] In this regard, efforts must be made to address those early childhood dynamics that form the politics of adolescent masculinities and male dominance at school and at home.

Admittedly, the breaking down of sex-based stereotypes is but a first step in a long process. Gay youth still need to know that "gay" exists, that we have a history, a community, and that there is nothing deviant about sexual relations between men. Without this, as many of the interveners in *Little Sisters* rightly argue, self-esteem cannot be assured. In addition to a safe space within which to have such a discussion, the discussion itself will require a level of openness not foreign in schools but all too often ignored by educators when dealing with gay sexuality. Similar tactics will need to be employed when dealing with the issue of HIV/AIDS and safer sexual practices. The question that thus far remains unanswered, however, is, why pornography? That is, if gay youth need to know that gay sex exists, what happened to gay liberation to ensure that the gay sexuality we offer them is a sexuality created by and for pornographers? More importantly, perhaps we need to ask why gay sex, as marketed through pornography, tends to look a lot like the heterosexual sex that results in the anti-gay backlash thrown at them in the first place, and how this is supposed to build safety and self-esteem.

There seems to be an assumption now rampant in our community that people need to see sex in order to know and feel valid about sex, and that pornography is the only way to educate and validate an ignorant and self-loathing mass of gay men longing to be sexually active. While I have no doubt that young gay need to feel less threatened by their sexual feelings and attractions, I fail to see how it is that exposure to pornography achieves this goal. It is also disappointing that a community that prides itself on creativity, innovation, and perseverance has abandoned sexual creativity for pornographic monotony – thereby abdicating sexual self-definition for definition by pimps. I find it difficult to believe that we cannot do better, cannot offer a sexuality that *does* build self-esteem and makes sexual arousal and equality no longer contradictions. If a frank, open discussion is needed, then let us provide *that*, rather than a vicious and deceptive array of sexual messages and stimuli that regulate desire through the threat of exclusion and promote desire through domination. Moreover, silencing those in need of a voice so that others can "know" sex cannot stand as a pillar of gay liberation. Similarly, insofar as condoms need to be seen in order to be used effectively, let us actually do that. Let us not, however, masquerade the call for safer sexuality with the use of "educative" mediums that make condom use secondary to a physical ideal that says visually, sexually, only physical perfection merits safety; these then are supplemented by others that dictate that once the physical ideal is achieved, safety is not needed because we are, as men, invincible.

In *Little Sisters,* much time was spent in convincing the courts that government efforts to regulate the harms of pornography are killing our youth. Heralded as a life elixir, gay male pornography was defended as the only way to protect and save a lost generation. While it is undoubtedly the case that young gay men today both access and learn much from the pornography sold by stores such as Little Sisters, why is so much effort now directed at protecting it? If self-confidence, better communication, and a sense of belonging result-ing in less harm, self-inflicted and inflicted on others, is our goal, we must ensure that the materials we promote as central to that goal can achieve it. In reviewing the pornography defended during the *Little Sisters* trial, I am left asking whether those who produce and market it have actually bothered to take the time to ask young gay men what they think of the gay sex offered them as validation. Knowing that gay pornography *was* all that we had as young men, I query now whether, in an attempt to justify our use of it and resulting reliance on it, we have simply adopted it as part of a rights platform without questioning its real roots and consequences. While I am aware that many do not want to give it up and fear life without it (it was, after all, all that many of us had), it may well be that the time has come to ensure that future generations do not suffer the pains we have. In doing so, we may also find that our own lives become more rewarding and freer, as well as more equal.

8 Controlling Pornographic Harm Post-*Butler*: Some Thoughts on Canada Customs, the Police, and Judicial Bias

Canada Customs has a long record of homophobic seizures, producing an equally long record of loud and justifiable outrage from the Canadian lesbian and gay community. There is no evidence that whatever is happening at the border now is different from what happened before the *Butler* decision except that *Butler* has made moralizing, homophobic customs seizures illegal.

Although we recognize that the equality test adopted by *Butler* is an improvement on Canada's criminal obscenity law, we still do not advocate criminal obscenity approaches to pornography. They empower the state rather than the victims, with the result that little is done against the pornography industry.

We are encouraged, however, that the *Butler* decision under Canada's new *Charter* makes it likely that our civil rights law against pornography would be found constitutional if passed there. And we are continuing our work to empower victims to fight back against the harm committed by pornographers.[1]

Catharine MacKinnon and Andrea Dworkin

I have argued that gay male pornography violates the sex equality standard outlined in *Butler* and responded to the argument that feminist anti-pornography efforts that limit the production and distribution of gay male pornography are homophobic. Having said this, like many feminist writers, I too am concerned that *Butler*, although theoretically and socially sound, has its limits, nowhere more apparent than with the almost complete unwillingness of Canada Customs and the Canadian police forces to use *Butler* against those who sell and profit from the harms of heterosexual pornography.

As noted earlier, in *Little Sisters*, the Supreme Court of Canada held that the *Butler* equality-based test applies to gay and lesbian pornography and that the harms of gay pornography do not cease to exist simply because the materials pair biological equals or are used by an oppressed sexual minority. The Court also recognized, however, that Canada Customs' procedures regarding the seizure and detention of pornography have been arbitrary and, as such, have discriminated against lesbians and gay men. It was also revealed in the course of this litigation that Canada Customs had failed to effectively implement the equality-based approach to pornographic harm outlined by the Canadian Supreme Court in *Butler*. Indeed, despite the minor changes already made to Customs procedures in an effort to rectify some its past wrongs, one is left to query whether non-harmful same-sex materials will not continue to be stopped at the border, while harmful heterosexual pornography is allowed to enter and be sold.

By reaffirming the equality rights test outlined in *Butler*, while at the same time recognizing the problems associated with present state efforts to regulate obscenity, it can be argued that the Court provided a victory for both lesbians and gay men concerned with the illegitimate exercise of state censorship and those who have fought to address the harms associated with the production and distribution of pornography. The question this final chapter poses is, where to from here? Thus far, I have argued that the equality analysis offered in *Butler*, now strengthened and clarified in *Little Sisters*, can be viewed as beneficial to gay men. I want here to argue that the conclusion of the courts in *Little Sisters* that Canada Customs had disparately applied Canada's obscenity provisions in a discriminatory fashion, such that much legitimate gay male expression had been wrongfully suppressed, provides a rare opportunity for the gay male community and those who support the *Butler* equality-based approach to pornography to work together to ensure that the real harms of pornography are addressed in a manner that fairly and effectively implements the Supreme Court of Canada's call for the elimination of anti-egalitarian expression only.

Feminist anti-pornography activists have long argued that pornography is a practice of sex discrimination. Gay men have long argued that gay pornography is a practice of sexual liberation – a medium with which to express and develop gay male identity and politic. Justifiably wary of state efforts to suppress gay male expression, gay men have reasoned that because pornography is a means with which to form and express this identity, efforts to restrict it must, of necessity, be challenged. The result has been considerable political division and animosity among persons committed to equality – a division most recently apparent following the Supreme Court of Canada's decision in *Butler* and the decisions of the lower courts in *Little Sisters*.

The review of gay male pornography offered throughout this book reveals that this tension is unwarranted. Admittedly, the reality of social ignorance and intolerance generally is such that *Butler* may be "deployed disproportion-ately against sexual depictions which contravene expressions of male hetero-sexual desire."[2] Indeed, in that police harassment and state suppression of legitimate lesbian and gay expression is a reality, concerns about continued harassment and state monitoring are justified and should serve as a rallying point around which to express political solidarity. In that gay male pornogra-phy undermines systemic equality by reinforcing those gender hierarchies that result in inequality, however, the issue should not be whether gay male por-nography should be exempt from the application of laws aimed at providing a space within which to express dissent and achieve equality, but why the state is not using this law to eliminate the harms resulting from the production and distribution of all pornography, gay and straight alike. Similarly, when the test and principles enunciated in *Butler* are judicially misapplied and construed in a moralistic, regressive manner, rather than pursuant to an equality-based harm approach, the issue is not the theory itself but the homophobic application of that theory. While concern and outrage are justified, our efforts are better directed at addressing judicial, administrative, and social bias, rather than at protecting those expressive mediums central to our own oppression.

The state, police, and some members of the judiciary, still embedded in moralistic ignorance, will continue to harass gay men simply because they are gay men, with or without what some clearly see as a legislative mandate (ex-cuse) to do so. Insofar that sex inequality hinders legitimate minority expres-sion and homophobia is but one means of ensuring sexism prevails, gay men and women must resist. When Canada's present criminal and Customs laws are used to discriminate against lesbians and gay men, those who have fought hard to achieve the recognition that pornography is an issue of sex discrimina-tion, not morality, must commit to ensuring that legal change that cannot be applied or interpreted disparately and in a homophobic manner is forthcom-ing. Homophobia, as long as it is permitted to silence dissent, will ensure that sex equality remains difficult to achieve. However, rather than supporting a medium that contributes to the real abuse of real people, that normalizes male sexual aggression, encouraging the subordination of one individual to the domination of a descriptively, more typically, "male" other – in sum, a medium which is itself homophobic – gay men should reject it.

I want in this chapter to attempt to build a bridge that allows two factions which need not be fragmented to move forward together. *Little Sisters* pro-vides an opportunity for gay men to rethink the role of pornography in our community, and the extent to which our defence of it continues to prevent us and others from achieving real justice. It also offers strong support for an approach to equality that gay men and their supporters have for too long rejected and on which more gay men would do well to focus, given the links between sex discrimination and homophobia. While legal solutions to the

problem of pornographic harm can prove complex, they can also prove remarkably simple if all parties with a vested interest in equality work together to ensure that strategies are developed and implemented that aim to
achieve it.

This chapter outlines some of the regulatory and legal problems arising from
the regulation of pornography post-*Butler* and concludes with an analysis of
some of the issues needing to be addressed if discrimination and ineffectiveness are to be avoided. The analysis offered includes an examination of the
MacKinnon-Dworkin anti-pornography civil rights ordinances first suggested
for use in the United States and now constitutionally sound in Canada – an
approach that circumvents police inaction insofar as prosecuting those who
produce and sell heterosexual pornography and that resolves the issue Crown
inaction made problematic post-*Butler* as a result of the *Hawkins* case discussed
in Chapter 1.[3] This chapter also examines strategies aimed at ensuring that
Canada Customs procedures are not applied in a discriminatory manner against
non-harmful same-sex materials.

What *Butler Can't* Do Alone: Judicial and Police Bias

Perhaps most frustrating and problematic about the ongoing post-*Butler* fight
for sex equality is just how little has been done to address the harms outlined
by the Court in that case. In Toronto, for example, there are at any given time
as many as one hundred stores on Yonge Street selling heterosexual pornography with misogynistic content so blatant that it can only accentuate the harms
anti-pornography activists have fought against and which the Supreme Court
finally recognized in *Butler.*

As noted in Chapter 1, because of the way the lower courts have interpreted
the Supreme Court of Canada's decision in *Butler* – specifically, finding that
harm be proven beyond a reasonable doubt each time a criminal prosecution
for pornography is heard by the courts – the Crown has all but refused to use
the criminal law to stop the sale of pornography (assuming perhaps that the
burden of proof is too high, too costly, and too time-consuming). Whatever
the reason for this inaction, the situation has not been helped by the police,
those charged with enforcing the Court's decision, who have done little if
anything to give the *Criminal Code* the teeth it needs to effect change. The end
result of both is that the number of charges laid has been so small as to receive
no press coverage and the number of guilty verdicts handed down by the
judiciary in the ten years following *Butler* has been so small as to be almost
insignificant.[4] It should not surprise us then that the stores catering to consumers of pornography continue to flourish, with many now marketing themselves as "*Butler*-proof."

The frustration experienced was further raised when the first post-*Butler*
case to go to trial so blatantly misapplied the Supreme Court's mandate as to

seriously undermine the entire approach taken by the Court. The case, *Glad Day Bookshop*,[5] also raised questions as to why the first case in which *Butler* was to be tested dealt with same-sex pornography. Why, many asked, given the sheer quantity of heterosexual pornography being sold in Canada, had nothing been done to shut down those distributors? Glad Day Bookshop is one of the largest distributors of lesbian and gay literature in Canada. It is also one of the country's most successful distributors of gay male pornography. On 3 October 1989, Canada Customs officials seized multiple copies of nine gay male pornographic publications Glad Day was importing for sale. The publications were initially deemed obscene pursuant to *Customs Tariff* code 9956, which incorporates the *Criminal Code* obscenity provision upheld by the Supreme Court in *Butler*.[6] In July 1990, Glad Day appealed this determination pursuant to the appeal provisions in the *Customs Tariff*. The deputy minister of Customs and Excise upheld the classification of the publications as obscene. Glad Day appealed this decision to the Ontario Court, General Division, as provided for in the *Customs Act*. The trial of this issue was heard by Hayes J. in May 1992, with the court finding that the original determination by Canada Customs was correct and that the Crown had proved beyond a reasonable doubt that the materials in question were obscene. Glad Day chose not to appeal the decision again, leaving Hayes J.'s decision to stand as a precedent, both for the interpretation of *Butler* and for the application of *Butler* to gay male pornography.

The materials in issue in *Glad Day* included publications such as *Oriental Guys*, *Playguy*, *Advocate Men*, *Movie Star Confidential*, *Hot Tricks*, *Sex Stop*, and *Bear Magazine*. Many of these magazines were later at issue in the *Little Sisters* trial. As such, they are the same materials that were subsequently found to breach the sex equality-based standard set by the Supreme Court in that case. Glad Day argued that the materials in question did not violate *Butler*, a claim I have already rejected. Here I want to focus on the considerable and justified concern expressed by many in the gay male and feminist communities about the reasons for Hayes J.'s decision to ban these materials.

Justice Hayes misapplied or ignored the judicial test for pornography set out by the Supreme Court of Canada in *Butler*. To repeat, *Butler* redefined pornography to restrict those materials which, when distributed, undermine an essential but as of yet unrealized respect for all members of society and equality in their relations with each other – specifically equality between women and men. Any application of *Butler* that fails to acknowledge that pornography is an issue of systemic inequality, rather than morality, seriously undermines its holding. The *Glad Day* determination that the publications were obscene was based more on a subjective, morality-based analysis of whether male-male sexual activity is appropriate and acceptable than on whether real harms of inequality result from the materials. Resting on a homophobic reaction to male-male sexual relations as such, rather than on specific harms of inequality, the decision served to obscure the role of pornography in sex equality, and the way in which it harms both women and gay men. As such, the decision did much to undermine efforts to expose the harms of pornography by appropriating that effort to promote homophobia. The decision is lacking legally and is socially regressive.

Justice Hayes's analysis of when publications will constitute obscenity, in particular his application of this analysis to the materials before him, was subjective, laden with heterosexist moralism, and far removed from the equality-based approach advanced in *Butler*. Hayes J. applied a subjective standard of taste. Post-*Butler*, it is clear that in determining whether publications are socially harmful, a judge is required to measure the materials against the sex equality standards of the community as a whole. This inquiry is distinguished from the application of the trier of fact's own subjective opinions about the tastefulness or impropriety of the publications. Specifically, judges must not base analysis on what they think or feel is tolerable.

In *Glad Day*, Hayes J. classified the materials seized as obscene because they "depicted" sexual activity which was described, among other things, as "casual, random, excessive, lewd and disgusting and without real human or relational dimension."[7] Much of his analysis focused on the fact that the materials before him depicted anal and oral sex – activities that, he alleged, were degrading and void of "any real meaningful human relationship."[8] He described the publications to contain "excessive, lewd and disgusting detail" and repeatedly commented on the "excessive descriptions" in them. His analysis did not, however, indicate why the materials harm the community as a whole. He did state that the materials were dehumanizing but again did not explain why. Indeed, his judgment was preoccupied with what he personally found unacceptable or "excessive," rather than with the harm done by the production and distribution of these materials. Hayes J.'s opinion almost completely ignored the *Butler* analysis.

Justice Hayes's assimilation of private morality to public harm is particularly evident in his description of those publications that are visual rather than verbal. Analyzing the magazine *Oriental Guys*, for example, he wrote:

> This magazine contains explicit descriptions of consensual oral and anal sex with oriental males. The article "Adonis" contains extensive excessive descriptions of the acts and professed pleasures and the appreciation of the physical activity. There is no description of violence. The description in the magazine of this sexual activity is degrading. I am of the opinion that this particular material does indicate a strong inference of a risk of harm that might flow from the community being exposed to this material. I am of the opinion that the community would not tolerate others being exposed to this item. The dominant characteristic is the undue exploitation of sex. It is obscene.[9]

Harm is not specified (just concluded), nor is the nature of what exactly is degrading or dehumanizing. It is impossible from Justice Hayes's analysis to determine if the magazine does constitute an undue exploitation of sex and hence whether it violates society's equality interest as recognized in *Butler.* His Honour's emphasis on anal and oral sex seems to indicate that the community will be harmed simply because anal and oral sex occur between men or because it is depicted visually and sold, not because persons were actually harmed in the making of the material or because some men may actually harm others in the production or as a result of the distribution of the material.

Similar deficiencies exist in Hayes J.'s analysis of *Spartan's Quest, Playguy, In Touch,* and *Advocate Men.* His Honour seems more concerned with "excessive descriptions" of same-sex sexual activity than with whether the descriptions are unduly exploitative of sex and harmful to the community because they result in inequality. For example, he made reference to one photograph in the magazine *Playguy* in which six men are shown engaging in oral sex. Specifically, three men are sitting on a couch while three other men are kneeling on the floor performing fellatio on them. Hayes J. said nothing about what this picture represents or implies, that is, how it was made, whether certain persons may have been forced to make it, what it does to a person to kneel to perform sex for a camera, what it says about domination and subordination, what attitudes about male sexuality are likely to arise as a result of exposure to it, how it is degrading or dehumanizing, and so on. The material was deemed obscene apparently because *he* believed its dominant characteristic to be the undue exploitation of sex, leaving unanswered exactly why this exploitation is undue, that is, how the harm of inequality might result from it.

Justice Hayes's analysis in *Glad Day* offered little more than a return to the morality-based standards specifically rejected in *Butler.* In essence, His Honour focused more on a perceived threat to Canadian morality by gay male sexuality than on specific harms of the material in question. As a result, he seriously failed to follow or implement the *Butler* test and seriously undermined *Butler's* potential for positive social change. His opinion also revealed what would soon become a series of evident flaws in an anti-pornography strategy reliant on the criminal law for enforcement.

After Hayes J.'s decision, Glad Day appealed to the Federal Court of Canada, arguing that Hayes J. had misapplied *Butler* and that *Butler* could not be used to regulate gay male pornography. LEAF was asked at this point by myself and American law professor Catharine MacKinnon to intervene, not because gay male pornography was not harmful but because it was felt that LEAF should not stand by and allow *Butler* to be so deliberately distorted. Many of the women and men who had supported LEAF in its campaign to fight pornography were concerned that Hayes J.'s decision, by smuggling morality back into pornography cases, would be used against materials that were not harmful while failing to stop the distribution of others that quite clearly were, since materials that do not offend conventional morality often do cause harm. LEAF declined to intervene, and Glad Day ultimately dropped its appeal to the Federal Court.

The reasons for LEAF's unwillingness to intervene in the *Glad Day* case are unclear. It may be that the group simply hoped the issue would go away. Savaged in the press post-*Butler* by gay activists and free speech libertarians alike, the group may simply have decided to withdraw from the issue for fear of being labelled "anti-sex" and "anti-gay." Its failure to intervene, clarify, and reaffirm its position, however, served only to fuel the rhetoric of those who soon began attacking (and who continue to malign) anti-pornography feminists and *Butler* as homophobic. In essence, LEAF stood by while its most committed supporters were libelled and discredited by those whose only agenda was the free distribution of pornography. Although Hayes J.'s moralistic approach to harm in *Glad Day* was subsequently repudiated by another judge in the same district,[10] the fact remained that with no comment from the group largely responsible for the decision in *Butler* as to the correct application of the test by the Supreme Court and those responsible for enforcing its decision, anti-pornography feminists were soon perceived as responsible for a judicial test that threatened legitimate sexual expression. Despite the content and likely effect of the pornography banned in *Glad Day*, anti-pornography activists hardly hailed the decision as a victory for equality. Quite the opposite. Many were alarmed at the tone of, and vilification inherent in, Hayes J.'s judgment. Without any intervention from the group first responsible for the decision Hayes J. so clearly misapplied, the women and men who had fought for the right to be free from pornography were soon scorned as responsible for the *Glad Day* decision itself and all it represented.

Despite LEAF's best efforts to ignore the issue, it was clear that it would not go away. The *Glad Day* decision, resulting in the seizure of materials that violate the *Butler* sex equality standard, made apparent the problems inherent in an anti-pornography approach that relies solely on the criminal courts for enforcement. It also raised serious questions about the effectiveness of a test applied by government agencies such as the police and Canada Customs. How, many queried, could these agencies ensure that women's voices and the voices of others harmed by pornography were heard and also ensure that systemic biases on the basis of sex and sexuality did not intervene to prevent the distribution of materials that were not harmful?

Without more public activism and calls for legal reform building on the ideas and sex equality theory outlined in *Butler* from the group responsible for *Butler*, it should have been obvious to everyone that the test for harm outlined in *Butler* simply could not do what needed to be done. This became particularly evident post–*Glad Day* as the police in every Canadian city continued to ignore their mandate while heterosexual pornography flourished but seizures of both lesbian and gay pornography and non-pornographic materials alike by Canada Customs continued unabated. Although first evident in the *Glad Day* trial, it soon became clear that *Butler,* as a test, was being ignored, as those charged with applying it were incapable or unwilling to do so. In this light, the *Little Sisters* case was inevitable. With gay activists continuing to insist on their right to pornography and with LEAF having refused to assist with and clarify its position in *Glad Day, Butler* would continue to be misapplied until this issue of discrimination in the application of this law against discrimination was faced.

Customs Procedures for Controlling Pornographic Harm: Some Thoughts on How *Not* to Achieve Systemic Equality

As noted earlier, Little Sisters Book and Art Emporium is a Vancouver-based bookstore catering to the lesbian and gay community. The store's inventory consists largely of books and magazines that include gay and lesbian literature, travel information, and academic studies related to sexuality and to gay and lesbian pornography. Since its establishment in 1983, the store has imported 80 to 90 percent of its inventory from the United States. In proceedings before the British Columbia Supreme Court in 1994, the store's directors argued that the materials sold in the store, and in particular gay pornography, did not violate the equality-based test for pornographic harm articulated in *Butler.*[11] Given this, the store argued, Canada Customs was not entitled to stop the importation of this pornography into Canada from the United States. The British Columbia Supreme Court and the British Columbia Court of Appeal rejected this claim,[12] as did the Supreme Court of Canada, finding that *Butler* did apply to same-sex pornography and that, as a result, Customs could stop the importation of materials that violate the sex equality interests undermined by pornography and protected in *Butler.*[13]

The preceding chapters of this book argue that the courts' conclusions are accurate and flow logically from the reasoning offered in *Butler.* An analysis of gay male pornography does not end here, however. For although the recognition that gay porn is socially harmful is a positive first step, further steps that effectively ensure that the equality standard in *Butler* is the *only* standard against which pornographic harm is measured must also be implemented. Moreover, it is imperative that this standard be applied fairly and correctly. If it is not, the potential remains for considerable error in applying the test. Specifically, the danger exists that minority sexual expression that does *not* violate the *Butler* equality test may be unlawfully regulated, while heterosexual pornography which does, may not.

This issue was examined by the Canadian courts in *Little Sisters* – their conclusion being that Canada Customs had unfairly targeted lesbian and gay importers and had violated the lesbian and gay male community's constitu-

tional guarantees of free speech and equality. With respect to Little Sisters'
claim that Canada Customs' procedures for limiting the sale and distribution
of obscenity violate its constitutional right to free speech, the British Columbia Supreme Court (hereinafter "the trial court") noted that, although the
aims of the Customs legislation itself are justified as but one means of protecting the public against the harms of pornography, the actual application of the
legislation had been used so as to unjustifiably violate free expression.[14] The
trial court relied on two evidentiary findings, both of which strongly support
the argument, advanced by the lesbian and gay male communities and anti-
pornography feminists alike, if for different reasons, that the methods used
for curtailing pornographic harm were ineffective.[15] Specifically, the trial court
noted that systemic shortcomings in Customs administrative procedures had
resulted in the prohibition of clearly admissible materials destined for Little
Sisters,[16] with the result that "the s. 2(b) rights of the authors and artists of
those materials, of those Canadian citizens who would have read and seen
them, and of Little Sisters and its proprietors [were] arbitrarily infringed."[17]
This finding was long overdue. Indeed, it is perhaps somewhat of an understatement to describe, as did the trial court, Canada Customs' procedures as
"difficult to understand,"[18] "arbitrary,"[19] "deficient,"[20] "unreasonable,"[21] "haphazard,"[22] and susceptible to "incorrect application."[23]

One of the trial court's more telling findings relates to those procedures by
which Customs officials seized and inspected obscenity at the Canada-United
States border before the trial. As noted in Chapter 3, the legislative scheme
governing the importation of goods into Canada is found in the *Canada
Customs Act*[24] and the *Customs Tariff*.[25] As explained in Chapter 3, this legislative scheme prohibits the importation of those materials that violate s. 163(8)
of the *Criminal Code*, that section of the *Code* judicially considered by the
Canadian Supreme Court in *Butler*. The Customs scheme thus forbids the
seizure of materials not caught by the *Butler* sex equality analysis.[26] As an aid
in this regard, Customs officials are asked to refer to *Customs Memorandum
D9-1-1*, a memorandum that incorporates an overview of the law relating to
obscenity, post-*Butler*, and is aimed at ensuring Customs officials apply *Butler* correctly and legally.[27] It prohibits, for example, materials that associate
sexual pleasure with pain and suffering, presentations of rape, sex without
consent, presentations of mutilation, and presentations of sex linked to submission and degradation. Unfortunately, although the legislation itself seems
clear enough, it is apparent that the Customs officials interpreting and applying it require training, guidance, and assistance to ensure its correct application, and a significant amount of time to ensure that their duties are
correctly fulfilled. As the trial court in *Little Sisters* noted, based on the evidence before it, neither the legislation nor those applying it tended to be
adequate to the task, providing results for Little Sisters and others that were
less than satisfactory and applications that were anything but fair. Materials

were seized that did not infringe *Butler* and materials – both heterosexual and homosexual – that did were not seized.

The trial court's findings revealed a complex administrative structure that was unable to fulfil the government's legislative mandate, and a system and method of censorship ripe for abuse and susceptible to discriminatory application. To begin with, the trial court noted that those junior officers (Customs inspectors)[28] initially responsible for culling materials to be inspected were given little or no guidance regarding how they were to determine which goods to inspect.[29] Customs inspectors obtained guidance for identifying possibly prohibited goods from s. 1 of *Memorandum D9-1-1*, which stated that

> 1. [u]pon presentations of appropriate documentation, Customs Officers must determine whether or not the goods may be classified under tariff code 9956. As a guide, the following information will be considered:
>
>   a   invoice description of the goods and any documentation available which describes the importation;
>   b   information obtained from the importer, especially concerning any previous determination which the goods may have had;
>   c   importers and exporters known to deal in pornographic goods;
>   d   geographic origin and production company of the goods (i.e., known sources of pornography);
>   e   intelligence information; and
>   f   other information known about the goods, for example, information obtained through the news media or any other source.[30]

The trial court found that these guidelines encouraged officers to detain goods on suspicions aroused solely by the title of the material imported. Occasionally, as suggested in s. 1(c) above, particular importers or foreign exporters would be formally identified, either locally or nationally, for heightened inspection simply because they were perceived as possible importers of illegal materials. At the same time, other importers of the same materials were ignored or overlooked. The guidelines thus failed to guarantee any systematic pattern of examination. As stated above, the trial court found that materials that often should have been examined were not, while those that should not have been, were. As the trial court noted, Little Sisters Bookstore had been identified at the Vancouver Mail Centre as a possible importer of obscenity, and almost all international mail, including that from the United States, addressed to the bookstore was routinely opened and examined. The store faced unwarranted harassment and experienced unjustified state interference in the operation of its business:

Customs' administration of code 9956(a) results in arbitrary consequences. Traditional bookstores do not have similar encounters with
Canada Customs. Helen Haggier, who operated a general-interest bookstore in Vancouver for many years, did not know that Customs inspected books for obscenity until she left that business and opened a
store catering to women, in which she stocked some material for lesbians. She had two shipments interrupted at the border and has never
received two of the books in the shipment, or any documents from
Customs in relation to them.

Duthies, one of Vancouver's oldest and best-known bookstores, has
had a section catering to homosexual tastes for many years. Duthies
carries many titles that were prohibited when Little Sisters attempted
to import them. The effect on Little Sisters of the special scrutiny of
shipments destined for them was strikingly illustrated in the testimony of Celia Duthie, the proprietor of Duthies. She was asked shortly
before the trial by the British Columbia Civil Liberties Association to
import several titles that were prohibited when Little Sisters had attempted to import them. The shipment was examined by Customs
but was delivered to her store.[31]

The trial court found that this discriminatory application was further exacerbated by the inadequate training given junior Customs officials initially responsible for determining the admissibility of imported materials. Inadequate
training in turn led to mistakes. When *Little Sisters* was first heard, pursuant
to s. 58 of the *Customs Act*, Customs inspectors, stationed predominantly at
Canadian ports of entry, were assigned the responsibility of detecting prohibited goods – including materials that might be deemed obscene under the
Customs Tariff. In addition to applying the *Customs Tariff*, these officers were
also expected to understand and monitor compliance with seventy-eight other
federal statutes administered by Canada Customs.[32] Too much was being expected of junior officials with little or no legal or administrative training – a
fact particularly alarming within the context of pornographic harm, given that,
of the sixteen weeks of training provided to these initial inspectors, only a few
hours were allocated to the interpretation of code 9956, which incorporates
the *Butler* sex equality analysis.[33] With little or no evidence on which to base
their findings, Customs officials thus ended up relying on their own suspicions and prejudices. As the trial court explained,

> [m]any publications, particularly books, are ruled obscene without
> adequate evidence. This highlights perhaps the most serious defect in
> the present administration of code 9956(a), that is, that classifying

officers are not adequately trained to make decisions on obscenity ...
There is no formal procedure for placing evidence of artistic or literary
merit before the classifying officers. Consequently, many publications
are prohibited entry into Canada that would likely not be found to be
obscene if full evidence were considered by officers properly trained to
weigh and evaluate that evidence.[34]

The trial court further found that Customs officers simply did not have
sufficient time to ensure their initial determinations were accurate, and that a
great many of the classifications made were questionable. Added to this was
an appeal procedure[35] for Customs decisions that was so onerous and confus-
ing that litigants resorted to the system of redetermination only rarely.[36] As a
result, those who believed that they had been wrongly accused of distributing
pornography and who had not been provided an opportunity to give evidence
to the contrary (the trial court noted that initial determinations were made
without the assistance of any evidence) were denied justice.[37] Believing that
they simply could not meet the demands of the appeal procedures in place,
many simply chose not to appeal decisions that were clearly incorrect.[38] The
trial court found that their frustration in this regard was not unfounded. Indeed, the costs involved in mounting an appeal,[39] the difficulty in understanding and fulfilling the administrative paperwork required by the *Customs Act*,[40]
and the delays inherent in the appeal process[41] made the entire appeal process
inaccessible. This, in turn, was further exacerbated by the fact that when appeals were launched and were successful, prohibitions on these redetermined
materials tended to reoccur, despite a previous finding that they were non-
harmful. As the trial court explained,

> Customs maintains a computerized database of prohibitions under
> code 9956, known as TRS. However, although this database is pres-
> ently accessible by all regional offices, it is not yet accessible by all
> ports of entry. Further, it is not entirely reliable. Since prohibited goods
> are listed by title, it has happened that admissible items have been
> prohibited entry because a previously prohibited item had the same
> title. Moreover, the TRS lists only prohibited titles and does not record
> items that have been examined and ruled admissible nor items that
> have been prohibited but re-determined as admissible. Such items may
> be unwittingly detained and prohibited again ... The plaintiffs identi-
> fied thirty-five publications that were prohibited *after* they had been
> ruled admissible by Customs.[42]

This evidence led the trial court to note that Canada Customs had disproportionately restricted many legitimate lesbian and gay male materials, such
that legally admissible materials were wrongly prohibited. Many of the mis-

takes noted at trial pointed to grave systemic problems in Customs' administration as it pertained to the regulation of harmful pornographic materials –
systemic problems and inconsistencies that had a far more negative impact on
lesbians and gay men than on any other identifiable group. The result, the
trial court concluded, was that the s. 2(b) *Charter* rights of Little Sisters Bookstore were routinely and arbitrarily infringed. As the Court explained,

> [t]o attribute the errors demonstrated in this trial entirely to human
> fallibility would be to ignore the grave systematic problems in the
> Customs administration ... Most homosexual pornography is imported
> from outside Canada. Homosexuals form a small minority group in
> society, probably less than 10% according to the evidence here, and
> there are only four bookstores in Canada dealing extensively in their
> literature. Imported shipments destined for those bookstores are me-
> thodically identified and scrutinized by customs officers. Moreover,
> estimates by customs officers of the proportion of all materials they
> detained and examined in relation to code 9956(a) that were pro-
> duced for homosexual audiences ranged from 20% to 75%, a propor-
> tion far in excess of the relative size of the group ... Further, a disturbing
> amount of homosexual art and literature that is arguably not obscene
> has been prohibited.[43]

Regarding those practices that specifically infringed the equality provisions
of the *Charter,* the practices of Canada Customs noted at trial stand out as
particularly discriminatory. It is clear, for example, from the trial court's findings that Canada Customs' procedures regarding gay male pornography (in
particular its approach to anal intercourse) reflected an undeniable anti-gay
bias. The trial court noted that despite clear law to the contrary, since 1990
alone (the year *Butler* was decided), twenty-nine publications destined for Little
Sisters had been held to be prohibited "solely on the ground that they described or depicted anal penetration, several on more than one occasion."[44]
While not willing to state unequivocally that Customs guidelines against anal
sex were deliberately aimed at restricting same-sex materials, the Court did
conclude that this unjustified focus on anal sex had this effect, thus discriminating against gay men: "The prohibition of representations of that practice
[anal sex] discriminated against male homosexuals. It deprived them of representations central to the values and culture of the minority group to which
they belong ... It [also] constituted an embargo on 'safe sex' guidelines within
Canadian homosexual communities at a time, in the context of the AIDS
epidemic, when such guidelines have been particularly important."[45]

It was also a clear violation of the law laid down in *Butler.* These shortcomings were further highlighted by the Supreme Court of Canada. Before that
Court, Little Sisters argued that Canada Customs' procedures regarding the

seizure and detention of pornography at the Canada-US border had been arbitrary and, as such, had discriminated against lesbians and gay men. The Court, reviewing the findings of the trial judge, accepted the trial court's finding to this effect and detailed the extent of this discrimination:

> The rights of the appellants under s. 2(b) and s. 15(1) of the *Charter* have been infringed in the following respects:
>
> (a) They have been targeted as importers of obscene materials despite the absence of any evidence to suggest that gay and lesbian erotica is more likely to be obscene than heterosexual erotica, or that the appellants are likely offenders in this regard;
>
> (b) In consequence of the targeting, the appellants have suffered excessive and unnecessary prejudice in terms of delays, cost and other losses in having their goods cleared (if at all) through Canada Customs;
>
> (c) The reasons for this excessive and unnecessary prejudice include:
>
>   (i) failure by Customs to devote a sufficient number of officials to carry out the review of the appellants' publications in a timely way;
>
>   (ii) the inadequate training of the officials assigned to the task;
>
>   (iii) the failure to place at the disposal of these officials proper guides and manuals, failure to update Memorandum D9-1-1 and its accompanying illustrative manual in a timely way, and the failure to develop workable procedures to deal with books consisting mostly or wholly of written text;
>
>   (iv) failure to establish internal deadlines and related criteria for the expeditious review of expressive materials;
>
>   (v) failure to incorporate into departmental guides and manuals relevant advice received from time to time from the Department of Justice;
>
>   (vi) failure to provide the appellants in a timely way with notice of the basis for detention of publications, the opportunity to make meaningful submissions on a re-determination, and reasonable access to the disputed materials for that purpose; and
>
>   (vii) failure to extend to the appellants the equal benefit of fair and expeditious treatment of their imported goods without discrimination based on sexual orientation.[46]

   This list of administrative failures, while not exhaustive, revealed an undeniable level of anti-gay prejudice. With respect to Little Sisters' claim that Canada Customs procedures for limiting the sale and distribution of pornography violated its constitutional right to free speech, the Canadian Supreme Court noted that although the aims of the legislation itself are justified as but one means of protecting the public against the harms of pornography, and although gay pornography is also harmful, the actual application of the Customs legislation in regulating harm had unjustifiably violated the right to free expression and equality to which all lesbians and gay men are entitled:

> Taking the evidence as a whole, it was clearly open to the trial judge to find, as he did, that the appellants suffered differential treatment when compared to importers of heterosexually explicit material, let alone more general bookstores that carried at least some of the same titles as Little Sisters.[47]

> The Customs treatment was high-handed and dismissive of the appellants' right to receive lawful expressive material which they had every right to import. When Customs officials prohibit and thereby censor lawful gay and lesbian erotica, they are making a statement about gay and lesbian culture, and the statement was reasonably interpreted by the appellants as demeaning gay and lesbian values. The message was that their concerns were less worthy of attention and respect than those of their heterosexual counterparts.[48]

> That having been said, there is nothing on the face of the Customs legislation, or in its necessary effects, which contemplates or encourages differential treatment based on sexual orientation. The definition of obscenity ... operates without distinction between homosexual and heterosexual erotica.[49]

The *Little Sisters* case poses some very real challenges for all persons and governments that want social equality. While it is clear that pornography is an affront to basic human rights, it is also clear that efforts to target it for elimination have posed a threat to the rights of persons not always protected by governments that do not fully protect those in need of equality. In arguments before the Supreme Court of Canada, Little Sisters and its interveners stated that, in light of the way in which the legislation was being applied, an appropriate remedy would be to invalidate the legislation in question. Fortunately, the Court rejected this claim, as the consequence of striking down the legislation would be that all pornography, whether it presents heterosexual or same-sex sexual acts, would have been allowed unrestricted importation into Canada. Fortunate because the Courts had already found that these materials as a class do significant harm to the equality rights of women and of all Canadians and, as the materials defended in *Little Sisters* show, there is little reason to accept the argument that same-sex materials as such cannot be distinguished as non-harmful. Similarly, striking down those sections of the *Customs Act* that give Customs officials the authority to determine the tariff classification of any class of goods, including child pornography and hate propaganda, regardless of the risk of harm they present, as Little Sisters' arguments supported, would have been highly detrimental.[50]

For its part, the Attorney General of Canada argued before the Supreme Court of Canada in *Little Sisters* that, with proper training and resources, Canada Customs inspectors could identify materials that promote inequality through violence and dehumanization. The submission of the appellants and the other pro-pornography interveners in *Little Sisters* to the contrary – that Customs officers are inherently incapable of applying the Customs legislation in a non-discriminatory manner – is arguably, to quote the only anti-pornography intervener in the case, Equality Now, "a capitulation to both homophobia and discrimination."[51] The Court appropriately required that Canada Customs administer the existing Customs regime in conformity with s. 15 of the *Charter*. Even better would be to implement measures ensuring that those responsible for making these determinations understand what pornography does and what harm means, and that they are given the guidance and resources needed to attack inequality, not immorality linked with sexual difference.

The majority of the Supreme Court of Canada in *Little Sisters* concluded that eliminating the legislative scheme itself would not be an appropriate remedy. Having said this, the Court refused to craft a remedy to ensure that Customs officials apply the legislation in a way that is not arbitrary and unconstitutional. The Court noted that it had not received any evidence to assist it in determining whether, post-1994 (the trial concluded on 20 December 1994), Customs had implemented measures to ensure that discrimination and inefficiency were avoided. Nor had Little Sisters provided any evidence that discrimination remained in place or informed the Court of the specific measures (short of declaring the legislation invalid or inoperative) that, in its view, would remedy any continuing problems.[52] Given the inadequate record before the Court, the Court simply refused to offer a solution insofar as the future application of this legislative scheme is concerned, ruling instead that to the extent that discrimination does continue, aggrieved parties will have an action against Canada Customs for failing to apply *Butler* correctly and for failing to respect the equality guarantees to which all Canadians are entitled. The question that remains is how best to ensure that discrimination and ineffectiveness are avoided.

In light of the *Little Sisters* ruling, all parties have a vested interest in working together to ensure that the collective interests of lesbian women and gay men are taken into account when regulating the systemic and individual harms arising from the distribution of those sexual materials that violate society's equality interests. But how best to do this? Following the decision of the BC Supreme Court, Canada Customs revealed that it had taken steps to address the administrative shortcomings identified at trial. For example, in dismissing a subsequent application by Little Sisters for an injunction to restrain Customs from enforcing the legislation, Smith J. noted that any book detained for examination must now be reviewed in its entirety by qualified officers and the proposed determination reviewed by one or more other qualified officers. If a book is prohibited entry into Canada, a designated tariff and values administrator and the director of prohibited importations must be notified. Provisions had been made for timely and clear advice to affected importers.[53] Customs has also implemented changes aimed at remedying some of the administrative defects outlined in the *Little Sisters* case. These include amendments aimed at making the administrative scheme less secretive, making the appeal procedures faster and less complicated, and allowing importers to submit written evidence as to why materials should not be prohibited once they have been detained. It has also issued a written instruction that Customs officers should resolve all doubts in favour of freedom of expression.[54]

Without evidence to the contrary, it is arguable that these amendments go some way toward addressing the administrative shortcomings revealed at trial. But without further evidence as to their success in avoiding anti-gay bias, one is left wondering whether these changes will be sufficient to ensure that the harms of pornography are addressed, while safeguarding non-harmful sexual expression. There is of yet no evidence post–*Little Sisters* that any efforts have been undertaken to ensure that the type of education and training needed to understand the *Butler*-based equality test is provided. Indeed, to date, there has been no consultation with those most aggrieved by past discriminatory practices – whether they be persons who have had legitimate, non-pornographic work censored or others who continue to suffer the effects of discrimination caused by those materials that, although pornographic and harmful, are still distributed and sold throughout Canada. This, to me, would seem a crucial first step in ensuring a more open and accountable legislative scheme.

It is worth noting here at least one other omission evident in the reforms thus far initiated by Canada Customs – specifically, its concern to protect speech, while offering little room for the voices of those muzzled by sexual degradation to question errors in judgment. While reforms aimed at introducing an easier appeal mechanism for Customs decisions that incorrectly target non-harmful sexual expression are to be applauded, it is troubling that no mechanism is being considered to allow those who are harmed by pornography to challenge the distribution of materials sold throughout Canada, despite Customs procedures aimed at ensuring their non-distribution. One need only enter any of a number of bookstores and pornography outlets in Canada to understand that, despite legislation aimed at halting the flood of pornography into the country, the flood still rages, with few signs of it ever subsiding. Add to this a police force that fails to prosecute those who sell pornography, despite their actions being a clear violation of the *Criminal Code*, and some judicial officers who continue to apply that *Code* according to outdated, morality-based standards,[55] and what one is left with is a system that risks failing those most in need of protection. Indeed, while there is of yet no evidence that Customs officials continued to discriminate against lesbians and gay men post-1994, the evidence clearly available on any shelf in any pornography store in Canada would seem to indicate that these same officials are not stopping those materials that do harm.

It may be that much of this is again due to a lack of understanding and training about what it is that pornography does. It may also be that, like the police and those charged with enforcing the law, they have simply chosen not to do what the law requires them to do. Unfortunately, no evidence has been forthcoming post–*Little Sisters* that anything has been done to alter this perception, with the risk being that the errors highlighted in *Little Sisters* will continue. In this regard, it is probably true that much can be achieved by allowing those harmed by pornography a space and role within which to educate those charged with protecting them against harm. With respect to the lesbian and gay community, for example, if the government is concerned with arresting the homophobic application of its legislation, it might want to provide a forum for those targeted by this discriminatory application to discuss and offer solutions as to how best to avoid a repeat of the past. It might also aim to provide similar forums for those harmed by pornography to explain to those charged with protecting them what pornography is, how best to identify it, and why.

Of course, discussion and consultation, while necessary, will not alone prove sufficient to ensure that many of the problems identified with the regulation of pornography exposed in *Little Sisters* are addressed. While at some level this may do much to ensure that harmful materials are denied entry or distribution, it is clear that if pornography is going to be tackled, border patrols and criminal penalties alone will not prove sufficient. While judicial and administrative education, implemented with the cooperation of those most aggrieved by incorrect decisions, is to be encouraged, it is evident that pornography must be dealt with in an arena that catches those materials not caught by criminal sanction. *Little Sisters* reaffirms the concern of many feminist women and pro-feminist men that little will actually be done to address the harms of pornography so long as the power to do so remains in the hands of those least harmed by it. Indeed, while the equality test adopted in *Butler,* and now strengthened and clarified in *Little Sisters*, is an improvement on Canada's criminal obscenity laws, the test alone, relying as it does on criminal sanction, and the mechanisms through which the criminal law is enforced, will not succeed in halting the production of pornography and the discrimination that results from its distribution.

What is needed is a multilayered approach, one similar to that presently being used to combat racial vilification, as discussed in the pages that follow. In this instance, what one needs is an approach that empowers pornography's victims – an approach that allows those most harmed by pornography to fight back against the agents of their harm and which, as such, puts some teeth into the *Butler* equality mandate. The civil rights, anti-pornography ordinances drafted by Catharine MacKinnon and Andrea Dworkin and first debated in the United States offer and make possible such an initiative in the Canadian context post-*Butler* and *Little Sisters*. *Butler* outlined the injury of pornography to be the injury to sex equality. This is a real harm. The ordinances put that into legal effect by making a real harm, recognized as one of sex inequality, actionable.

To do all this, of course, first requires that those gay men and lesbians most affected by the legislation learn to accept and accommodate the concerns of both those in and outside their community for whom pornography is not a source of liberation. As indicated throughout this book, there is an assumption within the lesbian and gay communities that if you are gay or lesbian, you must, of necessity, want and need pornography, that an affirmation of its existence is an affirmation of your identity, that an attack on it is an attack on you. And so exists the belief, now central to most gay rights strategies, that access to same-sex pornography is justice and equality. It is by now, one would hope, apparent that this is not the case. Herein then lies our greatest challenge. Until that assumption is laid to rest, until we drop pornography as a platform from which to gain equality, until we cease to defend all same-sex materials because we perceive their prohibition as an infringement on our right to speak, and until we recognize that considerable harm risks being inflicted on those who belong to a community that is failing to act on their behalf, it seems unlikely that the type of consultation, negotiation, and cooperation needed to avoid the inequalities that plague Customs procedures will ever be resolved.

To this one should also add that gay men, in particular, must learn to take seriously the anguish and pain of women harmed by pornography. For until their safety and full social participation are also guaranteed, our own struggle for human rights will prove futile. What is needed to ensure the successful and fair application of legislation aimed at building social equality is an open forum where all can speak freely, learn from each other, and work together to do what must be done to avoid the mistakes of the past. This cannot be accomplished if gay men continue a misguided campaign, masked as a fight for sexual freedom, that serves only to silence others also in need of sexual freedom and sex equality. The MacKinnon-Dworkin anti-pornography ordinances promise all of us both freedom and equality. Gay men would thus do well to support them.

Pornography as a Human Rights Violation

The Hate Speech Example
Most of the Canadian provincial human rights codes contain provisions that allow those vilified by hate speech to seek remedies aimed at stopping the

hate speech in question, while providing financial compensation to its victims. Lesbians and gay men have long lobbied for anti-gay hate speech to be included as speech that violates these and legislative protections.[56] With respect to the *Canadian Human Rights Act*, which specifically includes sexual orientation as a prohibited ground of discrimination, the courts have provided remedies against speech that vilifies on the basis of sexual orientation – a decision gay activists have applauded.[57] In *McAleer* v. *Canada (Canadian Human Rights Commission),* for example, an application was made to the Federal Court of Canada to overturn a decision of the Canadian Human Rights Tribunal ordering Canadian Liberty Net to shut down its telephone hate hotline.[58] The tribunal had ruled that the hate line was likely to expose gay people to hatred or contempt, undermining their right to equal participation in social life. Liberty Net argued that it had the right to freely express what it liked, when it liked. The respondent, McAleer, on the other hand, argued that Liberty Net's right to free speech could be curtailed if the message the group distributed caused discrimination against him as a gay man. The message on the phone line was clearly aimed at provoking anti-gay sentiment, making specific reference to the North American Man Boy Love Association (NAMBLA) and continuing with:

> I think the NAMBLA newsletter should be allowed in Canada but that child molesters, homo or otherwise, should be executed. This should decrease the possession or circulation within Canada of the newsletter. Hell, the ancient Celts used to take their queers and trample them into the peat bogs. That's not such a bad idea, maybe. Perhaps we have finally stumbled across the argument which will save Burns bog in Delta from development because it is the only bog big enough to service the needs of the progressive city of Vancouver.[59]

The Federal Court agreed with McAleer, holding that his right to non-discrimination had been violated by the distribution of material that was likely to expose him to contempt by reason of his sexual orientation.

The human-rights-based approach to hate speech has gained considerable support among gay scholars, both because it works and because it avoids many of the shortcomings of the criminal law. Richard Moon, for example, has argued that "the responsibility for hate propaganda should be civil, rather than criminal, in the form of a group defamation action or a human rights code complaint. The focus would then be on the harm done to the group members rather than on the wrongful intention of the speaker."[60] MacDougall, in turn, noting the very few successful prosecutions under the *Criminal Code*, supports those initiatives that build on the sanctions imposed by the *Code*. In this regard, it is important to note that, although the *Code* is sometimes problematic and difficult to apply, most of these authors do not call for the abolition of its provisions. Rather, they support "a panoply of provisions" aimed at fighting hate. Discussing the fight against racist speech, for example, Bruce Elman argues that "it is important for Canada to maintain criminal legislation sanctioning the promotion of hatred against minority groups," as "such legislation demonstrates the distaste of the public for hate propagandists and their message."[61] In addition, he contends that

> [a] panoply of provisions designed to combat rising racism is the most effective way for the state to deal with the problem. Customs and excise provisions can be used to prevent objectionable material from entering the country ... Human rights statutes and criminal sanctions can be employed to show Canadian society will not tolerate the promulgation of racist invective. By employing a combination of methods including public education, we will, hopefully, be able to combat the impact of racist speech by minimizing the credibility of the hate-monger and the susceptibility of the community to his racist message, and in the process we will create a just, tolerant society.[62]

Admittedly, getting this combination to work will require careful legislative drafting, a commitment to do so, and a willingness to listen to those most harmed by the inequality caused by hate speech. But this, of course, is the nature of law reform. Most importantly, these efforts provide an opportunity to combat the harms of sexism and homophobia caused by pornography. In this regard, the MacKinnon-Dworkin anti-pornography ordinances, to date rejected in the United States but now both constitutional and clearly much needed in Canada in light of the *Little Sisters* trial, merit consideration. Given the overwhelming support among lesbians and gay men in Canada for laws aimed at combating hate speech, there is little reason to now oppose legislative efforts that seek to allow women and men to take action against those who injure them through pornography. Indeed, given that the proof of harm arising from pornography is more scientifically sound than the proof of harm arising from hate speech, it would seem that there is no legitimate reason to oppose legislation that allows women and men to prove their harms, particularly since similar objections have rarely been raised to such remedies for hate speech. On the contrary, it is arguable that the opportunity to present this evidence does much to respond to the concerns of those who claim that no such evidence exists, without the fear of regulation on the basis of bias where no harm exists, so evident in the criminal sphere that is now relied on as the sole avenue for addressing these harms.

The MacKinnon-Dworkin Anti-Pornography Civil Rights Ordinances
In 1983, residents of two working-class areas in Minneapolis, Minnesota, asked American feminists Andrea Dworkin and Catharine MacKinnon to assist them

in stopping the distribution of pornography in their neighbourhoods.[63] Although the City initially intended to draft a zoning ordinance that would permit the sale of pornography only in specified (low-income) neighbourhoods, Dworkin and MacKinnon pointed out to the City's Zoning and Planning Committee that such a measure would only legitimize pornography. They urged the City to take a "civil rights" approach that would allow those harmed by the production and sale of pornography to sue those responsible for their harm. The idea was implemented as an amendment to the sex discrimination provisions of the Minneapolis Civil Rights Ordinance,[64] passed twice, but ultimately vetoed by then mayor Donald M. Fraser.[65]

In April 1984, similar legislation was passed in Indianapolis and signed into law by Mayor William H. Hudnut III. Before it went into effect, an alliance of booksellers challenged this legislation as unconstitutional. In *American Booksellers Association* v. *Hudnut*,[66] the US Court of Appeals for the Seventh Circuit held that the Indianapolis ordinance was an unconstitutional violation of free speech rights.[67] The Court accepted the factual premises of the ordinance, conceding that "depictions of subordination tend to perpetuate subordination,"[68] and that the "subordinate status of women in turn leads to affront and lower pay at work, insult and injury at home, battery and rape on the streets."[69] The Court also held that "racial bigotry, anti-Semitism, and violence on television influence the culture and shape our socialization. Yet all is protected speech, however insidious. Any other answer leaves the government in control of all of the institutions of culture, the great censor and director of which thoughts are good for us."[70]

The decision of the Canadian Supreme Court in *Butler* stands in stark contrast to *Hudnut*. The *Butler* Court, recognizing the need to link free speech with equality, justifies and permits legislative efforts aimed at preventing the sale of those pornographic materials that undermine sex equality. The Supreme Court of Canada's *Little Sisters* decision sustains this approach, while at the same time recognizing the many difficulties of putting the *Butler* theory into practice. The MacKinnon-Dworkin ordinances offer a solution to some of the problems exposed in *Little Sisters*. They offer a further method with which to combat pornographic harm – both homosexual and heterosexual. MacKinnon and Dworkin conceptualize pornography as a practice of sex discrimination, arguing that it actively promotes inequality between the sexes by eroticizing dominance and male supremacy. Their anti-pornography ordinances, outlined in Chapter 1, uniquely provide a specific and unambiguous definition of pornography, guarding against arbitrary and moralistic application. Most importantly, they locate the regulation of pornography within the context of eliminating sexualized gender hierarchies and the inequalities that result from them.[71]

Conceivably, the definition of pornography provided by MacKinnon and Dworkin, if added to the interpretive codes used by Customs officers and combined with reforms aimed at addressing the administrative shortcomings noted by the Court in *Little Sisters*, would go some way toward clarifying what these officers are meant to target and why. It would be particularly useful if accompanied by a forum aimed at providing those charged with stopping pornography with an opportunity to learn why and how pornography harms. Beyond the jurisdiction of the *Customs Act*, the ordinances, if enacted into Canadian law, would allow those harmed by pornography to bring a civil or human rights-based action against those responsible for their harm. The ordinances could be passed as an amendment to an already existing civil or human rights law or as a freestanding statute, with appropriate modifications to procedures for the setting.[72] They provide that it is sex discrimination to coerce, intimidate, or fraudulently persuade any person into performing for pornography.[73] The makers, sellers, exhibitors, and distributors of any pornography resulting from coercion, intimidation, or fraud can be sued for damages. Injunctive relief can also be sought to remove the product of the performance from public view.[74] It is also sex discrimination to produce, sell, exhibit, or distribute pornography, including through private clubs, and to force pornography on a person in any place of employment or education, and in any home or public place.[75] Victims of an assault, physical attack, or injury directly caused by specific pornography are entitled to file a complaint against the maker(s), seller(s), exhibitor(s), and distributor(s) of the pornography believed to have caused the assault.[76] Finally, traffickers in pornography, when proven to subordinate on the basis of sex, can be sued for damages and an injunction sought to stop the harm.

Lesbian feminist arts writer and journalist Susan Cole, who has been arguing for the use of the ordinances in Canada since their introduction in the United States in the early 1980s, posits that *Butler* offers an opportunity to adopt them into Canadian law. Advocating their use as part of the provincial and federal human rights codes, Cole writes:

> Now is the time for these kinds of legislative changes. We are at the precise point in our constitutional history when we can take advantage of what we know about pornography. We are just now developing a social contract for Canada ... Unlike our neighbours in the US, we do not have a 200-year history of constitutional law that has been imbedded in stone, or "freedoms" that have protected pornographers and have posed obstacles for women fighting against pornography. We have the chance to entrench human rights in a vocabulary that is distinctly Canadian and at a time when our decisions will define the basic constitutional priorities for the future.
>
> This human rights approach to pornography would pose no threat to the development of alternative erotic materials; nor would such a law make sex education materials subject to prosecution; it would not

allow the law to say that sex was dirty. It would allow the law to make
a strong statement in favour of equality; it would make it harder for
the consumers of pornography to think their sex-discriminatory practice had anything to do with freedom; it would allow women who are
dehumanized in the making and consumption of pornography to reclaim humanity through court action.[77]

Obviously, this legislative approach will not fix all the problems identified in
the *Little Sisters* proceedings, nor has anyone claimed that it will. It would not,
for example, have solved the many administrative shortcomings evident in the
way Canada Customs applied its legislation, as detailed in the *Little Sisters*
litigation, nor will it eradicate future discriminatory application of that legislation. This does not mean, however, that the approach offered is invalid. As
the courts have indicated, insofar as Canada Customs fails to target that which
should be targeted, the *Butler* equality-based test for pornographic harm will
continue to be violated. But many of the features of the ordinances specifically respond to the shortcoming of existing law. They are clear and concrete;
require proof of harm based on a civil standard, rather than allowing morals-
based attacks; and specifically promote equality of disadvantaged groups. They
also address harms that continue unaddressed under existing law.

Until all those affected by this legislation come together to develop strategies aimed at doing what must be done, the errors of the past will continue to
resurface, with further division and hostility inevitable. This will not occur,
though, until those opposed to the regulation of pornography cease to defend
those materials which, when assessed critically, can be seen to threaten their
own struggle to be treated as equals. In other words, we cannot expect to deal
with these shortcomings until we first deal with our own. Nor will it occur
until those harmed by pornography are offered a safe space within which to
talk about and do something about those materials and people that harm
them. The ordinance approach, adopted as part of a broader human rights
landscape, offers such a forum. Once adopted and used, this then leaves only
pro-pornography lesbians and gay men and their supporters to re-examine
their alliances and determine whether the silencing of many is worth the false
and short-lived liberation of a few.

Conclusion
As noted at the beginning of this book, the MacKinnon-Dworkin anti-
pornography ordinances have not been adopted in any Canadian jurisdiction.
The Supreme Court of Canada's decisions in *Butler,* now strengthened and
further clarified in *Little Sisters,* offer hope for those who believe that they
should be. By making freedom from pornographic harm a human right, a right
that takes precedence over any perceived right to unlimited speech, the ordinances put into practice the conceptual shift toward equality outlined in

Butler. Theirs is a legal strategy whose time has come, and it is one that poses no threat to those wanting sexual freedom for all. On the contrary, it offers those most disenfranchised by a lack of freedom, whether they be men or women, gay or non-gay, to confront and do what can be done about those who, in the name of free speech, market and profit from the distribution of inequality.

Whether or not this approach will be used remains to be seen. Will gay men hurt during the production of pornography claim compensation for this harm? Will those abused by their partners, those who are raped, those who are threatened, or those who are victimized on the basis of sex seek redress for the inequalities inflicted on them as a result of its distribution? As MacKinnon notes, they "might and they might not – but right now they can't."[78]

The MacKinnon-Dworkin anti-pornography ordinances do not profess to address all the inequalities that we experience. But it does offer hope for a future in which one man's freedom is not gained at the expense of another's personal safety. The harms documented by those hurt by sexual inequality are real and should not be trivialized as mere sexual theatre. By defending pornography, by opposing efforts to regulate it, by refusing to discuss ways to ensure that it is done effectively and fairly, however, gay men risk doing just this, leaving us with legislation that is ineffective and strategies that benefit few, while alienating many. Enabling victims to sue for damages and restricting the pornographer's financial gain, on the contrary, may ultimately have a considerable affect on the type of pornographic material that is produced and distributed, promoting equality. At a minimum, "framing the legal remedy as a violation of human rights emphasizes the political context of what otherwise appears as merely isolated, privatized incidents of sexual violence for pleasure and profit"[79] and offers some hope for a society in which sex equality is not a fiction. This is an approach from which gay men can only benefit. Combined with a concerted re-evaluation of where we want to go as a community and what we need to do to get there, it provides a positive first step for those committed to a gay male liberation based on compassion for others, reciprocity, and caring.

Conclusion

I came to New York to find a community. Well, I found one – one in which who I am is irrelevant and what I am is everything. And what I am, I am now told, is "a bottom," a role defined for me by men who don't give a damn about me as a person – men who care only about using me to make sure they are "on top." Men who would rather fuck than talk and for whom sexual gratification is one-sided.[1]

Ken, aged 21, 1995

The debate surrounding gay male pornography has of late become intense. This is particularly evident in the writings that have appeared since the Supreme Court of Canada's 1992 decision in *Butler,* through which the role of pornography in the lives of gay men has been firmly articulated within the gay male community itself. Many have found that they must either support pornography or assume the role of a pariah among those to whom they have traditionally turned for support and validation. Outside this community, feminist women long supportive of gay male equality – many of whom were central to the early articulation of gay male political rights discourse – have found themselves labelled homophobic simply for daring to support a judicial decision that affirms sex inequality.

This book offers a different perspective on the role of pornography in gay men's lives, in the hope of convincing at least some to align themselves with those feminist women and pro-feminist men who take sex equality seriously. The decision of the Supreme Court of Canada in *Little Sisters* provides a unique opportunity for gay men, who quite rightly oppose the unjustified state suppression of legitimate sexual expression, to support women committed to eliminating the many sources of sexual subordination and to assist them in gaining equality.

For too long gay men have campaigned heavily to defend their right to access pornography, something they believe is a central component in the struggle for gay male liberation. In the name of free speech, gay male pornography's importance has been held out as a reason to silence feminist-based efforts aimed at eliminating the sexual violence promoted through pornography's production and distribution. Pro-pornography activists claim that gay male pornography is subversive, liberating, and therefore integral to the formation and expression of gay male identity. As such, we are told it must be protected because to do otherwise is homophobic and anti-free speech.

As I see it and live it, something has gone terribly wrong with gay male liberation. What strikes me most about being gay today is that a lot of gay men are not all that "gay" about being gay. I am concerned about the often unquestioned results of its agenda, efforts, and liberation strategies. I have argued throughout this book that gay empowerment, encouraging a self-confidence that supports dissent and rejects values that result in all that is anti-gay, has been replaced with a selfish, misguided commitment to male dominance and the right to overpower. Equality in the form of compassion, mutual trust, and respect has been abandoned for a community ethic and identity politic that encourages and promotes the very essence of inequality: hyper-masculinity and the harms that arise from a system in which gender is polarized such that "male" equals top, equals power. This politic today is ex-emplified and inculcated by the sexuality promoted and defended in much of the pornography gay men produce, distribute, and purchase in the name of liberation. Rejecting this trend, I have argued in this book that there is little to be gained from sexualized conformity.

As a gay man in search of equality, liberation, and self-affirmation, I am acutely aware of the need for free speech. What I seek to examine throughout this work, however, is what exactly pornography has to do with my right to be free from homophobic attack, to express dissent, and to develop a gay male identity free from socially encouraged self-loathing. Gay male pornography offers a sexuality that is hierarchical and rarely compassionate or based on mutuality and respect. The picture of gay men offered in it is one of a community obsessed with physical and psychological masculinity and with obtaining and benefiting from male power and privilege. Its message, defended by gay male activists and academics alike as progressive, pervades all aspects of gay male culture, such that we now find ourselves promoting a model of behaviour more concerned with self-gratification and the right to dominate and control than with self-respect and respect for others. This adherence to power in the form of hyper-masculinity simply reinforces those models of behaviour that are the source of heterosexual male privilege and the homophobic rejection of any public expression that challenges it. It results in an identity that is far from liberating.

Gay men stand to benefit from the efforts of all persons committed to sex equality, whose agenda we would do well to emulate and join. By defending gay male pornography, we only stand in the way. In recognizing that state efforts to suppress gay male sexuality are often discriminatory and unjustified, the Supreme Court of Canada has in *Little Sisters* verified the need for speech that is both liberating and life-affirming. In acknowledging that pornography is not liberating, as pro-porn advocates would have us believe, the Court has also sent a clear message to its defenders that there are far more effective ways to achieve liberation than by advocating the distribution of materials that stimulate you to get it up by putting other people down.

The *Little Sisters* litigation has renewed the academic and political efforts on the part of many gay men to defend gay male pornography as representative of a sexual politics to which all gay men must have access. Adamant that pornography is necessary for the formation of a distinct gay male sexual identity, gay men have sought to justify its mass distribution. Indeed, defenders of gay male pornography have been so adamant that the right to access pornography is integral to the struggle for gay liberation that present gay rights strategies include an almost unquestioned assumption that any commitment to social equality for gay men must of necessity also include a commitment to the free production and distribution of gay male pornography. To be for gay male sexuality requires being for gay male pornography. This was apparent in the arguments advanced by gay men during the *Little Sisters* trial.

To these men – the same men who live in a society in which, for men, non-straight has come to mean non-male and in which gay men's perceived non-maleness has ensured that they remain both despised and oppressed – my analysis poses this question: what, exactly, is liberating about materials in which the descriptively straight man's right to "just fuck something" is an identity worth preserving, while "just being fucked" is something best "done" by women, or by those who, socially, are not "real" men? The pornography examined here displays the gay male identity politics defended by pro-porn advocates and applauded as liberation in *Little Sisters*. This identity should be rejected.

For many gay men, the *Little Sisters* case seemed to offer another opportunity for them to enshrine their right to equality. Until then, much had been done to ensure that the Canadian courts included lesbians and gay men in Canada's post-*Charter* efforts to build a more egalitarian and inclusive society. *Little Sisters*, we were told, was but another in a long line of litigation strategies aimed at securing gay equality. I have asserted throughout that, far from being a source of equality, this latest litigation effort represented a step backwards, one that can be rectified only by a radical rethinking of what it is gay men want and expect from those who claim to act on their behalf.

In the name of liberation, many gay men have ignored the claim that pornography does harm. Seen as an issue of "sexual freedom," gay male pornography has been defended as a base from which to challenge and subvert compulsory heterosexuality and develop gay male identity. A re-examination of the gay male pornography defended, however, reveals that there is little, if anything, liberating about a medium that encourages aggression as a sexual practice, that promotes physical harm as erotic and identity defining, and that reinforces an already entrenched system of sex discrimination on the basis of sexuality and gender. Gay men must instead construct a platform from which to begin a necessary reassessment of what gay male identity is and the models from whence that identity has been derived.

Both the *Butler* and *Little Sisters* cases offer gay men an opportunity to re-think the role of pornography in building this platform. Rejecting "immorality" as a social harm, choosing equality as a concrete constitutional standard, these cases offer a radical rethinking of the individual and systemic harms of pornography, sexism, and homophobia, and their interconnections. The issues these cases raise will require ongoing community consultation and co-operation. Without this, we will not ensure that the systemic and individual harms both *Little Sisters* and *Butler* identify are addressed in a way that is fair, effective, and non-discriminatory. Gay men have a central role to play in this discussion. But we cannot expect to do so as long as some of us continue to defend a "source of gay pride" that is central to the formation of a misogynist and heterosexually defined gay male identity. My objective has been to offer those who are looking for something more a chance to help define what that something more should look like. The model presently on offer does little more than sexualize a role play that rejects compassion, affection, and equality between gay men and that instead promotes, through sex, homophobia, and sexism, self-hate, hate for others, and harm to others. As such, it must be rejected.

Notes

Introduction

1 *Little Sisters Book and Art Emporium* v. *Canada (Minister of Justice)*, [2000] 2 S.C.R. 1120, hereinafter *Little Sisters*. The case can be found at <http://www.lexum.umontreal.ca/csc-scc/en/pub/2000/vol2/html/2000scr2_1120.html>. On appeal from the Court of Appeal for British Columbia (1998), 54 B.C.L.R. (3d) 306. Originally heard before the British Columbia Supreme Court (1996), 18 B.C.L.R. (3d) 241.

2 *R.* v. *Butler*, [1992] 1 S.C.R. 452 (S.C.C.), hereinafter *Butler*.

3 On the harms of lesbian pornography generally, see Sheila Jeffreys, *The Lesbian Heresy* (Melbourne: Spinifex Press, 1993) and Irene Reti, ed., *Unleashing Feminism: Critiquing Lesbian Sadomasochism in the Gay Nineties* (Santa Cruz: Her Books, 1993).

4 LEAF is Canada's leading and most respected legal feminist lobby group. Formed in 1984, a few months before s. 15 of Canada's *Charter of Rights and Freedoms* came into effect, the group has effectively shaped the way in which the *Charter*'s equality guarantees have been interpreted by the courts and has done so in a way that has done much to ensure real, substantive equality for Canadian women. LEAF is described by Sherene Razack as embodying three main features, all aimed at advancing the equality rights of Canadian women:

> the establishment of a single national fund, the direct sponsorship of (preferably winnable) cases and a complementary strategy of education and lobbying. As the epicenter of this strategy LEAF, Mary Eberts wrote, had a good chance of occupying the field of equality rights in the courtroom, but "expertise can be applied in ways other than this case-by-case approach. Counsel and volunteers from the organisation can become involved in legal writing, legal education, and continuing education of bench and bar. In this fashion, they may come to influence how decision makers view the legal issues involved. Just as important, however, they may influence how lawyers prepare and present cases they bring forward." "Occupying the field" on equality issues, doing pro-active litigation, influencing the influencers, were components of LEAF's vision.

See Sherene Razack, *Canadian Feminism and the Law: The Women's Legal Education and Action Fund and the Pursuit of Equality* (Toronto: Second Story Press, 1991), 47. An excellent compilation of the legal factums written by LEAF and a brief summary of each case can be found in Women's Legal Education and Action Fund, *Equality and the Charter: Ten Years of Feminist Advocacy Before the Supreme Court of Canada* (Toronto: Emond Montgomery, 1996).

5 *Butler, supra* note 2 at 493.

Chapter 1: Pornography as Inequality: A Perspective on Hate Speech and the Meaning of Sexism

1 *R.* v. *Butler*, [1992] 1 S.C.R. 452 (S.C.C.) at 493 (quoting House of Commons Standing Committee on Justice and Legal Affairs, *Report on Pornography* (Ottawa: 22 March 1978) at 18.

2 See Andrea Dworkin and Catharine MacKinnon, *Pornography and Civil Rights: A New Day for Women's Equality* (Minneapolis: Organizing against Pornography, 1988). A more detailed overview of the ordinances and their possible application in Canada is provided in Chapter 8.

3 Code of Indianapolis and Marion County, Ind., s. 16-3 (1984). For discussion, see Catharine MacKinnon, *Sex Equality* (New York: Foundation Press, 2001), 1517.

4 *Butler, supra* note 1.

5 See generally Chris Bearchell, "In Harm's Way: A Calculated Campaign Takes Aim at Sexual Imagery and Free Speech," in *XS: A Supplement to Xtra!* November 1992, 1; Chris Bearchell, "Gay Porn Censored from All Sides," *Toronto Star*, 15 January 1993, A23; John Leo, "Censors on the Left," *US News and World Report*, 4 October 1993, 30; Tim Kingston, "Canada's New Porn Wars," *San Francisco Bay Times*, 4 November 1993, 6; Leanne Katz, "Censors Helpers," *New York Times*, 4 December 1993, 21; "Censory Depravation," *Screw Magazine*, 27 December 1993, 10; Mickey Koivisto, "The Canadian Government's Big Chill on Queer Culture," *Gaze Magazine*, 1 April 1994, 16; Ted Fishman, "Northern Underexposure: Censorship in Canada," *Playboy*, June 1994, 58.

6 *R. v. Keegstra*, [1990] 3 S.C.R. 697.

7 *Butler* (S.C.C.), *supra* note 1 at 461.

8 *Canadian Criminal Code*, R.S. 1985, c. C-46.

9 *Butler* (S.C.C.), *supra* note 1 at 461. Butler was charged with 173 counts of illegal possession: 3 counts of selling obscene material contrary to s. 163(2)(a) of the *Code*, 41 counts of possessing obscene material for the purpose of distribution contrary to s. 163(1)(a) of the *Code*, 128 counts of possessing obscene material for the purpose of sale contrary to s. 163(2)(a) of the *Code*, and 1 count of exposing obscene material to public view contrary to s. 163(2)(a) of the *Code*. At trial, Butler was convicted on 8 counts relating to eight films. He was acquitted on all other counts. See *R. v. Butler* (1990), 50 C.C.C. (3d) 97 (Man. Q.B.). The Manitoba Court of Appeal allowed the appeal and entered convictions with respect to all counts. See *R. v. Butler* (1990), 60 C.C.C. (3d) 219 (Man. C.A.).

10 See *Canadian Constitution (Constitution Act, 1982)* [en. by the *Canada Act 1982* (U.K.), c. 11, s.1], pt. I *(Canadian Charter of Rights and Freedoms)* (hereinafter, the *Charter*). Section 2(b) of the *Charter* reads: "Everyone has the following fundamental freedoms: (b) freedom of thought, belief, opinion and expression, including freedom of the press and other media communication."

11 Although the protections provided in the *Charter* are expressed widely, the actual scope of these protections is determined by the first clause of the *Charter*, which requires the courts to recognize limits on the rights provided in it. Specifically, s. 1 of the *Charter* reads: "The Canadian Charter of Rights and Freedoms guarantees the rights and freedoms set out in it subject only to such reasonable limits prescribed by law as can be demonstrably justified in a free and democratic society." For the most part, s. 1 has been applied in a constrained and reasoned manner. This has resulted from the decision of the Supreme Court of Canada in *R. v. Oakes*, [1986] 2 S.C.R. 103 (S.C.C.). In *Oakes*, the Court articulated the judicial standard to be applied when determining whether proven *Charter* violations are justified. The standard is as follows: first, the objective of the legislation held to violate a *Charter* provision must be of sufficient importance to do so, and must relate to concerns which are pressing and substantial in a free and democratic society. Once the legislation passes these requirements, it is then scrutinized to determine: 1) whether the measures adopted and which infringe the right in question are rationally connected to the objective in question; 2) whether the measures employed impair as little as possible the right or freedom; and 3) whether the deleterious effects of the measures held to violate an alleged right are proportional to its objective or purpose. See Victor J. Ramraj, "Keegstra, Butler and Positive Liberty: A Glimmer of Hope for the Faithful" (1993) 51 *U. Toronto Fac. L. Rev.* 304 at 307. For a further analysis of *Oakes*, see Lorraine Eisenstat Weinrib, "The Supreme Court of Canada and Section One of the Charter" (1988) 10 *Sup. Ct. L. Rev.* 469.

12 *Canadian Criminal Code*, R.S. 1985, c. C-46.

13 *Butler* (S.C.C.), *supra* note 1 at 471.

14 *Ibid.* at 511. See note 11 above for an overview of the use and limits of s. 1 of the *Charter* – that section which allows the courts to uphold as reasonable and justified any violation of the *Charter*'s rights protections.

15 *Supra* note 1.

16 *Butler* (S.C.C.), *supra* note 1 at 479.

17 This is an impressive and thorough body of work. In addition to the authors cited throughout this book, a compilation of these findings can be found in MacKinnon, *Sex Equality, supra* note 3 at 1532-1630. See also Catharine MacKinnon and Andrea Dworkin, *In Harm's Way: The Pornography Civil Rights Hearings* (Cambridge: Harvard University Press, 1997) and Catherine Itzin, *Pornography: Women, Violence and Civil Liberties* (Oxford: Oxford University Press, 1992). See also Diana Russell, *Pornography: The Evidence of Harm* (Berkeley: Russell Publications, 1993); Gail Dines, Robert Jensen, and Ann Russo, *Pornography: The Production and Consumption of Inequality* (New York: Routledge, 1998); Susan Cole, *Power Surge: Sex, Violence and Pornography* (Toronto: Second Story Press, 1995); Andrea Dworkin, *Pornography: Men Possessing Women* (New York: Plume Books, 1989); Susanne Kappeler, *The Pornography of Representation* (Minneapolis: University of Minnesota Press, 1986).

18 For compilation of this evidence, see MacKinnon, *Sex Equality, supra* note 3 at 1532-1651. Of particular relevance are Susan Brownmiller, *Against Our Will: Men, Women and Rape* (New York: Simon and Schuster, 1985); Andrea Dworkin, "Pornography Is a Civil Rights Issue for Women" (1987/88) 21 *U. Michigan J.L. Ref.* 55; Diana Russell, *Pornography: The Evidence of Harm* (Berkeley: Russell Publications, 1993); Diana Russell, "Pornography and Rape: A Causal Model," in Diana Russell, ed., *Making Violence Sexy: Feminist Views on Pornography* (1993); Diana Russell, *Sexual Exploitation* (1984); Diana Russell, *Dangerous Relationships: Pornography, Misogyny and Rape* (1998).

19 Again, the reader is directed to the studies outlined in MacKinnon, *Sex Equality, supra* note 3 at 1532-1651.

20 See generally MacKinnon and Dworkin, *In Harm's Way, supra* note 17, and the victim-impact testimonies and work cited in MacKinnon, *Sex Equality, supra* note 3 at 1550-62. As MacKinnon notes (at 1550): "Laboratory studies have the benefit of controlling variables but the potential detriment of having been conducted in an artificial environment. With pornography, evidence from the real world shows the same results and dynamics as those found in laboratories and also documents a circular relation between production and consumption harms."

21 Factum of the Intervener Women's Legal Education and Action Fund, in the case of *R.* v. *Butler* (S.C.C.), File No. 22191, 1990 (hereinafter, LEAF Factum). Copies of the LEAF Factum are available from the LEAF national office, 415 Yonge Street, Suite 1800, Toronto, ON M5B 2B7.

22 For a thorough description of the content of pornography, see Dworkin, "Pornography Is a Civil Rights Issue for Women," *supra* note 18. See also Russell, *Pornography: The Evidence of Harm, supra* note 17; Neil Malamuth and Barry Spinner, "A Longitudinal Content Analysis of Sexual Violence in the Best-Selling Erotic Magazines" (1980) 16 *Journal of Sex Research* 226; Park Elliott Dietz and Barbara Evans, "Pornographic Imagery and Prevalence of Paraphilia" (1982) 139 *American Journal of Psychiatry* 1493; T.S. Palys, "Testing the Common Wisdom: The Social Content of Video Pornography" (1986) *Canadian Psychology* 22.

23 LEAF Factum, *supra* note 21 at para. 2. It should be noted that, despite the claims of some of the litigants in the *Little Sisters* case, some of the materials seized from Donald Butler's store were magazines and videos intended for sale to gay men. The nature and effect of these materials will be discussed in subsequent chapters. For now, however, it is sufficient to note only that these materials did exist and that LEAF was widely (and unfairly) criticized in the gay community for using them as part of its argument before the Court.

   An overview of LEAF's strategy and a response to the claim that the group appealed to judicial homophobia in order to win the case are found in Karen Busby, "LEAF and Pornography: Litigating on Equality and Sexual Representations" (1994) 9(1) *Can. J.L. and Soc.* 165. Regarding the gay male pornography relevant to the *Butler* case, Busby notes that, because the analysis LEAF offered was one based on equality (a point the Court accepted), to omit any discussion of gay pornography would be to omit a necessary discussion of the role these materials have, not only in gay communities but also within a broader social context. An analysis of the materials before the Court more than justifies this stance. As Busby explains (at 179), "[s]ome of the seized materials in *Butler* involved sex between men, and some of these materials were extremely violent. The depictions included gay bashing, penetration with a rifle, gang rape scenes, and prison rape scenes. None of the materials portrayed safe sex. One magazine featured a nude teenage boy surrounded by children's toys."

   Busby's justification is well founded. As such, one is left to query why LEAF, nine years later in the *Little Sisters* case, found itself able to justify a litigation strategy which, if accepted, would have allowed the unlimited circulation throughout Canada of the very materials the

group earlier criticized as a violation of society's sex equality interest. This is a point I will
return to in Chapter 6.
24 LEAF Factum, *ibid.* at para. 3. LEAF continues:

> Sex acts are presented being performed on subordinates by superiors or caretakers,
> including employer on employee, priest on penitent, doctor on nurse, and nurse on
> patient. Adult women are presented as children, with child-like (shaved) pubic areas,
> teddy bears, hair ribbons and saddle shoes. Some participants appear to be children.
> Women are shown having sex with women, as sex for men. An Asian woman is subjected
> to racist insults as part of forced fellatio and rape. Women are presented as being
> sexually insatiable. Women are simultaneously or serially penetrated in every orifice
> by penises or objects. Women are presented as gagging on penises down their throats.
> Women lick men's anuses. Women are bound with rings through their nipples and
> hung handcuffed from the ceiling. Men ejaculate all over women, including on their
> faces and into their mouths. In these contexts, women are referred to and described as
> "pussy," "cunt," "split beavers," "hole," "bitch," "hot titties and twats," "dyke meat," and
> "chocolate box."

25 *Ibid.* at para. 23, citing *Pornography and Prostitution in Canada: Report of the Special Committee on
Pornography and Prostitution*, 1985 (Fraser Report), 95-103 and chap. 6; *Final Report of the
Attorney General's Commission on Pornography* (US, 1986), 747-56, 767-1035, and chaps. 16
and 17; *Metro Toronto Task Force on Public Violence against Women and Children, Final Report*
(Canada, 1984), 66; *Report of the Joint Select Committee on Video Material* (Australia, 1988),
185-230; *Report of the Ministerial Committee of Inquiry into Pornography* (New Zealand, 1988),
38-45, 59-60, and 79-81; *Sexual Offences against Children: Report of the Committee on Sexual
Offences against Children and Youths* (Badgley Report) (US, 1984), chap. 55.
26 *Ibid.* at para. 7.
27 *Ibid.* at para. 22.
28 *Ibid.* at para. 30, citing *Final Report of the Attorney General's Commission, supra* note 25.
29 *Ibid.* at para. 31, citing Linda Lovelace, *Ordeal* (New Jersey: Citadel Press, 1980). LEAF
continues: "The pornography market provides a profit motive for physically harming people.
It is also a mechanism for proliferating and making permanent the societally imposed stigma
of sexual attacks. Pornography which is made from assaults and which exacerbates the injury
of those assaulted is no more worthy of protection as expression than are the assaults
themselves." An analysis of Linda Lovelace's ordeal, and a response to those who discount her
experiences, is offered in Chapter 4.
30 *Ibid.* at para. 34, citing E. Donnerstein, "Pornography: Its Effect on Violence against Women,"
in N. Malamuth and E. Donnerstein, eds., *Pornography and Sexual Aggression* (New York:
Academic Press, 1984), 53; N. Malamuth and L. Berkowitz, "Victim Reaction in Aggressive
Erotic Films as a Factor in Violence against Women" (1981) 41 *Journal of Personality and Social
Psychology* 710; N. Malamuth and J.V.P. Check, "The Effects of Mass Media Exposure on
Acceptance of Violence against Women: A Field Experiment" (1981) *Journal of Research in
Personality* 436; N. Malamuth, "Factors Associated with Rape as Predictors of Laboratory
Aggression against Women" (1983) 45 *Journal of Personality and Social Psychology* 432; N.
Malamuth and J.V.P. Check, "Aggressive Pornography and Beliefs in Rape Myths: Individual
Differences" (1985) 19 *Journal of Research in Personality* 299; M. McManus, *Introduction to
Report of Attorney General's Commission on Pornography* (Nashville: Rutledge Hill Press, 1986),
xviii; N. Malamuth and J.V.P. Check, "Penile Tumescence and Perceptual Responses to Rape
as a Function of the Victim's Perceived Reactions" (1980) 10 *Journal of Applied Social Psychology*
528; and D. Linz and J. Bryant, "Effects of Massive Exposure to Pornography," in N. Malamuth
and E. Donnerstein, eds., *Pornography and Sexual Aggression* (New York: Academic Press, 1984),
115.
31 LEAF factum, *supra* note 21 at para. 45, citing J.V.P. Check and T.H. Guloien, "Reported
Proclivity for Coercive Sex Following Repeated Exposure to Sexually Violent Pornography,
Nonviolent Dehumanizing Pornography and Erotica," in D. Zillman and J. Bryant, eds.,
Pornography: Research Advances and Policy Considerations (Hillsdale, New Jersey: Erlbaum, 1989);
D. Zillman and J. Bryant, "Effects of Massive Exposure to Pornography," in N. Malamuth and
E. Donnerstein, eds., *Pornography and Sexual Aggression* (New York: Academic Press, 1984),
115; J.V.P. Check and N. Malamuth, "Pornography and Sexual Aggression: A Social Learning
Theory Analysis" (1986) 9 *Communication Yearbook* 181; D. Zillman and J.B. Weaver,

"Pornography and Men's Sexual Callousness Toward Women," in D. Zillman and J. Bryant, eds., *Pornography: Research Advances and Policy Considerations* (Hillsdale, New Jersey: Erlbaum, 1989), 45; D.E.H. Russell, "Pornography and Rape: A Causal Model" (1989) 9 *Political Psychology* 41; D. Zillman and J. Bryant, "Effects of Prolonged Consumption of Pornography on Family Values" (1988) *A Journal of Family Issues* 518; J.G. Buchman, "Effects of Nonviolent Adult Erotica on Sexual Child Abuse Attitudes" (paper presented at meeting of the American Psychological Association, Boston, August 1990).

32 *Ibid.* at para. 46, citing *Public Hearings on Ordinances to Add Pornography as Discrimination against Women*, Minneapolis City Council, Government Operations Committee, 12 and 13 December 1983; Susan Cole, *Pornography and the Sex Crisis* (Toronto: Amanita Press, 1989), 44; C.Y. Yuen, "Women's Reactions to Violent Pornography, Nonviolent Pornography and Erotica" (master's thesis, University of Calgary, 1985); E. Sommers and J.V.P. Check, "An Empirical Investigation of the Role of Pornography in the Verbal and Physical Abuse of Women" (1987) 2 *Violence and Victims* 189; M.H. Silbert and A.K. Pines, "Pornography and Sexual Abuse of Women" (1984) 10 *Sex Roles* 857.

These findings are further supported by the victim-impact testimonies of those who have been pornography's victims – people who, when they do actually get a chance to speak about what pornography is and does, have a great deal to say about gender and the sexualization of dominance and subordination. From 1983 to 1992, Andrea Dworkin and Catharine MacKinnon, cooperating with various jurisdictions and at their initiative, provided this opportunity to both women and men for whom pornography is anything but a fantasy. The testimonies of these women and men bear witness to pornography as an act of inequality. See MacKinnon, *Sex Equality, supra* note 3; MacKinnon and Dworkin, *In Harm's Way, supra* note 17, and Dworkin and MacKinnon, *Pornography and Civil Rights: A New Day for Women's Equality*, *supra* note 2.

33 LEAF Factum, *supra* note 21 at para. 53. For, as LEAF notes, "pornography promotes systemic discrimination against women through systematic bias and subordination. The status and treatment of women is affected even for those who do not experience abuse related to pornography directly. When reduced to their sexual parts and seen in terms of how they can be sexually used, women are forced to live in a social climate of disrespect, denigration and comparative deprivation of human regard. Women's opportunities for autonomy and self-determination are undermined throughout society." *Ibid.* at para. 59.

34 US Department of Justice, *Attorney General's Commission on Pornography, Final Report* (Washington: US Government Printing Office, 1986). Since the commission's report in 1986 and LEAF's submission in 1991 were released, even more research has been conducted, conclusively establishing a causal connection between pornography and gender inequality. As MacKinnon summarizes:

A meta-analysis of almost thirty years of the major laboratory studies on aggression following exposure of normal men to pornography confirmed that exposure to pornography produces aggression, regardless of various moderating or mediating conditions such as level of sexual arousal, level of prior anger, type of pornography, medium used, or even, to some extent, the gender of the subject and the aggression's target. See Mike Allen et al., "A Meta-Analysis Summarizing the Effects of Pornography II: Aggression After Exposure," *Human Commun. Res.* Dec. 1995, at 258. This finding was strongest for materials that combine sex with violence but held true for sexually explicit material that does not show violence as well. Another meta-analysis concluded that, taken together, the body of experimental studies shows that exposure to pornography increases rape myth acceptance – again greater for violent pornography but also found to occur with non-violent pornography. See Mike Allen et al., "Exposure to Pornography and Acceptance of Rape Myths," 45 *J. Comm.* 5 (1995). The same outcome was found in Japan. See Ken-Ichi Ohbuchi et al., "Effects of Violent Pornography upon Viewers' Rape Myth Beliefs: A Study of Japanese Males," 1 *Psychol. Crime & L.* 71 (1994). In 2000 another meta-analysis of forty-six published studies including a total sample size of 12,323 people found "stable and generalizable," "clear and consistent results": "exposure to pornographic material puts one at increased risk for developing sexually deviant tendencies, committing sexual offenses, experiencing difficulties in one's intimate relationships, and accepting the rape myth." Elizabeth Oddone-Paolucci et al., "A Meta-Analysis of the Published Research on the Effects of Pornography," *The Changing Family and Child Development* 48, 51, 52-53 (Claudio Violato et al. eds., 2000). The authors urge that research move beyond the question of whether pornography influences violence and family functioning in light of the conclusive findings that it does. (*Sex Equality*, *supra* note 3 at 1549-50)

35 *Butler* (S.C.C.), *supra* note 1 at 497.
36 *Ibid*. at 509.
37 *Ibid*. at 496.
38 *Ibid*. at 500-8.
39 Note, for example, the experiences of Linda Marchiano (Lovelace), who was physically and psychologically abused during the production of the movie *Deep Throat*. Marchiano has described in detail how, during the production of this film, she was pimped, beaten, and forced at gunpoint to partake in sexual activities. See Lovelace, *supra* note 29. Marchiano's experiences are neither unusual nor unique. As Cole notes, "to the women who are in the pictures, it is real sex; it happened to them." Cole, *Power Surge: Sex, Violence and Pornography*, *supra* note 17 at 228. Marchiano's experiences and those of other women and gay men used to produce pornography are examined in more detail in Chapter 4.

There are, of course, those who, in addition to rejecting a link between what happened to these women during the production of pornography and the harms that result from the distribution of this abuse, doubt the claim that the violence documented by these women occurred because of pornography. See, for example, Nadine Strossen, *Defending Pornography: Free Speech, Sex and the Fight for Women's Rights* (New York: Scribner, 1995) and Brian McNair, *Mediated Sex: Pornography and Postmodern Culture* (London: Arnold Press, 1996), both of whom arguably question the testimonies offered by Marchiano and others in an attempt to discredit the link between pornography and personal harm. I will respond to these claims in Chapter 4.

40 Dworkin and MacKinnon note with respect to some of the testimony given at the Minneapolis hearings that

> [r]esearchers and clinicians documented what women know from life; pornography increases attitudes and behaviors of aggression and other discrimination by men against women ... Women testified that pornography was used to break their self-esteem, to train them to sexual submission, to season them to forced sex, to intimidate them out of job opportunities, to blackmail them into prostitution and keep them there, to terrorize and humiliate them into sexual compliance, and to silence their dissent. They told how it takes coercion to make pornography, how pornography is forced on women and children in ways that give them no choice about viewing the pornography or performing the sex. They told how pornography stimulates and condones rape, battery, sexual harassment, sexual abuse of children, and forced prostitution. We learned from the testimony that the more pornography men see, the more abusive and violent they want it to be; the more abusive and violent it becomes, the more they enjoy it, the more abusive and violent they become, and the less harm they see in it. In other words, pornography's consumers become unable to see its harm because they are enjoying it sexually. Men often think that they use pornography but do not do these things. But the evidence makes it clear that pornography makes it impossible for them to tell when sex is forced, that women are human, and that rape is rape. Evidence of a direct correlation between the rate of reported rape and consumption figures of major men's-entertainment magazines supports this. Pornography makes men hostile and aggressive toward women, and it makes women silent. Anyone who does not believe this should speak out against pornography in public some time. (*Pornography and Civil Rights*, *supra* note 2 at 47-8)

41 Canadian obscenity law originally developed within the context of preventing moral corruption through exposure to sexually explicit materials. An overlapping but broader purpose was to prevent offense to public sensibilities. Underlying assumptions informing these views were, and are, that women's naked bodies are indecent; sexual displays are immodest, unchaste, and impure; homosexuality is repulsive; and that sex outside traditional marriage or in other than traditional configurations is a sin. See LEAF Factum, *supra* note 21 at 3. In 1959, a significant step was taken to move beyond morality. At that time, the law was amended to define obscenity as "crime, horror, cruelty and violence," combined with sex, as well as the undue exploitation of sex. Unfortunately, this law was interpreted such that "undue exploitation of sex" depended upon sexual explicitness alone – not the actual harms resulting from sexual explicitness. See, for example, *R.* v. *Odeon Theatres Ltd. et al.* (1974), 16 C.C.C. (2d) 197 (Man. C.A.); *R.* v.

Kleppe (1977), 35 C.C.C. (2d) 168 (Ont. Prov. Ct.); *R. v. Gray* (1981), 65 C.C.C. (2d) 353 and 355 (Ont. H.C.). As LEAF explained in its factum in *Butler,* some courts assiduously and deliberately avoided identifying harm of any kind. Notwithstanding the accumulating evidence of harm, courts still took the approach of criminalizing "dirt for dirt's sake." See also *R. v. Coles Co. Ltd.* (1965), 2 C.C.C. 304, 322-3 (Ont. C.A.); *R. v. Prairie Schooner News Ltd.* (1970), 1 C.C.C. (2d) 252 (Man. C.A.); *R. v. Video World Limited* (1986), 22 C.C.C. (3d) 331 (Man. C.A.) at 342-3; *R. v. Periera-Vasquez* (1988), 64 C.R. (3d) 253 (B.C.C.A.) at 269; LEAF Factum, *supra* note 21 at 3-4. As LEAF noted, as long as the law remained concerned only with explicitness, it was unable to address the explosion of violent and abusive visual pornography in the 1970s and 1980s. This material featured incest, forced intercourse, sexual autilation, humiliation, beatings, bondage, and sexual torture, in which dominance and exploitation are directed at women. Some of this material did not necessarily contain the degree of explicitness the courts required for women but did cause real harm. For example, in the December 1984 issue of *Penthouse,* partially or fully naked Asian women are shown tightly bound and hanging from trees. Some courts convicted while others did not. LEAF argued that this occurred because the community standards test, focusing on explicitness only, was not properly anchored by a harms-based principle that found the harms to women to be determinative. LEAF Factum, *supra* note 21 at 4-5.

42 *Butler* (S.C.C.), *supra* note 1 at 492.
43 *Ibid.* at 495.
44 *Criminal Code, supra* note 8.
45 *R. v. Ramsingh* (1984), 14 C.C.C. (3d) 230 (Man. Q.B.), cited in *Butler* (S.C.C.), *supra* note 1 at 479.
46 *Butler* (S.C.C.) at 479 (quoting *Ramsingh* at 239).
47 *Ibid.*
48 *Ibid.* at 493.
49 *Ibid.*
50 Mari Matsuda, "Public Response to Racist Speech: Considering the Victim's Story" (1989) 87 *Mich. L. Rev.* 2320 at 2338. See also J.C. Love, "Tort Actions for Hate Speech and the First Amendment: Reconceptualizing the Competing Interests" (1992) 2 *Law & Sexuality* 29; Mari Matsuda et al., *Words That Wound: Critical Race Theory, Assaultive Speech and the First Amendment* (Boulder, CO: Westview Press, 1993). An excellent collection of papers on the effect of hate speech is found in Laura Lederer and Richard Delgado, eds., *The Price We Pay: The Case against Racist Speech, Hate Propaganda, and Pornography* (New York: Hill and Wang, 1995).
51 *Butler* (S.C.C.), *supra* note 1 at 462.
52 *Ibid.* at 464.
53 *Ibid.* at 466.
54 Chris Bearchell, "In Harm's Way: A Calculated Campaign Takes Aim at Sexual Imagery and Free Speech," *XS: A Supplement to Xtra!* November 1992.
55 See, for example, Chris Bearchell, "Proof: Who Needs Proof?" in *XS: A Supplement to Xtra!* November 1992, 3. In this regard, see also Bearchell, "Gay Porn Censored from All Sides," *Toronto Star,* 15 January 1993, A23; Chris Bearchell, "Harmed and Dangerous," *Xtra!* 15 February 1996, 8. Similar arguments have been a mainstay of gay journalism in Toronto. See, for example, the comments of Tim McCaskell, who writes in *Body Politic:* "There is no definitive evidence that pornography *causes* violence against women. In fact, wife-beating, rape and sexual harassment were epidemic in North America for years during which even the most soft-core pornography was largely banned. The disappearance of all pornography tomorrow would make no difference whatsoever in statistics of violence against women." Tim McCaskell, "Pornography and Prohibition," *Body Politic,* April 1983, 31.

See also the comments of Anna Marie Smith, who blames anti-pornography feminists for fictionalizing the link between porn and harm: "Using as evidence very controversial studies involving subjects who are bombarded with pornography and then quizzed about their attitudes towards violence against women, they have been extremely successful in making the notion of causality with porn a part of common sense. The acceptance of the slogan, 'Porn the theory, rape the practice' is now automatic." Anna Marie Smith, "Sex and Violence and Censorship," *Body Politic,* August 1986, 22.

See also "Pornography: The New Terrorism?" *Body Politic,* August 1978, 11; Chris Bearchell, "Pornography, Prostitution and Moral Panic," *Body Politic,* March 1984, 7; Chris Bearchell, "Not a Love Story and the Anti-Porn Crusade," *Body Politic,* July/August 1982, 11; Francis Gillis, "Monkey See, Monkey Rape?" *Body Politic,* December 1985, 13.

56 The hate propaganda provisions of the *Criminal Code* read:

318

1 Everyone who advocates or promotes genocide is guilty of an indictable offence and liable to imprisonment for a term not exceeding five years.

2 In this section "genocide" means any of the following acts committed with intent to destroy in whole or in part any identifiable group, namely,

a killing members of the group; or

b deliberately inflicting on the group conditions of life calculated to bring about its physical destruction.

3 No proceeding for an offence under this section shall be instituted without the consent of the Attorney General.

4 In this section "identifiable group" means any section of the public distinguished by colour, race, religion or ethnic origin.

319

1 Everyone who, by communicating statements in any public place, incites hatred against any identifiable group where such incitement is likely to lead to a breach of the peace is guilty of

a an indictable offence and is liable to imprisonment for a term not exceeding two years; or

b an offence punishable on summary conviction.

2 Everyone who, by communicating statements, other than in private conversation, wilfully promotes hatred against any identifiable group is guilty of

a an indictable offence and is liable to imprisonment for a term not exceeding two years; or

b an offence punishable on summary conviction.

3 No person shall be convicted of an offence under subsection (2)

a if he establishes that the statements communicated were true;

b if, in good faith, he expressed or attempted to establish by argument an opinion upon a religious subject;

c if the statements were relevant to any subject of public interest, the discussion of which was for the public benefit, and if on reasonable grounds he believed them to be true; or

d if, in good faith, he intended to point out, for the purpose of removal, matters producing or tending to produce feelings of hatred towards an identifiable group in Canada.

4 Where a person is convicted of an offence under section 318 or subsection (1) or (2) of this section, anything by means of or in relation to which the offence was committed, on such conviction, may, in addition to any other punishment imposed, be ordered by the presiding provincial court judge or judge to be forfeited to Her Majesty in right of the province in which that person is convicted, for disposal as the Attorney General may direct.

5 Subsection 199(6) and (7) apply with such modifications as the circumstances require to section 318 or subsection (1) or (2) of this section.

6 No proceeding for an offence under subsection (2) shall be instituted without the consent of the Attorney General.

7 In this section,

"communicating" includes communicating by telephone, broadcasting or other audible or visible means;

"identifiable group" has the same meaning as in section 318(4);

"public place" includes any place to which the public have access as of right or by invitation, express or implied;

"statements" includes words spoken or written or recorded electronically or electromagnetically or otherwise, and gestures, signs or other visible representations.

Although the *Code* does not prohibit hate propaganda directed against lesbians and gay men, legislation does exist which allows judges to impose harsher sentences in cases where evidence exists that an offence was motivated by bias, prejudice, or hate based on race, nationality, colour, religion, sex, mental or physical disability, or the sexual orientation of the victim. This has led activists to quite rightly query the omission of sexual orientation from the

Code's hate speech provisions. Others have queried the need for any "religious exemptions" (s. 319 (3)(b)), given the use of religious rhetoric to condemn homosexual identity. See Major, and Banks, *infra* note 65 at 233. See also "Rock to Beef Up Hate-Crimes Law," *Toronto Globe and Mail*, 11 June 1994, 4. The omission is unfounded given the Supreme Court of Canada's repeated findings that lesbians and gay men suffer the same level of prejudice, harm, abuse, and inequality as other groups protected as other socially disenfranchised groups.

As early as 1990, the Canadian courts noted in *Veysey* v. *Canada (Correctional Service)* (1990), 109 N.R. 300 at 317 that those groups offered protection under s. 15 of the *Charter of Rights and Freedoms* share similar characteristics: "Another characteristic common to the enumerated grounds is that the individuals or groups involved have been victimized and stigmatized throughout history because of prejudice, mostly because of fear or ignorance, as most prejudices are. This characteristic would also clearly apply to sexual orientation or, more precisely, to those who have deviated from accepted social norms, at least in the eyes of the majority."

Given this, the government's inaction with respect to amending the *Code* is cause for concern. This is a point discussed in more detail in Chapter 8.

57 Glenn Cooly, "Homophobic Bible Comic May Spark Legal Battle," *Now Magazine*, September 1992, 16. A similar earlier example is discussed in Gillian Rogerson, "They Only Want to Help Us: Christian Loonies Find an Unusual Route for Delivering Scurrilous Materials," *Body Politic*, July 1985, 21. In that case, classified advertisers in *Body Politic* reported receiving literature packages that included a booklet by American televangelist Jimmy Swaggart, entitled *Homosexuality: Its Causes and Its Cure*. In the booklet, Swaggart asserts, "The sex pervert is a gay or homosexual. I'm sick to death of words like 'gay' being used to amass respect for people who don't deserve respect. Why don't they use words descriptive of their chosen lifestyle, such as pervert, queer or faggot? There are plenty of appropriate words branding these people for what they really are." In response, the Coalition for Lesbian Gay Rights in Ontario (CLGRO) attempted to lay a complaint with the Ontario Human Rights Commission and with the Toronto police, after copies of the booklet were placed on car windshields throughout Toronto. A representative for CLGRO explained that "we are aware that this is not the strongest available form of hate literature against us, but we see that its function is to incite hatred against a class of people, regardless of their individual merits, by imputing to them everything from moral weakness to the deepest-dyed sin." Both the police and the commission replied that they were unable to act, as their governing statutes did not specifically prohibit anti-gay hate speech. This in turn led to calls for amendments to the *Criminal Code* and *Human Rights Act* hate speech provisions to include sexual orientation as a prohibited target of hate speech. The *Ontario Human Rights Code* has subsequently been amended. The use of human rights legislation to combat anti-gay hate speech is discussed in more detail in the final chapter.

58 Cooly, *ibid.*

59 *Ibid.*

60 *Ibid.*

61 Charles Moore, "Free Speech Challenge Based on Biblical Passages," *Calgary Herald*, 5 August 1998, A11.

62 Robert Matas, "Evangelicals Assailed over Anti-Games Ad.," *Globe and Mail*, 10 June 1990, 6.

63 Institute for the Scientific Investigation of Sexuality, *The Psychology of Homosexuality*, available from ISIS, P.O. Box 6725, Lincoln, NE 68506. The distribution of these and similar anti-gay pamphlets is not an uncommon occurrence in Canada. In October 1981, for example, literature proclaiming "God is on your side. Remember that the only good queer is a dead queer" turned up on the streets of Burnaby and other suburbs in British Columbia. As Chris Bearchell reported at the time, the pamphlet, distributed the night before Vancouver's gay and lesbian pride parade, instructs readers to "lobby to have the death penalty returned to any person convicted of being homosexual." It continued: "Meanwhile, if you see a queer on the street and there are no witnesses around, beat that queer so that he will never walk again." It concluded: "It is bad enough that we must put up with a lot of Asians, Jews and other filth. Must we also tolerate faggots?" See Chris Bearchell, "Beat That Queer: Hate Lit Spreads West," *Body Politic*, October 1991, 10.

64 REAL Women, *Laws Protecting Homosexuals or So-Called Sexual Orientation Legislation* (1988), available through REAL Women of Canada, 215 Victoria Street, Suite 509, Toronto, ON M5B 1T9. Noting that "the homosexual" must not be given rights protections because "he" poses a real threat to the proper functioning of society, the flyer continues:

Homosexuality has a harmful effect on society that can no longer be ignored. The new findings on AIDS have destroyed the idea that the gay rights movement doesn't injure anyone and that what they do is their own business. Homosexuals are a medical threat to their own sex, to those who require blood transfusions, to the promiscuous and their unknowing spouses. Homosexual food handlers are a frequent source of hepatitis outbreaks. Homosexual spouses expose their mates to a wide variety of diseases. In addition, the cost of medical research and treatment of AIDS is mounting daily and is being paid for by the taxpayer.

65 Kathleen Sam Banks, "Could Mom Be Wrong? The Hurt of Names and Wrongs: Hate Propaganda and Freedom of Expression" (June 1999) 6(2) *E Law – Murdoch University Electronic Journal of Law* <http://www.murdoch.edu.au/elaw/issues/v6n2/banks62nf.html>. See also Marie-France Major, "Sexual Orientation Hate Propaganda: Time to Regroup" (1996) 11(1) *Can. J.L. and Soc.* 221.

66 The *Canadian Human Rights Act* (R.S. 1985, c. H-6, ss. 2 and 13(1)) provides:

> 2   The purpose of this Act is to extend the laws in Canada to give effect, within the purview of matters coming within the legislative authority of Parliament, to the principle that all individuals should have an opportunity equal with other individuals to make for themselves the lives that they are able and wish to have and to have their needs accommodated, consistent with their duties and obligations as members of society, without being hindered in or prevented from doing so by discriminatory practices based on race, national or ethnic origin, colour, religion, age, sex, sexual orientation, marital status, family status, disability or conviction for an offence for which a pardon has been granted.

> **Hate messages**
> 13 (1)   It is a discriminatory practice for a person or a group of persons acting in concert to communicate telephonically or to cause to be so communicated, repeatedly, in whole or in part by means of the facilities of a telecommunication undertaking within the legislative authority of Parliament, any matter that is likely to expose a person or persons to hatred or contempt by reason of the fact that that person or those persons are identifiable on the basis of a prohibited ground of discrimination.

67 See *McAleer* v. *Canada (Human Rights Commission)* (1996), 132 D.L.R. (4th) 672 at 675 (F.C.T.D.) as quoted in Banks, *supra* note 65. The *McAleer* case and the use of Human Rights Code protections to fight hate speech are discussed in more detail in the final chapter.

68 The videotape, which seems to be distributed freely most often prior to lesbian and gay pride parades or marches throughout Canada and which was also distributed throughout Oregon and Colorado during those states' recent ballot initiatives aimed at curtailing the extension of basic human rights principles to lesbians and gay men, shows Jerry Falwell who, in referring to the 1993 March on Washington, states, "[I]t would have been hard not to use napalm." Directing his statements to gay men, he continues, "You send for my children. You want to sodomize and rape them and destroy them." See J. Kennedy, "Christians Advocate Violence," *Xtra! West*, 14 December 1996, 9.

69 Note, for example, statements made by Canadian member of Parliament Roseanne Skoke, who in 1994 was quoted as saying in Parliament that "homosexuality is based on an inhuman act, defiles humanity, destroys families ... and is annihilating mankind." See "Speaker Exits Robinson-Skoke Exchange," *Globe and Mail*, 1 October 1994, A3. As noted by Equality for Gays and Lesbians Everywhere (EGALE), the gay rights lobby group later responsible for trying to uphold pornographic speech as a constitutional right, prior to the comments made by Skoke, Reform Party Justice Critic Myron Thompson explained that "I don't hate thieves; I hate stealing. I do not hate murderers; I hate murdering. I do not hate homosexuals; I hate homosexuality." See EGALE, *Submissions to the House of Commons Standing Committee, House Committee on Justice and Legal Affairs, Regarding Bill c-41 Hate Crimes*, Ottawa, 1994.

70 As Banks explains, "gay men and lesbians are often portrayed as living an incomplete and sordid lifestyle, totally absorbed by illicit sex and AIDS is frequently cited as a form of deserved retribution for the 'sin against nature' of 'the destructive lifestyle' of homosexuality." Banks, *supra* note 65, quoting R. Brunet, "Tired of Celebrating an Obsession," *British Columbia Report*, 16 August 1993, 23.

71 Cited in M. Kirk and H. Madsen, *After the Ball* (New York: Doubleday, 1989), 101.

72 Banks, *supra* note 65. Arguing for the inclusion of sexual orientation in s. 319 of the *Criminal Code,* Banks continues:

> Hate propaganda represents a serious threat to a free and democratic society through its messages calculated to divide, demean and discriminate. Individuals who are the target of hate speech lose their dignity, self-worth and sense of belonging to the community, the targeted group suffers a loss of cultural identity and group reputation, and society as a whole is damaged by its messages encouraging division, prejudice and intolerance. Equality and inherent human dignity are not tentative concepts: without protection from the harms of hate propaganda, these ideas themselves are demeaned and marginalized. On balance, our commitments to equality, multiculturalism and social harmony are enhanced rather than diminished by expanding s.319 (2) of the *Criminal Code* to include sexual orientation within its prohibitions.

See also Major, *supra* note 65 at 234-40. As Major notes (at 227), there is little reason to believe that anti-gay prejudice does not manifest the same social and psychological damage as racial and other ethnic prejudices. See generally G. Herek, "Religious Orientation and Prejudice: A Comparison of Racial and Sexual Attitudes" (1987) 13 *Personality and Social Psychology Bulletin* 34; G. Herek, "Hate Crimes against Lesbians and Gay Men: Issues for Research and Policy" (1989) 44 *American Psychologist* 948; G.B. Meron, "Public Policy and Private Prejudice: Psychology and the Law on Gay Rights" (1989) *American Psychologist* 933.

73 Banks, *supra* note 65.
74 Factum of the Women's Legal Education Action Fund, in the case of *R. v. Keegstra,* Supreme Court of Canada (hereinafter S.C.C.), File No. 21116, 1 December 1989.
75 Patrick Lawlor, *Group Defamation: Submission to the Attorney General* (Toronto, March 1984). On file with author.
76 Kirk and Madsen, *supra* note 71 at 103-4. For further evidence, see Martin Kazu Hiraga, "Anti-Gay-and Lesbian Violence, Victimization, and Defamation: Trends, Victimization Studies and Incident Descriptions," in Laura Lederer and Richard Delgado, eds., *The Price We Pay: The Case against Racist Speech, Hate Propaganda, and Pornography* (New York: Hill and Wang, 1995); Gary Comstock, *Violence against Lesbians and Gay Men* (New York: Columbia University Press, 1991); Gregory Herek and Kevin Berrill, eds., *Hate Crimes: Confronting Violence against Lesbians and Gay Men* (New York: Sage Publications, 1992); Gail Mason and Stephen Tomsen, *Homophobic Violence* (Sydney: Hawkins Press, 1997); and People for the American Way, *Hostile Climate: A State by State Report on Anti-Gay Activity* (Washington: People for the American Way, 1997).
77 See generally Cynthia Petersen, "A Queer Response to Bashing: Legislating against Hate" (1991) 16 *Queen's L.J.* 237; Brief to the Members of the Ontario Legislature from the Coalition for Lesbians and Gay Rights in Ontario, *Discrimination against Lesbians and Gay Men: The Ontario Human Rights Omission* (1986); M. Sandler, "Hate Crimes and Hate Group Activity in Canada" (1994) 43 *U.N.B.L.J.* 269; Warren Kinsella, *Web of Hate: Inside Canada's Far Rights Network* (Toronto: HarperCollins, 1994).
78 Lawlor, *supra* note 75 at 5. See also Law Reform Commission of Canada, *Hate Propaganda* (Working Paper no. 50), Ottawa, 1986, 30.
79 Lawlor, *supra* note 75 at 6.
80 *Ibid.* at 17.
81 Scott Tucker, "Sex, Death and Free Speech: The Fight to Stop Friedkin's *Cruising,*" *Body Politic,* November 1979, 23 at 24.
82 *Ibid.*
83 They were, however, unwilling to question the possible negative message sent to gay men and everyone else by a film that shows us as little more than a community of fun-loving sadists, desiring to be sexually violated by other gay men. Indeed, many seem to now promote or defend these sexual stereotypes, a point I will return to in Chapter 6.
84 *Ibid.* at 25.
85 *Ibid.*
86 *Ibid.*
87 *Ibid.*
88 *Ibid.* at 26.
89 *Ibid.* at 27.
90 Note also, for example, recent legal actions aimed at shutting down phone lines that expose people to contempt or hatred because of their sexual orientation. For instance, the Federal Court of Canada recently upheld a Canadian Human Rights Tribunal decision that shut down

the telephone hotline of Vancouver's Canadian Liberty Net – a group committed to promoting hatred against lesbians and gay men. See "Federal Court Upholds Anti-Hate Ruling," *InfoFlash*, 15 February 1996. This issue is discussed in more detail in the final chapter.

91 Jane Rule, "Pornography," *Body Politic*, January/February 1984, 33.
92 See generally Chris Bearchell, "Proof, Who Needs Proof?" in *XS: A Supplement to Xtra!* November 1992, 3; Brian McNair, *Mediated Sex: Pornography and Postmodern Culture* (London: Arnold, 1996), chaps. 5 and 6; Alan Borovoy, "Beware the Bible or the 11 O'Clock News," *Globe and Mail*, 10 March 1992, A19; Vivian Smith, "Defending Pornography: Free Speech, Sex and the Fight for Women's Rights" (book review), *Globe and Mail*, 4 March 1995, C23; Christopher Hume, "The XXX Reality of Censorship," *Toronto Star*, 29 October 1994, L1; Chris Bearchell, "Gay Porn Censored on All Sides," *Toronto Star*, 15 January 1993, A23; and Nadine Strossen, *Defending Pornography: Free Speech, Sex and the Fight for Women's Rights* (New York: Scribner, 1995).
93 As Diana Russell explains, in responding to American Civil Liberties Union (ACLU) president Nadine Strossen's call for more proof, for example,

> [m]any people share Strossen's opinion that men who consume porn but who have never raped a woman disprove the theory that porn can cause rape. This is comparable to arguing that because some cigarette smokers don't die of lung cancer, there cannot be a causal relationship between smoking and lung cancer. Only members of the tobacco industry and some seriously addicted smokers consider this a valid argument today ... Although the scientific evidence that porn can cause rape is at least as strong as the evidence that smoking can cause lung cancer, many people are so ideologically committed to the view that porn is harmless that they find a multitude of excuses to disregard it. Strossen and the ACLU's strategy seems to be to ignore information, arguments and theories that they find too difficult to tackle, no matter how much dishonesty and misrepresentation it takes. ("Nadine Strossen: The Pornography Industry's Wet Dream," *On the Issues*, Summer 1995, 32)

94 *Butler* (S.C.C.), *supra* note 1 at 503.
95 *Ibid.* at 502 and 504.
96 *Keegstra, supra* note 6. *Keegstra* concerned the interpretation and application of ss. 318 and 319 of the *Canadian Criminal Code*. These provisions make it an indictable offence to communicate statements that wilfully promote hatred against any identifiable group. In *Keegstra*, the Canadian Supreme Court held that although these provisions do infringe the right to free expression, the infringement is nonetheless justified because of the threat to equality posed to target groups, and to society at large, from speech aimed at undermining equality. *Ibid.* at 747. Much has been written on the *Keegstra* decision. See generally Tamsin Solomon, "Antisemitism as Free Speech: Judicial Responses to Hate Propaganda in Zundel and Keegstra" (1995) 13(1) *Australian-Canadian Studies* 1; Kathleen Mahoney, "R. v. Keegstra: A Rationale for Regulating Pornography?" (1992) 37 *McGill L.J.* 242; Richard Moon, "Drawing Lines in a Culture of Prejudice: R. v. Keegstra and the Restriction of Hate Propaganda" (1992) *U.B.C. Law Rev.* 99; Bruce Elman, "Combatting Racist Speech: The Canadian Experience" (1994) 32(4) *Alta. L. Rev.* 621; Bruce MacDougall, *Queer Judgments: Homosexuality Expression and the Courts in Canada* (Toronto: University of Toronto Press, 2000), 147. See also the discussion provided in Chapter 8.
97 *Keegstra, supra* note 6 at 703.
98 *Ibid.* at 705.
99 *Ibid.* at 857.
100 *Ibid.* at 846.
101 *Butler* (S.C.C.), *supra* note 1 at 503.
102 Mark Hussey, "Defending Pornography: Free Speech, Sex and the Fight for Women's Rights" (book review), *On the Issues*, Summer 1995, 48.
103 Daniel Jonah Goldhagen, *Hitler's Willing Executioners: Ordinary Germans and the Holocaust* (New York: Random House, 1996). The sexualization of racism and anti-Semitism in pornography, and gay male pornography in particular, is discussed in Chapters 6 and 7 of this book.
104 *R. v. Hawkins; R. v. Jorgensen, R. v. Ronish et al, R. v. Jorgensen et al, R. v. Smeenk et al.* (1993) 15 O.R. (3d) 549 (Ont. C.A.) (indexed as *R. v. Hawkins*).
105 *Ibid.* at 564.
106 *Ibid.*
107 *Ibid.* at 567.

108 Specifically, the Court ruled that "[u]nder the *Butler* test, not all material depicting adults engaged in sexually explicit acts which are degrading or dehumanizing will be found to be obscene. The material must also create a substantial risk of harm to society. That risk is now an element of obscenity-based crimes. Like any element of a criminal allegation, it must be proved beyond a reasonable doubt and that evidence must be found in the evidence at trial." *Ibid.* at 566.

109 *Ibid.* at 566-7. The Court's analysis of what is harmful in *Hawkins* has now taken on an even more troubling dimension within the context of the harms of child pornography, a topic beyond the scope of this book but which merits a brief mention. In the case of *R.* v. *Sharpe*, [2001] 1 S.C.R. 45, the Supreme Court of Canada again appears to misunderstand the actual, real connection between *all* pornography and harm. In *Sharpe*, the Court ruled that it was a violation of the right to free expression to prohibit individuals from making and possessing some kinds of child pornography. As Professor Janine Benedet explains in an exceptional critique of the majority's judgment,

> [t]he majority relies on a few hypothetical cases to carve out two exceptions to the child pornography law: written works that are created by the person in possession of them – such as diaries, stories and drawings – and visual works made by or depicting the maker that depict only lawful sexual activity. The majority points to some hypothetical cases that would support each example focusing in particular on adolescents who keep a journal of their sexual experiences or who take sexual photos of each other as part of a consensual relationship ...
>
> The hypotheticals used by the majority to strike down portions of the provisions do not have a grounding in reality. Instead, they fall right in with the majority's abstract values approach to defining the contours of the appeal. They are ludicrous examples that are used to chop out substantial exceptions that cover a lot of real, harmful conduct ...
>
> [T]he Court is simply wrong to assume that written child pornography never involves real children. It is often important to the person making the written pornography that it be based on a real person. For example, in *R.* v. *R. W.*, the trial judge described the home environment of the accused's three children as one where their father was frequently if not almost constantly viewing pornography on videotape and through the Internet, and where drugs[,] alcohol and cigarettes were made available to these children and their friends. The accused repeatedly sexually assaulted both of his daughters, for example by refusing to let them leave the apartment unless he could first touch their breasts. The police also found in the accused's home approximately 100 pornographic photos and a 36 page story in two parts entitled "Making my Daughter Mine" and "Everyone Else's Play Toy" which describes his children by name and age and which contained "a fictional account" of how M. [one daughter] is made a sex slave ... set out in excruciating and horrifying detail. The details include incidents of rape, torture, forced sex with animals, prolonged periods of bondage, intercourse, non-consensual intercourse and fellatio with friends of the father as well as friends of the daughter, and the intended involvement of other friends of the daughter ...
>
> This exception ignores the fact that this is dangerous material and that the private sanctuary of the home is the most common location for abuse of women and children. M has a right to live in a home that does not contain positive presentations of her sexual abuse at the hands of her father, particularly as she is being forced to endure that abuse in real life. She also has a right not to worry that this story will be shown to others or that the acts described in it are what her father is planning for her and her friends next week or next month. We do not automatically allow people to make, use and store other kinds of dangerous items in their homes until they use them to do harm outside the home. Instead, we allow laws that ban possession of these items outright.
>
> Even more troubling is the reality of the second exception, privately created visual recordings of lawful sexual activity made by or depicting the person in possession and intended only for personal use. This exception also applies to both production and possession. This exception does not even require that the material depict the person in possession of it. Here, the Court's examples focus almost exclusively on adolescents who record their sexual acts as part of their sexual development in a mutual, consensual relationship. No evidence is discussed that might indicate if this ever happens, and, if so, under what conditions.

In fact, those adolescents whose lawful sexual activity is recorded often do not consent to that recording, are unaware of the recording, or consent to its recording under circumstances of deception or bribery. While the majority adds to its exception the condition that all parties must consent to the creation of the record, the Crown will now have to prove non-consent beyond a reasonable doubt. This will be extremely difficult where the children in the photo or tape cannot be traced and where they have been forced to smile. ("Children in Pornography After Sharpe" [2002] 43 *C. de D.* 327 at 338, 343, 344, and 345)

110 In addition to *Hawkins*, the reader should see the decision of the Alberta Provincial Court in *R. v. Erotica Video Exchange Ltd.* (1994), 163 A.R. 181 (Prov. Ct.).

111 Bruce MacDougall, *Queer Judgments: Homosexuality, Expression and the Courts in Canada* (Toronto: University of Toronto Press, 2000), 145. See also Derek Raymaker and David Kilgour, "The Freedom to Promote Hate: What We Learned from Jim Keegstra and Malcolm Ross" (1992) 41 *U.N.B.L.J.* 327 at 329.

Chapter 2: Sex Equality and Homophobia

1 Marilyn Frye, *The Politics of Reality* (Freedom, CA: Crossing Press, 1983), 146.

2 Catharine MacKinnon, *Toward a Feminist Theory of the State* (Cambridge: Harvard University Press, 1989), 114. See also Lise Oostergaard, who explains that

> [g]ender refers to the qualitative and interdependent character of women's and men's position in society. Gender relations are constituted in terms of the relations of power and dominance that structure the life chances of women and men. Thus gender divisions are not fixed biology, but constitute an aspect of the wider social division of labour and this, in turn, is rooted in the conditions of production and reproduction and reinforced by the cultural, religious and ideological systems prevailing in a society.
>
> The relations between men and women are socially constituted and not derived from biology. Therefore the term gender relations should distinguish such social relations between men and women from those characteristics which can be derived from biological differences.
>
> These relations are not necessarily nor obviously harmonious and non-conflicting. On the contrary, the socially constructed relations between the genders may be ones of opposition and conflict. But since such conflicts are not to be analyzed as facts of biology and nature but as being socially determined, they may take very different forms under different circumstances. They often take the form of male dominance and female subordination.
>
> In short, the concept of gender makes it possible to distinguish the biologically founded, sexual differences between women and men from the culturally determined differences between the roles given to or by women and men respectively in a given society. The first are unchangeable, like a destiny. The latter are workable and may be changed by political and opinion-shaping influences. (*Gender and Development: A Practical Guide* [London: Routledge, 1992], 6 and 7)

3 Katharine Franke, "The Central Mistake of Sex Discrimination: The Disaggregation of Sex from Gender" (1995) 144 *U. Pa. L. Rev.* 1 at 4.

4 See generally Adrienne Rich, "Compulsory Heterosexuality and Lesbian Existence" (1980) 5(4) *Signs: Journal of Women in Culture and Society* 63.

5 MacKinnon, *Toward a Feminist Theory of the State, supra* note 2 at 131 and 151.

6 *Ibid.* at 118. Building on MacKinnon's thesis, Sheila Jeffreys argues that gender becomes a desire, felt as sexual excitement, through which heterosexuality (read: the sexual pairing of male dominance and female submission) is maintained:

> The desire for gender, often felt as a visceral excitement, is a crucial component of heterosexuality as a political institution ... [It] is much more than just an annoyingly arbitrary and socially constructed classification system. Feminist theorists have shown how gender dynamically empowers heterosexuality, provides its most powerful pleasures through the sexuality of eroticised dominance and submission, and maintains the cruel power of men over women through turning it into just "sex." "Gender" is not an inert filing system but a vital force in constructing and maintaining heterosexuality as the scaffolding of male supremacy. The desire for gender is not just the desire to conform

and fit in ... but an excitement felt as sexuality in a male supremacist culture which eroticises male dominance and female submission ...

Masculinity and femininity, the genders of dominance and submission, are eroticised to create the sexuality of male supremacy which I call heterosexual desire. By the term "heterosexual desire" I do not mean desire for the opposite sex, but a desire that is organised around eroticised dominance and submission. It emerges from the political system of heterosexuality as the eroticised subordination of women and is seen as natural, as what sex is. The hetero in heterosexual desire means other; in such desire one participant is "othered," or reduced to subordinate status through dominant/submissive, objectifying sex. The "difference" between the sexes which is supposed to give the excitement to heterosexual sex, is not natural but political, a difference of power. Heterosexual desire is formed out of, and requires for its excitement and continuance, the subjection of women.

Thus gender is not simply the mould in which men and women learn different sexualities, but is a product of gender itself. The sexuality of male supremacy, heterosexual desire, requires the constant recreation of masculinity and femininity. ("Heterosexuality and the Desire for Gender," in Diane Richardson, ed., *Theorising Heterosexuality* [Buckingham: Open University Press, 1996], 74 at 74-77)

7   See Cass Sunstein, "Homosexuality and the Constitution" (1994) 70 *Ind. L.J.* 1 at 21. Sunstein argues that "[t]he evidence taken as a whole suggests that the prohibition on homosexual relations is best seen as an effort to insist on and rigidify so-called natural difference, in part by crisply separating gender roles ... The definition of men as essentially active in social and sexual arenas, and of women as essentially passive in both places, helps undergird sex inequality."

This point is particularly well documented by George Chauncey, whose work on the gay community in New York in the early 1900s does much to dispel the myth that gay oppression is disconnected from sexism. Indeed, Chauncey argues that it was not until women became more economically independent and socially empowered that the real animosity for things homosexual became socially ingrained and required:

Many men believed that women were threatening the sanctity of other male domains as well and were trying to take control of the nation's culture. The women's suffrage campaign seemed the most direct challenge, for many men interpreted women's demand for the vote as a renunciation of men's prerogative to represent the women in their families in the (male) public sphere ... On every front, women seemed to be breaching the division between the sexes' proper spheres and to be claiming or challenging the prerogatives of men.

The growing concern about the danger of over civilization and feminization of American men had manifold practical ramifications for men's everyday lives – and for their attitude toward fairies and queers ... The attack on women's influence on American culture led to an attack on men who seemed to have accepted that influence by becoming over civilized and men who did not do their part to uphold the manly ideal were subject to growing ridicule.

The insistence on exclusive heterosexuality emerged in part then in response to the crisis in middle-class masculinity precipitated by the manly comportment of working-class men and the subversion of manly ideals and sexualization of male social relations by the fairy. But heterosexuality became even more important to middle-class men because it provided them with a new, more positive way to demonstrate their manhood. Sexual style had long been a crucial aspect of gender style; both sexual aggressiveness and sexual self-control – as well as the ability to propagate and support children – had served as markers of manliness among different groups of men. But by the late nineteenth century, sexual personality – or "sexuality" – had emerged as a distinct domain of personhood and an independent basis for the assertion of manliness. (*Gay New York: Gender, Urban Culture, and the Making of the Gay Male World 1890-1940* [New York: Basic Books, 1994], 111-17)

See also Jonathan Ned Katz, *The Invention of Heterosexuality* (New York: Dutton, 1995) and Elizabeth Kennedy and Madeline Davis, *Boots of Leather, Slippers of Gold: The History of a Lesbian Community* (New York: Routledge, 1993). The themes and arguments covered in all these works are effectively summarized in Urvashi Vaid, *Virtual Equality: The Mainstreaming of Gay and Lesbian Liberation* (New York: Anchor Books, 1995).

8 Robert Goss, *Jesus Acted Up: A Gay and Lesbian Manifesto* (San Francisco: HarperCollins, 1993). As Marc Fajer notes, this notion that relationships need not be constructed on hierarchical gender roles is, socially, a threat to male power. Enforced heterosexuality thus becomes the norm: "[g]ay couples, operating without gender-based definitions of their proper roles during marriage, often create new roles for themselves based on sharing and equality, rather than on gender stereotypes. Thus, many gay relationships operate on a more equal basis than most heterosexual marriages and might well serve as a model of equality for marriage ... The rejection of gender based roles in relationships is part of a greater challenge to gender norms implicit in openly gay lives; the strict dichotomy between male and female." Marc A. Fajer, "Can Real Men Eat Quiche Together? Storytelling, Gender-Role Stereotypes and Legal Protections for Lesbians and Gay Men" (1992) 46 *U. Miami L. Rev.* 511 at 615.
    In other words, as Canadian legal academic Wendy Adams explains, we can see that the condemnation of homosexuality serves a broader purpose – that being the prohibition against blurring the lines between masculinity and femininity so essential to the social construct of heterosexuality and the institutionalized practice of heterosexism that results. The primacy of gender norms can thus be seen in both homophobia and sex discrimination, each one feeding off the other to the benefit of those for whom the constructs male/female, masculine/feminine, and heterosexual/homosexual, structured hierarchically, ensure male supremacy over all women and gay men. See Wendy A. Adams, "A Sex Equality Approach to Discrimination on the Basis of Sexual Orientation: A Comparative Analysis within the Context of US and Canadian Constitutional Regimes" (master's thesis, University of Michigan, 1999).
9 See Marylin Frye, *The Politics of Reality* (Freedom, CA: Crossing Press, 1983), 146. Frye continues:

> Any man who would be a friend to women must come to understand the values and principles of phallocratic culture and how his own life is interwoven with them, and must reject them and become disloyal to masculinity. Any man who would do this has to reinvent what being a man is. The initial intuition which many of us have had that gay men may be more prone than straight men to being friends to women has, perhaps, this much truth in it: for gay men, more than for straight men, the seeds both of some motive and of some resources for taking this radical turn are built into their cultural and political situation in the world. The gay man's difference can be the source of the friction which might mother invention and may provide resources for that invention.

> My comments should not be interpreted as implying that gay men do not presently benefit from the social, sexual, and economic subordination of women or that some gay men do not choose to participate in male privilege. On the contrary, what I am stating is that gay men have a choice and that the choice they must make is that which rejects those behaviour patterns that reinforce male dominance and that are central to both sexism and homophobia. This is a point I will return to throughout this text.

10 Suzanne Pharr, *Homophobia: A Weapon of Sexism* (Little Rock, AR: Chardon Press, 1988), 19. Pharr is not, of course, alone in her assertion that sexism and homophobia are interconnected. Indeed, many lesbian and gay academics write of the role of gender in the lives of gay men and lesbians and the impact that this has on both sexism and heterosexism. In addition to the other authors cited throughout this chapter, see in particular Diana Majury in her insightful article "Refashioning the Unfashionable: Claiming Lesbian Identities in the Legal Context" (1994) 7(2) *C.J.W.L.* 286; Lynne Pearlman, "Theorizing Lesbian Oppression and the Politics of Outness in the Case of *Waterman* v. *National Life Assurance:* A Beginning in Lesbian Human Rights/Equality Jurisprudence" (1994) 7(2) *C.J.W.L.* 454; Andrew Koppelman, "Why Discrimination against Lesbians and Gay Men Is Sex Discrimination" (1994) 69 *N.Y.U.L. Rev.* 197; Andrew Koppelman, "The Miscegenation Analogy: Sodomy Law as Sex Discrimination" (1988) 98 *Yale L.J.* 145; Marie Elana Peluso, "Tempering Title VII's Straight Arrow Approach: Recognizing and Protecting Gay Victims of Employment Discrimination" (1993) 46 *Vand. L. Rev.* 1533; Francisco Valdes, "Queers, Sissies, Dykes, and Tomboys: Deconstructing the Conflation of 'Sex,' 'Gender' and 'Sexual Orientation' in Euro-American Law and Society" (1995) 83 *C.L.R.* 3; Mary Anne Case, "Disaggregating Gender from Sex and Sexual Orientation: The Effeminate Man in the Law and Feminist Jurisprudence" (1995) *Yale L.J.* 1; E.R. Arriola, "Gendered Inequality: Lesbians, Gays and Feminist Legal Theory" (1994) 9 *Berkeley Women's L.J.* 103; Amelia Craig, "Musing about Discrimination on Sex and Sexual Orientation as 'Gender Role' Discrimination" (1995) 5 *S. Cal. Rev. L. and Women's Stud.* 105; James Wilets, "Conceptualizing Private Violence against Sexual Minorities as

Gendered Violence: An International and Comparative Law Perspective" (1997) 60 *Alb. L. Rev.* 989; Patricia Cain, "Feminist Jurisprudence: Grounding the Theories" (1989) 4 *Berkeley Women's L.J.* 191.

11 Pharr, *supra* note 10 at 8. As Pharr explains (at 8), homophobia is central to preserving sexism and ultimately patriarchy: "Patriarchy – an enforced belief in male dominance and control – is the ideology and sexism the system that holds it in place. The catechism goes like this: who do gender roles serve? Men and the women who seek power from them. Who suffers from gender roles? Women mostly and men in part. How are gender roles maintained? By the weapons of sexism: economics, violence, homophobia." Homophobia works to maintain gender roles because it silences those women and men whose sexual identity and behaviour, it is believed, will "bring down the entire system of male dominance."

12 Fajer, *supra* note 8 at 607.

13 Pharr, *supra* note 10 at 18. As Diana Majury also notes, "[l]esbians are discriminated against because they challenge dominant understandings and meanings of gender in our society. And the more overtly we challenge gender, the more overtly we are discriminated against. Gender differentiation, premised on the subordination of women, is as essential to heterosexualism as it is to sexism. Lesbian inequalities are sex inequalities because they are rooted in a highly circumscribed definition of gender and gender roles, according to which women are seen only in relation to men." Majury, *supra* note 10 at 311.

14 Pharr, *supra* note 10 at 19.

15 *Ibid.* at 17.

16 Gerda Lerner, *The Creation of Patriarchy* (New York: Oxford University Press, 1986), 239. Kathleen Gough in her essay "The Origin of the Family," in *Toward an Anthropology of Women* (New York: Monthly Review Press, 1975) lists six characteristics of male power historically enforced in family arrangements and through which male supremacy is maintained: "men's ability to deny women sexuality or to force it upon them; to command or exploit their labour to control their produce; to control or rob them of their children; to confine them physically and prevent their movement; to use them as objects in male transactions; or to withhold from them large areas of the society's knowledge and cultural attainments."
    These factors combined ensure and require that gender differences are maintained. They also regulate sexual relations such that heterosexuality remains compulsory, for without it, male dominance, assured through the characteristics outlined by Gough, would be undermined. This is a point developed in more detail by Robert Jensen, who writes: "Men in contemporary American culture are commonly trained to view sex as the acquisition of physical pleasure through the taking of women. Sex is a sphere in which men believe themselves to be naturally dominant and women naturally passive. Women are objectified, and women's sexuality is commodified; women become a thing to be fucked, fucking that can easily be purchased (for example, by paying for dinner or buying a prostitute) or taken by force if necessary. Sex is sexy because men are dominant and women are subordinate – power is eroticized." Robert Jensen, "Getting It Up for Politics: Gay Male Sexuality and Radical Lesbian Feminism," in Sara Miles and Eric Rofes, eds., *Opposite Sex* (New York: New York University Press, 1998), 149-50, citing the work of Lal Covney, Margaret Jackson, Sheila Jeffreys, Leslie Kay, and Pat Mahoney, *The Sexuality Papers: Male Sexuality and the Social Control of Women* (London: Hutchinson, 1984).

17 Bruce Ryder, "Straight Talk: Male Heterosexual Privilege" (1991) 16 *Queen's L.J.* 287 at 289.

18 Sylvia Law, "Homosexuality and the Social Meaning of Gender" [1988] *Wis. L. Rev.* 187 at 218. Andrew Koppelman provides further support for the notion that gay male relationships have the potential to undermine gender polarities when he writes: "Hostility to homosexuals is linked to other traditional, restrictive attitudes about sex roles. This suggests that Thomas Szasz is right: 'the homosexual does not threaten society by his actual behaviour but rather by the symbolic significance of his acts. Homosexuality threatens not the family as such, but a certain traditional ideology of the family. That ideology is one in which men, but not women, belong in the public world of work and are not so much members as owners of their families, while women, but not men, should rear children, manage homes, and obey their husbands.'" Andrew Koppelman, "The Miscegenation Analogy: Sodomy Law as Sex Discrimination" (1988) 98 *Yale L.J.* 145 at 159.
    For an analysis of the extent to which the changing definition of family post–Second World War resulted in an increased level of hostility against men and women who threatened the heterosexual family unit through which male dominance was and is maintained, see Chauncey et al., *supra* note 7.

19 Fajer, *supra* note 8 at 616.
20 See generally Gail Mason and Stephen Tomsen, *Homophobic Violence* (Sydney: Hawkins Press, 1997); Gregory Herek and Kevin Berrill, eds., *Hate Crimes: Confronting Violence against Lesbians and Gay* Men (New York: Sage, 1992); Gary Comstock, *Violence against Lesbians and Gay Men* (New York: Columbia University Press, 1991). Much of the literature on anti-gay violence draws out the link between violence and perceived gender violations or the need to prove gender adequacy. Herek and Berrill, for example, note that the ideological link between sexuality and gender has at least three consequences:

> First, gay people are stigmatized not only for their erotic behaviours but also for their perceived violation of gender norms. Second, because homosexuality is associated with deviation from something so "natural" as masculinity or femininity, its labelling as abnormal receives further justification. Heterosexuals with deep-seated insecurities concerning their own ability to conform to cultural standards for masculinity or femininity may even perceive homosexuality as threatening their own sense of self as a man or woman. Third, a dual pattern of invisibility and hostility, denial and condemnation, is associated with gender that parallels that for cultural heterosexism. People who do not conform to gender roles – regardless of their actual sexual orientation – often are labelled as homosexual and stigmatized or attacked. Fear of such labelling leads heterosexuals and homosexuals alike to monitor their own behaviour carefully to avoid any appearance of gender nonconformity. (*Ibid.* at 260)

21 K. Plummer, *Sexual Stigma: An Interactionist Account* (London: Routledge, 1975), 175.
22 Jeffrey Byrne, "Affirmative Action for Lesbians and Gay Men: A Proposal for True Equality of Opportunity and Workforce Diversity" (1993) 11 *Yale L. and Pol'y. Rev.* 47 at 56.
23 Clearly, the need to reinforce gender roles and in the process maintain sexism is not the only reason for the social rejection of same-sex relationships. As Marc Fajer explains, however, "[a]lthough most psychological studies of homophobia suggest that the strongest contributing factor is belief in the importance of maintaining gender-role stereotypes, a number of studies identify other factors that may be partially responsible as well. These factors include conservative attitudes about sexual issues in general, religious beliefs, and the belief that homophiles are dangerous. Notably, however, each of these factors can be attributed in part, or at least correlated to, fear of deviation from gender-role norms." Mark Fajer, "Can Two Men Eat Quiche Together? Storytelling, Gender-Role Stereotypes and Legal Protections for Lesbians and Gay Men" (1992) 46 *Miami L. Rev.* 511 at 518.

  While much of my work focuses on the extent to which anti-gay discrimination is an issue of sexism, I should not be seen here as implying that gender alone defines gay male identity. Indeed, to the best of my knowledge, very few of the authors who have attempted to articulate the role of gender in the lives of lesbians and gay men have ever made such a claim. All have to some extent recognized that gendered and sexualized relationships are, as Debbie Epstein explains, "complexly constructed in relation to other differences, such as those of age, race, ethnicity, class and/or disability." Debbie Epstein, "Keeping Them in Their Place: Hetero/Sexist Harassment, Gender and the Enforcement of Heterosexuality," in Alison Thomas and Celia Kitzinger, eds., *Sexual Harassment: Contemporary Feminist Perspectives* (Philadelphia: Open University Press, 1997), 158. While many of the authors cited here have focused their work on the role of gender and sex discrimination in the lives of lesbians and gay men, they have not done so at the expense of other types of discrimination, nor have they favoured one legal strategy above any other. Nonetheless, concern has been expressed by some authors that to talk of anti-lesbian and anti-gay discrimination as sex discrimination risks imposing an essentialist view on lesbian and gay identity, such that racial and class differences, for example, are ignored. See Cynthia Petersen, "Envisioning a Lesbian Equality Jurisprudence," in Didi Herman and Carl Stychin, eds., *Legal Inversions: Lesbians, Gay Men and the Law* (Philadelphia: Temple University Press, 1995).

  To the extent that someone might say that gender is all there is, this concern is probably justified. Fortunately, few have made such a claim. Nor am I. Neither am I saying that gender inequality impacts similarly on lesbians and gay men. To argue otherwise would be to deny the considerable benefit gay men, as men, receive from buying into gender male privilege and to deny the very real concerns many lesbians have with litigation strategies which risk denying this and other differences. In this regard, see generally Mary Eaton, "At the Intersection of Gender and Sexual Orientation: Toward Lesbian Jurisprudence" (1994) 3 *S. Cal. Rev. L. and*

Women's Stud. 183. What I am saying, however, is that within the context of a judicial decision such as *Butler,* which focuses on some of the harms of gender inequality, gay men would do well to re-examine the role of gender in their own lives. To that extent, I support Fajer's claim that society's fear of possible deviations from gender-role norms do play a significant role in the regulation of gay male sexuality. Indeed, it is probably accurate to conclude that with respect to the myriad ways in which discrimination is directed at gay men, although gender is not all there is, gender is never *not* there. Given this, gay men might want to rethink their attacks on any judicial attempt to subvert sex discrimination. They might also want to query the extent to which their defence of pornography undermines this judicial initiative. This is a theme developed in more detail in later chapters.

24 Pharr, *supra* note 10 at 18.
25 *Ibid.* at 19.
26 As outlined in the court brief of the National Organisation on Male Sexual Victimization, Inc. (and thirteen others) in the case of *Joseph Oncale* v. *Sundowner Offshore Services, Inc., John Lyons, Danny Pippen and Brandon Johnson,* US Supreme Court, October term 1996, No. 96-568, at 2-4. See also Catharine A. MacKinnon, "Oncale v. Sundowner Offshore Services, Inc., 96-568, Amici Curiae Brief in Support of Petitioner" (1997) 8 *U.C.L.A. Women's L.J.* 9; Marc S. Spindelman and John Stoltenberg, "Introduction: Exposing 'Manhood'" (1997) 8 *U.C.L.A. Women's L.J.* 3; Catharine MacKinnon, "Same-Sex Harassment: A Serious and Neglected Social Problem" (1998) 3 *Law Quadrangle Notes* 84; Richard F. Storrow, "Same-Sex Sexual Harassment Claims After Oncale: Defining the Boundaries of Actionable Conduct" (1998) 47 *Am. U. L. Rev.* 677; and Elise Harris, "Sex/Workers," *Out Magazine,* March 1998, 28.
27 Catharine A. MacKinnon, *Sexual Harassment of Working Women* (New Haven: Yale University Press, 1979), 206.
28 See Samuel Marcosson, "Harassment on the Basis of Sexual Orientation: A Claim of Sex Discrimination Under Title VII" (1992) 81(1) *Geo. L.J.* 1; Regina Stone-Harris, "Same-Sex Harassment – The Next Step in the Evolution of Sexual Harassment Law under Title VII" (1996) *St. Mary's L.J.* 269; Carolyn Grose, "Same-Sex Harassment: Subverting the Heterosexist Paradigm of Title VII" (1995) *Yale J.L. & Feminism* 375; Kara Gross, "Toward Gender Equality and Understanding: Recognizing That Same-Sex Sexual Harassment Is Sex Discrimination" (1996) *Brook. L. Rev.* 1165.
29 By which I mean that the courts have been reluctant to accept the extent to which same-sex harassment buys into and reinforces the gendered harms that arise within the context of opposite-sex harassment. This is made most evident in the case of *Goluszek* v. *Smith,* 697 F. Supp. 1452 (N.D. Ill. 1988). In that case, the court held that while women harassed at work by men have a Title VII remedy, because women are unequal to men at work, men sexually harassed by men have none, because all-male dominated environments cannot discriminate against a man as a man. Pursuant to this reasoning, sexually victimized men are denied access to civil rights remedies when sexually abused by other men in circumstances in which identically situated women do have a claim. As MacKinnon explains, this reasoning implies that same-sex harassment is only not gendered and, as such, supports the gender hierarchy of men over women in society only by ignoring the reality and systemic effects of gendered abuse:

> The *Goluszek* court held that a man cannot be made inferior as a Man in an all-male setting. But both Goluszek and Oncale were treated as inferior men in very standard ways – Oncale more violently. Oncale's attackers were asserting male dominance through imposing sex on a man with less power. Men who are sexually assaulted are thereby stripped of their social status as men. They are feminized: made to serve the function and play the role customarily assigned to women as men's social inferiors. In terms that apply to male-on-male rape generally, Susan Brownmiller describes prison rape of men as "an acting out of power roles within an all-male, authoritarian environment in which the weaker, younger inmate ... is forced to play the role that in the outside world is assigned to women." This lowers the victim's status, making him inferior as a man by social standards. For a man to be sexually attacked, by placing him in a woman's role, demeans his masculinity; he loses it, so to speak. This cannot be done to a woman. What he loses, he loses through gender, as a man.
> Often it is men perceived not to conform to stereotyped gender roles who are the targets of male sexual aggression. Goluszek was taunted for appearing unwilling to oppress women sexually. Because he did not conform to his male co-workers' view of

what his gender behavior ought to be, because he was not seen to be practicing sexual objectification and subordination of women, he was seen as less a man according to their sex-stereotyped standards. Goluszek was punished, ostracized, insulted, and forced to consume pornography to make him conform to their stereotype of how a man should be a man by subordinating women sexually. He was subjected to homophobic slurs reflecting the common assumption that if he is not "fucking" a woman, he is no longer a man as male supremacy defines it. "Having his gender questioned," marked Goluszek's abuse as sex-based. Title VII's goal of "strik[ing]" at the entire spectrum of disparate treatment of men and women resulting from sex stereotypes," clearly intercepts such acts.

See Catharine MacKinnon, *Brief of the National Organization on Male Violence et al in the case of Joseph Oncale v. Sundowner Offshore Services, Inc.*, US Supreme Court, No. 96-568, 11 August 1997, 9-11 (hereinafter, *Oncale Brief*).

30 The United States Court of Appeals for the Fifth Circuit had initially ruled that Oncale was not entitled to a civil rights remedy via Title VII (see *Oncale v. Sundowner Offshore Services, Inc.*, 83 F.3d 118 (5th Cir. 1996)). The Court felt bound by an earlier decision in *Garcia v. Elf Atochem No. Am.*, 27 F.3d 446 (5th Cir. 1994), in which the Court had held that "harassment by a male supervisor against a male subordinate does not state a claim against under Title VII even though the harassment has sexual overtones. Title VII addresses gender discrimination." Outlined in Adams, *supra* note 8 at 116, fn. 187.

As MacKinnon explains, in ruling that Title VII addresses "gender" discrimination, the Court was not referring to gender as socially defined. Rather, it conflated gender with sex, with biology, and avoided any analysis of the role of hierarchy, of dominance and submission, of gendered inequalities. Under this analysis, men cannot claim sexual harassment at the hands of other men because a man in an all-male context cannot be made subordinate on the basis of sex where the sexes are "equal" (read the same). Masculinity is thus assumed to be uniform, biological sex, making all men sufficiently equal to one another so that no man can be in a significant position of powerlessness to another man. On appeal in *Oncale*, Amici argued convincingly that the courts must move beyond this analysis and examine the way in which sexual acts premised on violence and inequality reinforce those social imbalances derived from rigid gender stereotypes that harm women and all men ridiculed for their inability to conform to hyper-masculinity:

> Much sexual harassment jurisprudence reasons that, had a sexually harassed woman been a man, she would not have been so treated, therefore she is harassed "because of sex." The present case poses the question, what if she had been a man and the same thing happened? The answer is at once sex-specific and sex-neutral: both sexes are covered for injuries through their gender. Women do not have sex equality rights only because men couldn't be treated in the same way, this case suggests, but because men could be and are not. And when they are? Had he been a woman, Mr. Oncale might not have been treated the way he was. But if he were, his sex equality rights would be recognized. (*Oncale Brief, supra* note 29 at 30)

31 Joan Biskupic, "Court Says Law Covers Same-Sex Harassment," *Washington Post*, 5 March 1998, A1.

32 Janet Halley, "Sexuality Harassment," in Reva Siegel and Catharine MacKinnon, eds., *Directions in Sexual Harassment Law* (New Haven: Yale University Press, 2004), 192.

33 *Ibid.* at 195.

34 *Ibid.* at 183.

35 A quite amazing response to Halley's criticism of the *Oncale* brief (and her misreading of Catharine MacKinnon's radical feminism in particular) is provided by Professor Marc Spindelman, who, rejecting Halley's assertion that radical feminists have undermined lesbian and gay sexual liberation by outlawing same-sex harassment, writes: "One of radical feminism's many lessons is that we don't have to tolerate *any* sexual violence in the name of good sex – or anything else. Notwithstanding widespread stories to the contrary, radical feminism opposes and seeks to end the definition of good sex and sexual violence, including sexual harassment and rape, as the same thing." See Marc Spindelman, "Discriminating Pleasures," in Reva Siegel and Catharine MacKinnon, eds., *Directions in Sexual Harassment Law* (New Haven: Yale University Press, 2004), 218.

36 As MacKinnon again argues:

> The sexual orientation of the parties inevitably arises in, and is implicated in ruling on, same-sex harassment. The sexual orientation of the parties is, however, properly irrelevant to the legal sufficiency of sexual harassment claims. An accused perpetrator's being gay or lesbian does not make that person's behavior sex-based, but sexual orientation may be pertinent in determining whether particular behavior is based on sex in the totality of the circumstances.
>
> By definition, sexual harassment is unwanted, so victim sexual orientation is as irrelevant on same-sex facial challenges on sex-basis as it is on opposite-sex ones. The sexual orientation of the victim cannot convert aggression that is sex-based into aggression that is not, or vice-versa.
>
> Only men are subject to denigration by gay-bashing taunts like "faggot." Only women are subject to denigration by the use of terms like "dyke" as epithet and insult. Such abuse is inherently socially gendered. Using sex with members of one's own sex as derision, insult, and hostility denigrates the target's gender-adequacy. Such terms, when part of sexual harassment, create a hostile environment for men *as men* and for women *as women*, whether directed at straights or gays. Because they attack individuals as members of their gender group, they are based on sex. (*Oncale Brief, supra* note 29 at 23, 25, and 26)

37 John Stoltenberg, "You Can't Fight Homophobia and Protect the Pornographers at the Same Time: An Analysis of What Went Wrong with Hardwick," in Leidholt and Raymond, *The Sexual Liberals and the Attack on Feminism* (New York: Pergamon Press, 1990).

38 Epstein, *supra* note 23 at 58.

Chapter 3: Sexualizing Masculinity, Normalizing Inequality

1 Factum of the Appellant Little Sisters Book and Art Emporium, in the case of *Little Sisters Book and Art Emporium* v. *Canada (Minister of Justice)*, S.C.C., File No. 26858, 19 July 1999, paras. 48 and 63.

2 *Little Sisters Book and Art Emporium* v. *Canada (Minister of Justice)* (1996), 131 D.L.R. 4th 486 (B.C. Sup. Ct.).

3 *Canada Customs Act*, R.S. 1985, c. 1.

4 *Canada Customs Tariff*, R.S. 1985, c. 41.

5 *R.* v. *Butler*, [1992] 1 S.C.R. 452.

6 Memorandum D9-1-1 outlines and explains the interpretation of *tariff* code 9956 of schedule VII to the *Customs Tariff* and provides procedures to be followed in this regard. It also reproduces code 9956 and, under the title "Guidelines and General Information," sets out detailed procedures to be followed in the classification process. The memorandum's main objective is to offer the following guidance to custom officers on code 9956(a):

> 5 Goods which are deemed to be obscene under the Criminal Code are those of [sic], a dominant characteristic of which, is the undue exploitation of sex, or of sex and any one or more of the following subjects, namely, crime, horror, cruelty and violence.
>
> 6 The following goods, insofar as they are deemed to be obscene ... within the meanings of the terms set forth above, are to be classified under tariff code 9956 and their importation into Canada prohibited:
> (a) goods which depict or describe sexual acts that appear to degrade or dehumanize any of the participants, including:
> (1) depictions or descriptions of sex with violence, submission, coercion, ridicule, degradation, exploitation or humiliation of any human being, whether sexually explicit or not, and which appear to condone or otherwise endorse such behaviour for the purposes of sexual stimulation or pleasure;
> (2) depictions or descriptions of sexual assault (previously, rape). Any goods that depict or describe a sexual activity between male/female, male/male or female/female which appears to be without his/her consent and which appears to be achieved chiefly by force or deception;
> (3) depictions or descriptions of bondage, involuntary servitude and the state of human beings subjected to external control, in a sexual context;
> (4) depictions or descriptions which appear to be associating sexual pleasure of [sic] gratification with pain and suffering, and with the mutilation of or

letting of blood from any part of the human body, involving violence, coercion and lack of basic dignity and respect for a human being;

(5) depictions or descriptions of sexual gratification gained through causing physical pain or humiliation, or the getting of sexual pleasure from dominating, mistreating or hurting a human being. This includes depictions and descriptions of physical force which appear to be used so as to injure, damage or destroy; of extreme roughness of action; of unjust or callous use of force or power; of spanking, beating or violent shoving in a sexual context;

(6) depictions or descriptions of mutilation or removal of any part of the human body or of the taking of human life, real or implied, for the purpose of sexual arousal; and

(7) depictions or descriptions of menstrual blood, faecal matter, urine or the inducement of faeces through enemas as part of sexual arousal.

(8) It should be emphasized that a book, film, videocassette, etc., is to be assessed in its entirety. It is to be considered as a whole and its overall nature and dominant characteristic must be assessed. A section containing subjects outlined in this Memorandum must be assessed as an integral part of the entire work and in the context of its theme. However, goods which in their essence are made up of many individual elements are not to be treated as a whole and may be prohibited on the basis of any one of their elements which fall within the prohibitory provisions of tariff code 9956. Similarly, a magazine or newspaper is to be considered on a segment-by-segment basis.

(9) Goods not classified under tariff code 9956 include the following:
   (a) goods which communicate in a rational and unsensational manner information about a sexual activity that is not unlawful are not to be prohibited;
   (b) sex aids and toys are not to be deemed obscene and, therefore, are not to be classified under tariff code 9956; goods are not to be prohibited solely on the basis of advertisements which simply promote the sale of various sex toys or sex aids. However, explicit textual descriptions or visual depictions in the advertisements deemed to be obscene will be prohibited. In assessing goods under tariff code 9956, full recognition should be given to freedom of expression.

7 *Little Sisters Book and Art Emporium* v. *Canada (Minister of Justice)*, [2000] 2 S.C.R. 1120 (S.C.C.) at 1155.
8 *Ibid.*
9 Factum of the Appellant Little Sisters Book and Art Emporium, *supra* note 1 at 14.
10 *Ibid.* at 14.
11 *Ibid.*
12 *Ibid.*
13 See *infra* notes 70 and 71.
14 Factum of the Intervener Women's Legal Education and Action Fund, in the case of *Little Sisters Book and Art Emporium* v. *A.G. Canada,* S.C.C., File No. 26858, 27 September 1999, at 7 (hereinafter, LEAF Factum, *Little Sisters*).
15 *Ibid.* at 8.
16 Factum of the Intervener Equality for Gays and Lesbians Everywhere (EGALE), in the case of *Little Sisters Book and Art Emporium* v. *Canada (Minister for Justice)*, S.C.C., File No. 26858, n.d., at 2.
   In concluding, the group again cites the work of Jerald Moldenhaur, who states: "[F]or gay people, literature is a very important bond, a kind of glue within our, community ... [T]he way that we connect with our community is often through our literature, through our newspapers, and through our books." *Ibid.* at 8.
17 *Ibid.* at 2.
18 *Ibid.* at 7.
19 *Ibid.* at 8.
20 *Ibid.*
21 *Ibid.*
22 *Ibid.* at 17, relying on the work of Carl Stychin, "Of Representation and Reality," in *Law's Desire: Sexuality and the Limits of Justice* (London: Routledge, 1995).

23 *Ibid.* at 14, relying on the work of Brenda Cossman and Bruce Ryder, "Customs Censorship and the Charter: The Little Sisters Case" (1996) 7(4) *Const. Forum Const.* 103 at 107-8.

24 LEAF Factum, *Little Sisters, supra* note 14, relying on Adrienne Rich, "Compulsory Hetero-sexuality and Lesbian Existence" (1980) 5(4) *Signs: Journal of Women in Culture and Society* 63, and Audre Lorde, "The Uses of the Erotic: The Erotic as Power," in Henry Abelove et al., eds., *The Lesbian and Gay Studies Reader* (New York: Routledge, 1993), 227 and 339.

25 Robert Jensen, "Getting It Up for Politics: Gay Male Sexuality and Radical Lesbian Feminism," in Sara Miles and Eric Rofes, eds., *Opposite Sex* (New York: New York University Press, 1998), 149-50.

26 Factum of the Intervener Equality Now, in the case of *Little Sisters Book and Art Emporium,* S.C.C., File No. 26858, 3 December 1999, at 10-11. In this regard, the reader should note the work of Audre Lorde and Susan Leigh Starr, "Interview with Audre Lorde," in Robin Linden et al., eds., *Against Sadomasochism: A Radical Feminist Analysis* (Palo Alto, CA: Frog in the Well, 1982), in which Lorde is again explicit in her rejection of the types of material defended in *Little Sisters* by LEAF and others – materials which, rather than challenge compulsory heterosexuality, reinforce it.

27 Equality Now Factum, *supra* note 26 at 16 and 17.

28 *Little Sisters Book and Art Emporium* v. *Canada,* [2000] 2 S.C.R. 1120 at 1159.

29 *Ibid.* at 1164.

30 *Ibid.* at 1223.

31 An excellent overview is also provided in Janine Benedet, "*Little Sisters Book and Art Emporium* v. *Minister of Justice:* Sex Equality and the Attack on *R.* v. *Butler*" (2001) 39 *Osgoode Hall L.J.* 187.

32 Much of the pornography quoted in this book comes from the pornography exhibits defended in the *Little Sisters* case, argued before the Supreme Court of Canada in 2001. What is offered is a sampling of magazines, videos, and books that had been detained by Canada Customs since 1985. In October 1999, I flew from Perth, Australia, to Vancouver, Canada, to view these exhibits. The exhibits had been classified illegal and were being detained at the Civil Exhibits Division of the British Columbia Court of Appeal. I was given permission by the Federal Department of Justice to view the exhibits. I had approximately two days to do so.

The quotations from those materials that were actually exhibits in the *Little Sisters* case were read into a tape recorder in Vancouver and later typed upon my return to Perth. As far as is possible, the quotations offered from these exhibits is an accurate summary of what appears in these materials. I say, "as far as possible" because I was working under a very tight time frame in legally constrained conditions. Each exhibit was bought to me individually in a locked room. I was then allowed to dictate into a tape recorder. I was not allowed to photocopy more than a few pages of the written materials because Canada Customs had ruled that these materials were illegal under Canadian law. I was not allowed to remove the materials from the courthouse and could view only one exhibit at a time. Some of these exhibits did not list the authors or years of publications, etc., because pages had been removed or blacked out in earlier court proceedings. If they did provide this material, I did not record all of this information because my aim was to use specific quotes for the purpose of critical analysis. I could not later return to find this bibliographic information because once the Supreme Court ruled that Canada Customs could detain these materials, they were either destroyed after subsequent court proceedings or returned to the United States, from whence they came. Many of these materials were also dated (as far back as 1985) and it was not possible to find the specific magazines in Canada, even in those stores that would have continued to sell them illegally. I have tried to track down some of the magazines in Australia but this is difficult without full bibliographic details. Many of the magazines are now out of stock and, I might add, also illegal in Western Australia. I am thus reluctant to purchase them even if I could find them. They would also now be illegal in Canada as a result of the *Little Sisters* case. While it is possible that some might still be sold in Canada, I am not keen to purchase materials that violate the *Canadian Criminal Code* provisions dealing with obscenity.

It is also worth noting that because of the nature of the pornography industry, the names of "authors" are often fictional. This makes getting verification from individual writers extremely difficult. In my summaries, I thus tended to simply provide the name of the magazine or book or video and the exhibit number. Because of its very nature, one simply cannot track down some authors and some writers by any of the usual means. These individuals change addresses and names regularly, and use pseudonyms. Also, given the nature of some of the material in question and its potentially illegal status, contact is even more difficult.

33 Brenda Cossman, "Return of the Loonies: Feminists Tell Supreme Court That Gay and Lesbian Porn Is Evil," *Xtra!* no. 396 (30 December 1999), 11.
34 William Willcox, "That Old Time Religion" (1995) no. 10 (11) *Manscape Magazine* at 15.
35 I am not suggesting that the type of harm arising from pictorial or video presentations is the same as that which arises from purely written or descriptive pornography. On the contrary, pornography that presents real people does just that – it presents and uses *real* people. (Regarding the abuse and exploitation of gay male pornographic models see the discussion in Chapter 4.) Having said this, however, I should also not be seen as saying that non-pictorial presentations are *not* a threat to gay equality, hence not socially harmful. This was a claim made by Little Sisters in its Supreme Court of Canada factum. Specifically, Little Sisters argued that

> the apprehension of harm supposedly avoided by the impugned *[Criminal Code]* provisions is further attenuated when textual material is involved. The trial Judge said *Butler* could not be distinguished on this basis since the material under consideration there included magazines. However, there were no books at issue in *Butler,* and most of the evidence in this case concerned books, a medium that strictly involves the imagination of both the writer and reader. No one is exploited or in any way harmed in the writing of a book. Even if text can give rise to a reasonable apprehension of harm, such texts will be sufficiently rare that they can be left to the normal criminal law process. (Little Sisters Factum, *supra* note 1 at 29)

This is a statement that, like many of the arguments advanced during this trial, seems to have been made with little or no appreciation of the materials in question. Within the context of this case, s. 163(8) of the *Criminal Code*, which defines "obscenity" and which is incorporated by reference into the *Customs Tariff*, applies equally to books and visual materials. *Butler* did not confine its analysis of harm to visual materials. Also, while the use of real people to make pornography can, of course, result in considerable harm to those people, it can also result in harm to other persons affected due to the attitudes conveyed by the presentation of another person's abuse. Similarly, when the abuse, torture, dehumanization, or sexual exploitation of people is promoted in such a way as to sexualize this abuse and inequality and to present it as positive and liberating, abusive and anti-egalitarian behaviour by its consumers is also promoted. The risk is not eliminated, however, simply because real people are not used to market the harm promoted.
36 Little Sisters Trial Exhibits, Exhibit 194, *Movie Star Confidential.*
37 Little Sisters Trial Exhibits, Exhibit 195, *Playguy,* vol. 13, no. 12 (December 1989), published by Modernismo Publications.
38 *Ibid.* at 58.
39 Little Sisters Trial Exhibits, Exhibit 198, *Advocate Men*, December 1989, published by Liberation Publications.
40 *Ibid.* at 66.
41 *Ibid.* at 39.
42 *Ibid.* at 40.
43 *Ibid.* at 56.
44 *Ibid.*
45 Little Sisters Trial Exhibits, Exhibit 49, *MAC II 19: A Drummer Super Publication,* vol. 19 (January 1990), published by Desmotis Publishers.
46 *Ibid.* at 24.
47 Little Sisters Trial Exhibits, Exhibit 197, *Bear: Masculinity without the Trappings,* no. 9 (1989), published by COA Publishers.
48 *Ibid.*
49 Catharine MacKinnon, *Toward a Feminist Theory of the State* (Boston: Harvard University Press, 1989), 141.
50 Little Sisters Trial Exhibits, Exhibit 262, *Oriental Guys*, no. 4 (Spring 1999).
51 Little Sisters Trial Exhibits, Exhibit 6, *Oriental Guys*, no. 6 (Spring 1990).
52 *Oriental Guys, supra* note 50.
53 Note, for example, the letters to the editor in *Oriental Guys, ibid.*
54 Little Sisters Trial Exhibits, Exhibit 200, *Sex Stop: True Revelations and Strange Happenings from 18 Wheeler,* vol. 3.
55 Little Sisters Trial Exhibits, Exhibit 211, *Cut/Uncut: True Gay Experiences of Foreskin and Circumcision,* vol. 1 (1986), published by G.S. Press.

56 Little Sisters Trial Exhibits, Exhibit 202, *Sex Stop: True Homosexual Experiences*, vol. 3.
57 *Ibid.*
58 *Ibid.*
59 *Ibid.*
60 *Ibid.*
61 Little Sisters Trial Exhibits, Exhibit 212, *Humongous: True Gay Encounters*, vol. 5 (1989), published by Leyland Publications.
62 Little Sisters Trial Exhibits, Exhibit 213, *Juice: True Homosexual Experiences*, vol. 5 (1984).
63 *Ibid.*
64 Little Sisters Trial Exhibits, Exhibit 19, John Preston, *Entertainment for a Master*, 1986.
65 Little Sisters Trial Exhibits, Exhibit 48, *Dungeon Master: The Male S/M Publication*, no. 39 (1990), published by Desmotis Publishers.
66 Little Sisters Trial Exhibits, Exhibit 216, *Mr. S/M 65.*
67 Little Sisters Trial Exhibits, Exhibit 192, Film: *Headlights and Hard Bodies*, Zeus Video Production.
68 Little Sisters Trial Exhibits, Exhibit 49, *MAC II 19, supra* note 45.
69 Men against Rape and Pornography, *Looking at Gay Porn* (1993), available from MARAP, P.O. Box 8181, Pittsburgh, PA 1517.
70 Factum of the Intervener Women's Legal Education and Action Fund, in the case of *R. v. Butler*, S.C.C., 1991, File No. 22191, 1990, at para. 5.
71 *Ibid.* at para. 48.
72 Mickey Skee, "Tricks of the Trade," *Frontiers Magazine*, 22 August 1997, 43. See also Will Harris, "Porn Again," *Campaign Magazine*, December 1993, 47 at 48. An excellent overview of the economics of the pornography industry is provided by Ann Russo, "Feminists Confront Pornography's Subordinating Practices," in Gail Dines, Robert Jensen, and Ann Russo, eds., *Pornography: The Production and Consumption of Inequality* (New York: Routledge, 1998). See also Catherine Itzin, "'Entertainment for Men': What It Is and What It Means," in Itzin, ed., *Pornography: Women, Violence and Civil Liberties* (London: Oxford University Press, 1992).
73 Harris, *supra* note 72 at 48.
74 Pornography on the Internet is big business and, if recent international findings are any indication, immensely popular. Indeed, trading in sexually explicit material is now one of the biggest recreational applications of users of computer networks, with frequently visited newsgroups sporting names such as "alt.sex.stories," "rec.arts.erotica," and "alt.sex.bondage" – newsgroups which, in addition to providing materials now readily available via mail order, offer the online browser materials featuring pedophilia (the use of children in sexual acts), hebaphilia (the use of youths in sexual acts), and paraphilia (material that includes images of bondage, sado-masochism, urination, defecation, and sex acts with animals). An excellent overview of the use of Internet pornography and the types of pornography available electronically is found in Philip Elmer-Dewitt, "On a Screen Near You: Cyberporn," *Time Magazine*, 10 July 1995, 48 at 53, and Marty Rimm, "Marketing Pornography on the Information Superhighway" (1995) 83 *Geo. L.J.* 1849. See also Catharine A. MacKinnon, "Vindication and Resistance: A Response to the Carnegie Mellon Study of Pornography in Cyberspace" (1995) 83 *Geo. L.J.* 1959 at 1966-7; Frederick Lane, *Obscene Profits: The Entrepreneurs of Pornography in the Cyber Age* (New York: Routledge, 2000) and Catharine MacKinnon, *Sex Equality* (New York: Foundation Press, 2001), 1509.
    Internet pornography was not in issue in either *Butler* or *Little Sisters,* and I provide these examples only for the purpose of showing the pornography that is available worldwide. In *Little Sisters*, Little Sisters argued that the Court should take judicial notice of the availability of obscenity and hate propaganda on the Internet, but not for the purpose of recognizing the pervasiveness of pornographic harm and hate speech. Rather, the Court should do so in order to recognize that "the fact that Parliament has refrained from enacting legislation to regulate the Internet is persuasive evidence that Parliament does not consider the suppression of obscenity crossing the border by electronic means to be a pressing and substantial legislative objective." This, of course, is not why Parliament has failed to regulate Internet pornography. To date, no nation has adequately addressed the control of Internet pornography, primarily, it is argued, because the technology to do so does not exist. This should not be seen as indicative of a lack of concern. On the contrary, many countries, including Canada, do recognize the need for regulation. The question posed by this new technology, however, is how best to ensure that it is done in a way that meets the objective of social equality. To the extent that this is the objective (as it is in Canada), the *Butler* sex equality standard for pornography will

serve as the standard for Internet regulation – as it will for the regulation of non-Internet materials. It may be that other means of regulating Internet porn (e.g., via human/civil rights claims) will need to be addressed, given the nature of the Internet regulation, but this certainly does not stand as a reason to invalidate *Butler*. On the contrary, *Butler* and *Little Sisters* should be seen as the base from which to construct a remedy that does what it should do.

75 As found on the Internet at <http://www.gayfarm.com/guests/>.
76 As found on the Internet at <http://toptwinks.com>; <http://www.web-boys.com>and <http://www.gaympegs.com/tts/twinks.html>; <http://boytwinks.youngest.web.com/index.html>.
77 The content of gay male porn magazines does not differ from gay male video porn. See Edisol Wayne Dotson, *Behold the Man: The Hype and Selling of Male Beauty in Media and Culture* (New York: Harrington Park Press, 1999), 134.
78 Doug Lawrence, *1999 Adam Gay Video Directory, 9th Annual Edition* (Los Angeles: Knight Publishing, 1998).
79 *Ibid.* at 97.
80 *Ibid.* at 91.
81 Andrea Dworkin, *Women Hating* (New York: Plume, 1974), 89. Dworkin, discussing a 1970s magazine, *Suck*, in which the story "Tough Young Dicks for Hot Tricks" appears, continues:

> Five young toughs are cruising; they pick up a long-haired boy, shove him in the back seat of the car and order him to blow them all; the boy considers refusing, since he'd love to be beaten then and there, but instead submits since greater abuse can always be had through submission than through resistance; the young toughs brutally rape the long-haired boy, then piss and shit all over him. He is, of course, ecstatic: "Gee did I smell of come and teenage sweat and urine and I had two more toss-offs myself thinking about their tough young faces and dicks enjoying me for hot kicks."
>
> The stereotype of the homosexual that emerges from the general run of *Suck* fiction is not very different from the stereotype of woman. The homosexual is queer, asshole, cocksucker, faggot; the woman is hole, hot wet fuck tube, hot slit, or just plain ass. He thrives on pain and so does she. Gangbanging is their mutual joy. Huge, throbbing, monster, atom-smashing cock is god and master to them both. The parts they play in the sado-masochistic script are the same: so are the costumes, attitudes, and other conventional cultural baggage. It is not hard to see that the struggle for gay male liberation and women's liberation is a common struggle: both mean freedom from the stigma of being female. The fantasies (indicative of structural mental sets) oppress male homosexuals and women alike. Women and male homosexuals are united in their queerness, a union that is real and verifiably affirmed by *Suck*, which contributes to the cultural oppression of both. (*Ibid.* at 89 and 90)

82 Andrea Dworkin, *Pornography: Men Possessing Women* (New York: Plume, 1989), 61.
83 John Stoltenberg, "Gays and the Pro-Pornography Movement: Having the Hots for Sex Discrimination," in Michael Kimmel, ed., *Men Confront Pornography* (New York: Crown Publishers, 1990), 248-50.
84 *Ibid.* at 251.
85 Paul Gallant, "Editorial: I Thought Pro-Sex Feminists Had Won," *Xtra!* 13 January 2000, 15.
86 Seymour Kleinberg, "The New Masculinity of Gay Men, and Beyond," in Kaufman, ed., *Beyond Patriarchy* (Toronto: Oxford University Press, 1987), 123.

Chapter 4: Abusing Real People
1 As quoted in Charles Isherwood, *Wonder Bread and Ecstasy: The Life and Death of Joey Stefano* (Los Angeles: Alyson Publications, 1996).
2 As Catharine MacKinnon and Andrea Dworkin explain within the context of their proposed legal ordinances aimed at defining the production of pornography as a violation of civil rights,

> [t]he first victims of pornography are those in it. Pornography indelibly makes those it uses into its presentation of them, so that no matter who they are or what they say about how they really felt, to those who have seen them in pornography, they are pornography for life ... Pornographers promote an image of free consent because it is good for business. But most women in pornography are poor, were sexually abused as children, and have reached the end of this society's options for them, options that were biased against them as women in the first place. This alone does not make them coerced for purposes of the Ordinance; but the fact that some women may "choose"

pornography from a stacked deck of life pursuits (if you call a loaded choice a choice, like the "choice" of those with brown skin to pick cabbages or the "choice" of those with black skin to clean toilets) and the fact that some women in pornography say they made a free choice does not mean that women who are coerced into pornography are not coerced. (*Pornography and Civil Rights: A New Day for Women's Equality* [Minneapolis: Organizing against Pornography, 1988], 42-3)

3 In this regard, see generally Factum of the Intervener Women's Legal Education and Action Fund, in the case of *R. v. Butler*, S.C.C., File No. 22191, 1990.
4 Ms. Marchiano's complete testimony is provided in Catharine MacKinnon and Andrea Dworkin, *In Harm's Way: The Pornography Civil Rights Hearings* (Cambridge: Harvard University Press, 1997). She has also documented her experiences in her book, *Ordeal* (Secaucus, NJ: Citadel Press, 1980).
5 MacKinnon and Dworkin, *In Harm's Way*, *ibid.* at 62.
6 See Marchiano's complete account in her book *Ordeal*, *supra* note 4.
7 Ms. Marchiano described this incident as follows:

> During the filming of *Deep Throat*, actually after the first day, I suffered a brutal beating in my room for smiling on the set. It was a hotel room and the whole crew was in one room. There was at least 20 people partying, music going, laughing, and having a good time. Mr. Traynor started to bounce me off the walls. I figured out of 20 people, there might be one human being that would do something to help me and I was screaming for help, I was being beaten, I was being kicked around and, again, bounced off of walls. And all of a sudden the room next door became very quiet. Nobody, not one person came to help me.
>
> The greatest complaint the next day was the fact that there was bruises on my body. So many people say that, in *Deep Throat*, I have a smile on my face, and I look as though I am really enjoying myself. No one ever asked me how those bruises got on my body. (MacKinnon and Dworkin, *In Harm's Way*, *supra* note 4 at 62)

8 *Ibid.* at 65. See also Catharine MacKinnon, "Linda's Life and Andrea's Work," *Feminism Unmodified: Discourses on Life and Law* (Boston: Harvard University Press, 1987).
9 See Catharine MacKinnon, *Sex Equality* (New York: Foundation Press, 2000), chaps. 10 and 11 and Laura Lederer, "Then and Now: An Interview with a Former Pornography Model," in Laura Lederer, ed., *Take Back the Night* (New York: William Morrow, 1980), 57.
10 MacKinnon, *Sex Equality*, *ibid.* at 1537; MacKinnon and Dworkin, *In Harm's Way*, *supra* note 4 at 114 and Mimi Halper Silbert, "The Effect on Juveniles of Being Used for Pornography and Prostitution," in D. Zillmann and J. Bryant, eds., *Pornography: Research Advances and Policy Considerations* (Hillsdale, New Jersey: Erlbaum, 1989).
11 United States Department of Justice, *Attorney General's Commission on Pornography Final Report* (US Government Printing Office, 1986); MacKinnon and Dworkin, *In Harm's Way*, *supra* note 4; MacKinnon, *Sex Equality*, *supra* note 9 at 1538, 1550-5.
12 Nadine Strossen, *Defending Pornography: Free Speech, Sex, and the Fight for Women's Rights* (New York: Scribner, 1995), 183-4.
13 Linda Marchiano has never claimed to have married Traynor of her own free will. According to Marchiano, Traynor's lawyer recommended that Traynor marry her so that she could not testify against him in a pending criminal drugs trial. When she declined, Marchiano writes, Traynor kicked, choked, and attempted to strangle her until she had no choice but to marry him by force. This and similar abuse is well documented in Marchiano's 1980 autobiography *Ordeal* (Secaucus, NJ: Citadel Press, 1980).
14 As Marchiano's testimonies and book make clear, she was keen to escape the pressures of a family that was less than functional. She further explains that Traynor took advantage of this and, once he had successfully forced her into prostitution, used it against her to produce pornography. Once the films had been made, Traynor could, according to Marchiano, then use them against his victim as blackmail and as a marketing tool for further abuse. See Lovelace, *supra* note 4. In this regard, Marchiano's life experience is not atypical of those of many of the women who find themselves used in pornography. As Ann Russo explains,

> [s]ome women work in the pornography industry because they are running away from sexually and physically violent homes, and pornographers offer them food, shelter, money, promises of love, and a home. Some may get into it because their fathers, uncles, husbands, brothers, or boyfriends prostitute them or make pornography of

them, and then act as their "agents"; sometimes the pornography is used to blackmail young girls into continuing their life in the sex industry. In a study by Mimi Silbert and Ayala Pines of 200 street prostitutes in San Francisco, 10 percent of the women stated that they had been used in pornographic films and magazines as children [under age thirteen], and 38 percent reported that explicit photographs had been taken of them when they were children for commercial reasons or the personal gratification of the photographer. ("Feminists Confront Pornography's Subordinating Practices," in Gail Dines et al., *Pornography: The Production and Consumption of Inequality* [New York: Routledge, 1998], 26)

See also Evelina Giobbe, "Connections between Prostitution and Pornography" (1993) 7(1) *Whisper* 3.

15 In her book Marchiano details how Traynor had planned to take her to Juarez, Mexico, so that he could make money from her having public sex with a donkey. His knowledge and insights into the use of women in this way is revealing. As Marchiano writes, the conversation in the car en route proceeded as follows:

"I hope you like Donkeys," he said.
"Donkeys are fine."
"There's no fucking reason you should like Donkeys," he said. "It's just that it'd be a good thing if you did like Donkeys is all. It'd be better for you."
"What would be better if I liked donkeys?"
"Donkeys'd be better," he said.
"*Why* would it be better if I liked donkeys?" –
"Because you're going to be fucking them in Juarez," he came to the point. "That's what I've been telling you, that's the reason we're going to Juarez. To fuck donkeys." He had to be kidding. Didn't he? His eyes were off the road and on my face. Evidently I didn't register sufficient shock because he felt compelled to describe all the wonders waiting for us in Juarez. He talked about an arena similar to the pit used for a cockfight – hundreds of men sitting around a ring, yelling out their wagers. In the middle of the ring, naked women and a donkey. The men would be betting on the various women. Specifically on how many centimetres of donkey penis each woman would be able to contain in her vagina.
"You're *made* for this contest," Chuck said. "I'm telling you, you'll clean up. Shee-yit, the last chick I brought to Juarez made us three thou and she was nothin'."
This was surely just another story, another of Chuck's little on-the-road entertainments. However, there were too many details. If it was all make-believe, he had given it a lot of thought.
"The chicks go in one at a time," he was saying. "And the crowd cheers, just like when prize-fighters come into a ring. And then they strap the chick up on this contraption and then they bring out their trained donkey and they lead the donkey right into the fucking cunt."
"You're lying!" I said. "How could a donkey do anything with a woman?"
"Oh, he gets a little fucking help," Chuck said, obviously pleased that I was finally reacting. "They've got to point him right, you dig? Sometimes the chick gets ripped up a little – I'm telling you, you haven't lived 'till you've seen one of those donkey dongs. Those suckers are *huge!* And the guys are all bidding like they're at some fucking auction – 'I'll bet a thousand on the redhead,' like that."
"That would kill a woman."
"Nah, they got the medicos right there," Chuck said. "If the bleeding gets too bad, they unstrap the chicks and give them medical assistance right on the spot. Some of those chicks are really haemorrhaging, too." (Linda Lovelace, *Ordeal* [Secaucus, NJ: Citadel Press, 1980], at 93-5; all rights reserved; reprinted by permission of Citadel Press/Kensington Publishing Corp., www.kensingtonbooks.com).

The sexual arena Traynor describes is not fictional. It and others like it do exist and women are physically mutilated because of them. Often these encounters are filmed, with the films in turn sold as pornography. It is clear from a reading of *Ordeal* that Traynor's knowledge of these events was not haphazard. The man was well versed in the comings and goings of the sex trade. This allowed him to exploit Marchiano, through force, in turn allowing him to make the types of connections needed to ensure the eventual success of films such as *Deep Throat*.

He was, as is clear from Ms. Marchiano's accounts, a small-time pimp who profited immensely from selling his product to the larger pimps who were able to benefit from the abuse inflicted on Linda Marchiano and that resulted in Linda Lovelace.

16 *Ibid.* at 140-1.
17 Lovelace, *supra* note 4 at 190.
18 *Ibid.* at 190.
19 *Ibid.*
20 As Ms. Marchiano writes, "Two weeks of making a movie, even a pornographic movie, was better than two weeks of being a hooker. And being with other people, just listening to others talk, that was nice." (*Ibid.* at 137.) While to some this might be representative of a form of liberation, statements like these should not be taken out of context. They certainly should not be seen as advocating the use of women in porn. Nor should they been seen as a sign that Marchiano made these movies by choice or that she would have chosen to do them had she not been physically abused, assaulted, and forced at gunpoint into making them. Thus, while "liberating" insofar as the interaction with others offered an albeit brief break from Chuck Traynor's physical abuse, Ms. Marchiano is certainly not, as some would have us believe, advocating the pornographic use of women as a means of finding salvation after victimization at the hands of an abusive husband or partner. As Ms. Marchiano herself makes clear, the two are inseparable.
21 *Ibid.* at 110-15.
22 Brian McNair, *Mediated Sex: Pornography and Postmodern Culture* (London: Arnold, 1996), 75. Emphasis in original.
23 *Ibid.* at 76.
24 Lovelace, *supra* note 4 at 251.
25 Contrary to the claims of some that Linda Marchiano is a "one-off" or "an exception," other women have experienced similar patterns of abuse within the industry. As Ann Russo again notes:

> The stories of women who have left the industry are evidence of the mistreatment, coercion, and violence that many experience. No doubt, there are also stories of women who do sex work and feel it offers them an arena in which to express their power. However, these are in sharp contrast to stories of others who report that the sex often is experienced as "abusive" and "like rape," others who learn to cope with it by disassociating themselves from their bodies by using drugs and alcohol to numb physical and emotional pain. Many women do not make substantial sums of money, and they are often abused by those who profit from their work. Micki Garcia, former director of Playmate Promotions, was for six years a supervisor, friend, and confidante to the "Playmates." She "saw and felt the grim realities of the Playboy lifestyle: alienation from family and friends, drug abuse, attempted suicide, prostitution, unnecessary cosmetic surgery, mental and physical abuse, rape, attempted murder and murder." (Russo, *supra* note 14 at 26)

See also Evelyn Radinson, "New Playboy Club Folds in New York City" (1986) (Spring/Summer) *WAP Newsreport* 1; Peter Bogdanovich, *The Killing of the Unicorn: Dorothy Stratten (1960-1980)* (New York: William Morrow, 1984); "Statement of Whisper Action Group Members" (1992) (Winter/Spring) *Whisper* 3.
26 Having said this, I should state that I am not at all convinced that as many women are "doing well" out of pornography as Strossen and McNair would have us believe. If the testimonies of women such as Linda Marchiano are credible (and there is no reason to doubt them), it would seem that the only women who are "doing well" out of pornography are those who have become the pimps they once worked for, who now work on the other side of the camera, and who now themselves profit from the use of other women. Others, however, while they might "do well" initially by marketing their own violation for a few years, risk finding that they are "used up." Some then find that they are being used in the production of other less "attractive" forms of pornography (S&M, anal rape, excrement, bestiality, and so on) until they are forced to drop out – by which point many are addicted to drugs and alcohol, taken in order to get through the day; burdened with jail records; and untrained, hence unemployable. *This* is the reality of what many women's "doing well" in porn turns into, and the appallingly limited vision of women's possibilities that emerges from this defence is nothing if not steeped in misogynistic rhetoric. See Russo, *supra* note 14 at 24; Vednita Nelson, "Black Women and

Prostitution" (1992) 6 (Summer/Fall) *Whisper* 1 and "Working in the Body Trade" (1981) (Autumn) *Aegis* 19; Laura Lederer, "Then and Now: An Interview with a Former Pornography Model," in Laura Lederer, ed., *Take Back the Night* (1980); US Department of Justice, *Attorney General's Commission on Pornography Final Report* (US Government Printing Office, 1986), 780-2.

27 Factum of the Intervener EGALE, in the case of *Little Sisters Book and Art Emporium* v. *A.G. Canada*, S.C.C., File No. 26858, 1999, at 14-15.

28 Factum of the Appellant Little Sisters Book and Art Emporium, in the case of *Little Sisters Book and Art Emporium* v. *A.G. Canada*, S.C.C., File No. 26858, 30 July 1999, at 24.

29 See discussion in Chapter 3.

30 John Burger, *One-Handed Histories: The Eroto-Politics of Gay Male Video Pornography* (New York: Harrington Park Press, 1995), 71.

31 *Ibid.* at 72.

32 The use of the word "model" or "actor" risks glamorizing the very real experiences of many of the people presented as "actors" and the reality that they, as real people, do experience. The seriousness of this point should not be underestimated. Those who support gay male pornography tend to overlook that the "images/models" in gay male pornography are real people, upon many of whom direct physical contact, often in the form of violence presented through sex, is frequently inflicted in order to produce that which is defended as fantasy – a political euphemism or cover for abuse. It should not be assumed that these young men are always willing participants, particularly when free will is largely defined by one's ability to exercise some social and economic independence. The young men who appear in gay male pornography do so for a number of reasons, but "choice" is not always a factor. This corresponds to the findings of those who have documented the lives of the women used in heterosexual pornography. In this regard, see Russo, *supra* note 14 at 24. See also Vednita Nelson, "Black Women and Prostitution" (1992) 6 (Summer/Fall) *Whisper* 1 and "Working in the Body Trade" (1981) (Autumn) *Aegis* 19.

33 The sexual trauma many of these men experience and the ways in which it should be dealt with by those wanting to assist young men struggling to survive the emotional and physical abuse often associated with male prostitution and prostitution generally is discussed in more detail in Christopher Kendall and Rus Funk, "Gay Pornography's 'Actors': When 'Fantasy' Isn't," in Melissa Farley, ed., *Prostitution, Trafficking, and Traumatic Stress* (Binghamton, NY: Haworth, 2003), 89-110.

34 On the effects of childhood sexual abuse on adult sexuality see C.M. Meston, J.R. Heiman, and P.D. Trapnell, "The Relationship between Early Abuse and Adult Sexuality" (1999) 36(4) *Journal of Sex Research* 385.

35 Christopher Kendall, "Real Dominant, Real Fun: Gay Male Pornography and the Pursuit of Masculinity" (1993) 57(1) *Sask. L. Rev.* 21 at 33 and 34, citing *Gay Pornography: Sometimes Men Possess Men* (hereinafter, *1985 U.C.L.A. Study*), 20. The author of this study has chosen to remain anonymous and to change the names of those interviewed because he wanted to ensure confidentiality to his sources, as well as his own anonymity. In 1993 the author granted me permission to publish some of his findings, on the condition that I did not identify him or the men interviewed. I agreed to this request and continue to do so.

Jim Y.'s description of fisting, as first promoted in his films and then copied by gay men, is reminiscent of the forced oral penetration inflicted on Linda Marchiano in the film *Deep Throat* – a sexual practice later copied by men and directed at their female partners, many of whom suffered considerable physical harm as a result. Note the testimony of the many sexual assault counsellors who noted a marked increase in the number of throat rapes after the release of the film *Deep Throat*. As one counsellor explained during the Minneapolis Anti-Pornography Hearings, "I have been alarmed by the increasing numbers of women and gay men who have reported to me that they have been throat raped. In one incident the woman reported hearing one of her attackers state, 'I'll Deep Throat her' before losing consciousness. Gay men have reported similar assaults. It is important to note, however, that although we know about most of the murders that include sexual assaults, we don't know how many were caused by the victims suffocating during a throat rape." Letter of Flora Colao, Certified Social Worker, reprinted in MacKinnon and Dworkin, *In Harm's Way*, *supra* note 4 at 215.

36 *Ibid.* at 34.

37 Dale Reynolds, "Documenting America's Schizoid Sexuality," *Outrage* 178 (March 1998), 58 at 59.

38 *Ibid.*
39 Isherwood, *supra* note 1 on back cover.
40 Scott-Patrick Mitchell, "Ifs and Butts: The Life and Death of a Porn Star on the Stage," *Westside Observer*, 4 February 2000, 9.
41 *Ibid.*
42 *Ibid.* at 9. Stefano's use of hustling to feed his drug habit is well documented by Isherwood. Initially, Stefano's status as *the* gay porn star commanded huge prostitution fees. The higher fees did not, however, command any more self-respect:

> The decision to escort wasn't exactly an agonizing one for Stefano. He had hustled for drug money in Philadelphia from an early age ... One of LA's biggest music moguls used to pay him $1,000 to go have sex with him ... It was on a call to the same music mogul that it was brought home to Stefano that if he had moved up the scale in his own eyes, an expensive prostitute, in the eyes of others, he was hardly different from a cheap one. "He came home really hurt and upset. He felt like now he was a big porn star, but people still treated him the same way: 'Here's the money – do your thing.'"

As Isherwood explains, Stefano's already fragile self-esteem would suffer even more when, after his status as one of the best had vanished, he was left having to hustle for far less money in order to pay for a drug habit which had peaked during his heyday as a performer. Although Stefano had sworn he would not return to the industry, he soon felt and found that sex was all he had and all he was wanted for. Desperate, he again found himself turning to an industry quick to exploit his vulnerability:

> attempts to locate steady employment in Miami had, of course, not been fruitful. Even with Trigoura's support, he couldn't muster the confidence to pursue attempts to find alternative work, and he had to support himself with the occasional trick or dance gig in Miami or Key West. He swore to Trigoura that he wanted nothing more to do with the porn-star lifestyle, but he had to keep earning a living. It was clear to Smith, who was still booking dance gigs for him, that his desire to quit the business was genuine. Stefano was so tired of the routine that he required significant infusions of drugs to be able to perform. "At clubs the only time he was really messy was when he had to perform," Smith says. "I'd drive him down to Key West, and he'd get all fucked up, barely make it, and then want me to drive him right home." (Isherwood, *supra* note 1 at 178)

43 *Ibid.* at 191.
44 Carl Stychin, *Law's Desire: Sexuality and the Limits of Justice* (London: Routledge, 1995), 83.
45 F.G. Torres, "Lights, Camera, Actionable Negligence: Transmission of the AIDS Virus during Adult Motion Picture Production" (1989) 13 *Hastings Comm. and Ent. L.J.* 89 at 99.
46 Mickey Skee, "Laid Bare: A Return to Unsafer Sex in Gay Adult Video?" *Frontiers Magazine* 16, no. 8 (August 1997), 53.
47 *Ibid.* at 54.
48 Roger Edmonson, *Boy in the Sand: Casey Donovan – All American Sex Star* (Los Angeles: Alyson Books, 1998), 223-4.
49 Culver's experience is not unique. In documenting the life of Joey Stefano, for example, Isherwood notes that any non-pornography career promises made to Stefano were soon forgotten once the men who made them had used him sexually. See Isherwood, *supra* note 1 at 111-12. In this regard, too, the experiences of the men used to produce gay pornography mimic the life experiences of many of the women used to produce heterosexual porn. See Russo, *supra* note 14 at 23-4.
50 Edmonson, *supra* note 48 at 223-4. See also Peter Jordan, "The Naked VCR," *Outrage* 131 (April 1994), 45 at 47. As Jordan explains in regard to Donovan,

> Donovan's last film, the appropriately titled *Fucked Up*, was released the year before his death from AIDS in 1987 ... It's one of the scariest films ever made. It's [sic] director, Christopher Rage specialized in sleaze filmed with a clear-eyed stare, and here – with the main title spelt out in lines of cocaine – he embodied a human being who had fallen off the edge of the universe. It's a place far beyond orgasm, let alone emotion. Drugged to his glassy eyeballs, Donovan is a mere receptacle – a human sex bin that self destructs before your eyes in an increasingly incoherent guttermouth monologue. To call it the last act of a morality play would be foolish, but as a record

of a once Golden Boy rocketing to oblivion, there's nothing quite like it. (Peter Jordan, *ibid.* at 47)

51 Dale Reynolds, "The Gay Porn Industry: Hot, Dirty and Sometimes Sad," *Outrage* 147 (August 1995), 12 at 15.

52 See Torres, *supra* note 45; Skee, *supra* note 46.

53 For information on the harms of prostitution generally, see MacKinnon, *Sex Equality, supra* note 9; Melissa Farley, "Prostitution and the Invisibility of Harm" (2003) 26(1-4) *Women and Therapy*; Evelina Giobbe, "Confronting the Liberal Lies about Prostitution," in D. Leidholdt and J. Raymond, eds., *The Sexual Liberals and the Attack on Feminism* (New York: Pergamon Press, 1990); Kathleen Barry, *Female Sexual Slavery* (New York: New York University Press, 1979); Kathleen Barry, *The Prostitution of Sexuality* (New York: New York University Press, 1995). Within the context of male prostitution, see Donald West, *Male Prostitution* (London: Harrington Park Press, 1993). See also K.W. Elifson, "Seroprevalence of Human Immunodeficiency Virus among Male Prostitutes" (1989) *New England Journal of Medicine* 321.

54 Factum of the Intervener Women's Legal Education and Action Fund, in the case of *R. v. Butler,* S.C.C., File No. 22191, 1990.

55 See, for example, Carl Stychin, "Exploring the Limits: Feminism and the Legal Regulation of Gay Male Pornography" (1992) 16 *Vt. L. Rev.* 857 at 898. Stychin argues that a liberatory approach to pornography will replace "the marketplace with regulation sensitive to sexual differences and historical experience. This liberatory approach further ensures that failures of the market will be rectified. In pornography, the effect is a focus on employment standards rather than moral sanction ... Finally, this regulatory approach provides for greater participation and control of the pornography industry."

56 On the challenge of gay male consumerism generally, see Dennis Altman, "What Changed in the Seventies?" in Gay Left Collective, ed., *Homosexuality, Power and Politics* (London: Alyson and Busby, 1980). Altman writes (at 57): "In essence the commercial gay scene represents not so much the liberation of the homosexual as his co-option into mainstream consumerist society. To speak cynically, it represents the triumph of the capitalist entrepreneur over traditional morality ... There is often a defacto collusion between the police, who prevent cruising parks and the businessman who offer the same facilities at a price." To this one could add that gay male pornography, once controlled by gay men, represents a de facto collusion between straight male society and those businessmen who will profit by selling an identity politic which straight male society has always encouraged.

57 Richard Fung, "Looking for My Penis: The Eroticized Asian in Gay Video Porn," in Bad Object Choices, eds., *How Do I Look? Queer Film and Video* (Seattle: Bay Press, 1991), 160.

58 Doug Seto, "Caste and Castaways: Welcome to Polk St.," *Bay Area Reporter,* 29 July 1993, 18.

Chapter 5: Gay Male Pornography and Violence

1 MacKinnon and Dworkin, *In Harm's Way: The Pornography Civil Rights Hearings* (Cambridge: Harvard University Press, 1997), 107-8.

2 Factum of the Appellant Little Sisters Book and Art Emporium, in the case of *Little Sisters Book and Art Emporium* v. *A.G. Canada,* S.C.C., File No. 26858, 30 July 1999, at 24.

3 (14 July 1992), (Ont. Ct. (Gen. Div.)).

4 See discussion *infra* at note 42.

5 Michael Scarce, *Male on Male Rape: The Hidden Toll of Stigma and Shame* (New York: Insight Books, 1997), 67-8.

6 *Ibid.* at 68.

7 Factum of the Intervener Women's Legal and Education Action Fund, in the case of *R. v. Butler,* S.C.C., File No. 21116, 1 December 1989.

8 Factum of the Intervener EGALE, in the case of *Little Sisters Book and Art Emporium* v. *A.G. Canada,* S.C.C., File No. 26858, 1999.

9 Little Sisters Factum, *supra* note 2 at 23.

10 EGALE Factum, *supra* note 8, para. 39, quoting Brenda Cossman, "Feminist Fashion or Morality in Drag? The Sexual Subtext of the Butler Decision," in B. Cossman, S. Bell, L. Gotell, B.L. Ross, eds., *Bad Attitude/s on Trial: Pornography, Feminism and the Butler Decision* (Toronto: University of Toronto Press, 1997), 128.

11 EGALE Factum, *supra* note 8 at para. 40. In concluding, EGALE relied on the work of Professor L. Green, who has argued that

whatever role straight pornography plays in the complex causal network that keeps women in their place, gay pornography obviously plays a much different role [if any] in keeping gay people in their place, for that is by and large the work of straight people. Here, the oppressor class, if there is one, is in the wrong socio-erotic location ... [I]f we begin with the new paradigm's view of the harm that pornography causes women, we will find that the analogous harms suffered by gay men are not in the main caused by gay men. They are caused by heterosexual women and men whose attitudes are not significantly influenced by gay male pornography. Thus, while in the gender-dominance theory of pornography the oppressor class and the class of consumers of pornography strongly overlap, in the reality of lesbian and gay life, the oppressor class and the class of consumers of gay pornography are disjointed. (*Ibid.*, citing L. Green, "Pornographies" [1999] 7 *Journal of Political Philosophy* 8.1 at 8.16)

12 Factum of the Intervener Equality Now, in the case of *Little Sisters Book and Art Emporium* v. *A.G. Canada*, S.C.C., File No. 26858, 3 December 1999, at 8, para. 19. See generally Karen Busby, "LEAF and Pornography: Litigating on Equality and Sexual Representations" (1994) 9 *Can. J.L. and Soc.* 165 at 179-80; LEAF Factum, *R.* v. *Butler, supra* note 7 at para. 5.

13 Noted in the Factum of the Attorney General of Canada, in the case of *Little Sisters Book and Art Emporium* v. *A.G. Canada*, S.C.C., File No. 26858, 29 October 1999, at para. 40.

14 *Ibid.*

15 Note, for example, the comments of Paris J. in *R.* v. *Scythes*, [1993] O.J. No. 537 D.R.S. 93-06432 Toronto, 16 January 1993, at para. 6. Quoted in the Factum of the Attorney General of Canada, *ibid.* at para. 42.

16 [1985] 1 S.C.R. 494.

17 Factum of the Attorney General of Canada, *supra* note 13 at para. 58.

18 *Ibid.* at para. 59.

19 *Ibid.* at para. 59.

20 Testimony of Dr. Neil Malamuth, in the case of *R.* v. *Scythes* (16 January 1993) (Ont. C.J. (Prov. Div.)).

21 Scarce, *Male on Male Rape, supra* note 5 at 67. See also Michael Scarce, "The Reality of Male Rape" (1993) (Winter) *National Coalition against Sexual Assault Journal* 7; Michael Scarce, "Same-Sex Rape of Male College Students" (1997) 45(4) *Journal of American College Health* 171; Michael Scarce, "Harbinger of Plague: A Bad Case of Gay Bowel Syndrome" (1997) 34(2) *Journal of Homosexuality* 1.

22 Caroline Waterman et al., "Sexual Coercion in Gay Male Relationships: Predicators and Implications for Support Services" (1989) 26(1) *Journal of Sex Research* 118. As noted in Scarce, *Male on Male Rape, supra* note 5 at 67.

23 David F. Duncan, "Prevalence of Sexual Assault Victimization among Heterosexual and Gay/Lesbian Students" (1990) *Psychological Reports* 66. As noted in Scarce, *supra* note 5 at 65.

24 Ford C.I. Hickson et al., "Gay Men as Victims of Non-consensual Sex" (1994) 23(3) *Archives of Sexual Behaviour* 281. As noted in Scarce, *ibid.* at 65.

25 Outlined in Scarce, *supra* note 5 at 127-32. See also Fred Pelka, "Raped: A Male Survivor Breaks His Silence," in Patricia Searles and Ronald Berger, eds., *Rape and Society: Readings on the Problem of Sexual Assault* (Boulder, CO: Westview Press, 1995), 250.

26 Richie J. McMullen, *Male Rape: Breaking the Silence on the Last Taboo* (London: G.M.P. Publishers, 1990), 25, citing Groth and Burgess, "Male Rape: Offenders and Victims" (1980) 137 *American Journal of Psychiatry* 806. It is not my purpose here to offer a detailed analysis of male rape. This has been done elsewhere, most recently by Michael Scarce, *supra* note 5. See also Rus Funk, *Stopping Rape: A Challenge for Men* (Philadelphia: New Society Publishers, 1993); Arthur Kaufman et al., "Male Rape Victims: Non-Institutional Assault" (1980) 137 *American Journal of Psychiatry* 221; Deryck Calderwood, "The Male Rape Victim" (1987) 7 *Medical Aspects of Human Sexuality* 53; Caroline Mezey, *Male Victims of Sexual Assault* (London: Oxford University Press, 1992); Peter Goyer and Henry Eddleman, "Same Sex Rape of Nonincarcerated Men" (1984) 141 *American Journal of Psychiatry* 576.

27 *Ibid.* at 26. As McMullen further notes: "[i]n many cases, it is the feared or actual loss of positive power and aggression which motivates the offender to behave negatively. It is as though the offender is over compensating for any other potential hurts to his otherwise already fragile masculinity. Being unable to find the resources in himself to deal with feared or actual loss, he must act out or externalize his fears in such a way as to be seen as more dominant, more masculine." *Ibid.* at 28.

28 *Ibid.* at 26.
29 Susan Brownmiller, *Against Our Will: Men, Women and Rape* (New York: Simon and Schuster, 1985), 258. See also Mary Willcox, "The Sexually Assaulted Prisoner" (1986) 12 *New Eng. J. on Crim. and Civ. Confinement* 355; Peter Nacci and Thomas Kane, "The Incidence of Sex and Sexual Aggression in Federal Prisons" (1984) 48 *Federal Probation* 35; David Heilpern, *Fear or Favour: Sexual Assault of Young Prisoners* (Lismore, NSW: Southern Cross Press, 1998).
30 Catharine MacKinnon, Brief of National Organization on Male Violence et al., in *Joseph Oncale v. Sundowner Offshore Services, Inc. et al*, US Supreme Court, No. 96-568, 11 August 1997, at 10.
31 McMullen, *supra* note 26 at 26.
32 Little Sisters Trial Exhibits, Exhibit 49, *MAC II 19: A Drummer Super Publication*, January 1990, at 56.
33 Little Sisters Trial Exhibits, Exhibit 48, *Dungeon Master, No. 39 – The Male S/M Publication*, 1990, at 13.
34 Noted in a pamphlet distributed by Men against Rape and Pornography, *Looking at Gay Porn* (1993), available from MARAP, P.O. Box 8181, Pittsburgh, PA 15217.
35 A stereotype brilliantly debunked by Michael Scarce, *supra* note 5 at 69-70. In this regard, see also my critique of the work of Janet Halley, discussed in Chapter 3. See also Marc Spindelman, "Discriminating Pleasures," in Reva Siegel and Catharine MacKinnon, eds., *Directions in Sexual Harassment Law* (New Haven: Yale University Press, 2004), 218. More analysis of the rape myths outlined here is found in Allson Salmon, Sharon Isle, and Trevor Morton, "Sexual Assault in the Gay and Lesbian Community," *Westside Observer* (Perth, Western Australia), October 1994, 11.
36 Although sexualized as such in pornography, the opposite is in fact the case. As Scarce again explains within the context of one victim's testimony,

> T.J., a male survivor in his mid-20s was raped by a date in his dorm room while attending college. The man had torn T.J.'s clothing off, turned him around, and was raping him when T.J.'s roommate, Ted, came home and interrupted the assault. T.J. recalled that during the assault, the man raping him "had reached around and was rubbing me. When I'm scared, I'm usually erect too. It's that adrenaline flow. It [the rape] was really hard to deal with after that." Later that evening as T.J. talked with Ted, he wondered aloud if he had done enough to prevent the rape, or if he had really wanted to have sex. "One of the ways my roommate tried to help me was by saying, 'You know you were not to blame. You didn't have an erection.' and I said, 'No, but I did.'" Ted had made the assumption that T.J. did not experience an erection, and attempted to use that information as a strategy for affirming the validity of the rape. Although Ted remained admirably supportive even after learning of the erection, this situation is a prime example of falsely equating an erection with consent, and lack of erection with violence. (Scarce, *supra* note 5 at 61)

See also D.E. Redmund et al., "Spontaneous Ejaculation Associated with Anxiety" (1983) 140(9) *American Journal of Psychiatry* 1163.
37 Susan Cole, *Pornography and the Sex Crisis* (Toronto: Amanita Press, 1989), 44.
38 Ronald Weitzer, *Sex for Sale: Prostitution, Pornography and the Sex Industry* (New York: Routledge, 2000), 49-50.
39 *Ibid.* at 61.
40 See Frederick S. Lane III, *Obscene Profits: The Entrepreneurs of Pornography in the Cyber Age* (New York: Routledge, 2000), xiv. See also Catharine MacKinnon, *Sex Equality* (New York: Foundation Press, 2001), 1509, and Marti Rimm, "Marketing Pornography on the Information Superhighway" (1995) 83 *Geo. L.J.* 1849.
41 David Island and Patrick Letellier, *Men Who Beat the Men Who Love Them* (New York: Harrington Park Press, 1991). For more information on gay male domestic abuse, see also Caroline Waterman and Lori Dawson, "Sexual Coercion in Gay Male Relationships: Predicators and Implications for Support Services" (1989) 26(1) *Journal of Sex Research* 118; "Battered Lovers," *Advocate*, 4 March 1986, 42-5; H. Donat, "Domestic Violence Strikes Gay Relationships," *Sentinel*, 2 August 1990, 5; Pierce Reed, "Naming and Confronting Gay Male Battering," *Gay Community News*, 16-22 April 1989; T. Kingston, "Breaking the Silence: Gay Domestic Violence," *Coming Up!* February 1989, 10-11.
42 As Island and Letellier explain, "domestic violence is a big problem for America's 9.5 million adult gay men. We estimate that as many as 500,000 gay men are victims, and, of course,

226 Notes to pages 102-6

equal numbers are also perpetrators. Thus, only substance abuse and AIDS adversely affect more gay men, making domestic violence the third largest health problem facing gay men today." Island and Letellier, *supra* note 41 at 1.
43 *Ibid.* at 50.
44 *Ibid.* at 52.
45 *Ibid.* at 52-3.
46 *Ibid.* at 51.
47 *Ibid.*
48 *Ibid.*
49 Edisol Wayne Dotson, *Behold the Man: The Hype and Selling of Male Beauty in Media and Culture* (New York: Harrington Park Press, 1999).

Chapter 6: Gay Male Pornography
1 Seymour Kleinberg, "The Masculinity of Gay Men and Beyond," in Michael Kaufman, ed., *Beyond Patriarchy* (Toronto: Oxford University Press, 1987), 123.
2 *R. v. Butler*, [1992] 1 S.C.R. 452 at 493. LEAF's factum is available from the Supreme Court of Canada, Ottawa, File No. 22191.
3 I should not be understood here as implying that inequality in itself is not a form of violence. As Leo Bersani notes, "inequality doesn't have to be enforced with whips to be violent: the denial to Blacks of equal seating privileges on public buses was rightly seen as a form of racial violence." *Infra* note 33 at 253. Rather, in referring here to "non-violent" pornography, I refer only to those materials that do not present violent behaviour as traditionally recognized (i.e., rape, sexual submission enforced with whips, burning with hot wax, bondage) and which have been distinguished as such by the courts and those who defend these materials. These materials can and do result in the types of gendered and racial stereotypes that result in inequality – inequality which in turn allows for the further sexualization of violence. In this regard, it is somewhat futile to distinguish between violent and non-violent materials, as both result in inequality. I draw such a distinction here, however, only to respond to those who would argue that non-violence eliminates the risk of harm found in inequality.
4 See generally John Burger, *One-Handed Histories: The Eroto-Politics of Gay Male Video Pornography* (New York: Harrington Park Press, 1995); Brenda Cossman, "Feminist Fashion or Morality in Drag? The Sexual Subtext of the Butler Decision," in B. Cossman, S. Bell, L. Gotell, B.L. Ross, eds., *Bad Attitude/s on Trial: Pornography, Feminism and the Butler Decision* (Toronto: University of Toronto Press, 1997); Brenda Cossman and Bruce Ryder, "Customs Censorship and the Charter: The Little Sisters Case" (1996) 7(4) *Const. Forum* 103; Richard Dyer, "Coming to Terms," *Jump Cut*, no. 30 (1985), 28; L. Green, "Pornographies" (1999) 7 *Journal of Political Philosophy* 8.1; Jeffrey Sherman, "Love Speech: The Social Utility of Pornography" (1995) 47 *Stan. L. Rev.* 661; Carl Stychin, "Exploring the Limits: Feminism and the Legal Regulation of Pornography" (1992) 16 *Vt. L. Rev.* 857; Ted Fishman, "Northern Underexposure: Censorship in Canada," *Playboy*, June 1994, 58; Thomas Waugh, "Men's Pornography: Gay vs. Straight," *Jump Cut*, no. 30 (1985), 33; Chris Bearchell, "In Harm's Way: A Calculated Campaign Takes Aim at Sexual Imagery and Free Speech," *XS: A Supplement to Xtra!* November 1992; Chris Bearchell, "Invisibility Equals Death: Canada Customs and the Butler Decision May Erase Us for Good," *XS: A Supplement to Xtra!* October 1992, 15; Chris Bearchell, "Proof, Who Needs Proof?" *XS: A Supplement to Xtra!* November 1992, 3; Chris Bearchell, "Gay Porn Censored from All Sides," *Toronto Star*, 15 January 1993, A23; Brenda Cossman, "Return of the Loonies: Feminists Tell Supreme Court That Gay and Lesbian Porn Is Evil," *Xtra!* no. 396 (30 December 1999), 11; Paul Gallant, "Editorial: I Thought Pro-Sex Feminists Had Won," *Xtra!* 13 January 2000, 15; Jared Mitchell, "Leather Boy and the Sex Police: Porn/Gay Porn – Without All That Oppression," *Xtra!* 13 January 2000, 4.
5 Thomas Waugh, "Men's Pornography: Gay vs. Straight," *Jump Cut*, no. 30 (1985), 33. In the same article, Waugh writes: "The spectator's positions in relation to the representations are open and in flux. These include: non-viewing with the images functioning as background visual muzak; direct unmediated look at image-object, especially in solo-jerk films; look mediated by narrative – spectator's position fluctuates or is simultaneously multiple, among different characters and types, roles etc. Spectator's indentificatory entry into the narrative is not predetermined by gender divisions; mise en scene does not privilege individual roles, top or bottom, inserter or insertee, in any systematic way." *Ibid.* at 33.
6 Thomas Waugh, *Hard to Imagine: Gay Male Eroticism in Photography and Film from Their Beginnings to Stonewall* (New York: Columbia University Press, 1996), 48-9. Cited in the Factum of the

Appellant Little Sisters, in the case of *Little Sisters Book and Art Emporium* v. *A.G. Canada*, S.C.C., File No. 26858, 30 July 1999, at para. 63.

7 Factum of the Intervener EGALE, in the case of *Little Sisters Book and Art Emporium* v. *A.G. Canada*, S.C.C., File No. 26858, 1999, at para. 40.

8 *Ibid.* Elsewhere Waugh again relies on the absence of women in gay life generally to argue that

> [u]nlike straight male porn, gay porn does not directly and systematically replicate the heterosexist patriarchal order in its relations of production, exhibition, consumption or representation. Kathleen Barry's assertion that "homosexual pornography acts out the same dominant and subordinate roles of heterosexual pornography" cannot be shown to be true of any of these terms. Produced by, depicted and consumed exclusively by gay men, the fantasy universe of gay porn resembles the gay ghetto in its hermeticism as well as in its contradictory mix of progressive and regressive values, in its occupancy of a defensible enclave within heterosexist society. It subverts the patriarchal order by challenging masculinist values, providing a protected space for non-conformist, non-reproductive and non-familial sexuality, encouraging many sex-positive values and declaring the dignity of gay people. (Waugh, *supra* note 6 at 34)

9 As Island and Letellier report within the context of gay male domestic abuse, there is nothing normal or acceptable about men physically assaulting or abusing other men, and it is the myth of acceptability that daily results in gay men abusing their same-sex partners: "the boys being boys idea may have been harmless when we were all six years old, but when a man is 26 years old, is in the hospital with broken bones, and his lover broke them, this is not normal! This is much more than boys being boys. It is violence. Unfortunately, this myth is pervasive in the gay male community. With few positive relationship role models available, many gay men tend to view and accept violence by their partners as the norm." David Island and Patrick Letellier, *Men Who Beat the Men Who Love Them* (New York: Harrington Park Press, 1991), 26.

10 Philip Galanes, "More Male Than Not: A Consideration of Gay Male Pornography and the Dworkin/MacKinnon Pornography Ordinance" (student paper presented 1 August 1990). I would like to thank Philip for providing me with a copy of his work and for allowing me to learn from, cite, and rely on his extraordinary insights into the harms of gay pornography and the links between homophobia and sexism. His strength and courage in this regard have allowed me and motivated me to do that which, as he rightly argues, must be done: challenge the many inequalities that presently exist in our community.

11 Michael Bronski, "Gay Publishing: Pornography," in Bronski, *Culture Clash: The Making of Gay Sensibility* (Boston: South End Press, 1984), 160 at 165.

12 Bronski in particular relies on the different types of men shown in gay porn to distinguish it from straight porn, explaining:

> Gay pornography often features men who are unusually good looking, or examples of a sexually desirable "type": muscle builder, preppy, leatherman, or jock. These are glorifications of the male figure. However, sometimes, the models fall into the ordinary realm of good looks, instilling in the viewer a sort of boy-next-door feeling. The variety of "types" in gay male porn is indicative of the impulse to eroticize as many images of men as possible. While certain magazines feature a certain style – *Drummer* capitalizes on the older, mature, hirsute man, while *In Touch* is more interested in the smooth-skinned, late adolescent – a wide variety of pornographic gay images are being produced and appreciated. (*Ibid.* at 166-7)

13 Galanes, *supra* note 10 at 12. This is a question asked and answered by Seymour Kleinberg, "The New Masculinity of Gay Men and Beyond," in Michael Kaufman, ed., *Beyond Patriarchy: Essays by Men on Pleasure, Power and Change* (Toronto: Oxford University Press, 1987).

14 John Burger, *One-Handed Histories: The Erotic-Politics of Gay Male Video Pornography* (New York: Harrington Park Press, 1995), 103.

15 Factum of the Intervener EGALE, *supra* note 7 at para. 41.

16 Carl Stychin, "Exploring the Limits: Feminism and the Legal Regulation of Pornography" (1992) *Vt. L. Rev.* 857 at 878.

17 *Ibid.* at 883-4.

18 Judith Butler, *Gender Trouble: Feminism and the Subversion of Identity* (New York: Routledge, 1990).

19 Sheila Jeffreys, *The Lesbian Heresy* (Melbourne: Spinifex Press, 1993), 84-5, critiquing Judith Butler, *supra* note 18. A similarly tough-minded demystification of these postmodern scholars is offered in Somer Brodribb, *Nothing Mat(t)ers: A Feminist Critique of Postmodernism* (Melbourne: Spinifex Press, 1992). See also Sheila Jeffreys, "Heterosexuality and the Desire for Gender," in Diane Richardson, ed., *Theorising Heterosexuality* (Buckingham: Open University Press, 1996).

20 Galanes, *supra* note 10 at 17. Galanes' argument is echoed in the Factum of Equality Now in arguments before the Supreme Court of Canada in *Little Sisters*. In particular, writing within the context of lesbian pornography, the group argues that materials that sexualize acts of coercion, violence, pain, and domination between women sexually condition lesbian women to eroticize abusing, and being abused by, other women. The real violence that can occur in lesbian relationships is also minimized by the degree that the women abused in lesbian pornography are perceived as enjoying that abuse. The idea that some women want to be the slaves of other women is patterned on racist and sexist notions that it is right to dominate certain individuals or groups – because they want or deserve to be dominated. Black women and Jewish women, for example, have written of the inequality they experience when acts of slavery and Nazism are promoted as sexual. The abuse of women as sex remains abusive whether the perpetrator is a woman or a man. The argument of the appellants that lesbian and gay male sado-masochism is not harmful because it is consensual simply replicates the myth expressed in heterosexual pornography that women and children enjoy being raped and sexually tortured. It also replicates the racist ideology that members of minority groups are in control of their subordination and therefore deserve and even enjoy the abuse they experience. See Factum of the Intervener Equality Now, in the case of *Little Sisters Book and Art Emporium v. A.G. Canada*, S.C.C., 3 December 1999, at paras. 27 and 29. Relying on the work of Audre Lorde and Susan Leigh Starr, "Interview with Audre Lorde"; Maryel Norris, "An Opinionated Piece on Sadomasochism"; Susan Leigh Starr, "Swastikas: The Street and the University," in Robin Linden et al., eds., *Against Sadomasochism: A Radical Feminist Analysis* (Palo Alto, CA: Frog in the Well, 1982), 66-71, 106-8, 131-5.

   In this regard, it is again worth quoting the work of Sheila Jeffreys, who, confronting the myth of implied consent within the context of sado-masochistic pornography writes:

> In a male supremacist culture where sex is constructed from the eroticisation of the inequality between men and women, traditional heterosexual sex is, as MacKinnon puts it "an aggressive intrusion on those with less power." Where sex is so constructed the idea of consent serves to smooth over the real barbarity that can take place in sexual practice. Catharine MacKinnon points out that although malestream thought on sexuality tends to see the woman's right to withhold consent as affording the woman a power equal to that which a man gains from his custom of sexual initiation, there is no equality in these practices. Where sex is constructed to be eroticised inequality, the idea of consent can be an incitement, both to men's violence and to sadomasochism. The idea of consent constructs a taboo to be broken. The transgression of consent becomes an exciting possibility. Sadomasochism exists because of the construction of male supremacist sexuality around consent. It then uses the same idea to justify its existence. (*Supra* note 19 at 43, quoting the work of Catharine MacKinnon, *Toward a Feminist Theory of the State* [Cambridge: Harvard University Press, 1989], 127)

   See also Carole Reeves, "Serious Porn, Serious Protest," *All the Rage: Reasserting Radical Lesbian Feminism* (London: Teachers College Press, 1996), 65-70, and Irene Reti, ed., *Unleashing Feminism* (Santa Cruz: Her Books, 1993). Insofar as gay porn, like lesbian porn, is gendered, there is little reason to believe that the notion of implied consent is any less dangerous within the gay male context. Many of us do not need, want, or seek out our oppression, and the consequences of pornographic materials that say otherwise are far too serious to ignore or justify as mere role play or sexual theatre.

21 Jeffrey Sherman, "Love Speech: The Social Utility of Pornography" (1995) 47 *Stan. L. Rev.* 661 at 683-5. Sherman notes: "The issue in a young man's quest for self acknowledgment and self-acceptance is not holding hands or hugging or kissing or running through a meadow in slow motion. The issue is the sexual act. A gay adolescent encounters many examples of male-male affection but they fail to provide the validation he needs if they do not explicitly acknowledge male-male sex." *Id.* at 683. This is an argument to which I will respond in more detail in Chapter 7.

22 *Ibid.* at 685.

23 As Dotson notes, gay porn is not simply an issue of showing us oral and anal sex. There is often a clear message attached to the penetrative sex demanded by men such as Sherman:

> Frank Browning writes, "A few minutes into almost any gay leather porn flick, one encounters the macho dudes who 'beat' their boys into submission, slapping them hard across the jaw and the ass, yanking a mouth to a macho crotch, as the yanked-on one moans, 'Yeah, Daddy, yeah!'" In many of these videos, men who sometimes look more like young boys than mature adults are forced into submissive, helpless situations, such as being tied facedown on a bed or hammock with their legs spread wide apart, while a group of stronger men, often dressed in leather and carrying whips or riding crops, stand in a circle and masturbate. Eventually, the submissive man is penetrated with a large artificial penis or a man's fist and lower arm. Next, the men standing in the circle each take their turn at having intercourse with the man who is tied down. When the camera shows the submissive man's face, it is difficult to determine if his expression is one of excitement and pleasure or one of fear and pain. (Wayne Edisol Dotson, *Behold the Man: The Hype and Selling of Male Beauty in Media and Culture* [New York: Harrington Park Press, 1999], 133-4, quoting Frank Browning, *The Culture of Desire* [New York: Crown Publishers, 1993], 51)

It is also worth noting the work of Robert Jensen, who questions whether the liberatory potential of watching and performing anal sex is undermined by the social meaning attached to "fucking" or "being fucked." Given that gay porn asks us to "fuck" in order to find strength and validation, is the subversive nature of the medium not jeopardized given what "fucking" means socially? Jensen writes:

> Attention to the meaning of the principal male slang term for sexual intercourse – fuck – is instructive. To fuck a person is to penetrate him or her. To fuck someone in another context ("he really fucked me over on that deal") means to hurt or cheat someone. When hurled as a simple insult ("fuck you"), the intent is denigration, and the remark is often a prelude to violence or the threat of violence. People continue to use the same word for sex and aggressive or violent behavior, even though there is great resistance to the notion that sex as fucking is linked to domination, aggression, and violence. (Robert Jensen, "Getting It Up for Politics: Gay Male Sexuality and Radical Lesbian Feminism," in Sara Miles, ed., *Opposite Sex* [New York: New York University Press, 1998], 159)

24 "My First Lesson," *Manscape Magazine* 10, no. 11 (January 1995), 112.
25 Kleinberg, *supra* note 1 at 123-4.
26 Seymour Kleinberg, *Alienated Affections: Being Gay in America* (New York: St. Martin's Press, 1980), 196.
27 Richard Dyer, "Coming to Terms," *Jump Cut*, no. 30 (1985), 28. Dyer continues:

> The basis of gay porn is a narrative sexuality, a construction of male sexuality as the desire to achieve the goal of visual climax. In relation to gay sexual politics, it is worth signalling that this should give pause to those of us who thought/hoped that being a gay man meant that we were breaking with the gender role system. At certain levels this is true, but there seems no evidence that in the predominant form of how we represent our sexuality to ourselves (in gay porn) we in any way break from the norms of male sexuality.
> ... In so far as porn is part of the experimental education of the body, it has contributed to and legitimized the masculine model of gay sexuality, a model that always implies the subordination of women. (*Ibid.* at 28)

28 Marc Simpson, *Male Impersonators: Men Performing Masculinities* (New York: Routledge, 1994), 134. Writing of Stryker's role model status as the epitome of what gay men think a "real man" should be like, Simpson continues:

> Not only does his name connote thrusting violence (one of his most famous films is called *Stryker Force*), but his penis is celebrated for its ability to inflict pain; it is slapped across faces, rammed down throats (accompanied by the sweet nothing line, "Choke on dat fat cock"), and jammed up rectums without so much as a "please" or "thank you." His name is synonymous with a certain sadism towards his "partners" (who never approach the equality this word suggests); they are always total "bottoms" to his

total "top" ... In porn, it would seem, gay men demand that the fucker and the fucked remain distinct categories ... Stryker is a gay man's idea of what a straight man should be: a stud without anality, a prick without an arse, a top man *who does not have a bottom of his own.* (*Ibid.* at 135)

29 John Stoltenberg, *Refusing to Be a Man* (New York: Meridian Books, 1989), 110.
30 On the use of sexist slang within the gay community, see Julia P. Stanley and Susan Robins, "Sexist Slang and the Gay Community: Are You One, Too?" *The Michigan Occasional Papers Series*, no. 14 (Ann Arbor: University of Michigan, Department of Women's Studies, 1991).
31 Kevin Koffler, "Sex, Videotape and Maybe Lies: An Interview with Gay Icon Jeff Stryker," *Advocate*, 12 September 1989, 26.
32 Richard Fung, "Looking for My Penis: The Eroticized Asian in Gay Video Porn," in Bad Object Choices, eds., *How Do I Look? Queer Film and Video* (Seattle: Bay Press, 1991).
33 Leo Bersani, "Is the Rectum a Grave?" in Jonathan Goldberg, ed., *Reclaiming Sodom* (New York: Routledge, 1994), 249 at 249.
34 *Ibid.* at 262.
35 *Ibid.* at 258.
36 *Ibid.* at 257.
37 *Ibid.* at 250.
38 *Ibid.* at 253 and 254.
39 *Ibid.* at 255.
40 Richard Rambuss, *Closet Devotions* (London: Duke University Press, 1998), 154 n. 75.
41 Stychin, *supra* note 16 at 876.
42 Suzanne Pharr, *Homophobia: A Weapon of Sexism* (Little Rock, AR: Chardon Press, 1988), 18.
43 *Ibid.* at 19.
44 Tim Carrigan, Bob Connell, and John Lee, "Hard and Heavy: Toward a New Sociology of Masculinity" (1985) 14 *Theory and Society* 551 at 562.
45 Admittedly, the argument can be made that those who, internalizing self-hate, become the feminized other that pornography tells them they should be, no longer challenge patriarchy because they *are* below other men in a gender hierarchy. They become, in essence, the "female" in the male/female gender polarity necessary for male supremacy. Hence, it might be argued, they will not be the recipients of abuse because they are not a threat.
      In that these men are identified as "female," it is true they are not as much of a threat as those who refuse to accept gender categories. Nonetheless, to the extent that these men are recognized as a non-threat, it is because they are no longer seen as undermining inequality. Hence, because of homophobia, they become exactly what is required by straight men in order for them to maintain male supremacy. At a political level, this is disastrous for any group committed to social equality. At another level, however, it is naïve to assume that these men will no longer be attacked simply because they are theoretically no longer a threat to social hierarchies. As feminized "others," they will remain the target of considerable abuse, ensuring that those who are closeted fear the results of being labelled female. Add to this the abuse of those men who, politically, do dare challenge patriarchal expectations, and this ensures that closeted gay men stay closeted out of fear, or that they adopt masculine mimicry. The effect of either is invisibility, and this is exactly what homophobia aims to do – render gay male sexuality deviant and ultimately invisible.
46 Kleinberg, *supra* note 1 at 123.
47 Leo Bersani, "Is the Rectum a Grave?" in Douglas Crimp, ed., *AIDS: Cultural Analysis, Cultural Activism* (Cambridge, MA: MIT Press, 1987), 208.
48 As Kleinberg again explains, "men in leather are already the easiest marks for violent teenagers on a drunken rampage in Greenwich Village or on Mission Street on a Saturday night. The lessons of Negroes who disliked blackness, or Jews who insisted they were assimilated, really German, are ignored. To some whites, everything not black is black; to Nazis Jews are Jews, sidelocks or not. Telling the enemy one is as good as him because one is like him does not appease him; often it makes him more vicious, furious because somehow his victim seems to approve his scorn." Kleinberg, *supra* note 1 at 132.
49 Factum of the Intervener Women's Legal Education and Action Fund, in the case of *R. v. Butler* (S.C.C.), File No. 22191, 1990, at para. 46.
50 Little Sisters Trial Exhibits, Exhibits 29 and 30, *Tom of Finland Retrospective I and II.*
51 Little Sisters Trial Exhibits, Exhibit 202, *Sex Stop: True Homosexual Experiences,* vol. 3.
52 Little Sisters Trial Exhibits, Exhibit 33, *Martie: Black Summer, White Heat.*

53 Simon Obendorf, "OG" Oriental Guys/Occidental Gaze: Towards a Feminist Critique of Western Homosexual Pornographic Depictions of Asian Men" (student paper, University of Melbourne, 1997), on file with the author.
54 Within the context of pornography, the argument most commonly advanced is that any call for political change which asserts that pornography is an issue of sexual inequality is "essentialist" because it assumes that all women are the same, that gender is *the* source of oppression for all women, and, as a result, ignores the differing realities caused by racial difference, class difference, difference on the basis of sexuality, and so on. Of course, this is not a claim made by those feminists who oppose and fight against pornography. These women, many of whom have written outstanding work on the use of race and sexuality in pornography, are not arguing that gender is *all* there is to pornography. Rather, what they are arguing is that gender is never *not* there. It, like other systems of oppression, intersects with other oppressions. It is, however, something that all women (and, I would argue, all gay men) have in common. This is not to say that all women and all gay men are similarly situated. Quite the contrary. Nor should we be seen as arguing that some men do not and will not continue to rely on gendered and racial inequalities to themselves find some sense of empowerment. What we are saying, however, is that their "playing" with inequality will not subvert it or eradicate the very real harms that result in the discrimination experienced by women and other gay men. Nor will it necessarily eradicate the power of gender inequality when turned on, and used against, themselves. In this regard, and within the specific context of those lesbian women who argue that to paint gender as an issue for *all* women is essentialist because some women can and do play with gender, thereby subverting it, see Sheila Jeffreys, *Lesbian Heresy* (Melbourne: Spinifex Press, 1993). Within the context of gender and race, see Andrea Dworkin, *infra* note 57 at 122-5. See also Aminatta Forna, "Pornography and Racism: Sexualizing Oppression and Inciting Hatred," in Catherine Itzin, ed., *Pornography: Women, Violence and Civil Liberties* (Oxford: Oxford University Press, 1992), and Gloria Cowen, "Racism and Sexism in Pornography," in Laura Lederer and Richard Delgado, eds., *The Price We Pay: The Case against Racist Speech, Hate Propaganda, and Pornography* (New York: Hill and Wang, 1995).
55 See bell hooks, "Eating the Other," in *Black Looks: Race and Representation* (Boston: South End Press, 1992). See also Thelma Golden, *Black Male: Representations of Masculinity in Contemporary American Art* (New York: Whitney Museum of American Art, 1994).
56 Catharine MacKinnon, *Toward a Feminist Theory of the State* (Cambridge: Harvard University Press, 1989), 138.
57 Andrea Dworkin, *Right Wing Women* (New York: Perigee Books, 1978), 122. See also Dworkin's work in *Pornography: Men Possessing Women* (New York: E.P. Dutton, 1981). For further analysis of the role of racism in pornography, see Patricia Hill Collins, *Black Feminist Thought* 166-80 (1990); Alice Walker, "Coming Apart," in Walker, *You Can't Keep a Good Woman Down* (New York: Harcourt, 1981), 41; Catharine MacKinnon, *Sex Equality* (New York: Foundation Press, 2001), 1537 and 1581.
58 *Ibid.* at 124.
59 *Ibid.* at 124.
60 Obendorf, *supra* note 53 at 11-12. The article to which the writer refers is "Hitchhiker Kidnapped?" *OG: Oriental Guys* no. 19 (1997), 53-72.
61 Fung, *supra* note 32 at 151-2.
62 As Obendorf explains, the stereotype becomes reality such that Asian men are conflated with and become anus, buttocks, passivity, and vulnerability:

> Nowhere is this more obvious than in the letters page of *OG: Oriental Guys*, where Caucasian readers compliment the magazine on models or photo spreads which they have found particularly arousing. One such letter, and its reply from the *OG* editorial staff will demonstrate the point at hand:
>
> *Reader:* I have recently received back issues of *OG* and you are to [be] congratulated for the high quality of the editorial, design and editorial content. Would it be possible to include more "pink" that is explicit butthole pictures in each issue? Perhaps I am not alone in thinking the rosebud part of Asian men's anatomies is choice.
>
> *Reply:* No Peter you are not alone and we have already taken steps to rectify the situation. (Obendorf, *supra* note 53 at 14, citing "Letter to the Editor," [1995] 14 *OG: Oriental Guys* 5)

63 Tony Ayres, "Undesirable Aliens," *HQ Magazine* (Sydney), March-April 1998, 110 at 112.

64 Fung, *supra* note 32 at 155.
65 Ayres, "Undesirable Aliens," *HQ Magazine*, March-April 1998, 110 at 115.
66 Interestingly, LEAF makes a similar argument with respect to lesbian pornography in its factum in the *Little Sisters* trial. Unlike Fung, however, LEAF does not highlight problems with the way in which race *is* used in pornography, arguing only that women of colour need the types of pornography at issue in the trial: "Lesbians of colour and Aboriginal lesbians find that they are often marginalized from mainstream and LGBT cultures and from communities of colour and Aboriginal communities. Discriminatory censorship of their expression impedes the struggle of lesbians of colour and Aboriginal lesbians for full participation in social and political life." Factum at the Intervener Women's Legal and Action Fund (LEAF), in the case of *Little Sisters Book and Art Emporium v. A.G. Canada*, S.C.C., File No. 26858, 27 September 1999.
    Although LEAF does not address the reality of non-white gay men, it is worth questioning whether the use of women of colour results in the freedom LEAF advocates and whether the women the group professes to represent can in fact find freedom insofar as gay men continue to suffer from the racial harms so evident in gay male pornography. That is, can the racism that harms these women be eradicated if the same racial harms are perpetuated elsewhere?
    An excellent analysis of the use of lesbians of colour in pornography is provided in Jeffreys, *supra* note 19 at 186. Within the context of lesbian sado-masochistic pornography, for example, Jeffreys writes: "We must see and challenge clearly any attempt to make racist and fascist values or behaviour acceptable. The eroticizing of power and oppression in the sexuality of cruelty that is S/M trains us to be turned on by the trappings of fascism. The erotic appeal of fascism, structured into our sexuality as we learn our sexual responses under male supremacy, is enhanced by the politics of S/M. The sexuality of cruelty that is S/M is neither innate nor inevitable."
    See also Audre Lorde and Susan Leigh Starr, "Interview with Audre Lorde," in Robin Linden, ed., *Against Sadomasochism: A Radical Feminist Analysis* (Palo Alto, CA: Frog in the Well, 1982).
67 Fung, *supra* note 32 at 196.
68 Kleinberg, *supra* note 1 at 132.
69 Carl Gopal, "Gay Racism," *Independent Monthly*, May 1994, 14.
70 Letter to *Body Politic*, no. 96 (September 1983), 5.

Chapter 7: "Protecting" Gay Youth

1 Iain Clacher, "Silence Is Where the Hate Grows" (8 September 1997) <http://www.youth.org/loco/PERSONProject/Alerts/International/suicide3.html>.
2 Gavin Pitts, "Couch Potato," *Westside Observer*, 11 April 1996, 16.
3 Jeffrey Sherman, "Love Speech: The Social Utility of Pornography" (1995) 47 *Stan. L. Rev.* 661 at 683.
4 See US Department of Health and Human Services statistics, as quoted in Kevin Jennings, *Becoming Visible* (Boston: Alyson Publications, 1994), 264. See also Christopher Bagely, "Suicidal Behaviours in Homosexual and Bisexual Males" (1997) 18(1) *Crisis* 24; Gary Remafedi, "Risk Factors for Attempted Suicide in Gay and Bisexual Youth" 87(6) *Paediatrics* 869; USA Task Force on Youth Suicide *Final Report*, specifically the chapter by P. Gibson, "Gay Male and Lesbian Youth Suicide" (US Department of Health and Human Services, 1989); A. Martin, "The Stigmatization of the Gay and Lesbian Adolescent" (1988) 16 *Journal of Homosexuality* 163; V. Urbine, "Addressing the Needs of Lesbian, Gay and Bisexual Youth" (1992) 24 *Journal of Homosexuality* 9; M. Rotheram, "Suicidal Behaviour and Gay Related Stress among Gay and Bisexual Male Adolescents" 87(8) *American Journal of Public Health* 1; Ron MacDonald and Trudi Cooper, "Young Gay Men and Suicide" (1998) 17(4) *Youth Studies Australia* 23; Jonathon Nicholas and John Howard, "Better Dead Than Gay" (1998) 17(4) *Youth Studies Australia* 28; Gary Remafedi et al., "The Relationship between Suicide Risk and Sexual Orientation" (1997) 87(8) *American Journal of Public Health* 1; Neil Buhrich and Carlson Loke, "Homosexuality, Suicide and Parasuicide" (1988) 10 *Journal of Homosexuality* 113.
5 A 1993 report by the San Francisco Health Commission found that "almost 12% of 20 to 22 year old gay men surveyed were HIV positive, as were 4% of 17 to 21 year olds. If those figures are not quickly reversed, health officials say, the current generation of young urban gay men will have as high an infection rate by the time they reach their mid 30s as middle age gay men are thought to have today – close to 50%." Outlined in Chris Bull, "The Lost Generation: The Second Wave of HIV Infections among Young Gay Men," *Advocate*, May 1994, 36.

6 Jennings, *supra* note 4 at 262.
7 *Ibid.*
8 James Sears, *Growing Up Gay in the South* (New York: Harrington Park Press, 1991), cited in Jennings, *supra* note 4 at 263.
9 *Ibid.* at 263.
10 As quoted in S. Jeffrey-Poulter, "A Smell of Weimar 1987-8," in Stephen Jeffrey-Poulter, ed., *Peers, Queers, and Commons* (London: Routledge, 1991), 222.
11 Iain Clacher, "Silence Is Where the Hate Grows: Gay Teenagers and the Frightening Final Solution," *Campaign Magazine* (Sydney), September 1997, 27. Research worldwide supports these findings, such that it can now be concluded that gay and lesbian youth are at least three times more likely than heterosexual youth to attempt suicide. See P. Gibson, *Gay Male and Lesbian Youth Suicide, Report of the Secretary's Task Force on Youth Suicide (*US Department of Health and Human Services, 1989); A. Bell and M. Weinberg, *Homosexualities: A Study of Diversity among Men and Women* (New York: Simon and Schuster, 1978); K. Jay and A. Young, *The Gay Report: Lesbian and Gay Men Speak Out about Their Sexual Experiences and Lifestyles* (New York: Summit, 1977); T. Roesler and R. Deisher, "Youthful Man Homosexuality" (1972) *Journal of the American Medical Association* 1018; G. Remafedi and J.A. Farrow, "Risk Factors for Attempted Suicide in Gay and Bisexual Youth" (1991) *Paediatrics* 87.
12 Jennings, *supra* note 4 at 263.
13 Government of Western Australia, *Making a Difference: Youth Suicide Prevention Manual,* Health Department of Western Australia, Perth, 1994.
14 A recent LaTrobe University survey of 750 young people between the ages of fourteen and twenty-one reveals that almost half reported they had been verbally or physically assaulted because they were attracted to people of the same sex. Almost 70 percent experienced this abuse at school; 60 percent of this abuse was inflicted by other students. See "Same Sex Attraction Meets School Hostility," *Australian,* 23 November 1998, 17, and "Much Delayed Report Due at Last," *Westside Observer,* 20 November 1998, 3. See also Richard Yallop, "Playground Prejudice," *Australian,* 3 April 1997, 9; Katherine Glascott, "Student's Harsh Lesson in Sex Education," *Australian,* 3 April 1997, 9; Katherine Glascott, "Gay Schoolboy Tests Vilification," *Australian,* 2 April 1997, 3.
15 A recent report by the Western Australian AIDS Council, entitled *Here for Life: Youth Sexuality Project,* reveals similar findings. Specifically, the report notes that "the process of realising a same-sex orientation typically results in: damaged self esteem, distancing from family and peers, attempts to avoid disclosure, distortion of nearly all relationships, increasing sense of isolation and a sense of inferiority and self loathing." A copy of the report is available from the Western Australian AIDS Council, 664 Murray Street, West Perth, WA, Australia 6005 or via e-mail at waac@highway1.com.au.
16 National Gay and Lesbian Task Force, National Anti-Gay/Lesbian Victimization Report, New York, 1984, reported in Jennings, *supra* note 4 at 263.
17 Massachusetts Governor's Commission on Gay and Lesbian Youth, *Making Schools Safe for Gay and Lesbian Youth,* Boston, 1993, reported in Jennings, *ibid.* at 263.
18 G. Remafedi, "Male Homosexuality: The Adolescent's Perspective" (unpublished paper, University of Minnesota, Adolescent Health Program, 1985), reported in Jennings, *ibid.*
19 Jennings, *supra* note 4 at 263-4. These findings are also reported and discussed in the Massachusetts Commission on Gay and Lesbian Youth, *Making Our Schools Safe for Gay and Lesbian Youth* (1993). There is little reason to doubt the validity of the findings in other countries such as Canada and Australia. It should be noted that in 1997 an Australian House of Representatives Standing Committee report entitled *Aspects of Youth Suicide* included confusion over sexuality or rejection of suicide as being a factor that may trigger suicidal behaviour. See House of Representatives Standing Committee, *Aspects of Youth Suicide* (Canberra: Australian Government Publishing Service, 1997), 9. The report was, however, shamefully inadequate insofar as providing any recommendations for dealing with the specific needs of lesbian and gay youth. An excellent overview of the seriousness of the problem in Australia is provided in Iain Clacher, "Silence is Where the Hate Grows: Gay Teenagers and the Frightening Final Solution," *Campaign* (Sydney), September 1997, 27. See also Ben Widdcombe, "Can We Catch Our Falling Stars?" *Outrage,* November 1997, vol. 174, 52.
20 Jennings, *supra* note 4 at 264.
21 *Id.*
22 Geraldo Lima et al., "The Relationship between Homophobia and Self-Esteem in Gay Males with AIDS" (1993) 25(4) *Journal of Homosexuality* 69.

23   Iwan Bloch, *The Sexual Life of Our Time* (New York: Rebman, 1937) cited in A. Damien Martin and Emery Hetrick, "The Stigmatization of the Gay and Lesbian Adolescent" (1988) 15(1) *Journal of Homosexuality* 163.

24   A. Damien Martin and Emery Hetrick, "The Stigmatization of the Gay and Lesbian Adolescent" (1988) 15(1) *Journal of Homosexuality* 163 at 167. As Martin and Hetrick explain, the effect of these stereotypes on a naïve, developing adolescent is a cognitive dissonance that will radically affect that person's sense of self. As Goffman also notes, "[t]he standards he has incorporated from the wider society equip him to be intimately alive to what others see as his failing, inevitably causing him to agree that he does indeed fall short of what he really ought to be. Shame becomes a central possibility, arising from the individual's perception of one of his own attributes as being a defiling thing to possess." Martin and Hetrick at 167, citing E. Goffman, *Stigma: Notes on the Management of Spoiled Identity* (Englewood Cliffs, NJ: Prentice Hall, 1963).

25   Martin and Hetrick, *supra* note 24 at 164, citing G. Allport, *The Nature of Prejudice* (Garden City, NY: Doubleday, 1958); E.S. Hetrick and A.D. Martin, "Ego-Dystonic Homosexuality: A Developmental View," in E.S. Hetrick and T.S. Stein, eds., *Innovations in Psychotherapy with Homosexuals* (Washington: APA Press, 1984); A.D. Martin, "The Emperor's New Clothes: Modern Attempts to Change Sexual Orientation," in Hetrick, *ibid.*; R. Blair, *Ex-Gay* (New York: Homosexuality Counselling Center, 1982); D. Baker, *Beyond Rejection: The Church, Homosexuality and Hope* (Portland: Multnomah Press, 1985).

26   Martin and Hetrick, *ibid.* at 168. As the authors further explain, this sense of self-hate can in turn result in considerable social isolation:

>   The awareness of inferiority means that one is unable to keep out of consciousness the formulation of some chronic feeling of the worst sort of insecurity ... The fear that others can disrespect a person because of something he shows means that he is always insecure in his contact with other people; and this insecurity arises, not from mysterious and somewhat disguised sources, as a great deal of our anxiety does, but from something which he knows he cannot fix. Now that represents an almost fatal deficiency of the self-system, since the self is unable to disguise or exclude a definite formulation that reads, "I am inferior. Therefore, people will dislike me and I cannot be secure with them." (*Ibid.* at 167, citing H. Perry, M. Gawel, and M. Gibbon, *Clinical Studies in Psychiatry* [New York: Norton, 1956], 145)

27   G.J. MacDonald, "Individual Differences in the Coming Out Process for Gay Men: Implications for Theoretical Models" (1982) 8(1) *Journal of Homosexuality* 1 at 1 and 4.

28   Debra Boyer, "Male Prostitution and Homosexual Identity" (1989) 17(1) *Journal of Homosexuality* 151 at 167.

29   Ritch Savin-Williams, "Coming Out to Parents and Self-Esteem among Gay and Lesbian Youths" (1989) 17(1) *Journal of Homosexuality* 1 at 2. Research indicates that the majority of male prostitutes are gay men between the ages of fifteen and twenty-three. In another study, it was noted that "the majority were either gay identified, struggling to find a place in the gay male subculture, or both. Only 15% of the youth regarded themselves as 'straight.' Although many of the habitual and situational prostitutes in the study identified themselves as gay, few were able to report any kind of permanence in their homosexual relationships. The researchers found that for many of these boys, intimacy was thwarted by their fears of closeness and affection, their 'promiscuous past,' and their dislike for control or restriction in relationships." Eli Coleman, "The Development of Male Prostitution Activity among Gay and Bisexual Adolescents" (1989) 17(1) *Journal of Homosexuality* 131 at 137.
      Many of the young gay men who end up on the street flee their homes for fear of negative reaction from their parents, while others flee as a direct result of the violence inflicted on them by their families once their sexual orientation is revealed. Many turn to prostitution because it promises a sole outlet through which to meet other gay people or because they have internalized society's expectation that this is what gay people do.

30   Boyer, *supra* note 28 at 172. For an excellent overview of some of the many problems associated with homeless gay youth, see G. Kruks, "Gay and Lesbian Homeless/Street Youth: Special Issues and Concerns" (1991) 12 *Journal of Adolescent Health* 515.

31   *Ibid.* at 176-7.

32   As Coleman explains, many of the young gay men now prostituting themselves on the streets turn to drug use – a factor which ensures only that they remain there as they find themselves unable to pay for their drug addiction:

In one of the studies on male juvenile prostitution, Schick found that 20 percent of his 144 subjects eventually overdosed on heroin. Furnold, in his study of male juvenile prostitution, also found a significant history of drug abuse among the subjects, especially after entry into hustling. Similarly, Allen found that 29 percent of his sample were regular users of hard drugs and 42 percent were heavy drinkers or alcoholics. Drug dealing is common. Allen and Fischer et al. found that the degree of drug use is related to the type of prostitution – with habitual prostitutes being the heaviest users. Many of these boys use drugs while they are hustling (76 percent in the URSA study).

See Coleman, *supra* note 29 at 140, citing F. Schick, "Service Needs of Hustlers," unpublished manuscript, available from author, 111 N. Wabash Avenue, Suite 1320, Chicago 60602; R. Furnold, "Male Juvenile Prostitution" (master's thesis, University of Southern California, 1978); D.M. Allen, "Young Male Prostitutes: A Psychological Study" (1980) 9 *Archives of Sexual Behaviour* 399; and B. Fischer et al., *Report on Adolescent Male Prostitution* (San Francisco: Urban Associates, 1982).

33 Boyer, *supra* note 28 at 178.
34 Richard Troiden, "The Formation of Homosexual Identities" (1989) 17(1) *Journal of Homosexuality* 43 at 62.
35 *Ibid.* at 62.
36 Raymond Berger, "Passing and Social Support among Gay Men" (1992) 23(3) *Journal of Homosexuality* 85 at 89.
37 Martin and Hetrick, *supra* note 24 at 171.
38 Robert Kus, "Alcoholism and Non-Acceptance of Gay Self: The Critical Link" (1988) 15(1) *Journal of Homosexuality* 25.
39 See Gabriel Rotello, *Sexual Ecology: AIDS and the Destiny of Gay Men* (New York: Dutton, 1997), and Lynette Lewis and Michael Ross, *A Select Body: The Gay Dance Party Subculture and the HIV/AIDS Pandemic* (Cassell: London, 1995). Lewis and Ross at 18, citing R. Stall and J. Wiley, "A Comparison of Alcohol and Drug Use Patterns of Homosexual and Heterosexual Men; The San Francisco Men's Health Study" (1988) *Drug and Health Dependence*.
40 Robert J. Kus, "Alcoholics Anonymous and Gay American Men" (1987) 14(2) *Journal of Homosexuality* 253.
41 *Ibid.* at 32-3.
42 Troiden, *supra* note 34 at 57.
43 Rotello, *supra* note 39 at 139. Similar findings are reported by Lewis and Ross who, in investigating the use of the drug ice among young gay men at dance parties, report a need for self-control, increased sexual ability, and a desire to hide the shame attached to gay sex as major factors in increased drug use among gay men. See in particular Lewis and Ross, *supra* note 39 at 114, 119-20.
44 Factum of the Intervener Canadian AIDS Society, *Little Sisters Book and Art Emporium*, S.C.C., No. 26858, para. 4, quoting Canadian AIDS Society, *Spring 1999 National AIDS Awareness Campaign, Young Gay Men and HIV/AIDS* at 1. See in particular Kevin Cranston, "HIV Education for Gay, Lesbian and Bisexual Youth: Personal Risk, Personal Power, and the Community of Conscience" (1992) 22(3) *Journal of Homosexuality* 247 at 251-2.
45 This is a point again best articulated by Cranston, who writes: "[L]esbian, gay, and bisexual youth are at increased risk because of their lower self-esteem. A body of evidence exists to document higher rates of suicidal ideation and suicide attempts in this population compared to heterosexual adolescents, a problem believed by most researchers to be secondary to low self-esteem ... A person with a poor sense of personal worth has less ability to pursue healthy behavioural options. And if the use of alcohol or other drugs is linked with sexual activity, unsafe sexual practices are more likely to occur." *Ibid.* at 253.
46 Rotello, *supra* note 39 at 259.
47 *Ibid.* at 289.
48 Clacher, *supra* note 11 at 30.
49 Cranston, *supra* note 44.
50 *Ibid.* at 251. A similar analysis is offered by de Bruyn, who notes that because "homosexuality identity is not acknowledged, permitted and supported as a natural development of human personality ... [this] inevitably leads to negative self-esteem and a lack of negotiating skills and consequently to a heightened vulnerability to HIV infection amongst gay men."
See T. de Bruyn, "HIV/AIDS and Discrimination: A Discussion Paper," Canadian HIV/ AIDS Legal Network and Canadian AIDS Society (1998) <http://www.aidslaw.ca/elements/

disc/DISCdiv.html>, 1 at 12. See also *Report of the Evaluation of the National HIV/AIDS Strategy*, National Evaluation Steering Committee (Canberra: Commonwealth of Australia, 1992) and R. Sanatioso, "A Social Psychological Perspective on HIV/AIDS and Gay or Homosexually Active Asian Men" (1999) 36 *Journal of Homosexuality* 76. An excellent overview of these issues is found in Darryl Pereira, "HIV/AIDS and Its 'Willing Executioners': The Impact of Discrimination" (1999) 6(4) *E Law – Murdoch University Electronic Journal of Law* <http://www.murdoch.edu.au/elaw/issues/v6n4/pereira64.html>.

51 Cranston, *ibid.* at 256.
52 Factum of the Canadian AIDS Society, *supra* note 44 at para. 8.
53 *Ibid.* at para. 9. CAS continued: "There is a need for safer sex educational messages to be tailored to the realities of the sexual practices of men who have sex with men; such messages need to be eroticized in order to be effective in not merely informing but encouraging behavioural change."
54 Factum of the Intervener EGALE, in the case of *Little Sisters Book and Art Emporium* v. *A.G. Canada*, S.C.C., File No. 26858, 1999, at para. 4.
55 Testimony of Thomas Waugh in *Little Sisters*, cited by EGALE, *ibid.* at para. 4.
56 *Ibid.* at para. 5.
57 Factum of the Intervener Legal Education and Action Fund, in the case of *Little Sisters Book and Art Emporium* v. *A.G. Canada*, S.C.C., File No. 26858, 27 September 1999, at para. 15.
58 *Ibid.* at para. 19.
59 *Ibid.* at para. 18.
60 Factum of the Intervener Canadian AIDS Society, *supra* note 44 at para. 23.
61 *Ibid.* at para. 57.
62 *Ibid.* at para. 1.
63 *Ibid.* at para. 58.
64 Evidence of Thomas Waugh, cited by EGALE, *supra* note 54 at para. 5.
65 Evidence of Becki Ross, cited by EGALE, *ibid.* at para. 5.
66 Evidence of Chris Bearchell, cited by EGALE, *ibid.* at para. 5.
67 EGALE, *ibid.* at para. 7.
68 Evidence of Karen Mitstysyn, cited by EGALE, *ibid.* at para. 7.
69 Evidence of Chris Bearchell, cited by EGALE, *ibid.* at para. 8.
70 LEAF, *supra* note 57 at para. 16.
71 Evidence of Nino Ricci, cited by LEAF at para. 19.
72 Roger Myrick, *AIDS, Communication and Empowerment: Gay Male Identity and the Politics of Public Health Messages* (New York: Harrington Park Press, 1993).
73 *Ibid.* at 52.
74 David L. Chambers, "Gay Men, AIDS and the Code of the Condom" (1994) 29(2) *Harv. C.R.-C.L.L. Rev.* 353.
75 *Ibid.* at 368-9.
76 For, as Chambers himself explains, the response from other gay men to such a suggestion is usually one of disbelief or anger:

> I had a conversation recently with the associate director of education of a large AIDS service organization that conveyed gay men's intense feelings about sex and sexual freedom. I asked whether, given the high rates of unprotected sex occurring even among men who intend to use a condom on all occasions, he thought that the best advice to a young person just coming out might be to try to develop a lively sexual life that did not include anal intercourse. His response was abrupt and unequivocal. His organization, he said, would never recommend avoiding anal intercourse. To him, a gay man who told another gay man to avoid anal intercourse had probably absorbed the larger society's hatred of gay sexuality or was himself ashamed of the allure of anal sex. At a minimum, he said, advice of this sort would be ineffective because it would be seen as coming from such a person. I suddenly felt that in raising the subject, I became the chaperone at the prom. I became Nancy Reagan, urging, "Just say no."

Chambers continues that the conversation reminded him of the amount of effort gay men have put into asserting their right to sexual freedom – freedom equated with the right to have anal intercourse – and queries whether, given the extent to which our liberation platform has been built on sexual liberty, the condom alone will save lives. He writes:

[D]uring the 1970s, gay men and lesbians asserted with passion their right to have sex in the ways that pleased them. In the 1980s, as their friends began to die, many men felt a pall cast over all sexual acts and particularly anal intercourse, even though gay organizations remained consistent advocates for safe but full sexual lives. Some men, for rational or irrational reasons, chose celibacy. A mild counter-revolution began in the late 1980s. Queer Nation urged gay men to rejoice in their sexual lives, distributing stickers proclaiming "Buttfucking Is Fun." ACT-UP printed T-shirts and posters with the intertwined thighs of two muscular men obviously having intercourse to show us that "Safe Sex Is Hot Sex." In this celebration of sex and the condom, gay men were responding to our frustration with the saltpeter in our brains after more than a decade of an epidemic. We wanted a life.

Through the condom strategy, we are asserting a belief in our capacity to gain some control over this terrible disease by our repeated act of putting on a condom. The question for us is whether we can hold onto these beliefs in our capacities and hold onto our lives at the same time. (*Ibid.* at 359-60)

77 *Ibid.* at 385.
78 Rotello, *supra* note 39 at 204.
79 Quoted by David Menadue, "The Nouveau Cowboys of Barebacking," in *Positive Living: A Magazine for People Living with HIV/AIDS*, Perth, Western Australia, 26 March 1999, 8. Menadue's article is also posted at <http://gaytoday.badpuppy.com/garchive/viewpoint/031599vi.html>. Other pro-barebacking arguments are advanced by Tony Valenzuela, "Bareback Sex and HIV: A Young Man's Choice," in *Gay Today: A Global Site for Daily Gay News* at <http://gaytoday.badpuppy.com/garchive/viewpoint/031599vi.html>. See also Gordan Nary, "The Risks of Bareback Sex" at <http://www.japoc.org/policy/viewpoints/jun98edit.html> and Gregory Freeman, "Bug Chasers: The Men Who Long to be HIV+," *Rolling Stone* (6 February 2003) <http://Rolling.Stone.com>.
80 Menadue, *ibid.* at 10.
81 *Ibid.* at 10.
82 *Ibid.* at 10.
83 Signorile, *Life Outside: The Signorile Report on Gay Men* (New York: HarperCollins, 1997), 67.
84 Carl Stychin, *Law's Desire: Sexuality and the Limits of Justice* (London: Routledge, 1995), 90.
85 See Lewis and Ross, *supra* note 39. As Lewis and Ross note, evidence of this can be seen in the desirability of masculine attributes mirrored in the classified personal advertisements section of the inner city gay media, which are biased in favour of "straight looking and acting" gay men.

Dotson also notes a similar theme in the advertisements for male contact lines, and queries the effect these have on men who do not conform to the image and theme presented. See Edisol Wayne Dotson, *Behold the Man: The Hype and Selling of Male Beauty in Media and Culture* (New York: Harrington Park Press, 1999), 135.

A similar analysis is offered by Daniel Harris, who, reviewing the gay male classifieds, queries whether anything but self-hate and contempt can arise from the messages conveyed:

For the last 30 years, many men have attracted their mates, not by describing their own attributes, but by issuing a steady stream of self-righteous denigrations of other homosexuals, whom they dismiss in advertisements that amount to a public disavowal of gay life, a faithless defection from the subculture in which they brandish like "no trespassing" signs an interminable series of homophobic epithets including "no fats," "no fems," and "no fags." Gay personal ads are often organized around a parade of antitypes, a procession of effeminate monstrosities who are marched out and heckled by men who grovel before heterosexual society by referring to themselves as "straight-acting" and "straight-appearing," terms that reveal a degree of self-hatred unique among even the most conformist of ethnic groups, who would never stoop to such slavish behavior, fawning over the virility of their white masters. The picture of gay culture that emerges in many post-Stonewall advertisements is not that of the utopic consensus of a united group of committed freedom fighters but the furious enmity and self-loathing of a highly fractured society, torn apart by internal divisions. (*The Rise and Fall of Gay Culture* [New York: Ballantine Books, 1997], 59)

86 See, for example, Stychin, *supra* note 85. Specifically, Stychin refers to the interview with a young man used during the production of gay porn (discussed in Chapter 4). Recall that when interviewed, this young man explained how his films made popular the sexual practice of fisting. To this, Stychin queries why anyone would care. At a basic level, the young man used to produce the film probably cared a great deal, particularly if his participation in its production was less than consensual. It is also interesting to note that in asking why anyone cares whether gay men copied the sexual acts presented in the film, Stychin implies that he accepts that the pornography in question may have encouraged gay men to mimic the actions in it. In other words, the films did serve as a learning tool. Stychin tries to justify the use of this sexual material by stating that my purpose in using this example was to imply that some sexual practices are more morally acceptable than others. This was not, of course, my objective. My reason in using this example was merely to demonstrate that those who observe gay male pornography are influenced to do what it tells them to do – a point Stychin apparently accepts as accurate. As another writer notes, while it is one thing to justify the presentation of certain sexual practices because viewers want it, it is irresponsible to do so once we accept that people might actually imitate it. Writing specifically within the context of the porn industry's return to unsafe sex, for example, the same author argues:

> [T]here is a move among some in the porn industry to depict unsafe sex – they say viewers want it. The problem is, viewers may want to imitate it. In a *Frontiers* survey, 92 respondents said they do not imitate unsafe sex practices, 39 said they do, and 66 said they do sometimes; while it's encouraging that 92 respondents do not imitate on-screen unsafe sex practices, when you add 39 and 66, that's 105 respondents risking their lives and the lives of their sex partners, and who knows how many others.
>
>   Safe sex practices and clean-needle exchange are what will help save lives – to give out any other message is unconscionable. The porn industry is a billion a year industry ... If first one company and then another turns to unsafe sex practices, they will drive others to follow suit. And if fans rent and buy more videos featuring unsafe sex than videos featuring safer sex, they will send a message to the porn industry to keep depicting unsafe sex ... Without the porn industry's help, fewer people will adhere to safer-sex guidelines and the statistics will soon show that HIV among gay and bisexual men is again on the rise. (Editor, "The Serious Side of Porn," *Frontiers Magazine*, 22 August 1997, 10)

  See also Austin Foxx, "That Type of Guy," *Frontiers Magazine*, 22 August 1997, 65.

87 See Dave Ford, "Write Stuff," *San Francisco Bay Times*, 24 September 1992, 9. Ford notes that this recipe is quite clearly laid out, with step-by-step instructions, pictures and all, in gay male pornography: "In its dehumanization, porn has influenced the way we perceive ourselves, our bodies and our fellow men. Objectification is exciting; simple visual stimulation fuels lust. Nothing like a nice chest, or butt, or pair of thighs, or – fill in the blank ... Since we mistake Sexland for real life, and thereby let it dictate our tastes, we run the risk of choosing and cruising based on total objectification by Sexland dictates."

88 Signorile, *supra* note 83 at 28.

89 Rotello, *supra* note 39 at 254.

90 Will Harris, "Porn Again," *Campaign Magazine*, December 1993, 49. Harris continues: "Fifteen years ago, to be a porn star, you needed a dick and that was about it. It was ok if you had a hairy chest and didn't have pecs to die for. Today the producers of porn are looking for a specific look – and that is usually with lots of muscles with little hair. If you're even slightly overweight, a bit puny, thinning on top, have a hairy back, you'll have to dig deep in the bargain box of a porn video store to find yourself." *Ibid.* On the equation of body hair with age and the promotion of youth in gay porn, see Dotson, *supra* note 85 at 132.

91 *Id.*

92 Ford, *supra* note 87 at 9. Ford continues:

> By confusing Sexland and life, we could do ourselves eventual psychic harm. After all, mainstream advertising and info-tainment tell us we shouldn't exist at all. Since our cultural identity is based at least partly on our sexuality, and since porn is one avenue by which we communicate to ourselves about sex, the danger remains that by believing porn in any way, we're viewing ourselves in only the most narrow terms at our core – that is, with regards to ourselves as sexual/sensual beings. It's easy to believe our human

worth resides in how closely we [fit] to the pornographic ideal: impossibly fit, young, tall, brainless, whatever.

A similar point is raised by Daniel Harris, who argues that gay porn can only lead to a community in which self-respect and respect for others takes a back seat:

> Pornography ... vitiates our sense of touch and exaggerates our sense of sight, promoting dissatisfaction with our real-world lovers and distancing us from the actual sensations of an experience that many now perceive exclusively through the stylized representations of it available on the store shelves. Because advertising often works by infecting the consumer with fear and insecurity, as we have seen in the case of the cosmetics industry, the commercialization of the gay community almost invariably means that homosexuals will become more fearful and insecure. The achievement of our economic viability as a market entails an enormous loss of self-confidence. We exchange guilt about our sexuality for apprehension, growing out of remorse and maturing into anxiety. (Harris, *supra* note 85 at 133)

93 Signorile, *supra* note 83 at 24. And why would he? As Rotello explains, the gay community certainly has not done its share to ensure that gay men develop those attitudes that demand respect for others. Noting in particular the trend among gay male academics to intellectualize sexual entitlement, Rotello argues that the notions that it is appropriate to do so, "would be considered scandalous if they were coming from straight men talking about women." Rotello, *supra* note 39 at 268.

94 *Ibid.* at 24-5.

95 Blade Thompson, quoted in Will Harris, *supra* note 85 at 50. To which another porn star is quoted as adding, "sex is one of life's strongest drives. Who would want to look at someone who is ugly in a porn video or magazine?" *Ibid.*

96 Bob Tremble, Margaret Schneider, and Carol Appathurai, "Growing Up Gay or Lesbian in a Multicultural Context" (1989) 17(3) *Journal of Homosexuality* 253 at 263.

97 Body Politic Collective, "31 Words," *Body Politic*, April 1985, 29.

98 *Ibid.* at 30.

99 *Ibid.* at 31. It is also worth noting the words of Tim McCaskell, who, echoing concerns similar to those voiced by feminist women regarding the gay male commitment to pornography, asks, "We have required that our classified advertisers act responsibly in terms of the Criminal Code and in terms of exclusionary language which we feel is destructive of our community. Why is it suddenly such an issue to require that they continue to act responsibly in our pages in terms of objectionable racial stereotyping which is damaging to individuals, sets the stage for further discrimination, cuts off our paper from minority sections of our community and undermines our goal of helping build that community?" *Ibid.* at 45.

100 Tremble et al., *supra* note 96 at 263.

101 Letter to the editor, *Campaign Magazine,* January 1992, quoted in Tony Ayres, "Undesirable Aliens," *HQ Magazine*, March-April 1998, 110 at 114-15.

102 "Letter to the Editor," *Body Politic*, no. 113 (April 1985), 31.

103 Lewis and Ross, *supra* note 39.

104 *Ibid.* at 200.

105 *Ibid.* at 183. As Lewis and Ross note:

> Many of the respondents personally identified with the new "straighter-than straight" gay identity symbol, although most of them were concerned about its degenerative effects on the social legitimization and future self-determination of the gay subculture. Respondent 25 suggested that this normalizing symbol masked the gay identity through the process of assimilation:
>
> "[s]traight acting is exactly what it is ... it involves them closing themselves in a box."
>
> This new gay stereotype symbol was similar to Hans Christian Anderson's story of the Emperor's New Clothes in which the Emperor only exchanged one form of oppression for another (in this case a similarly scantily-clothed one to the dance party patron). Most of the respondents indicated that many gay dance party patrons denied their stigmatized gay identity by "passing" as straight men. Respondent 29 denied his association with the stigmatized gay stereotypic symbol:
>
> "I'm not like other gay men as you can see ... I'm very straight." (*Ibid.* at 183)

106 *Ibid.* at 199.
107 Signorile, *supra* note 83 at 137.
108 As reported in Greg Callaghan, "Worst Days of Their Lives," *Australian*, 10 April 2000, 11.
109 *Ibid.*
110 *Ibid.*
111 Some ideas for change and education strategies in this regard are discussed in the work of Wayne Martino, "Cool Boys, Party Animals, Squids and Poofters: Interrogating the Dynamics and Politics of Adolescent Masculinities in School" (1999) 20(2) *British Journal of Sociology of Education* 239. See also Wayne Martino, "Masculinity and Learning: Exploring Boys' Underachievement and Under-Representation in Subject English" (1985) 27(2) *Interpretations* 22; Wayne Martino, "'A Bunch of Arseholes': Exploring the Politics of Masculinity for Adolescent Boys in Schools" (1997) 16(3) *Social Alternatives* 39; S. Askew, *Boys Don't Cry: Boys and Sexism in Education* (Milton Keynes, UK: Open University Press, 1988); E. Jordan, "Fighting Boys and Fantasy Play: The Construction of Masculinity in the Early Years of School" (1995) 7(1) *Gender and Education* 69; J. Kenway, "Masculinities in Schools: Under Siege, on the Defensive and Under Reconstruction?" (1995) 16(1) *Discourse: Studies in the Cultural Politics of Education* 59; J. Kenway, "Boys' Education, Masculinity and Gender Reform: Some Introductory Remarks" (1997) 17(1) *Curriculum Perspectives* 57; S. Kessler et al., "Gender Relations in Secondary Schooling" (1995) 58 *Sociology of Education* 34; L. Laskey and C. Beavis, *Schooling and Sexualities* (Geelong: Deakin University, 1985); C. McLean, "Men, Masculinity and Heterosexuality," in L. Laskey and C. Beavis, eds., *Schooling and Sexualities: Teaching for a Positive Sexuality* (Geelong: Deakin University, Centre for Education and Change, 1995); A. Nickson, "Keeping a Straight Face: Schools, Students and Homosexuality, Part 1," in Laskey and Beavis, *supra;* C. Skelton, "Learning to Be Tough: The Fostering of Maleness in One Primary School" (1996) 8(2) *Gender and Education* 185.

Chapter 8: Controlling Pornographic Harm Post-*Butler*

1 Catharine MacKinnon and Andrea Dworkin, "Statement on Canadian Customs and Legal Approaches to Pornography," in Diane Bell and Renate Klein, eds., *Radically Speaking: Feminism Reclaimed* (Melbourne: Spinifex Press, 1996), 218.
2 Sheila Noonan, "Harm Revisited: R. v. Butler" (1992) 4(1) *Const. Forum Const.* 12 at 16.
3 *R. v. Hawkins* (1993) 15 O.R. (3d) 549 (C.A.).
4 See *R. v. Hawkins, supra* note 3; *R. v. Jacob* (1996), 112 C.C.C. (3d) 1 (Ont. C.A.); *R. v. Erotica Video Exchange Ltd.* (1994), 163 A.R. 181 (Prov. Ct.).
5 *Glad Day Bookshop Inc. v. Canada (Deputy Minister of National Revenue, Customs and Excise)* (14 July 1992) (Ont. Ct. (Gen. Div.)).
6 See discussion, *supra* Chap. 3.
7 *Glad Day, supra* note 5.
8 *Ibid.*
9 *Ibid.*
10 See *R. v. Ronish* (1993) 18 C.R. (4th) 165 (Ont. C.J. Prov. Div.).
11 *Little Sisters Book and Art Emporium v. A.G. Canada* (1996), 131 D.L.R. (4th) 486 at 536 (B.C.S.C.).
12 *Little Sisters Book and Art Emporium v. Canada* (1996), 18 B.C.L.R. (3d) 241 (B.C.C.A.).
13 *Little Sisters Book and Art Emporium v. Canada (Minister of Justice),* [2000] 2 S.C.R. 1120.
14 *Little Sisters* (B.C.S.C.), *supra* note 11 at 532-5.
15 Lesbian and gay male activists, for example, argue that the means chosen to regulate pornography unjustifiably restrict the flow of pornographic materials that, in their opinion, should not be censored, an argument refuted throughout this book. Anti-pornography feminists, on the other hand, argue that the means chosen do not effectively restrict the flow of those materials that do harm. Generally, anti-pornography feminists have agreed with lesbian and gay activists that present methods do unjustifiably restrict the sale and distribution of many non-harmful lesbian and gay publications. These same feminists have also argued quite forcefully that Customs procedures in particular, to the extent that they do not adhere to the *Butler* harms-based test, are discriminatory and ineffective. In this regard, see MacKinnon and Dworkin, *supra* note 1.
16 *Little Sisters* (B.C.S.C.), *supra* note 11.
17 *Ibid.* at 556.
18 *Ibid.*
19 *Ibid.*

20 *Ibid.* at 546.
21 *Ibid.* at 560.
22 *Ibid.* at 518.
23 *Ibid.* at 546.
24 *Canada Customs Act*, R.S. 1985, c. 1.
25 *Canada Customs Tariff*, R.S. 1985, c. 41.
26 Section 114 of the *Customs Tariff* prohibits the importation of "any goods enumerated or referred to in Schedule VII" of that statute. Schedule VII lists classes of prohibited goods and assigns each class a code number. Code 9956(a) deals with obscene material and prohibits the importation of those materials deemed to be obscene under s. 163(8) of the *Criminal Code*, that section of the code judicially considered by the Canadian Supreme Court in *Butler*. Code 9956(a) thus forbids the seizure of materials not caught by the *Butler* sex equality analysis.
27 A full outline of the memorandum is provided in Chapter 3 at footnote 6.
28 Pursuant to s. 58 of the *Customs Act*, Customs officers are authorized to determine the tariff classification of imported goods at Canadian ports of entry. Initially, this determination is made by relatively junior Customs officials, referred to as Customs inspectors. Inspectors at this level are required to undergo only a sixteen-week training session before commencing their duties, during which they spend only a few hours on the interpretation and application of code 9956. See *Little Sisters* (B.C.S.C.), *supra* note 11 at 501-2.
29 Not all imported materials are inspected, as the examination of all goods and mail presented at ports of entry would be a practical impossibility. *Ibid.* There are approximately 240 ports of entry in Canada, and in the fiscal year 1993-4, for example, almost 230,000 shipments, made up of about 330 million goods, were imported through them. *Ibid.* Customs officials estimate that there are approximately 10.5 million entry transactions each year and that between 20,000 and 40,000 items of mail enter the Customs Mail Centre daily in Vancouver alone. Customs tries to examine approximately 8 percent of the goods imported. *Ibid.* at 502.
     As Customs is predominantly concerned with ensuring compliance with the law and with detecting contraband, goods unlikely to contravene applicable legislation are examined less frequently. An example of such goods are books, which are not subject to Customs duty and which ordinarily do not fall within schedule VII of the *Customs Tariff*. This is not to say that books have not been seized. Indeed, the fact that many books (predominantly those indicating lesbian and gay male content) have initially been determined to be obscene but later permitted clearly shows that lesbian and gay materials have been treated disparately. Many of the seized materials did not violate the *Butler* test for obscenity. Specifically, they could not be deemed harmful applying the equality-based test articulated in that case. What is most troubling about the restrictions imposed on their distribution, however, is that many of them are central to the development and articulation of those lesbian and gay male identities necessary for the eventual undermining of gender inequality – the type of inequality that the Court in *Butler* attempted to address. See the discussion in Chapters 2 and 6 for an explanation as to how the public expression of lesbian and gay relationships and identities might potentially undermine patriarchy and the inequalities that arise from it. The trial court in *Little Sisters* recognized this and noted that the results are less than fair. Indeed, they lead to the discriminatory targeting of those bookstores that specialize in the sale of lesbian and gay male materials:

> Little Sisters' choice of carrier affects their ability to import material. Because of the scrutiny their shipments receive at the Vancouver Mail Centre, Little Sisters uses United Parcel Services as much as possible for cross-border deliveries. They have not had a book carried by that carrier prohibited in the last two years, while virtually every shipment to them through the mail is inspected and many items are prohibited. On one occasion, a package of domestic mail from Ontario was opened and inspected by Customs. This understandably contributed immensely to the perception of the principals of Little Sisters that they are being persecuted by Customs. Although I am satisfied that this incident was the result of inadvertent human error by customs officers, it was caused by the systematic targeting of Little Sisters' importation in the Customs Mail Centre. (*Little Sisters* (B.C.S.C.), *supra* note 11 at 518)

30 *Ibid.* at 503.
31 *Ibid.* at 517.
32 *Little Sisters* (B.C.S.C.), *supra* note 11 at 501.
33 *Ibid.*

34 *Ibid.* at 519. The trial court further noted that junior Customs inspectors were provided no evidence with which to assist them in distinguishing between those materials that are harmful and those that are of value because of their literary or artistic merit: "In a system that relies on inspection and detection of illegal importation at the border, it is essential that the importer be afforded an opportunity to place relevant evidence before the classifying officer to facilitate an informed decision. There is presently no formal procedure in place for achieving that." *Ibid.* at 553. The trial court also noted that if importers chose to submit extrinsic evidence, such as expert opinion, to redetermination officers, these tariff administrators would consider it. Unfortunately, such evidence was "not routinely invited and oral evidence was never permitted." *Ibid.* at 506.

35 Appeals from the decisions of Customs inspectors are made as follows:

> Section 59 permits any officer designated by the Minister, or any officer within a class of officers so designated, to re-determine tariff classifications under, inter alia, s.60. This delegation has been made to a class of officers known as Tariff and Values Administrators.
>
> Section 60 affords the importer the right to have the classification of prohibited goods re-determined as follows:
>
> > 60(1) The importer ... may ...
> > (a) within ninety days, or
> > (b) where the Minister deems it advisable, within two years after the deter-mination ... was made in respect of the goods under section 58, request a re-determination of the tariff classification ...
> > (2) A request under this section shall be made to a designated officer in the prescribed manner and in the prescribed form containing the prescribed information.
> > (3) On receipt of a request under this section, a designated officer shall, with all due dispatch, re-determine the tariff classification ... and give notice of this decision to the person who made the request.
>
> Section 63 grants a right to a further re-determination by the Deputy Minister of National Revenue for Customs and Excise:
>
> > 63(1) Any person may,
> > (a) within ninety days after the time he was given notice of a decision under section 60 ... , or
> > (b) where the Minister deems it advisable, within two years after the time a determination ... was made under section 58, request a further re-determination of the tariff classification ... re-determined ... under section 60 ...
> > (2) A request under this section shall be made to the Deputy Minister in the prescribed manner and in the prescribed form containing the prescribed information.
> > (3) On receipt of a request under this section, the Deputy Minister shall, with all due dispatch, re-determine the tariff classification ... and give notice of his decisions to the person who made the request.
>
> Section 67 grants a right of appeal from the Deputy Minister's re-determination to the Canadian International Trade Tribunal, which must hold a hearing and may then make "such order, finding or declaration as the nature of the matter may require." Section 71 substitutes the superior court of the relevant province or territory for the Canadian International Trade Tribunal where the goods in question have been prohibited pursuant to, inter alia, code 9956. (*Ibid.* at 498-9)

36 The statistics presented at trial suggested that importers submitted few initial classification decisions for redetermination pursuant to ss. 60, 63, and 67 of the *Customs Act*. Of those that were taken, a small number resulted in reclassification of the initially prohibited material. An even smaller proportion of decisions were appealed to the courts, as provided for in s. 71 of the *Customs Act. Ibid.* at 512-13.

37 *Ibid.* at 506.

38 The trial court found that appeals were rare, and those that were considered revealed an appalling rate of error. As the trial court noted within the context of the appeal provision in the *Customs Act:*

> The plaintiffs identified 261 titles detained from imported shipments destined for Little Sisters since 1984, seventy-seven of them on more than one occasion. Of those, sixty-two were released for delivery after examination pursuant to s.58. Little Sisters sought re-determination pursuant to s.60 on 210 prohibitions and were successful on twenty-eight. Of 150 re-determinations sought pursuant to s.63, they were successful on forty-six. As mentioned, they were successful on their one appeal pursuant to s.67. Thus, roughly 20% of prohibitions at the s.58 level were considered to be incorrect by Tariff and Values Administrator acting pursuant to s.60, and roughly 30% of the decisions of lower-ranking officers were considered to be incorrect by Tariff Administrators reviewing the materials pursuant to s.63. (*Ibid.* at 516)

39 The trial court found that the entire process was expensive, particularly for small businesses like those that cater to the lesbian and gay male communities:

> [a]s expected, Little Sisters began to experience delayed deliveries of imported material and prohibitions of some items. In the early years, Mr. Deva and Mr. Smyth [owners of Little Sisters] accepted these difficulties passively. However, they believed that Customs was prohibiting important work that was not obscene, and when Customs prohibited two issues of *The Advocate*, they decided to resort to the re-determination procedures provided by the legislation. They felt they were being singled out by Customs since the magazine was available in Vancouver by subscription and on various news-stands.
>
> Lawyers employed by Little Sisters unsuccessfully invoked ss. 60 and 63. Mr. Deva and Mr. Smyth considered the issue sufficiently important to justify the expense of an appeal under s. 67. On the day of the hearing of the appeal, counsel for Canada Customs consented to a judgment allowing the appeal. The federal Crown justified this result at this trial by stating that the Deputy Minister had changed his mind after the s. 63 re-determination was made but that there was no statutory procedure for him to formalize that decision except by a judgment granted pursuant to an appeal under s. 67. It seems the impending appeal caused those responsible to look more carefully at the publication. In any event, Little Sisters' position was eventually vindicated some sixteen months after the initial prohibition. In the meantime, Little Sisters lost the ability to sell the two shipments prohibited and the intervening thirty issues of the periodical. (*Ibid.* at 515)

40 The trial court found that Little Sisters and other bookstores were often dissuaded from seeking redetermination as a result of the complexities involved in doing so and the cost involved in hiring lawyers:

> Little Sisters has sought re-determinations on several occasions since then, but they have often been frustrated by the obscurity of Customs' forms and procedures and by the cost of legal services ... The ubiquitous customs forms are difficult to understand, a fact that was conceded even by representatives of Canada Customs. There is merit to the complaints of the plaintiffs and others that they do not pursue redetermination because they are not clearly apprised of their rights and the procedures available to them. (*Ibid.* at 556)

41 Redeterminations requested by Little Sisters Bookstore under s. 60 of the *Customs Act* generally took about three to four months to complete. Some redeterminations under s. 63 took more than a year to complete. The delays and disruptions caused by detained and prohibited shipments affected Little Sisters financially and in other ways:

> Often, material is dated by the time it is received and has lost its sales value. Publications denied entry to Little Sisters are often successfully imported and sold by other stores. Planned events, like book launches, are sometimes jeopardized when Customs interrupts shipment of the publications involved. The proprietors often refer customers to local general-interest stores to obtain publications that Little Sisters is unable to import. More subtly, Mr. Deva and Ms. Fuller [Little Sisters manager] must be very circumspect in their ordering. (*Ibid.* at 516)

Importers were not the only persons denied justice. The trial court found that the appeal process was designed to "accommodate" only those who wished to argue that their imported materials were not harmful. It offered no recourse to those who wished to argue that non-prohibited materials were harmful. Legislators seemed to have completely overlooked this factor. I will return to this point shortly when addressing possible legislative reforms.

42 *Ibid.* at 518 (emphasis added). The trial court continued by noting that "a striking example of this is the collection of short stories entitled *Macho Sluts* (1988) by Pat Califia. It has been prohibited pursuant to s. 58 on four set occasions since October 23, 1989, when it was re-determined under s. 63 to be admissible." *Ibid.*

43 *Ibid.* at 553.
44 *Ibid.* at 557.
45 *Ibid.* at 558.
46 *Little Sisters* (S.C.C.), *supra* note 13 at 1202.
47 *Ibid.* at 1185.
48 *Ibid.* at 1188.
49 *Ibid.* at 1189.
50 This was a remedy sought by the Appellant Little Sisters, which asked specifically that ss. 58 and 71 of the *Customs Act* be struck out as unconstitutional. These sections allow Customs officers to detain goods suspected of being illegal in Canada. This includes pornography and hate speech. Fortunately, the Court rejected this request.
51 Factum of the Intervener Equality Now, in the case of *Little Sisters Book and Art Emporium* v. *A.G. Canada*, S.C.C., File No. 26858, 3 December 1999, at para. 28.
52 *Little Sisters* (S.C.C.), *supra* note 13 at 1204.
53 Noted in Factum of the Minister of Justice and Attorney General of Canada, in hearings before the Supreme Court of Canada, *Little Sisters Book and Art Emporium* v. *A.G. Canada*, S.C.C., File No. 26858, 29 October 1999, at 8.
54 *Ibid.* at paras. 9 and 10. Specifically, the Supreme Court of Canada in *Little Sisters* noted that, since the case was first heard at trial, Customs had amended its administrative procedures as follows:

(a) Memorandum D9-1-1 was re-written with particular attention being given to s. 2(b) *Charter* rights, artistic merit and importers rights.

(b) A series of Information Bulletins were issued by the Prohibited Importations Unit of Customs, with the purpose of clarifying issues relating to the administration of [the Tariff Code]. These Bulletins are available to the public through the Prohibited Importations Unit.

(c) The somewhat complicated B2 form by which an importer appealed a determination was replaced by a simple written request for re-determination or review.

(d) Importers may submit with their re-determination request any evidence which they view as relevant.

(e) When goods are detained and suspected of being obscene, the importer receives a written notice containing the following information: a brief description of the goods; port of entry; date of detention; statement of reasons for the detention, and a contact name and telephone number. The importer is also invited to view the materials and submit evidence in writing attesting to their admissibility.

(f) If the goods are determined to be obscene according to the legislation, the importer receives a written notice of determination containing the following information: a brief description of the goods; the reasons for prohibition; a contact name and telephone number; a list of options available, including instructions for appeal. If the goods are not obscene, they are forwarded immediately to the importer after any duties and taxes, if applicable, are paid.

(g) Customs officers are instructed to resolve all doubts in favour of freedom of expression. (*Little Sisters* (S.C.C.), *supra* note 13 at 1255-6)

55 See generally *Glad Day Bookshop Inc.* v. *Canada*, *supra* note 5.
56 See generally Kathleen Sam Banks, "Could Mom Be Wrong? The Hurt of Names and Wrongs: Hate Propaganda and Freedom of Expression" (June 1999) 6(2) *E Law – Murdoch University Electronic Journal of Law*, <http://www.murdoch.edu.au/elaw/issues/v6n2/banks62nf.html> and Marie-France Major, "Sexual Orientation Hate Propaganda: Time to Regroup" (1996) 11(1) *Can. J.L. and Soc.* 221.

57 The *Canadian Human Rights Act* (*Canadian Human Rights Act*, R.S. 1985, c. H-6, ss. 2 and 13(1)) provides:

> 2 The purpose of this Act is to extend the laws in Canada to give effect, within the purview of matters coming within the legislative authority of Parliament, to the principle that all individuals should have an opportunity equal with other individuals to make for themselves the lives that they are able and wish to have and to have their needs accommodated, consistent with their duties and obligations as members of society, without being hindered in or prevented from doing so by discriminatory practices based on race, national or ethnic origin, colour, religion, age, sex, sexual orientation, marital status, family status, disability or conviction for an offence for which a pardon has been granted.

> **Hate messages**
> 13. (1) It is a discriminatory practice for a person or a group of persons acting in concert to communicate telephonically or to cause to be so communicated, repeatedly, in whole or in part by means of the facilities of a telecommunication undertaking within the legislative authority of Parliament, any matter that is likely to expose a person or persons to hatred or contempt by reason of the fact that that person or those persons are identifiable on the basis of a prohibited ground of discrimination.

58 (1996) 132 D.L.R. 4th 672 (F.C.T.D.).
59 Detailed in Bruce MacDougall, *Queer Judgments: Homosexuality, Expression and the Courts in Canada* (Toronto: University of Toronto Press, 2000), 147.
60 *Ibid.* at 146, referring to Richard Moon, "Drawing Lines in a Culture of Prejudice: R. v. Keegstra and the Restriction of Hate Propaganda" (1992) 26 *U.B.C. Law Rev.* 99.
61 Bruce Elman, "Combatting Racist Speech: The Canadian Experience" (1994) 32(4) *Alta. L. Rev.* 621 at 664. Elman continues: "Further, criminal sanctions confirm society's perception that minority groups are both in need of and deserving of protection against the hatred caused by such messages. However, criminal sanctions prohibiting racist speech are not easily employed, and should not be applied indiscriminately. Criminal trials are time consuming and expensive and, because of exacting standards of proof, success is always in doubt." *Ibid.* at 665.
62 *Ibid.* at 665. Many of the advantages of the human rights commissions approach were noted and supported by the Supreme Court of Canada in its decision in *Canada (Human Rights Commission)* v. *Taylor* (1990), 3 C.R.R. (2d) 116, wherein the Court noted:

> It is essential to recognize that, as an instrument especially designed to prevent the spread of prejudice and to foster tolerance and equality in the community, the *Canadian Human Rights Act* is very different from the *Criminal Code*. The aim of human rights legislation, and of s. 13(1), is not to bring the full force of the state's power against a blame worthy individual for the purpose of imposing punishment. Instead, provisions found in human rights statutes generally operate in a less confrontational manner, allowing for a conciliatory settlement if possible and, where discrimination exists, gearing remedial responses more towards compensating the victim.

See also in this regard Susan Cole, *Power Surge: Sex, Violence and Pornography* (Toronto: Second Story Press, 1995).
63 See Catharine MacKinnon and Andrew Dworkin, *In Harm's Way: The Pornography Civil Rights Hearings* (Cambridge: Harvard University Press, 1997) for more information on the facts surrounding the history of the Minneapolis ordinance.
64 Outlined in Andrea Dworkin and Catharine MacKinnon, *Pornography and Civil Rights: A New Day for Women's Equality* (Minneapolis: Organizing against Pornography, 1988), 99-105. See also Catharine MacKinnon and Andrea Dworkin, *In Harm's Way, ibid.*
65 See Paul Best and Ann Vandenberg, "Politics, Feminism and the Constitution: The Anti-Pornography Movement in Minneapolis" (1987) 39 *Stan. L. Rev.* 607 for a detailed account of the history of the Minneapolis ordinances. See also Robert Jensen, "A Review of In Harm's Way: The Pornography Civil Rights Hearings"; Steven Hill and Nina Silver, "Civil Rights Anti-Pornography Legislation: Addressing the Harm to Women"; David Orthmann, "A Review of Pornography and Civil Rights: A New Day for Women's Equality," all located at the ACLU Web page <http://www.nostatusquo.com/ACLU/Porn/>.
66 *American Booksellers Association* v. *Hudnut*, 771 F.2d 323 (7th Cir. 1985).
67 *Ibid.* at 328.

68 *Ibid.*
69 *Ibid.* at 329.
70 *Ibid.* at 329. See Catharine MacKinnon, *Only Words* (Cambridge: Harvard University Press, 1993); John Stoltenberg, "Confronting Pornography as a Civil-Rights Issue," in *Refusing to Be a Man: Essays on Sex and Justice* (New York: Meridian Press, 1990), and Cass Sunstein, "Pornography and the First Amendment" (1986) 22 *Duke L.J.* 589 for an overview of the *Hudnut* case.
71 For further discussion, see Stoltenberg, *ibid.* See also Andrea Dworkin, "Pornography Is a Civil Rights Issue for Women" (1988) 21 *U. Mich. J.L.* Ref. 55; Marian Leslie Klausner, "Redefining Pornography as Sex Discrimination: An Innovative Civil Rights Approach" (1984-5) 20 *New Eng. L. Rev.* 721; Jocelynne Scutt, "Incorporating the Dworkin/MacKinnon Approach into Australian Law" (1991) 5 *Inkwel* 3 (1991); "Pornography: Freedom v. Censorship?" (1991) *C.L.B.* 14; Mary Horniblow, "Power Undressing" (1993) *Polemic* 17; Chilla Bulbeck, "Words Can Never Hurt Me?" (1990) 15(2) *L.S.B.* 79. The leading advocate for the implementation of the ordinances in Canada has been Cole, *supra* note 62.
72 The ordinances set up procedures that provide that investigation and conciliation should follow complaints of discriminatory practices. Unresolved complaints can proceed to a public hearing at which an order to cease and desist can be made, along with the payment of damages to the complainant. An overview of how this works legally is provided in Dworkin and MacKinnon, *Pornography and Civil Rights*, *supra* note 64 at 101.
73 See, for example, *Minneapolis Ordinance*, section 4(m), as provided in MacKinnon and Dworkin, *In Harm's Way*, *supra* note 63 at 429. See also Dworkin and MacKinnon, *Pornography and Civil Rights*, *supra* note 64 at 41.
74 Outlined in Dworkin and MacKinnon, *Pornography and Civil Rights*, *ibid.* at 45.
75 *Ibid.* at 49.
76 *Ibid.* at 50.
77 Cole, *supra* note 62 at 87.
78 Mary Blakely, "Is One Woman's Sexuality Another Woman's Pornography?" *Ms Magazine*, April 1985, 37 (quoting Catharine A. MacKinnon).
79 Elizabeth Spahn, "On Sex and Violence" (1984-5) 20 *New Eng. L. Rev.* 629.

Conclusion
1 Personal interview by author, New York, 10 September 1995.

Bibliography

Publications by the Author

Kendall, Christopher, "Teen Suicide, Sexuality and Silence" (1988) 23(5) *Alternative Law Journal* 216.

–, "Gay Male Pornography and the Pursuit of Masculinity" (1993) 57 *Saskatchewan Law Review* 21.

–, "Gay Male Pornography's Harms: An Issue of Sex Discrimination" (1995) 5 *Australian Feminist Law Journal* 81.

–, "Gay Male Pornography and the Sexualization of Masculine Identity," in L. Lederer and R. Delgado, eds., *The Price We Pay: The Case against Racist Speech, Hate Propaganda and Pornography* (New York: Farrar, Strauss & Giroux, 1995), 102.

–, "Homophobia as an Issue of Sex Discrimination: Lesbian and Gay Equality and the Systemic Effects of Forced Invisibility" (1996) 3(3) *E Law – Murdoch University Electronic Journal of Law*.

–, "Gay Male Pornography after Little Sisters Book and Art Emporium: A Call for Gay Male Cooperation in the Struggle for Sex Equality" (1997) 12 *Wisconsin Women's Law Journal* 21.

–, "HIV/AIDS Education and the (Mis)Representation of Safe Sex" (1997) 22(3) *Alternative Law Review* 130.

–, "A Review of Western Australia's New Censorship Legislation in Light of Recent North American Pronouncements on Pornographic Harm" (1997) 1 *Southern Cross Law Review* 1.

–, "Sexism, Homophobia and the Meaning of Community: A Gay Male Perspective on Why Sex Equality Matters" (1998) 3 *Sister in Law* 175.

–, "Gay Male Pornography/Gay Male Community: Power without Consent, Mimicry without Subversion," in J. Kuypers, ed., *Men and Power* (Halifax: Fernwood Press, 1999), 86-105.

–, "The Harms of Gay Male Pornography: A Sex Equality Perspective Post *Little Sisters Book and Art Emporium*" (2001) 2 *Gay and Lesbian Law Journal* 1.

–, "Educating Gay Male Youth: Why Pornography Isn't a Path towards Self Respect," forthcoming (2004), *Journal of Homosexuality*.

–, "Gay Male Liberation Post *Oncale:* Since When Is Sexualized Violence Our Path to Liberation?" in Catharine MacKinnon and Reva Siegal, eds., *Directions in Sexual Harassment Law* (New Haven: Yale University Press, 2004), 221-46.

–, "Gay Male Pornography and Sexual Violence: A Sex Equality Perspective on Gay Male Rape and Partner Abuse," forthcoming (2004), *McGill Law Journal*.

–, and Russel Funk, "Gay Male Pornography's 'Actors': When 'Fantasy' Isn't," in Melissa Farley, ed., *Prostitution, Trafficking, and Traumatic Stress* (New York: Haworth Press, 2003).

Books

Allport, G., *The Nature of Prejudice* (Garden City, NY: Doubleday, 1958).

Askew, S., *Boys Don't Cry: Boys and Sexism in Education* (Milton Keynes, UK: Open University Press, 1988).

Barry, Kathleen, *Female Sexual Slavery* (New York: New York University Press, 1979).

–, *The Prostitution of Sexuality* (New York: New York University Press, 1995).

Bell, A., and M. Weinberg, *Homosexualities: A Study of Diversity among Men and Women* (New York: Simon and Schuster, 1978).

Bell, Diane, and Renate Klein, eds., *Radically Speaking: Feminism Reclaimed* (Melbourne: Spinifex Press, 1996).

Bogdanovich, Peter, *The Killing of the Unicorn: Dorothy Stratten (1960-1980)* (New York: William Morrow, 1984).

Brodribb, Somer, *Nothing Mat(t)ers: A Feminist Critique of Postmodernism* (Melbourne: Spinifex Press, 1992).

Bronski, Michael, *Culture Clash: The Making of Gay Sensibility* (Boston: South End Press, 1984).

Browning, Frank, *The Culture of Desire* (New York: Crown Publishers, 1993).

Brownmiller, Susan, *Against Our Will: Men, Women and Rape* (New York: Simon and Schuster, 1985).

Burger, John, *One-Handed Histories: The Eroto-Politics of Gay Male Video Pornography* (New York: Harrington Park Press, 1995).

Butler, Judith, *Gender Trouble: Feminism and the Subversion of Identity* (New York: Routledge, 1990).

Champions Video of Australia, *Video Release Catalogue* (Canberra: Champions, 1993).

Chauncey, George, *Gay New York: Gender, Urban Culture, and the Making of the Gay Male World 1890-1940* (New York: Basic Books, 1994).

Cole, Susan, *Pornography and the Sex Crisis* (Toronto: Amanita Press, 1989).

–, *Power Surge: Sex, Violence and Pornography* (Toronto: Second Story Press, 1995).

Crimp, Douglas, ed., *AIDS: Cultural Analysis, Cultural Activism* (Cambridge, MA: MIT Press, 1987).

Dines, Gail, Robert Jensen, and Ann Russo, *Pornography: The Production and Consumption of Inequality* (New York: Routledge, 1998).

Dotson, Edisol Wayne, *Behold the Man: The Hype and Selling of Male Beauty in Media and Culture* (New York: Harrington Park Press, 1999).

Dworkin, Andrea, *Women Hating* (New York: Plume Books, 1974).

–, *Right Wing Women* (New York: Perigee Books, 1978).

–, *Pornography: Men Possessing Women* (New York: Plume Books, 1989).

Dworkin, Andrea, and Catharine MacKinnon, *Pornography and Civil Rights: A New Day for Women's Equality* (Minneapolis: Organizing against Pornography, 1988).

Edmonson, Roger, *Boy in the Sand: Casey Donovan: All American Sex Star* (Los Angeles: Alyson Books, 1998).

Edwards, Tim, *Erotics and Politics: Gay Male Sexuality, Masculinity and Feminism* (London: Routledge, 1994).

Farley, Melissa, ed., *Prostitution, Trafficking, and Traumatic Stress* (Binghamton, NY: Haworth, 2003).

Fischer, B., et al., *Report on Adolescent Male Prostitution* (San Francisco: Urban Associates, 1982).

Frye, Marilyn, *The Politics of Reality* (Freedom, CA: Crossing Press, 1983).

Funk, Rus, *Stopping Rape: A Challenge for Men* (Philadelphia: New Society Publishers, 1993).

Goss, Robert, *Jesus Acted Up: A Gay and Lesbian Manifesto* (San Francisco: HarperCollins, 1993).

Harris, Daniel, *The Rise and Fall of Gay Culture* (New York: Ballantine Books, 1997).

Heilpern, David, *Fear or Favour: Sexual Assault of Young Prisoners* (Lismore, NSW: Southern Cross Press, 1998).

Herek, Gregory, and Kevin Berrill, eds., *Hate Crimes: Confronting Violence against Lesbians and Gay Men* (New York: Sage Publications, 1992).

hooks, bell, *Black Looks: Race and Representation* (Boston: South End Press, 1992).

Isherwood, Charles, *Wonder Bread and Ecstasy: The Life and Death of Joey Stefano* (Los Angeles: Alyson Publications, 1996).

Island, David, and Patrick Letellier, *Men Who Beat the Men Who Love Them* (New York: Harrington Park Press, 1991).

Itzin, Catherine, ed., *Pornography: Women, Violence and Civil Liberties* (Oxford: Oxford University Press, 1992).

Jay, K., and A. Young, *The Gay Report: Lesbian and Gay Men Speak Out about Their Sexual Experiences and Lifestyles* (New York: Summit, 1977).

Jeffreys, Sheila, *Anticlimax: Feminist Perspectives on the Sexual Revolution* (New York: New York University Press, 1990).

–, *The Lesbian Heresy* (Melbourne: Spinifex Press, 1993).

Jennings, Kevin, *Becoming Visible* (Boston: Alyson Publications, 1994).
Kappeler, Susanne, *The Pornography of Representation* (Minneapolis: University of Minnesota Press, 1986).
Katz, Jonathan Ned, *The Invention of Heterosexuality* (New York: Dutton, 1995).
Kennedy, Elizabeth, and Madeline Davis, *Boots of Leather, Slippers of Gold: The History of a Lesbian Community* (New York: Routledge, 1993).
Kinsella, Warren, *Web of Hate: Inside Canada's Far Rights Network* (Toronto: HarperCollins, 1994).
Kirk, M., and H. Madsen, *After the Ball* (New York: Doubleday, 1989).
Kleinberg, Seymour, *Alienated Affections: Being Gay in America* (New York: St. Martin's Press, 1980).
Laskey, L., and C. Beavis, *Schooling and Sexualities* (Geelong: Deakin University, 1985).
Lawrence, Doug, *1999 Adam Gay Video Directory, 9th Annual Edition* (Los Angeles: Knight Publishing, 1998).
Lederer, Laura, and Richard Delgado, eds., *The Price We Pay: The Case against Racist Speech, Hate Propaganda, and Pornography* (New York: Hill and Wang, 1995).
Lerner, Gerda, *The Creation of Patriarchy* (New York: Oxford University Press, 1986).
Lewis, Lynette, and Michael Ross, *A Select Body: The Gay Dance Party Subculture and the HIV/AIDS Pandemic* (London: Cassell, 1995).
Lovelace, Linda, *Ordeal* (Secaucus, NJ: Citadel Press, 1980).
MacDougall, Bruce, *Queer Judgments: Homosexuality, Expression and the Courts in Canada* (Toronto: University of Toronto Press, 2000).
MacKinnon, Catharine, *Sexual Harassment of Working Women* (New Haven: Yale University Press, 1979).
–, *Feminism Unmodified: Discourses on Life and Law* (Cambridge: Harvard University Press, 1987).
–, *Toward a Feminist Theory of the State* (Cambridge: Harvard University Press, 1989).
–, *Only Words* (Cambridge: Harvard University Press, 1993).
–, *Sex Equality* (New York: Foundation Press, 2001).
MacKinnon, Catharine, and Andrea Dworkin, *In Harm's Way: The Pornography Civil Rights Hearings* (Cambridge: Harvard University Press, 1997).
McMullen, Ritchie J., *Male Rape: Breaking the Silence on the Last Taboo* (London: GMP Publishers, 1990).
McNair, Brian, *Mediated Sex: Pornography and Postmodern Culture* (London: Arnold, 1996).
Mason, Gail, and Stephen Tomsen, *Homophobic Violence* (Sydney: Hawkins Press, 1997).
Matsuda, Mari, Charles Lawrence III, Richard Delagado, and Kimberle Crenshaw, *Words That Wound: Critical Race Theory, Assaultive Speech and the First Amendment* (Boulder, CO: Westview Press, 1993).
Mezey, Caroline, *Male Victims of Sexual Assault* (London: Oxford University Press, 1992).
Oostergaard, Lise, *Gender and Development: A Practical Guide* (London: Routledge, 1992).
People for the American Way, *Hostile Climate: A State by State Report on Anti-Gay Activity* (Washington: People for the American Way, 1997).
Pharr, Suzanne, *Homophobia: A Weapon of Sexism* (Little Rock, AR: Chardon Press, 1988).
Reti, Irene, ed., *Unleashing Feminism: Critiquing Lesbian Sadomasochism in the Gay Nineties* (Santa Cruz, CA: Her Books, 1993).
Rotello, Gabriel, *Sexual Ecology: AIDS and the Destiny of Gay Men* (New York: Dutton, 1997).
Russell, Diana, *Pornography: The Evidence of Harm* (Berkeley: Russell Publications, 1993).
Scarce, Michael, *Male on Male Rape: The Hidden Toll of Stigma and Shame* (New York: Insight Books, 1997).
Sears, James, *Growing Up Gay in the South* (New York: Harrington Park Press, 1991).
Signorile, Michelangelo, *Life Outside: The Signorile Report on Gay Men* (New York: HarperCollins, 1997).
Simpson, Marc, *Male Impersonators: Men Performing Masculinities* (New York: Routledge, 1994).
Stoltenberg, John, *Refusing to Be a Man* (New York: Meridian Books, 1989).
Strossen, Nadine, *Defending Pornography: Free Speech, Sex, and the Fight for Women's Rights* (New York: Scribner, 1995).
Stychin, Carl, *Law's Desire: Sexuality and the Limits of Justice* (London: Routledge, 1995).
Vaid, Urvashi, *Virtual Equality: The Mainstreaming of Gay and Lesbian Liberation* (New York: Anchor Books, 1995).

Waugh, Thomas, *Hard to Imagine: Gay Male Eroticism in Photography and Film from Their Beginnings to Stonewall* (New York: Columbia University Press, 1996).
Weeks, Jeffrey, *Sexuality and Its Discontents* (London: Routledge and Kegan Paul, 1985).
Weitzer, Ronald, *Sex for Sale: Prostitution, Pornography and the Sex Industry* (New York: Routledge, 2000).
West, Donald, *Male Prostitution* (London: Harrington Park Press, 1993).

Book Chapters
Altman, Denis, "What Changed in the Seventies?" in Gay Left Collective, ed., *Homosexuality, Power and Politics* (London: Alyson and Busby, 1980).
Bersani, Leo, "Is the Rectum a Grave?" in Douglas Crimp, ed., *AIDS: Cultural Analysis, Cultural Activism* (Cambridge, MA: MIT Press, 1987).
–, "Is the Rectum a Grave?" in Jonathan Goldberg, ed., *Reclaiming Sodom* (New York: Routledge, 1994).
Check, J.V.P., and T.H. Guloien, "Reported Proclivity for Coercive Sex Following Repeated Exposure to Sexually Violent Pornography, Nonviolent Dehumanizing Pornography and Erotica," in D. Zillman and J. Bryant, eds., *Pornography: Research Advances and Policy Considerations* (Hillsdale, New Jersey: Erlbaum, 1989).
Cossman, Brenda, "Feminist Fashion or Morality in Drag? The Sexual Subtext of the Butler Decision," in B. Cossman, S. Bell, L. Gotell, and B.L. Ross, eds., *Bad Attitude/s on Trial: Pornography, Feminism and the Butler Decision* (Toronto: University of Toronto Press, 1997).
Cowen, Gloria, "Racism and Sexism in Pornography," in Laura Lederer and Richard Delgado, eds., *The Price We Pay: The Case against Racist Speech, Hate Propaganda, and Pornography* (New York: Hill and Wang, 1995).
Donnerstein, E., "Pornography: Its Effect on Violence against Women," in N. Malamuth and E. Donnerstein, eds., *Pornography and Sexual Aggression* (New York: Academic Press, 1984).
Epstein, Debbie, "Keeping Them in Their Place: Hetero/Sexist Harassment, Gender and the Enforcement of Heterosexuality," in Alison Thomas and Celia Kitzinger, eds., *Sexual Harassment: Contemporary Feminist Perspectives* (Philadelphia: Open University Press, 1997).
Forna, Aminatta, "Pornography and Racism: Sexualizing Oppression and Inciting Hatred," in Catherine Itzin, ed., *Pornography: Women, Violence and Civil Liberties* (Oxford: Oxford University Press, 1992).
Fung, Richard, "Looking for My Penis: The Eroticized Asian in Gay Video Porn," in Bad Object Choices, eds., *How Do I Look? Queer Film and Video* (Seattle: Bay Press, 1991).
Giobbe, Evelina, "Confronting the Liberal Lies about Prostitution," in D. Leidholdt and J. Raymond, eds., *The Sexual Liberals and the Attack on Feminism* (New York: Pergamon Press, 1990).
Halley, Janet, "Sexuality Harassment," in Reva Siegel and Catharine MacKinnon, eds., *Directions in Sexual Harassment Law* (New Haven: Yale University Press, 2004).
Itzin, Catherine, "Entertainment for Men: What It Is and What It Means," in Itzin, ed., *Pornography: Women, Violence and Civil Liberties* (London: Oxford University Press, 1992).
Jeffrey-Poulter, S., "A Smell of Weimar 1987-8," in S. Jeffrey-Poulter, ed., *Peers, Queers, and Commons* (London: Routledge, 1991).
Jeffreys, Sheila, "Heterosexuality and the Desire for Gender," in Diane Richardson, ed., *Theorising Heterosexuality* (Buckingham: Open University Press, 1996).
Jensen, Robert, "Getting It Up for Politics: Gay Male Sexuality and Radical Lesbian Feminism," in Sara Miles and Eric Rofes, eds., *Opposite Sex* (New York: New York University Press, 1998).
Kazu Hiraga, Martin, "Anti-Gay and Lesbian Violence, Victimization, and Defamation: Trends, Victimization Studies and Incident Descriptions," in Laura Lederer and Richard Delgado, eds., *The Price We Pay: The Case against Racist Speech, Hate Propaganda, and Pornography* (New York: Hill and Wang, 1995).
Kendall, Christopher, and Russell Funk, "Gay Male Pornography's 'Actors': When 'Fantasy' Isn't," in Melissa Farley, ed., *Prostitution, Trafficking, and Traumatic Stress* (Binghamton, NY: Haworth, 2003).
Kleinberg, Seymour, "The New Masculinity of Gay Men, and Beyond," in Michael Kaufman, ed., *Beyond Patriarchy* (Toronto: Oxford University Press, 1987).
Linz, D., and J. Bryant, "Effects of Massive Exposure to Pornography," in N. Malamuth and E. Donnerstein, eds., *Pornography and Sexual Aggression* (New York: Academic Press, 1984).

Lorde, Audre, "The Uses of the Erotic: The Erotic as Power," in Henry Abelove et al., eds., *The Lesbian and Gay Studies Reader* (New York: Routledge, 1993).

Lorde, Audre, and Susan Leigh Starr, "Interview with Audre Lorde," in Robin Linden et al., eds., *Against Sadomasochism: A Radical Feminist Analysis* (Palo Alto, CA: Frog in the Well, 1982).

MacKinnon, Catharine, and Andrea Dworkin, "Statement on Canadian Customs and Legal Approaches to Pornography," in Diane Bell and Ranate Klein, eds., *Radically Speaking: Feminism Reclaimed* (Melbourne: Spinifex Press, 1996).

McLean, C., "Men, Masculinity and Heterosexuality," in L. Laskey and C. Beavis, eds., *Schooling and Sexualities: Teaching for a Positive Sexuality* (Geelong: Deakin University, Centre for Education and Change, 1995).

Norris, Maryel, "An Opinionated Piece on Sadomasochism," in Robin Linden et al., eds., *Against Sadomasochism: A Radical Feminist Analysis* (Palo Alto, CA: Frog in the Well, 1982).

Pelka, Fred, "Raped: A Male Survivor Breaks His Silence," in Patricia Searles and Ronald Berger, eds., *Rape and Society: Readings on the Problem of Sexual Assault* (Boulder, CO: Westview Press, 1995).

Petersen, Cynthia, "Envisioning a Lesbian Equality Jurisprudence," in Didi Herman and Carl Stychin, eds., *Legal Inversions: Lesbians, Gay Men and the Law* (Philadelphia: Temple University Press, 1995).

Reeves, Carol, "Serious Porn, Serious Protest," in Lynne Harned and Elaine Miller, eds., *All the Rage: Reasserting Radical Lesbian Feminism* (London: Teachers College Press, 1996).

Russo, Ann, "Feminists Confront Pornography's Subordinating Practices," in Gail Dines, Robert Jensen, and Ann Russo, eds., *Pornography: The Production and Consumption of Inequality* (New York: Routledge, 1998).

Spindelman, Marc, "Discriminating Pleasures," in Reva Siegel and Catharine MacKinnon, eds., *Directions in Sexual Harassment Law* (New Haven: Yale University Press, 2004).

Stanley, Julia, and Susan Robins, "Sexist Slang and the Gay Community: Are You One, Too?" in *The Michigan Occasional Papers Series*, no. 14 (Ann Arbor: University of Michigan, Department of Women's Studies, 1991).

Starr, Susan Leigh, "Swastikas: The Street and the University," in Robin Linden et al., eds., *Against Sadomasochism: A Radical Feminist Analysis* (Palo Alto, CA: Frog in the Well, 1982).

Stoltenberg, John, "Gays and the Pro-Pornography Movement: Having the Hots for Sex Discrimination," in Michael Kimmel, ed., *Men Confront Pornography* (New York: Crown Publishers, 1990).

–, "You Can't Fight Homophobia and Protect the Pornographers at the Same Time: An Analysis of What Went Wrong with Hardwick," in D. Leidholt and J. Raymond, eds., *The Sexual Liberals and the Attack on Feminism* (New York: Pergamon Press, 1990).

Zillman, D., and J. Bryant, "Effects of Massive Exposure to Pornography," in N. Malamuth and E. Donnerstein, eds., *Pornography and Sexual Aggression* (New York: Academic Press, 1984).

Zillman, D. and J.B. Weaver, "Pornography and Men's Sexual Callousness Toward Women," in D. Zillman and J. Bryant, eds., *Pornography: Research Advances and Policy Considerations* (Hillsdale, New Jersey: Erlbaum, 1989).

Journal Articles

Allen, D.M., "Young Male Prostitutes: A Psychological Study" (1980) 9 *Archives of Sexual Behaviour* 399.

Arriola, E.R., "Gendered Inequality: Lesbians, Gays and Feminist Legal Theory" (1994) 9 *Berkeley Women's L.J.* 103.

Bagely, Christopher, "Suicidal Behaviours in Homosexual and Bisexual Males" (1997) 18(1) *Crisis* 24.

Banks, Kathleen Sam, "Could Mom Be Wrong? The Hurt of Names and Wrongs: Hate Propaganda and Freedom of Expression" (June 1999) 6(2) *E Law – Murdoch University Electronic Journal of Law.* <http://www.murdoch.edu.au/elaw/issues/v6n2/banks62nf.html>.

Benedet, Janine, "*Little Sisters Book and Art Emporium* v. *Minister of Justice*: Sex Equality and the Attack on *R.* v. *Butler*" (2001) 39 *Osgoode Hall L.J.* 187.

–, "Child Pornography after *Sharpe*" (2002) 43 *C. de D.* 327.

Berger, Raymond, "Passing and Social Support among Gay Men" (1992) 23(3) *Journal of Homosexuality* 85.

Best, Paul, and Ann Vandenberg, "Politics, Feminism and the Constitution: The Anti-Pornography Movement in Minneapolis" (1987) 39 *Stan. L. Rev.* 607.
Boyer, Debra, "Male Prostitution and Homosexual Identity" (1989) 17(1) *Journal of Homosexuality* 151.
Bulbeck, Chilla, "Words Can Never Hurt Me?" (1990) 15(2) *L.S.B.* 79.
Busby, Karen, "LEAF and Pornography: Litigating on Equality and Sexual Representations" (1994) 9(1) *C.J.L.S.* 165.
Byrne, Jeffrey, "Affirmative Action for Lesbians and Gay Men: A Proposal for True Equality of Opportunity and Workforce Diversity" (1993) 11 *Yale L. and Pol'y. Rev.* 47.
Cain, Patricia, "Feminist Jurisprudence: Grounding the Theories" (1989) 4 *Berkeley Women's L.J.* 191.
Calderwood, Deryck, "The Male Rape Victim" (1987) 7 *Medical Aspects of Human Sexuality* 53.
Cameron, Jamie, "Abstract Principle v. Contextual Conceptions of Harm: A Comment on R v. Butler" (1992) 37 *McGill L.J.* 1135.
Carrigan, Tim, Bob Connell, and John Lee, "Hard and Heavy: Toward a New Sociology of Masculinity" (1985) 14 *Theory and Society* 551.
Case, Mary Anne, "Disaggregating Gender from Sex and Sexual Orientation: The Effeminate Man in the Law and Feminist Jurisprudence" (1995) *Yale L.J.* 1.
Chambers, David L., "Gay Men, AIDS and the Code of the Condom" (1994) 29(2) *Harv. C.R.-C.L.L. Rev.* 353.
Check, J.V.P., and N. Malamuth, "Pornography and Sexual Aggression: A Social Learning Theory Analysis" (1986) 9 *Communication Yearbook* 181.
Coleman, Eli, "The Development of Male Prostitution Activity among Gay and Bisexual Adolescents" (1989) 17(1) *Journal of Homosexuality* 131.
Cossman, Brenda, and Bruce Ryder, "Customs Censorship and the Charter: The Little Sisters Case" (1996) 7(4) *Const. Forum* 103.
Craig, Amelia, "Musing about Discrimination on Sex and Sexual Orientation as 'Gender Role' Discrimination" (1995) 5 *S. Cal. Rev. L. and Women's Stud.* 105.
Cranston, Kevin, "HIV Education for Gay, Lesbian and Bisexual Youth: Personal Risk, Personal Power, and the Community of Conscience" (1992) 22(3) *Journal of Homosexuality* 247.
Dietz, Park Elliott, and Barbara Evans, "Pornographic Imagery and Prevalence of Paraphilia" (1982) 139 *American Journal of Psychiatry* 1493.
Duncan, David, "Prevalence of Sexual Assault Victimization among Heterosexual and Gay/Lesbian Students" (1990) *Psychological Reports* 66.
Dworkin, Andrea, "Pornography Is a Civil Rights Issue for Women" (1987/88) 21 *U. Mich. J.L. Ref.* 55.
Eaton, Mary, "At the Intersection of Gender and Sexual Orientation: Toward Lesbian Jurisprudence" (1994) 3 *S. Cal. Rev. L. and Women's Stud.* 183.
Elifson, K.W., "Seroprevalence of Human Immunodeficiency Virus among Male Prostitutes" (1989) *New England Journal of Medicine* 321.
Elman, Bruce, "Combatting Racist Speech: The Canadian Experience" (1994) 32(4) *Alta. L. Rev.* 621.
Fajer, Marc A., "Can Real Men Eat Quiche Together? Storytelling, Gender-Role Stereotypes and Legal Protections for Lesbians and Gay Men" (1992) 46 *U. Miami L. Rev.* 511.
Farley, Melissa, "Prostitution and the Invisibility of Harm" (2003) 26 *Women and Therapy* 1.
Franke, Katherine, "The Central Mistake of Sex Discrimination: The Disaggregation of Sex from Gender" (1995) 144 *U. Pa. L. Rev.* 1.
–, "What's Wrong With Sexual Harassment?" (1997) 49 *Stan. L. Rev.* 691.
Freung, Richard, "Older Lesbian and Gay People: A Theory of Successful Aging" (1991) *Journal of Homosexuality* 99.
Giobbe, Evelina, "Connections between Prostitution and Pornography" (1993) 7(1) *Whisper* 3.
Goyer, Peter, and Henry Eddleman, "Same Sex Rape of Nonincarcerated Men" (1984) 141 *American Journal of Psychiatry* 576.
Green, L., "Pornographies" (1999) 7 *Journal of Political Philosophy* 8.1.
Grose, Carolyn, "Same-Sex Harassment: Subverting the Heterosexist Paradigm of Title VII" (1995) *Yale J.L. & Feminism* 375.
Gross, Kara, "Toward Gender Equality and Understanding: Recognizing That Same-Sex Sexual Harassment Is Sex Discrimination" (1996) *Brook. L. Rev.* 1165.

Groth, A., and A.W. Burgess, "Male Rape: Offenders and Victims" (1980) 137 *American Journal of Psychiatry* 806.

Herek, G., "Religious Orientation and Prejudice: A Comparison of Racial and Sexual Attitudes" (1987) 13 *Personality and Social Psychology Bulletin* 34.

–, "Hate Crimes against Lesbians and Gay Men: Issues for Research and Policy" (1989) 44 *American Psychologist* 948.

Hickson, Ford C.I., et al., "Gay Men as Victims of Non-consensual Sex" (1994) 23(3) *Archives of Sexual Behaviour* 281.

Horniblow, Mary, "Power Undressing" (1993) *Polemic* 17.

Hunter, Ian, "*R. v. Butler:* Feminism Trumps Morality" (1993) 35 *Crim. L.Q.* 147.

Jordan, E., "Fighting Boys and Fantasy Play: The Construction of Masculinity in the Early Years of School" (1995) 7(1) *Gender and Education* 69.

Kaufman, Arthur, et al., "Male Rape Victims: Non-Institutional Assault" (1980) 137 *American Journal of Psychiatry* 221.

Kenway, J., "Masculinities in Schools: Under Siege, on the Defensive and Under Reconstruction?" (1995) 16(1) *Discourse: Studies in the Cultural Politics of Education* 59.

–, "Boys' Education, Masculinity and Gender Reform: Some Introductory Remarks" (1997) 17(1) *Curriculum Perspectives* 57.

Klausner, Marianne Leslie, "Redefining Pornography as Sex Discrimination: An Innovative Civil Rights Approach" (1984-85) 20 *New Eng. L. Rev.* 721.

Koppelman, Andrew, "The Miscegenation Analogy: Sodomy Law as Sex Discrimination" (1988) 98 *Yale L.J.* 145.

–, "Why Discrimination against Lesbians and Gay Men Is Sex Discrimination" (1994) 69 *N.Y.U.L. Rev.* 197.

Kramer, Richard, "R. v. Butler: A New Approach to Obscenity Law or Return to Morality Play?" (1993) 35 *Crim. L.Q.* 77.

Kruks, G., "Gay and Lesbian Homeless/Street Youth: Special Issues and Concerns" (1991) 12 *Journal of Adolescent Health* 515.

Kus, Robert, "Alcoholics Anonymous and Gay American Men" (1987) 14(2) *Journal of Homosexuality* 253.

–, "Alcoholism and Non-Acceptance of Gay Self: The Critical Link" (1988) 15(1) *Journal of Homosexuality* 25.

Law, Sylvia, "Homosexuality and the Social Meaning of Gender" (1988) *Wis. L. Rev.* 187 at 218.

Lima, Geraldo, "The Relationship between Homophobia and Self-Esteem in Gay Males with AIDS" (1993) 25(4) *Journal of Homosexuality* 69.

Love, J.C., "Tort Actions for Hate Speech and the First Amendment: Reconceptualizing the Competing Interests" (1992) 2 *Law & Sexuality* 29.

McAllister, Debra, "Butler: A Triumph for Equality Rights" (1992/1993) 2 *N.J.C.L.* 118.

MacDonald, G.J., "Individual Differences in the Coming Out Process for Gay Men: Implications for Theoretical Models" (1982) 8(1) *Journal of Homosexuality* 1.

MacDonald, Ron, and Trudi Cooper, "Young Gay Men and Suicide" (1998) 17(4) *Youth Studies Australia* 23.

MacKinnon, Catharine, "Vindication and Resistance: A Response to the Carnegie Mellon Study of Pornography in Cyberspace" (1995) 83 *Geo. L.J.* 1959.

–, "Oncale v. Sundowner Offshore Services, Inc., 96-568, Amici Curiae Brief in Support of Petitioner" (1997) 8 *U.C.L.A. Women's L.J.* 9.

–, "Same-Sex Harassment: A Serious and Neglected Social Problem" (1998) 3 *Law Quadrangle Notes* 84.

Mahoney, Kathleen, "R. v. Keegstra: A Rationale for Regulating Pornography?" (1992) 37 *McGill L.J.* 242.

Major, Marie-France, "Sexual Orientation Hate Propaganda: Time to Regroup" (1996) 11(1) *Can. J.L. and Soc.* 221.

Majury, Diana, "Refashioning the Unfashionable: Claiming Lesbian Identities in the Legal Context" (1994) 7(2) *C.J.W.L.* 286.

Malamuth, Neil, "Factors Associated with Rape as Predictors of Laboratory Aggression against Women" (1983) 45 *Journal of Personality and Social Psychology* 432.

Malamuth, Neil, and L. Berkowitz, "Victim Reaction in Aggressive Erotic Films as a Factor in Violence against Women" (1981) 41 *Journal of Personality and Social Psychology* 710.

Malamuth, Neil, and J.V.P. Check, "The Effects of Mass Media Exposure on Acceptance of Violence against Women: A Field Experiment" (1981) *Journal of Research in Personality* 436.

Malamuth, Neil, and Barry Spinner, "A Longitudinal Content Analysis of Sexual Violence in the Best-Selling Erotic Magazines" (1980) 16 *Journal of Sex Research* 226

Marcosson, Samuel, "Harassment on the Basis of Sexual Orientation: A Claim of Sex Discrimination under Title VII" (1992) 81(1) *Geo. L.J.* 1.

Martin, A. Damian, and Emery Hetrick, "The Stigmatization of the Gay and Lesbian Adolescent" (1988) 15(1) *Journal of Homosexuality* 163.

Martino, Wayne, "Masculinity and Learning: Exploring Boys' Underachievement and Under-Representation in Subject English" (1985) 27(2) *Interpretations* 22.

–, "A Bunch of Arseholes': Exploring the Politics of Masculinity for Adolescent Boys in Schools" (1997) 16(3) *Social Alternatives* 39.

–, "Cool Boys, Party Animals, Squids and Poofters: Interrogating the Dynamics and Politics of Adolescent Masculinities in School" (1999) 20(2) *British Journal of Sociology of Education* 239.

Matsuda, Mari, "Public Response to Racist Speech: Considering the Victim's Story" (1989) 87 *Mich. L. Rev.* 2320.

Meron, G.B., "Public Policy and Private Prejudice: Psychology and the Law on Gay Rights" (1989) *American Psychologist* 933.

Meston, C.M., J.R. Heiman, and P.D. Trapnell, "The Relationship between Early Abuse and Adult Sexuality" (1999) 36(4) *Journal of Sex Research* 385.

Moon, Richard, "Drawing Lines in a Culture of Prejudice: R. v. Keegstra and the Restriction of Hate Propaganda" (1992) *U.B.C. Law Rev.* 99.

–, "R. v. Butler: The Limits of the Supreme Court's Feminist Re-Interpretation of Section 163" (1993) 25 *Ottawa L. Rev.* 361.

Nacci, Peter, and Thomas Kane, "The Incidence of Sex and Sexual Aggression in Federal Prisons" (1984) 48 *Federal Probation* 35.

Nelson, Vednita, "Working in the Body Trade" (1981) (Autumn) *Aegis* 19.

–, "Black Women and Prostitution" (1992) 6 (Summer/Fall) *Whisper* 1.

Nicholas, J., and John Howard, "Better Dead Than Gay" (1998) 17(4) *Youth Studies Australia* 28.

Noonan, Sheila, "Harm Revisited: R. v. Butler" (1992) 4(1) *Const. Forum Const.* 12.

Palys, T.S, "Testing the Common Wisdom: The Social Content of Video Pornography" (1986) *Canadian Psychology* 22.

Pearlman, Lynne, "Theorizing Lesbian Oppression and the Politics of Outness in the Case of Waterman v. National Life Assurance: A Beginning in Lesbian Human Rights/Equality Jurisprudence" (1994) 7(2) *C.J.W.L.* 454.

Peluso, Marie Elena, "Tempering Title VII's Straight Arrow Approach: Recognizing and Protecting Gay Victims of Employment Discrimination" (1993) 46 *Vand. L. Rev.* 1533.

Pereira, Darryl, "HIV/AIDS and Its 'Willing Executioners': The Impact of Discrimination" (1999) 6(4) *E Law – Murdoch University Electronic Journal of Law*. <http://www.murdoch.edu.au/elaw/issues/v6n4/pereira64.html>.

Petersen, Cynthia, "A Queer Response to Bashing: Legislating against Hate" (1991) 16 *Queen's L.J.* 237.

"Pornography: Freedom v. Censorship?" (1991) *C.L.B.* 14.

Radinson, Evelyn, "New Playboy Club Folds in New York City" (1986) (Spring/Summer) *WAP Newsreport* 1.

Ramraj, Victor J., "Keegstra, Butler and Positive Liberty: A Glimmer of Hope for the Faithful" (1993) 51 *U. Toronto Fac. L. Rev.* 304.

Rich, Adrienne, "Compulsory Heterosexuality and Lesbian Existence" (1980) 5(4) *Signs: Journal of Women in Culture and Society* 63.

Redmund, D.E., et al., "Spontaneous Ejaculation Associated With Anxiety" (1983) 140(9) *American Journal of Psychiatry* 1163.

Remafedi, Gary, "Risk Factors for Attempted Suicide in Gay and Bisexual Youth" 87(6) *Paediatrics* 869.

Remafedi, Gary, et al., "The Relationship between Suicide Risk and Sexual Orientation" (1997) 87(8) *American Journal of Public Health* 1.

Rimm, Marty, "Marketing Pornography on the Information Superhighway" (1995) 83 *Geo. L.J.* 1849.

Roesler, T., and R. Deisher, "Youthful Man Homosexuality" (1972) *Journal of the American Medical Association* 1018.

Rotheram, M., "Suicidal Behaviour and Gay Related Stress among Gay and Bisexual Male Adolescents" 87(8) *American Journal of Public Health* 1.

Russell, Diana, "Pornography and Rape: A Causal Model" (1989) 9 *Political Psychology* 41.

Ryder, Bruce, "Straight Talk: Male Heterosexual Privilege" (1991) 16 *Queen's L.J.* 287.

Sanatioso, R., "A Social Psychological Perspective on HIV/AIDS and Gay or Homosexually Active Asian Men" (1999) 36 *Journal of Homosexuality* 76.

Sandler, M., "Hate Crimes and Hate Group Activity in Canada" (1994) 43 *U.N.B.L.J.* 269.

Savin-Williams, Ritch, "Coming Out to Parents and Self-Esteem among Gay and Lesbian Youths" (1989) 17(1) *Journal of Homosexuality* 1.

Scales, Ann, "Avoiding Constitutional Depression: Bad Attitudes and the Fate of Butler" (1994) 7(2) *C.J.W.L.* 349.

Scarce, Michael, "The Reality of Male Rape" (1993) *National Coalition against Sexual Assault Journal* 7.

–, "Harbinger of Plague: A Bad Case of Gay Bowel Syndrome" (1997) 34(2) *Journal of Homosexuality* 1.

–, "Same-Sex Rape of Male College Students" (1997) 45(4) *Journal of American College Health* 171.

Scutt, Jocelynne, "Incorporating the Dworkin/MacKinnon Approach into Australian Law" (1991) 5 *Inkwel* 3.

Sherman, Jeffrey, "Love Speech: The Social Utility of Pornography" (1995) 47 *Stan. L. Rev.* 661.

Silbert, M.H., and A.K. Pines, "Pornography and Sexual Abuse of Women" (1984) 10 *Sex Roles* 857.

Skelton, C., "Learning to Be Tough: The Fostering of Maleness in One Primary School" (1996) 8(2) *Gender and Education* 185.

Solomon, Tamsin, "Antisemitism as Free Speech: Judicial Responses to Hate Propaganda in Zundel and Keegstra" (1995) 13(1) *Australian-Canadian Studies* 1.

Sommers, E., and J.V.P. Check, "An Empirical Investigation of the Role of Pornography in the Verbal and Physical Abuse of Women" (1987) 2 *Violence and Victims* 189.

Spahn, Elizabeth, "On Sex and Violence" (1984-5) 20 *New Eng. L. Rev.* 629.

Spindelman, Marc, and John Stoltenberg, "Introduction: Exposing 'Manhood'" (1997) 8 *U.C.L.A. Women's L.J.* 3.

Stone-Harris, Regina, "Same-Sex Harassment – the Next Step in the Evolution of Sexual Harassment Law Under Title VII" (1996) *St. Mary's L.J.* 269.

Storrow, Richard, "Same-Sex Sexual Harassment Claims After Oncale: Defining the Boundaries of Actionable Conduct" (1998) 47 *Am. U.L. Rev.* 677.

Stychin, Carl, "Exploring the Limits: Feminism and the Legal Regulation of Pornography" (1992) 16 *Vt. L. Rev.* 857.

Sunstein, Cass, "Pornography and the First Amendment" (1986) 22 *Duke L.J.* 589.

–, "Homosexuality and the Constitution" (1994) 70 *Ind. L.J.* 1.

Tremble, Bob, Margaret Schneider, and Carol Appathurai, "Growing Up Gay or Lesbian in a Multicultural Context" (1989) 17(3) *Journal of Homosexuality* 253.

Troiden, Richard, "The Formation of Homosexual Identities" (1989) 17(1) *Journal of Homosexuality* 43.

Urbine, V., "Addressing the Needs of Lesbian, Gay and Bisexual Youth" (1992) 24 *Journal of Homosexuality* 9.

Valdes, Francisco, "Queers, Sissies, Dykes, and Tomboys: Deconstructing the Conflation of 'Sex', 'Gender' and 'Sexual Orientation' in Euro-American Law and Society" (1995) 83 *C.L.R.* 3.

Waterman, Caroline, and Lori Dawson, "Sexual Coercion in Gay Male Relationships: Predicators and Implications for Support Services" (1989) 26(1) *Journal of Sex Research* 118.

Weinrib, Lorraine, "The Supreme Court of Canada and Section One of the Charter" (1988) 10 *Sup. Ct. L. Rev.* 469.

Whisper, "Statement of Whisper Action Group Members" (1992) (Winter/Spring) *Whisper* 3.

Wilets, James, "Conceptualizing Private Violence against Sexual Minorities as Gendered Violence: An International and Comparative Law Perspective" (1997) 60 *Alb. L. Rev.* 989.

Willcox, Mary, "The Sexually Assaulted Prisoner" (1986) 12 *New Eng. J. on Crim. and Civ. Confinement* 355.

Magazine Articles
Ayres, Tony, "Undesirable Aliens," *HQ Magazine*, March-April 1998, 110.
Baker, John, "Canada Customs a Continuing Problem for Bookstores and Distributors; Trial Postponed," *Publishers Weekly*, 20 December 1993, 12.
"Battered Lovers," *Advocate*, 4 March 1986, 42.
Bearchell, Chris, "Not a Love Story and the Anti-Porn Crusade," *Body Politic*, July/August 1982, 11.
–, "Pornography, Prostitution and Moral Panic," *Body Politic*, March 1984, 7.
–, "Beat That Queer: Hate Lit Spreads West," *Body Politic*, October 1991, 10.
Blakely, Mary, "Is One Woman's Sexuality Another Woman's Pornography?" *Ms Magazine*, April 1985, 37.
Body Politic Collective, "31 Words," *Body Politic*, April 1985, 29.
Brunet, R., "Tired of Celebrating an Obsession," *British Columbia Report*, 16 August 1993, 23.
Bull, Chris, "The Lost Generation: The Second Wave of HIV Infections among Young Gay Men," *Advocate*, May 1994, 36.
"Censory Depravation," *Screw Magazine*, 27 December 1993, 10.
Clacher, Iain, "Silence Is Where the Hate Grows: Gay Teenagers and the Frightening Final Solution," *Campaign Magazine* (Sydney), September 1997, 27.
Cooly, Glenn, "Homophobic Bible Comic May Spark Legal Battle," *Now Magazine*, September 1992, 9.
Donat, H., "Domestic Violence Strikes Gay Relationships," *Sentinel*, 2 August 1990, 5.
Dyer, Richard, "Coming to Terms," *Jump Cut*, no. 30 (1985), 27.
Editor, "The Serious Side of Porn," *Frontiers Magazine*, 2 August 1997, 10.
Elmer-Dewitt, Philip, "On a Screen Near You: Cyberporn," *Time Magazine*, 10 July 1995, 48.
"Federal Court Upholds Anti-Hate Ruling," *InfoFlash*, 15 February 1996.
Fishman, Ted, "Northern Underexposure: Censorship in Canada," *Playboy*, June 1994, 58.
Foxx, Austin, "That Type of Guy," *Frontiers Magazine*, 22 August 1997, 65.
Gillis, Francis, "Monkey See, Monkey Rape?" *Body Politic*, December 1985, 13.
Gopal, Carl, "Gay Racism," *Independent Monthly*, May 1994, 14.
Harris, Elise, "Sex/Workers," *OUT Magazine*, March 1998, 28.
Harris, Will, "Porn Again," *Campaign Magazine*, December 1993, 47.
Holleran, Andrew, "The Wrinkle Room," *New York Times Magazine*, 1 September 1996, 60.
Hussey, Mark, "Defending Pornography: Free Speech, Sex and the Fight for Women's Rights" (book review), *On the Issues*, Summer 1995, 48.
Jeffreys, Sheila, "How Orgasm Politics Has Hijacked the Women's Movement," *On the Issues*, Spring 1996, 21.
Jordan, Peter, "The Naked VCR," *Outrage* 131 (April 1994), 45.
Kingston, T., "Breaking the Silence: Gay Domestic Violence," *Coming Up!* February 1989, 10.
Koffler, Kevin, "Sex, Videotape and Maybe Lies: An Interview with Gay Icon Jeff Stryker," *Advocate*, 12 September 1989, 26.
Koivisto, Mickey, "The Canadian Government's Big Chill on Queer Culture," *Gaze Magazine*, 1 April 1994, 16.
"Letter to the Body Politic," *Body Politic*, no. 96 (September 1983), 5.
McCaskell, Tim, "Pornography and Prohibition," *Body Politic*, April 1983, 31.
Moldenhaur, Jerald, "Glad Day Bookshop and the Glad Day Censorship Fund," *Censorship Bulletin* 4 (1986), 13.
Narvil, Jeffrey, "The New Custom at Customs," *Authors League Bulletin*, Summer 1994, 22.
"Pornography: The New Terrorism?" *Body Politic*, August 1978, 11.
Reed, Pearce, "Naming and Confronting Gay Male Battering," *Gay Community News*, 16-22 April 1989, 3.
Reynolds, Dale, "The Gay Porn Industry: Hot, Dirty and Sometimes Sad," *Outrage* 147 (August 1995), 12.
–, "Documenting America's Schizoid Sexuality," *Outrage* 178 (March 1998), 58.
Rogerson, Gillian, "They Only Want to Help Us: Christian Loonies Find an Unusual Route for Delivering Scurrilous Materials," *Body Politic*, July 1985, 21.
Rosen, Jeffrey, "Men Behaving Badly: The Incoherence of Sexual Harassment Law," *New*

Republic, 29 December 1997, 10.

Rule, Jane, "Pornography," *Body Politic*, January/February 1984, 33.

Russell, Diana, "Nadine Strossen: The Pornography Industry's Wet Dream," *On the Issues*, Summer 1995, 32.

Skee, Mickey, "Laid Bare," *Frontiers Magazine* 16(8) (August 1997), 53.

–, "Tricks of the Trade," *Frontiers Magazine* 16(8), (August 1997), 43.

Smith, Anna Marie, "Sex and Violence and Censorship," *Body Politic*, August 1986, 22.

Strossen, Nadine, "Big Sister Is Watching You," *Advocate*, 14 November 1995, 62.

Tucker, Scott, "Sex, Death and Free Speech: The Fight to Stop Friedkin's Cruising," *Body Politic*, November 1979, 23.

Waugh, Thomas, "Men's Pornography: Gay vs. Straight," *Jump Cut*, no. 30 (1985), 33.

Widdcombe, Ben, "Can We Catch Our Falling Stars?" *Outrage* 174 (November 1997), 52.

Newspaper Articles

Bearchell, Chris, "Invisibility Equals Death: Canada Customs and the Butler Decision May Erase Us for Good," *XS: A Supplement to Xtra!* October 1992, 15.

–, "In Harm's Way: A Calculated Campaign Takes Aim at Sexual Imagery and Free Speech," *XS: A Supplement to Xtra!* November 1992, 9.

–, "Proof, Who Needs Proof?" *XS: A Supplement to Xtra!* November 1992, 3.

–, "Gay Porn Censored from All Sides," *Toronto Star*, 15 January 1993, A23.

Biskupic, Joan, "Court Says Law Covers Same-Sex Harassment," *Washington Post*, 5 March 1998, A1.

Borovoy, Alan, "Beware the Bible or the 11 O'Clock News," *Globe and Mail*, 10 March 1992, A19.

Callaghan, Greg, "Worst Days of Their Lives," *Australian*, 10 April 2000, 11.

Cossman, Brenda, "Return of the Loonies: Feminists Tell Supreme Court That Gay and Lesbian Porn Is Evil," *Xtra!* 30 December 1999, 11.

Ford, Dave, "Write Stuff," *San Francisco Bay Times*, 24 September 1992, 9.

Gallant, Paul, "Editorial: I Thought Pro-Sex Feminists Had Won," *Xtra!* 13 January 2000, 15.

Glascott, Katherine, "Gay Schoolboy Tests Vilification," *Australian*, 2 April 1997, 3.

–, "Student's Harsh Lesson in Sex Education," *Australian*, 3 April 1997, 9.

"Harmed and Dangerous," *Xtra!* 15 February 1996, 8.

Hume, Christopher, "The XXX Reality of Censorship," *Toronto Star*, 29 October 1994, L1.

Katz, Leanne, "Censors Helpers," *New York Times*, 4 December 1993, 21.

Kennedy, J., "Christians Advocate Violence," *Xtra! West*, 14 December 1996, 9.

Kingston, Tim, "Canada's New Porn Wars," *San Francisco Bay Times*, 4 November 1993, 6.

Leo, John, "Censors on the Left," *US News and World Report*, 4 October 1993, 30.

Matas, Robert, "Evangelicals Assailed over Anti-Games Ad," *Globe and Mail*, 10 June 1990, 6.

Mitchell, Jared, "Leather Boy and the Sex Police: Porn/Gay Porn – Without All That Oppression," *Xtra!* 13 January 2000, 4.

Mitchell, Scott-Patrick, "Ifs and Butts: The Life and Death of a Porn Star on the Stage," *Westside Observer*, 4 February 2000, 9.

Moore, Charles, "Free Speech Challenge Based on Biblical Passages," *Calgary Herald*, 5 August 1998.

"Much Delayed Report Due at Last," *Westside Observer*, 20 November 1998, 3.

Pitts, Gavin, "Couch Potato," *Westside Observer*, 11 April 1996, 16.

Salmon, Allson, Sharon Isle, and Trevor Morton, "Sexual Assault in the Gay and Lesbian Community," *Westside Observer*, 10 October 1994, 11.

"Same Sex Attraction Meets School Hostility," *Australian*, 23 November 1998, 17.

Seto, Doug, "Caste and Castaways: Welcome to Polk St.," *Bay Area Reporter*, 29 July 1993, 18.

Smith, Vivian, "Defending Pornography: Free Speech, Sex and the Fight for Women's Rights" (book review), *Globe and Mail*, 4 March 1995, C23.

"Speaker Exits Robinson-Skoke Exchange," *Globe and Mail*, 1 October 1994, A3.

Yallop, Richard, "Playground Prejudice," *Australian*, 3 April 1997, 9.

Internet Sites

de Bruyn, T., "HIV/AIDS and Discrimination: A Discussion Paper," Canadian HIV/AIDS Legal Network and Canadian AIDS Society (1998), <http://www.aidslaw.ca/elements/disc/DISCdiv.html>.

Freeman, Gregory, "Bug Chasers: The Men Who Long to Be HIV +," *Rolling Stone* (6 February 2003) <http://Rolling.Stone.com>.

Hill, Steven, and Nina Silver, "Civil Rights Anti-Pornography Legislation: Addressing the Harm to Women," Always Causing Legal Unrest Web page (1998), <http://www.nostatusquo.com/ACLU/Porn/>.

Jensen, Robert, "A Review of In Harm's Way: The Pornography Civil Rights Hearings," Always Causing Legal Unrest Web page (1998), <http://www.nostatusquo.com/ACLU/Porn/>.

Menadue, David, "The Nouveau Cowboys of Barebacking," *Positive Living: A Magazine for People Living with HIV/AIDS* (26 March 1999), 8. Menadue's article is also posted at <http://gaytoday.badpuppy.com/garchive/viewpoint/031599vi.html>.

Orthmann, David, "A Review of Pornography and Civil Rights: A New Day for Women's Equality," Always Causing Legal Unrest Web page (1995), <http://www.nostatusquo.com/ACLU/Porn/>.

Valenzuela, Tony, "Bareback Sex and HIV: A Young Man's Choice," *Gay Today: A Global Site for Daily Gay News* (1997), <http://gaytoday.badpuppy.com/garchive/viewpoint/031599vi.html>.

Government Reports and Documents

EGALE, Brief to the members of the Ontario Legislature from the Coalition for Lesbians and Gay Rights in Ontario, *Discrimination against Lesbians and Gay Men: The Ontario Human Rights Omission*, 1986.

–, *Submissions to the House of Commons Standing Committee, House Committee on Justice and Legal Affairs, Regarding Bill C-41 Hate Crimes*, Ottawa, 1994.

Gibson, P., *Gay Male and Lesbian Youth Suicide, Report of the Secretary's Task Force on Youth Suicide*, U.S. Department of Health and Human Services, 1989.

Government of Canada, *Pornography and Prostitution in Canada: Report of the Special Committee on Pornography and Prostitution* (Fraser Report), 1985.

Government of Western Australia, *Making a Difference: Youth Suicide Prevention Manual*, Health Department of Western Australia, Perth, 1994.

House of Commons Standing Committee on Justice and Legal Affairs, *Report on Pornography*, Ottawa, 22 March 1978.

House of Representatives Standing Committee, *Aspects of Youth Suicide*, Canberra, 1997.

Law Reform Commission of Canada, *Hate Propaganda* (Working Paper no. 50), Ottawa, 1986.

Lawlor, Patrick, *Group Defamation: Submission to the Attorney General*, Toronto, March 1984.

McManus, M., *Introduction to Report of Attorney General's Commission on Pornography* (Nashville: Rutledge Hill Press, 1986), xviii.

Metro Toronto Task Force on Public Violence against Women and Children, *Final Report*, 1984.

Public Hearings on Ordinances to Add Pornography as Discrimination against Women, Minneapolis City Council, Government Operations Committee, 12 and 13 December 1983.

Report of the Evaluation of the National HIV/AIDS Strategy, National Evaluation Steering Committee, Canberra, 1992.

Report of the Joint Select Committee on Video Material, Canberra, Australia, 1988.

Report of the Ministerial Committee of Inquiry into Pornography, Wellington, New Zealand, 1988.

Sexual Offences against Children: Report of the Committee on Sexual Offences against Children and Youths (Badgley Report), US, 1984, chap. 55.

US Attorney General's Commission, *Final Report of the Attorney General's Commission on Pornography*, Washington, DC, 1986.

Court Documents

Factum of the Appellant, Little Sisters Book and Art Emporium, in the case of *Little Sisters Book and Art Emporium v. A.G. Canada*, Supreme Court of Canada, File No. 26858, 19 July 1999.

Factum of the Appellant Little Sisters Book and Art Emporium, in the case of *Little Sisters Book and Art Emporium v. A.G. Canada*, Supreme Court of Canada, File No. 26858, 30 July 1999.

Factum of the Attorney General of Canada, in the case of *Little Sisters Book and Art Emporium v. A.G. Canada*, Supreme Court of Canada, File No. 26858, 29 October 1999.

Factum of the Intervener Canadian AIDS Society, *Little Sisters Book and Art Emporium*, Supreme Court of Canada, File No. 26858, 16 September 1999.

Factum of the Intervener EGALE, Supreme Court of Canada, in the case of *Little Sisters Book and Art Emporium* v. *A.G. Canada*, Supreme Court of Canada, File No. 26858, 1999.

Factum of the Intervener Equality Now, in the case of *Little Sisters Book and Art Emporium* v. *A.G. Canada*, Supreme Court of Canada, File No. 26858, 3 December 1999.

Factum of the Intervener Women's Legal Education and Action Fund, in the case of *Little Sisters Book and Art Emporium* v. *A.G. Canada,* Supreme Court of Canada, File No. 26858, 27 September 1999.

Factum of the Intervener Women's Legal Education and Action Fund, in the case of *R.* v. *Butler,* Supreme Court of Canada, File No. 22191, 1990.

Factum of the Minister of Justice and Attorney General of Canada, in hearings before the Supreme Court of Canada, *Little Sisters Book and Art Emporium* v. *A.G. Canada*, Supreme Court of Canada, File No. 26858, 29 October 1999.

Factum of the Women's Legal and Education and Action Fund, in the case of *R.* v. *Keegstra,* Supreme Court of Canada, File No. 21116, 1 December 1989.

MacKinnon, Catharine, *Brief of National Organization on Male Violence et al in Joseph Oncale* v. *Sundowner Offshore Services, Inc. et al,* US Supreme Court, File No. 96-568, 11 August 1997.

Unpublished Works

Adams, Wendy A., "A Sex Equality Approach to Discrimination on the Basis of Sexual Orientation: A Comparative Analysis within the Context of US and Canadian Constitutional Regimes" (master's thesis, University of Michigan, 1999).

Galanes, Philip, "More Male Than Not: A Consideration of Gay Male Pornography and the Dworkin/MacKinnon Pornography Ordinance" (speech, 1 August 1990).

Gay Pornography: Sometimes Men Possess Men, (1985) UCLA study.

Institute for the Scientific Investigation of Sexuality, *The Psychology of Homosexuality*, available from ISIS, P.O. Box 6725, Lincoln, NE 68506.

Men against Rape and Pornography, *Looking at Gay Porn* (1993), available from MARAP, P.O. Box 8181, Pittsburgh, PA 15217.

Obendorf, Simon, "OG: Oriental Guys/Occidental Gaze: Towards a Feminist Critique of Western Homosexual Pornographic Depictions of Asian Men," (student paper, University of Melbourne, 1997).

REAL Women, *Laws Protecting Homosexuals or So-Called Sexual Orientation Legislation* (1988), available from REAL Women of Canada, 215 Victoria Street, Suite 509, Toronto, ON M5B 1T9.

Yuen, C.Y., "Women's Reactions to Violent Pornography, Nonviolent Pornography and Erotica" (master's thesis, University of Calgary, 1985).

Cases

American Booksellers Association v. *Hudnut,* 771 F.2d 323 (7th Cir. 1985).

Canada (Human Rights Commission) v. *Taylor* (1990), 3 C.R.R. (2d) 116.

Garcia v. *Elf Atochem No. Am.,* 27 F.3d 446 (5th Cir. 1994).

Glad Day Bookshop Inc. v. *Canada (Deputy Minister of National Revenue, Customs and Excise)* (14 July 1992)(Ont. Ct. (Gen. Div.)).

Goluszek v. *Smith,* 697 F. Supp. 1452 (N.D. Ill. 1988).

Joseph Oncale v. *Sundowner Offshore Services, Inc., John Lyons, Danny Pippen and Brandon Johnson* (Supreme Court of the United States, October term 1996, No. 96-568).

Little Sisters Book and Art Emporium v. *A.G. Canada* (1996), 18 B.C.L.R. (3d) 241 (B.C.S.C).

Little Sisters Book and Art Emporium v. *A.G. Canada* (1998) 54 B.C.L.R. (3d) 306 (B.C.C.A).

Little Sisters Book and Art Emporium v. *Canada (Minister of Justice),* [2000] 2 S.C.R. 1120.

McAleer v. *Canada (Human Rights Commission)* (1996), 132 D.L.R. (4th) 672 (F.C.T.D.).

New York v. *Ferber,* 458 U.S. 747 (1982).

Oncale v. *Sundowner Offshore Services, Inc.,* 83 F.3d 118 (5th Cir. 1996).

Osborne v. *Ohio,* 110 S. Ct. 1691, 1697 (1990).

R. v. *Butler* (1990), 50 C.C.C. (3d) 97 (Man. Q.B.).

R. v. *Butler* (1990), 60 C.C.C. (3d) 219 (Man. C.A.).

R. v. Butler, [1992] 1 S.C.R. 452.
R. v. Coles Co. Ltd. (1965), 2 C.C.C. 304, 322-23 (Ont. C.A.).
R. v. Fringe Product Inc. et al. (1990), 53 C.C.C. (3d) 422.
R. v. Gray (1981), 65 C.C.C. (2d) 353 (Ont. H.C.).
R. v. Keegstra, [1990] 3 S.C.R. 697 (S.C.C.) 758.
R. v. Kleppe (1977), 35 C.C.C. (2d) 168 (Ont. Prov. Ct.).
R. v. Oakes, [1986] 2 S.C.R. 103 (S.C.C.).
R. v. Odeon Theatres Ltd. et al. (1974), 16 C.C.C. (2d) 197 (Man. C.A.).
R. v. Periera-Vasquez (1988), 64 C.R. (3d) 253 (B.C.C.A.).
R. v. Prairie Schooner News Ltd. (1970), 1 C.C.C. (2d) 252 (Man. C.A.).
R. v. Ramsingh (1984), 14 C.C.C. (3d) 230 (Man. Q.B.).
R. v. Ronish, (1993) 18 C.R. (4th) 165 (Ont. Ct. Prov. Div.).
R. v. Video World Limited (1986), 22 C.C.C. (3d) 331 (Man. C.A.).
Towne Cinema Theatres v. The Queen, [1985] 1 S.C.R. 494.
Veysey v. Canada (Correctional Service) (1990), 109 N.R. 300.

Legislation
Canadian Constitution (Constitution Act, 1982) [en. by the *Canada Act 1982* (U.K.), c. 11, s.1], pt. I (*Canadian Charter of Rights and Freedoms*).
Canadian Criminal Code, R.S. 1985, c. C-46.
Canada Customs Act, R.S. 1985, c. 1.
Canada Customs Tariff, R.S. 1985, c. 41.
Canadian Human Rights Act, R.S. 1985, c. H-6.
Saskatchewan Human Rights Code, S.S. 1979, c. S-24.1 as am.

Permissions

All reasonable attempts have been made to secure permission to reproduce all material used in this book and if there are errors or omissions they are wholly unintentional and the publisher would be grateful to learn of them.

The following individuals and/or publishers kindly gave permission to quote excerpts from their works in this book:

Janine Benedet, "Child Pornography after *Sharpe*" (2002) 43 *Cahiers de Droit*. 327.

Andrea Dworkin and Catharine MacKinnon, *Pornography and Civil Rights: A New Day for Women's Equality* (Minneapolis: Organizing against Pornography, 1988).

Philip Galanes, "More Male than Not: A Consideration of Gay Male Pornography and the Dworkin/MacKinnon Pornography Ordinance" (speech, 1 August 1990).

Linda Lovelace (with Mike O'Grady), *Ordeal* (Secaucus, NJ: Citadel Press, 1980). [All rights reserved. Reprinted by permission of Citadel Press/Kensington Publishing Corp., www.kensingtonbooks.com].

Catharine MacKinnon, *Sex Equality* (New York: Foundation Press, 2001) at 1550.

Catharine MacKinnon and Andrea Dworkin, *In Harm's Way: The Pornography Civil Rights Hearings* (Cambridge: Harvard University Press, 1997).

Simon Obendorf, "OG: Oriental Guys/Occidental Gaze: Towards a Feminist Critique of Western Homosexual Pornographic Depictions of Asian Men" (student paper, University of Melbourne, 1997).

Michael Scarce, *Male on Male Rape: The Hidden Toll of Stigma and Shame* (New York: Insight Books, 1997).

It is worth noting that getting permission to use the pornographic materials cited in this book was extremely difficult. Much of the pornography quoted in the book comes from the pornography exhibits defended in the *Little Sisters* case, argued before the Supreme Court of Canada in 2001. What is offered is a sampling of magazines, videos, and books that had been detained by Canada Customs since 1985.

There were approximately 200 exhibits in the *Little Sisters* litigation. Of these, this book offers a summary of or quotations from a small sample. I also offer other examples of materials that Little Sisters would have sold if it had proven victorious before the Supreme Court of Canada. In October 1999, I flew from Perth, Australia, to Vancouver, Canada, to view these exhibits. The exhibits had been classified illegal and were being detained at the Civil Exhibits Division of the British Columbia Court of Appeal. I was given permission by the Federal Department of Justice to view the exhibits and I had approximately two days to do so.

The quotations provided from those materials were read into a tape recorder in Vancouver and later typed upon my return to Perth. As far as is possible, the quotations offered from these exhibits are an accurate summary of what appears in these materials. I say "as far as possible" because I was working under a very tight time frame in legally constrained conditions. Each exhibit was bought to me individually in a locked room. I was then allowed to dictate into a tape recorder, and I was not allowed to photocopy more than a few pages of the written materials because Canada Customs had ruled that these materials were illegal under Canadian law. I also was not allowed to remove the materials from the court house and could only view one exhibit at a time.

Some of these exhibits did not list the author or year of publication, etc., because pages had been removed or blacked out in earlier court proceedings. If these details were provided, I did not record all of them because my aim was to use specific quotes for the purpose of critical analysis. I could not later return to find this bibliographic information because once the Supreme Court ruled that Canada Customs could detain these materials, they were either destroyed after subsequent court proceedings or returned to the United States, from whence they came.

Many of these materials were also dated (as far back as 1985) and it was not possible to find the specific magazines in Canada, even in those stores that would have continued to sell them illegally. I have tried to track down some of the magazines in Australia but this was difficult without full bibliographic details. Many of the magazines are now out of stock and, I might add, illegal in Western Australia. I was thus reluctant to purchase them, even if I could find them. They would also now be illegal in Canada as a result of the *Little Sisters* case. While it is possible that some might still be sold in Canada, I was not keen to purchase materials that violate the Canadian Criminal Code provisions dealing with obscenity.

It is also worth noting that because of the nature of the pornography industry, the names of "authors" are often fictional. This makes getting verification from individual writers extremely difficult. Thus, in my summaries, I tended to simply provide the name of the magazine, book, or video, and the exhibit number from the case. Because of its very nature, one simply cannot track down some authors and writers by any of the usual means. These individuals change addresses and names regularly, and often use pseudonyms. Also, given the nature of some of the material in question and its potentially illegal status, contact is made even more difficult.

Index

Fajer, Marc, 34
feminine role: gay men as socially feminized, 35; gendered concept of femininity, 31, 111, 205n2, 205n6; submissive
gender role, 31-2; status of submissive
male, 67, 97-8, 116-17, 118-19, 121,
147-8, 229n23, 230n45; use of Asian
men, 123, 125-8, 156
feminist anti-pornography activists: allies
in gay liberation movement, 130;
arguments re harassment as sexually
abusive behaviour, 40; criticized as
homophobic, 12, 21-2, 169, 188; harms
of gender inequality, 41; pornographic
harm, 70, 90-1, 163, 180; pornography
as sex discrimination, 130, 163, 188;
racial inequality, 123. *See also* Dworkin,
Andrea; MacKinnon, Catharine
Ford, Dave, 152, 238n92
Fraser, Donald M., 184
Fraser Report (of Special Committee on
Pornography and Prostitution, 1985),
91
free speech. *See* freedom of expression
freedom of expression: in anti-gay hate
speech case *(McAleer)*, 182; civil rights
ordinances *vs.* pornography (US), 184;
limitations on, 9, 11; pornography as,
3-4, 6, 21-5, 189; *vs.* right to equality,
3-4, 6, 9-11, 184. See also *Butler, R. v.*
Friedkin, William, 19-20
Frontiers Magazine, 101
Frye, Marylin, 30, 32, 207n9
Fucked Up (film), 83-4, 222n50
Fung, Richard, 85, 116, 126-8, 154-5

Galanes, Philip, 108-9, 112
Gallant, Paul, 68
gay male identity: argument re need for gay
male pornography, xiii, 47-9, 52, 53, 67,
103, 109, 114, 130, 140-3, 160-1, 163,
181, 189-91, 238n86; arguments re role
play in pornographic materials, 29, 40,
108-9, 113, 116, 157-8, 189; counter-
argument re need for non-pornographic
education materials, 141; normalized and
sexualized physical standards, 151-3;
sexual objectification in gay male pornography, 108-9, 114-15, 238n92; shame
instilled by homophobia and pornography's role in instilling self-hate, 138;
when rape equals sex, 100
gay male liberation: arguments re pornography as source of sexual freedom, 145,
150-1, 236n76; feminists as allies, 130;
gay male pornography defended as
liberation, 55, 103, 122, 159, 163, 189;
masculine mimicry as, 157-8; need for
equality, xiv-xv, xvii, xix, 150, 181,

189-90; portrayal of gay male sex to gay
male youth, 139-43, 159-60
gay male pornography. *See* pornography,
gay male
gay men: alcoholism and drug use, 137-8;
appropriation of hyper-masculinity, 120-
2; argument re gay male sexual identity as
challenge to gender norms, 32-4, 42, 103,
121, 207n8, 209n23; argument re role
options promoted shown in pornography
and subversive nature of role play, 29, 40,
108-9, 113, 116, 157-8, 189; coming out,
fear of and reaction to, 33-5, 103, 121;
condom as stigma, 144-53; conformity
as invisibility, 33-5, 42, 103, 120, 121,
136, 157-8, 239n105; identity *(see* gay
identity); physical appearance ("body
fascism"), 151-3; self-hatred, xv, 93,
101-3, 109, 133, 152, 157, 237n85;
silenced by homophobia, xvi, 33-5, 42,
103, 120, 121, 136, 208n11; socially
feminized, 35; as threat to male supremacy, 33-5, 103, 120-1, 157, 207n8,
208n18, 209n20. *See also* gay youth
Gay Video Guide, 64
gay youth: abuse, verbal and physical,
133-4, 135-6, 158; alcoholism and drug
use, 137-8, 234n32; attempts to "pass,"
135, 136-7; coming out, fear of and
reaction to, 135-6; condom use, 144-5,
147, 150; ethnic gay youth, 153-7; gay
male sexual imagery, 113-14, 228n21;
HIV/AIDS and, 132, 138, 140-1, 147-8;
homophobia, 132-6, 158; isolation and
lack of support, 132-4, 136-7; myths
re homosexuality, 100, 102-3, 135-6,
225n36; need for safe sex sexual education, 138, 139-43, 148, 159-60; pornography as "education," 140-3, 159-61;
prostitution, 136, 234n29; self-hate,
133-5, 137, 139-40, 157, 234n26,
235n45; suicide rates, 132, 133, 134, 141,
235n45; unsafe sex promoted by gay
male pornography, 145-8. *See also* gay
male identity; gay men
gender inequality: compulsory heterosexuality, 31-2, 114; gender as social
construct, 31, 111, 205n2, 205n6;
gendered nature of rape, 97-8; heterosexual male privilege and, 33-5, 68,
120-1; hierarchy of dominance and
submission, 31-2, 40-1, 68, 105-6,
112-13, 120-1, 206n7; maintained by
homophobia, 32-5, 59, 103, 120-1;
patriarchy and, 34; pornography as sex
inequality issue, 2-4, 5-6, 8-9, 11-12,
24-5, 42, 70, 129, 177, 196n34; same-sex
harassment, 37-41, 210n29, 212n36; as
sex discrimination *(see* sex discrimination)

misogyny: effect on women not acknowledged by gay men, 21, 181; feminization
of submissive gay male, 67, 97-8, 103,
116-17, 118-19, 121, 147-8, 229n23,
230n45; in gay male subculture, 30, 35;
in gay male pornography, 44, 56, 88,
90-1; in heterosexual pornography, 20,
44, 88, 90-1, 196n33, 197n40; and
homophobia, 35, 120-1; *MacGuigan
Report* on right of Parliament to limit, 6
Mitstysyn, Karen, 48, 142
Moldenhaur, Jerald, 47-8
Moon, Richard, 182
moral codes. *See* community standards
Mr. S/M 65, 63
Myrick, Roger, 144

NAMBLA (North American Man Boy Love
Association), 182
National Gay and Lesbian Task Force, 133
Nazi hate propaganda, 25

Obendorf, Simon, 125-6
obscenity laws: Canada Customs' enforcement, 46, 54, 162, 163-4, 170-6, 240n15;
constitutionality of *(Butler),* 2-4, 5-6, 22-
3, 45-6; *Glad Day* decision, 166; s. 163 of
Criminal Code, 5-6, 10, 25-7, 45, 52-3,
171, 197n41; SCC ruling re application
by Canada Customs, 175-7
Oncale, Joseph: homophobia or male
supremacy, 35-6; ordeal classified as
"homosexual panic," 38-9; rape in
context of society, 39-42; ruling re civil
rights remedy, 37, 201n29, 211n30,
212n36
Ordeal (by Marchiano, 1980), 70, 72
Oriental Guys magazine, 60, 123, 125-6,
167

Partner abuse, 88-9, 101-2
Pharr, Suzanne, 32-3, 35, 120-1
Playguy magazine, 57, 168
police: homophobic behaviour, 164; non-
enforcement of *Butler* test, 165-70,
179-80
Poppart, Ken, 154
pornographic harm: argument re inapplica-
bility to same-sex pornography, 28-9,
45, 49, 67-8, 88, 90-1, 105-7, 189-90;
Bearchell in *Butler* case, 12-13; Bearchell
in *Little Sisters* case, 142-3; *Butler* decision,
3, 4-5, 22-8, 70, 92-3, 163, 166; civil or
human rights approach, 1-2, 13-14, 28,
181, 183-7; degradation and, 6-8, 10-11,
26; denial by gay community, 4, 12-14,
21-5, 28-9, 42-3, 45-9, 67-8, 93, 130;
equality-based approach, 2, 6-7, 9-12, 24-
5, 42, 70, 129, 163, 166, 177; evidence

in *MacGuigan Report,* 6-7; gay male
pornography and, 29, 45-9, 67-8, 88,
91-4; heterosexual pornography and, 3,
4-5, 22-8, 89-90, 93, 196n33, 197n40;
as human rights violation, 181-3; LEAF's
factum on harm (in *Butler),* 7-8, 12-13,
63-4, 85, 90, 105, 122, 194n23, 195n24;
pornography as behavioural model, 107-
8; production of (*see* "actors" in pornography); *Sharpe* decision, 204n108; See
also *Little Sisters;* standard of proof
pornography: child pornography, 204n108;
civilly actionable, 2, 13-14, 181, 183-5;
definition in civil rights ordinances (US),
1-2, 5, 184; different from hate speech
for gay rights activists, 4, 14, 21-5, 28-9,
93; as freedom of expression, 3-4, 6,
21-5, 189; heterosexual and gay male
distinguished by gay community, 44-5,
49; as human rights violation, 181-3; as
inequality issue, 2-4, 5-6, 8-9, 11-12,
24-5, 42, 70, 129, 177, 196n34; production (*see* "actors" in pornography); profits
from, 64; as sex discrimination, xvi, 2, 6-
8, 129-30, 163, 184. *See also Little Sisters;*
pornographic harm; standard of proof
pornography, gay male: "actors" in (*see*
"actors" in pornography); "annihilation
of the self," 117-20; argument re inappli-
cability of harm-based test, 3-4, 45, 49,
88, 90-1, 106-8, 189; argument re it
exposing the artificial nature of gender,
110-11; argument re reciprocal abuse as
equality, 109-13; argument re role options
offered to gay men, 29, 40, 108-9, 113,
116, 157-8, 189; argument re sexual
penetration as positive and subversive,
113-20; childhood abuse sexualized,
61-2, 113-14; as distinguished from
heterosexual pornography, 44-5, 49,
88; economics of, 64, 76-7, 85, 101;
examples of specific content, 54-67,
214n32; gay male identity formation
and, 47-9, 52, 53, 67, 103, 109, 114,
130, 140-3, 160-1, 163, 181, 189-90,
238n86; harm denied by gay community,
4, 12-14, 21-5, 28-9, 42-3, 45-9, 67-8,
93, 130; harms-based standard (*Little
Sisters* decision), 46, 52-3, 69-70;
hierarchy of dominance and submission,
xv-xvi, 29, 68, 105-7, 112-21, 129-30,
147-8, 189; homophobic in nature,
129-30, 164; impact on sex equality
interests of gay men and society, 47, 100;
misapplication of *Butler* test by Canada
Customs, 162, 164, 171-2, 241n29;
normalization of rape, 62, 67, 95-100;
physical appearance of men, 227n12;
pornographic harm, 29, 45-9, 67-8, 88,

Set in Arrus and News Gothic by Artegraphica Design
Printed and bound in Canada by Friesens
Copy editor: Judy Phillips
Proofreader: Deborah Kerr
Indexer: Patricia Buchanan